Observing
Development
of the
Young Child
Second Edition

Janice J. Beaty
Elmira College

Merrill, an Imprint of
Macmillan Publishing Company
New York

Collier Macmillan Canada, Inc.
Toronto

Maxwell Macmillan International Publishing Group
New York   Oxford   Singapore   Sydney

Cover Photo: Jeff Greenberg

This book was set in Trump Mediaeval.

Administrative Editor: David K. Faherty
Production Coordinator: Linda Kauffman Peterson
Art Coordinator: Lorraine Woost
Cover Designer: Cathy Watterson
Photo Editor: Gail Meese

Photo credits: pp. 2, 180, 202, 222, 228, 246, 267, Janet Gagnon; pp. 13, 102, 128, 150, 189, 235, 280, 284, 300, 320, 324, 346, Lloyd Lemmerman/Merrill Publishing; pp. 42, 55, 70, 108, 118, 140, 144, 156, 167, 197, 215, 256, 259, 292, 308, 309, 336, 348, Janice Beaty; pp. 44, 74, Ben Chandler/Merrill Publishing; p. 95, Larry Hamill/Merrill Publishing.

Macmillan Publishing Company
866 Third Avenue, New York, New York 10022

Collier Macmillan Canada, Inc.
1200 Eglinton Avenue East
Suite 200
Don Mills, Ontario, M3C 3N1

Library of Congress Catalog Card Number: 89−60935
International Standard Book Number: 0−675−21140−9
Printed in the United States of America
3 4 5 6 7 8 9 − 93 92 91 90

To my mother and father

The Author

Janice J. Beaty, professor of Human Services at Elmira College in Elmira, New York, is director of the Human Services Program and project manager of the Head Start CDA Training Program. Dr. Beaty teaches undergraduate and graduate courses in early childhood education, children's literature, and Mark Twain storytelling. She is an author of children's books (*Nufu and the Turkeyfish, Plants in his Pack,* and *Seeker of Seaways*), coauthor of adult books (*Mark Twain Walking America Again* and *Storytelling Mark Twain Style*), and author of teacher-training textbooks (*Skills for Preschool Teachers* and *The Computer as a Paintbrush*). Dr. Beaty has developed training materials and films for the Child Development Associate (CDA) program and has made presentations at CDA Training Institutes and workshops around the country. Her interest in people of other cultures has lured her to such diverse locations as the island of Guam in the western Pacific and San Salvador in the Bahamas. Her present studies focus on young children's learning through self-discovery with materials in the classroom setting.

Preface

This textbook presents a unique system for observing and recording the development of young children ages two to six years old in an early childhood classroom setting. The text is designed to be used by college students preparing to be teachers in prekindergarten programs, nursery schools, day-care centers, Head Start classes, preschools of all kinds, and kindergarten classrooms. The book can also be used by teachers and assistant teachers in such programs who want to learn more about children in order to make plans for individuals. Staff members who are preparing a Child Development Associate (CDA) portfolio will find this textbook especially helpful in its suggestions for activities that are developmentally appropriate for young children.

The text focuses on observation of the six major aspects of child development: emotional, social, motor, cognitive, language, and creative. Each of these aspects is further divided into two specific areas: self-identity and emotional development; social play and prosocial behavior; large and small motor development; cognitive development of skills in classification and seriation and of skills in number, time, space, and memory; spoken and written language; and art skills and imagination.

These areas of child development are outlined in a *Child Skills Checklist*, which includes specific, observable child behaviors in the sequence in which they occur. Each of twelve chapters discusses one of these areas, giving ideas for classroom activities for children who have not shown the specified behavior. The most recent child development research in each area is presented as background for the checklist items as they are discussed. Each chapter concludes with a discussion of an actual child observation in the particular area and an interpretation of the data gathered.

The text may serve college students as a guide for observing and recording the development of young children in their student teaching and course work. The book is especially well suited to be a supplementary text for child development courses. It also can be used by in-service teachers and assistants who are upgrading their skills in observing children, as well as learning to plan for individuals based on developmental needs.

Unique aspects of this edition of *Observing Development of the Young Child* include the latest information on the development of human emotions from babyhood through kindergarten, a new look at moral development (prosocial behavior) in young children, a discussion of written language as a natural development of emergent literacy rather than as something that has to be taught to children, and a section on the development of the imagination as an important aspect of creativity.

Perhaps the most useful features of this textbook are the activities for children described after each checklist item. Included are activities highlighting the latest children's books on each of the topics discussed.

NEW FEATURES IN THE SECOND EDITION

The *Child Skills Checklist* has been redesigned to include space for the observer to record evidence for each of the checklist items, together with the date. (See Appendix A, *Child Skills Checklist.*)

Use of a *running record* for the initial gathering of observational data is presented. How to transfer the data to the *Child Skills Checklist* and then to develop a learning prescription for the child are described. (See Appendix B, *Learning Prescription.*)

New checklist items include large motor material on using legs, feet, arms, and hands in rhythm and creative movement activities, plus new cognitive items involving singing and musical games.

Each chapter concludes with a discussion of an actual observation of a child in the particular area. Where appropriate, sample checklists are included to allow the student to see how an observer might record the observational evidence. An interpretation of the data gathered is discussed, and suggestions are given for activities to help the individual child, based on his or her strengths.

USE AS A COMPANION TEXT

This second edition of *Observing Development of the Young Child* is designed to be used as a companion volume with the author's text *Skills for Preschool Teachers* (Columbus, OH: Merrill, 1988). While *Observing Development of the Young Child* is intended as a child development textbook, *Skills for Preschool Teachers* is a teacher development book, focusing on thirteen areas of teacher competencies.

Like this textbook, *Skills for Preschool Teachers* is also based on an observational checklist, the Teacher Skills Checklist, which documents teacher competencies in the thirteen CDA Functional Areas of safety, health, learning environment, physical, cognitive, communication, creative, self, social, guidance, families, program management, and professionalism.

Together, the two textbooks form a cohesive, whole training program for pre-service teachers, beginning teachers, and in-service teachers preparing for the CDA credential. Both of these books focus on positive behaviors in children and teachers. Thus, in both the development of children and the training of teachers, these books look at "areas of strength and confidence" and "areas needing strengthening" in order to set up individualized training plans.

ACKNOWLEDGMENTS

Many thanks to Bonny Helm, Elmira College CDA Field Supervisor, who read the original text; to Elmira College undergraduate students in my class "Observing and Recording Child Development" and graduate students in my class "The Young Child: Aspects of Development," who offered suggestions and practical applications of the checklist; to Ellen Wohl, who allowed my students to observe children in the Head Start classrooms of the Chemung County Child Development Program; to Debbie Peterson and the parents of children in the Arnot Art Museum Preschool who allowed me to photograph their children; to the Gannett Tripp Learning Center and its research librarians at Elmira College; and to the many people in the field who have used the text and offered their constructive criticism for this revised edition. Finally I would like to thank the reviewers of this text: Barbara Nilsen, Broome Community College; Lee Allen, University of Wisconsin—Milwaukee; Myra Adler Lesser, Pennsylvania State University; and Douglas Kennard, College of Charleston.

Janice Beaty

Contents

Checklists
and Tables

Checklists

Tables

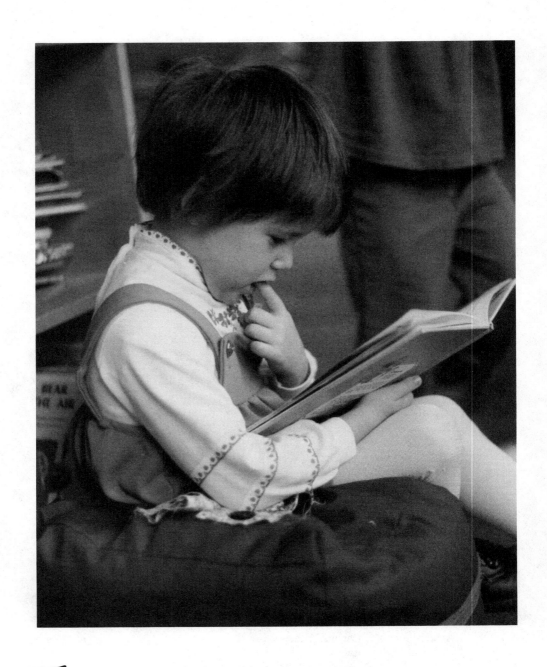

1 Observation of Development

A|ll children go through a sequence of development that can be observed. From large to small motor coordination, from simple ideas to complex thinking, from one-word utterances to lengthy sentences, from scribbles to representational drawings . . . all children everywhere seem to proceed through a step-by-step sequence of development that can be traced by a knowledgeable observer, one who knows what to look for.

This textbook gives students of child development and teachers of young children primarily ages three to five a method for observing and recording this natural development as the children work and play in the environment of the early childhood classroom. This method will help observers determine specifically where each child stands in the areas of emotional, social, physical, cognitive, language, and creative development.

The purpose for observing children's development in this manner is twofold: (1) for students of child development to gain an in-depth understanding of real children and their sequences of growth, and (2) for teachers of young children to become aware of each child's growth, in order to support individual development and to give special help where developmental lags are apparent.

Many similar textbooks teach observational skills and strategies. These techniques are particularly important for researchers and child psychologists. However, this text will go beyond that level to teach the non-specialist observer to understand children through the gathering and interpreting of objective data about children's development. The *Child Skills Checklist* at the conclusion of this chapter will assist the observer in focusing on particular aspects and sequences of development. Each of the following chapters will expand on one aspect of that development as outlined in the checklist:

Emotional
    1. Self-Identity
    2. Emotional Development
Social
    3. Social Play
    4. Prosocial Behavior
Physical
    5. Large Motor Development
    6. Small Motor Development
Cognitive
    7. Cognitive Development (Classification and Seriation)
    8. Cognitive Development (Number, Time, Space, Memory)
Language
    9. Spoken Language
    10. Written Language
Creative
    11. Art Skills
    12. Imagination

Each chapter treats one of these twelve areas of development, and each area contains eight items based on recognized developmental sequences. Not every detail of development is included. The eight representative items, however, make the observations inclusive enough to be meaningful without becoming so detailed as to be cumbersome. For items the observer does not check as apparent when observing a child, there is a section of ideas following each item that should be useful in planning for individual needs. These ideas are also listed in an index following Chapter 14.

Observational assignments at the end of each chapter will include not only use of the *Child Skills Checklist* for individuals and groups of children, but also use of anecdotal records, running records, specimen records, time sampling, event sampling, and rating scales.

WHY OBSERVE YOUNG CHILDREN

Many people are curious about how children grow. Parents want to know if their children are developing normally, or how they compare with siblings. Grandparents and relatives want to know what clever new things the young child is doing or saying. Teachers would like to find out why their students behave the way they do or why they are not doing what they should be. Psychologists often observe troubled children in a natural setting to determine their problems and prescribe help. Pediatricians need to observe children in a clinical setting to assess health problems. Researchers observe young children in both natural and clinical settings in order to test hypotheses about development and to formulate new theories.

Systematic observation of children (that is, observation using a particular system) is different from informal observation, which is really little more than watching. In systematic observation there is a specific purpose for gathering information about the children, as well as a particular method for collecting and recording it. For teachers and students who wish to learn more about the youngsters they work with, the following may be among their own particular reasons for systematic observing and recording.

1. To make an initial assessment of the child's abilities.
2. To determine a child's areas of strength and which areas need strengthening.
3. To make individual plans based on observed needs.
4. To conduct an ongoing check on the child's progress.
5. To learn more about child development in particular areas.
6. To resolve a particular problem involving the child.
7. To use in reporting to parents or specialists in health, speech, mental health.
8. To gather information for the child's folder for use in ongoing guidance and placement.

WHAT TO LOOK FOR

What kinds of children's actions are important for observers to watch and record? In each of the six principal areas of child development, there are particular behaviors that observers should look for and record. Under *emotional development*, for instance, the observer needs to pay special attention to nonverbal cues. What facial expressions are exhibited? What do the eyes look like, the eyebrows, the mouth? Are the eyes staring, downcast, slit, closed? Are the eyebrows raised, lowered, straight? Is the mouth in a pout, a smile, a scowl? What about the posture? Is it ramrod straight, slumped, swaggering, slouched? What kinds of gestures are made with the hands, arms, feet? Are the hands to the sides, fists clenched, arms swinging free, feet together? Does the child walk with a swing, a shuffle, a skip?

Under *social development*, the observer should be aware of how children interact and get along with one another. Is she alone or a part of the group? Is he a leader or a follower? Popular with the others or often excluded? What roles does he play when pretending? How does she respond to sharing or taking turns? Is he cooperative and helpful? How?

Under *physical development*, the observer needs to watch how the child walks, runs, climbs, jumps, and balances. Does he have eye-hand coordination in using tools, making puzzles, painting? Can she dress herself and tie her shoes? These questions need to be answered with more than a "yes" or "no." In all observations the observer needs to be recording detailed evidence to tell "how." When she walks, the child may amble, stroll, skip, strut, clump, shuffle, stumble, trudge, or tiptoe. What happens with her legs and feet when she "clumps"?

In *cognitive development*, it is obvious the observer cannot know what the child is thinking but must rely on classroom responses and reactions that demonstrate reasoning ability, problem solving, and memory. Even language ability is intertwined with cognitive development as, in fact, are all developmental aspects. No single aspect of development truly stands alone but should be considered brush strokes on the intricate picture of the whole child being drawn by the observer.

Language development can be observed by listening closely to the child and recording on paper or tape. Does the child initiate conversations or is he a listener? Can she speak complete sentences? Are they understandable? Can he print his own name? Does she recognize the names of others?

What about *creativity*? Is she manipulating the medium by swishing paint around the paper, or can she represent people and buildings? How far does his pretending go? Must she have a physical prop in order to play a role, or will her imagination do?

We need, then, to look for and be aware of physical gestures, movements, and features, as well as verbal and nonverbal communication and interactions with people and materials.

METHODS FOR OBSERVING AND RECORDING

Systematic observation always implies recording. Not only must the observer have a particular reason to look at the child and know what to look for, but he also needs a method for recording the information gathered. A number of useful methods have been developed over the years by observers of young children. The following will be included for discussion and use in this text: anecdotal records, running records, specimen records, time sampling, event sampling, and the use of observation tools such as rating scales and checklists.

Anecdotal Records

Anecdotal records are brief narrative accounts describing an incident of a child's behavior that is important to the writer. Anecdotes describe what happened in a factual, objective manner, telling how it happened, when and where it happened, and what was said and done. Sometimes they include reasons for the child's behavior, but "why" is better kept in the commentary part of the record. These accounts are most often written *after* the incident has occurred, by someone who witnessed it informally, rather than *while* it was occurring, by someone who was formally observing and recording.

Anecdotal records have long been made by teachers, physicians, psychologists, social workers, and even parents who record when their babies first walk and talk. Sometimes these are referred to as "baby biographies."

Although anecdotal records are brief, describing only one incident at a time, they are cumulative. A series of them over a period of time can be extremely useful in providing rich details about the person being observed. Other advantages for using anecdotal records include

1. The observer needs no special training in order to record.
2. The observation is open-ended. The recorder writes anything and everything he or she witnesses and is not restricted to one kind of behavior or one type of recording.
3. The observer can catch an unexpected incident no matter when it occurs, for it will be recorded later.
4. The observer can look for and record the significant behavior and can ignore the rest.

As in all observational methods, there are disadvantages, too. Observers need to decide why they are observing, what they want to find out, and which method will be most useful. Some of the disadvantages of the anecdotal record method are

1. It does not give a complete picture because it records only incidents of interest to the observer.
2. It depends too much on the memory of the observer. Witnesses to events are notoriously poor on details.
3. Incidents may be taken out of context and thus interpreted incorrectly or used in a biased manner.
4. It is difficult to code or analyze narrative records like this; thus, the method may not prove useful in a scientific study.

Such records can be more useful if recorded on a vertically divided page, with the anecdote on the left side and a space for comments on the right; or the page can be divided horizontally, with the anecdote at the top and commentary at the bottom. (See the example on the next page.)

This anecdote tells what happened in an objective manner. Especially good are the direct quotes. The anecdote could have included more details about the child's facial expression, tone of voice, and gestures. The reader does not get the feeling of whether the boy was enjoying himself as a helper, trying to ingratiate himself with another child who was not paying much attention, or trying desperately to gain the attention of the other boy. Such details are sometimes missing from anecdotes because they have not been written down until the end of the day or even later, and by then are forgotten.

Anecdotal Record

Child's Name *Stevie* Age *4* Date *2-23*
Observer *Anne* Place *S. nursery* Time *9:00 - 10:00*

Incident

Stevie went over to the block corner and asked two boys, Ron and Tanner, if he could help them build. They told him it was okay. As they were building, he accidentally knocked some blocks down. "I can put it back up," he said, and handed the blocks to Ron. For awhile he watched Ron build and then said, "I found a smoke stack, Ron," and handed him a cylinder block. Ron told him where to put it, and Stevie then began getting cylinders off the shelf and handing them to Ron and Tanner to place. Finally he started placing his own cylinders around the perimeter of the building. The teacher asked him if he wanted to finger paint, but he replied, "I'm not gonna finger paint unless Ron finger paints."

Comment

Stevie is often involved in a lot of dramatic play with several other boys. He especially likes to be near or playing with Ron. He seems to look up to him. Whatever rules Ron sets in the play, Stevie follows. Once engaged in play, he likes to continue, and he will usually not let another child or even the teacher distract him.

The comments contain several inferences and conclusions based on insufficient evidence. Obviously, this observer has spent some time watching Stevie, as indicated by her comments, "Stevie is often involved" and "Once engaged in play, he likes to continue and will usually not . . ." She would need an accumulation of such anecdotes in order to make valid statements of this nature based on evidence. If this were one page in an accumulation of anecdotes about Stevie, the comments would perhaps be more accurate.

The observer infers that Stevie "likes to be near or playing with Ron," although there is not sufficient evidence here to make so definite an inference. Perhaps she should have said, "Whatever rules Ron sets in the play, Stevie follows," if Stevie actually placed a cylinder block where directed. However, this was only hinted at and not stated. Particular words are very important in objective recording. Her conclusion about Stevie's not letting another child or even the teacher distract him is only partially accurate, since no evidence about another child is recorded.

If you were writing the comment about this particular anecdotal record, what things might you infer from the incident? Can you make any conclusions based on this information alone, or is it too limited? Are there things you might want to look for in the future when observing this boy that you should include in the commentary?

It is also helpful to indicate what the purpose is for the particular observation. Most observation forms do not provide a space for this, but the usefulness of the observation is enhanced if it is included. In this case, the observer was looking for evidence of involvement in social play for this child.

Running Records

Another popular type of observing and recording method is the *running record*. It is a detailed narrative account of behavior recorded in a sequential manner as it happens. The observer writes down everything that occurs over a specified period of time, which may be as short as several minutes or from time to time during a full day. The running record is different from the anecdotal record because it includes all behavior and not just selected incidents, and it records behavior as it occurs, instead of later.

As with all factual recording, the observer must be careful not to use descriptive words or phrases that are judgmental. For instance, if the observer sees the child "acting grumpy this morning," he needs to avoid this judgment and instead record the actual details that explain what happened. For example, "Jonathan would not respond to the teacher's greeting at first, and when he did, he muttered 'good morning,' in a low voice with his head bent down."

The running record has a number of advantages for persons interested in child development.

1. It is a rich, complete, and comprehensive record not limited to particular incidents.
2. It is open-ended, allowing the observer to record everything he or she sees, and not restricting the observations to a particular kind of behavior.
3. It does not require the observer to have special observational skills and therefore is particularly useful to the classroom teacher.

There are also several disadvantages to using this method, once again depending on the purpose for gathering the information.

1. It is very time-consuming, and it is difficult for observers to find periods of uninterrupted time.
2. It is difficult to record everything for any length of time without missing important details.
3. It works best when observing an individual, but it is very inefficient and difficult when observing a group.
4. Observers must keep themselves apart from the children, which is sometimes difficult if they are the teachers.

Running records are more useful if recorded on a form where the observer can make comments later. It is difficult for the observer to record every word of all that is said and every facet of all that occurs when children are busily playing together. In the example of a running record, the observer has caught the essence. The dialogue is especially well recorded. His inferences and conclusions are carefully kept on the commentary side of the record. Although we cannot make the same conclusion about Katy being

---

Running Record

Child's Name *Katy* Age *4* Date *2/9*
Observer *Rob* Place *S. Nursery* Time *9–10:00*

Observation	Comments
Katy is playing by herself with plastic blocks, making guns; she walks into other room: "Lisa, would you play with me; I'm tired of playing by myself." They walk into other room to slide & climbing area.	Clips blocks together to make gun, then copies it to make one for Lisa. Cleverly done. Intricate. Shows creativity. (Does teacher allow guns?)
K: "I am Wonder Woman."	
L: "So am I."	
K: "No, there is only one Wonder Woman. You are Robin."	Seems to be the leader here as in other activities I have observed. Lisa is the friend she most often plays with.
L: "Robin needs a Batman because Batman & Robin are friends."	
All this takes place under slide & climber. Lisa shoots block gun which Katy has given to her. Katy falls on floor.	
L (to teacher): "We're playing superfriends, and Wonder Woman keeps falling down."	
Katy opens eyes, gets up, and says: "Let's get out our batmobile and go help the world." She runs to other room and back making noises like a car.	Katy switches roles here. She shows good concentration and spends much time on one play episode.

L: "Wonder Woman is died. She fell out of the car." She falls down.

K: "It's only a game, wake up. Lisa, you be Wonder Woman. I'll be . . ."

She can distinguish reality from fantasy.

L: "Let's play house now."

Katy begins sliding down the slide.

K: "We have a lot of superfriends to do." She says this while sliding. "Robin is coming after you!" she shouts to Lisa, running from the slide and into the other room.

Shows good large motor coordination. Spends much time every day like this, running and skipping around room. Seems to know she is good at this and spends a lot of time doing it.

Lisa has gone into the housekeeping area and says to Katy: "Katy, here is your doll's dress." (Lost yesterday.)

John joins the girls.

L: "I'm Wonder Woman."

K: "I'm Robin."

J: "I'm Batman. Where is the batmobile?"

K: "It's in here." They run into the other room, and Katy points under the slide telling John what the batmobile can do. Then all run to the other room and back again. Then Katy says: "John, we are not playing superfriends any more."

Seems to be more comfortable playing with only one child at a time.

more comfortable playing with only one child at a time based on this evidence, the observer had been gathering this evidence for several weeks and perhaps felt he could. Such an explanation should then be included here. It also would be helpful to record the time that the various incidents occurred in order to know how much time had elapsed on the gun play, the slide play, and the running back and forth.

Because the running record captures so much important developmental behavior of the preschool child, it has been chosen as the primary recording method to be used with the *Child Skills Checklist* in the assessment of an individual child's development as discussed in this textbook. Its use in combination with the checklist is discussed at the end of the chapter.

Specimen Records

Specimen records, or *specimen descriptions,* as they are sometimes called, are similar to running records but more detailed and precise. They are most often used by researchers who want a full and complete description of behavior, whereas the running record is used especially by teachers in a more informal way. The observer is definitely not a part of the classroom activities with the specimen records method and must keep aloof from the children.

Like the running records, specimen records are narrative descriptions of behavior or events as they happen, but descriptions usually based on predetermined criteria such as the time of day, the person, and the setting (Irwin & Bushnell, p. 103). The amount of detail to be recorded depends upon the purpose for the observation. Enough detail should be recorded to give the reader of the observation a sense of how things actually happened. The test of a good specimen record is whether it can be dramatized. Does the description tell how the children moved, what their facial expressions and gestures were, and not only what they said but how they said it? It is better to record too much detail than not enough. Here is a sample extraction.

> Mark's friend Rob is playing in the play grocery store taking empty food boxes off the shelves, so Mark watches him for a moment, begins to take the boxes off the shelves, and places them in a toy shopping cart. Two girls proceed over to where Mark is, and they knock his boxes over (which were teetering because there were so many in the cart). Mark then opens his eyes wide, grits his teeth, and places his hands on his hips, saying, "You guys, why do you knock it down like that?" Meanwhile, the girls appear little affected by his question and walk off. Meanwhile, his friend Rob is still taking the boxes off the shelves, and he says to Mark, "We are stealing stuff." So Mark joins the act, hiding the boxes in the rear by the playhouse. It appears that no one pays any attention to their act of "stealing," so Mark loses interest.

Can you dramatize this specimen record? It tells us neither exactly how the girls took action nor what Mark does to show his loss of interest, but otherwise it is rich in detail.

Specimen records are later coded by researchers to elicit findings regarding kinds of behavior, lengths of incidents, interaction patterns, or other information relevant to the purpose of the observation. Advantages and disadvantages of this particular method are the same as for the running record.

Objective Recording of Narrative Data

Objective recording of the narrative data gained from observing young children—a process required with anecdotal, running, and specimen records—is not a simple task. We are used to observing what happens around us and making simultaneous interpretations about it. In objective recording, we must separate these two roles and guard against confusing them. What we record must be the objective facts only, no judgments, inferences, or conclusions. Perhaps if we think of ourselves as witnesses at a trial, we can more easily discern what information is acceptable and what is not.

If we see a child come into the room in the morning, for instance, refuse to greet the teacher, walk over to a table and sit down, push away another child who tries to join him, and shake his head in refusal when the teacher suggests an activity, how can we record it? An anecdotal record might read like this:

> Jonathan walked into the room this morning as if he were mad at the world. He would not look up at the teacher or respond to her greeting. He

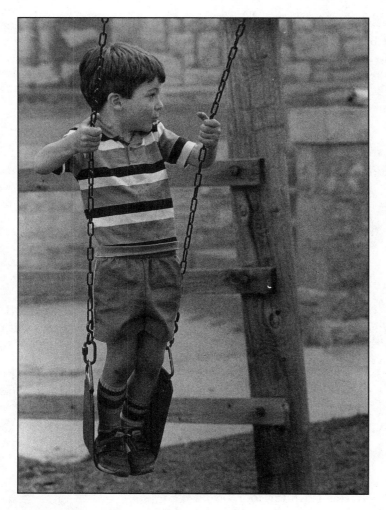

What we record about children must be the objective facts only, no judgments, inferences, or conclusions.

sort of slumped as he walked across the room and plunked himself down in a chair at one of the activity tables. Richie tried to join him but was pushed away. The teacher went over and asked him if he wanted to help mix play dough, but he shook his head no.

This record is rich enough in detail for us to visualize it, but is it factually objective? No. The words "as if he were mad at the world" are a conclusion based on insufficient evidence. The recorder might better have described his entrance objectively.

Jonathan walked into the room this morning with a frowning kind of look on his face. He lowered his head when the teacher greeted him, and did not respond.

This behavior was unusual for Jonathan. Later the teacher found out that he was not "mad at the world," but sad because his pet cat had been killed by a car the night before. We realize then that frowning looks, lowered head, and refusal to speak or participate may be the result of emotions other than anger. It is up to us to sift out our inferences and judgments, then, and make sure we record only the facts.

The following are judgmental phrases and sentences sometimes found in observation records. Should they ever be used? If not, what could you substitute for them?

He was a good boy today.
Marcie was mad at Patty.
shouted angrily
showed his strength
lost his temper
got upset
would never talk like that

Other observer errors include (1) omitting some of the facts, (2) recording things that did not happen, and (3) recording things out of order. Here is the "Jonathan incident" again with some of these errors included. Can you find them?

Jonathan walks in the classroom this morning. He doesn't look at the teacher but goes straight to a seat at one of the tables. The teacher wants him to help mix play dough, but he refuses. Richie comes over to play with him, but he pushes him away.

Omitted facts include the following:

1. Has frowning look on face.
2. Does not respond to teacher's greeting.

   3. Walks across room with shoulders slumped.
   4. Drops himself down into seat at activity table.
   5. Shakes his head no when teacher asks him to help mix play
   dough.

Added facts include

   1. Richie comes over "to play with him."

A fact recorded out of order is

   1. Richie tries to join him before teacher asks him to help mix
   play dough.

   Such errors can creep into an observation almost without the recorder being aware. You need to practice with at least two observers recording the same incident and then to compare results. If you find discrepancies
between the records, check carefully that you have observed the following
guidelines for objective recording.

Guidelines for Objective Recording

   1. Record only the facts.
   2. Record every detail without omitting anything.
   3. Do not interpret as you observe.
   4. Do not record anything you do not see.
   5. Use words that describe but do not judge or interpret.
   6. Record the facts in the order that they occur.

Time Sampling

In the *time sampling* method, the observer records the frequency of a behavior's occurrence over time. The behavior must be overt and frequent (at least
once every fifteen minutes) to be a candidate for sampling (Irwin & Bushnell,
p. 149). For example, talking, hitting, and crying are such behaviors, because
they can be clearly seen and counted. Problem solving is not a good candidate for time sampling because this behavior is not always clear to the observer, nor can it be counted easily.
   Time sampling thus involves observing specified behavior of an
individual or group and recording the presence or absence of this behavior
during short time intervals of uniform length. The observer must prepare
ahead of time, determining what specific behavior he will look for, what
time interval he will use, and how he will record the presence or absence of
the behavior.
   For example, in order to help an aggressive child named Jamie
change his ways, the teacher wants to know how frequently Jamie's negative

behavior occurs. First, Jamie's aggressive behavior must be specifically defined. It includes

> hitting
> pushing
> kicking
> holding another child against his will
> taking another child's toy

These particular behaviors are usually determined by previous formal or informal observations made to discover exactly what the observer needs to be concerned with in the sampling. Jamie, for instance, did not use words aggressively. Another child might have expressed aggression quite differently, and the observer would sample that.

Next the decision is made about what time intervals to use. The observer may decide to sample Jamie's behavior for five minute intervals during the first half hour of the morning for a week. The teacher already knows that this seems to be the most difficult time for him.

The teacher then must decide what and how to record on the sheet, which is blocked into time intervals. Often a time sampling observer simply records "1" after the interval if the behavior occurs and "0" if it does not. This is called *duration recording* and is concerned with the presence or absence of the behavior (Bell & Low, p. 65).

Check marks or tally marks can also be used if the teacher wants to know how many times the behavior occurred, rather than its presence or absence. This is called *event recording* and is concerned with the frequency of the behavioral event.

Furthermore, the teacher may be more concerned with specific categories of aggression rather than just aggression in general. In that case each of the categories can be given in code.

> h = hitting
> p = pushing
> k = kicking
> hd = holding
> t = taking

The teacher will be doing event recording of specific categories rather than frequency of occurrence. The observation form can be set up like any of the following examples or in the teacher's own manner, depending on the information desired. The observation for Jamie's first half hour of one morning could look like any one of those in Figure 1.

From this the teacher might conclude that Jamie's aggressive actions on this morning occurred mainly during the first fifteen minutes and involved mostly hitting and pushing of the other children. If this turned out

	Time Intervals (5 minutes each)					
Duration Recording (presence or absence)	1	2	3	4	5	6
	1	1	1	0	0	0
Event Recording (frequency)	𝚃𝙷𝙻	|||			0	0	0
Event Recording (presence or absence)	h,p	h,p,t	h	0	0	0

FIGURE 1. Event recording of specific categories

to be the pattern for the rest of the week, the teacher might want to plan an interesting transition activity for Jamie to do by himself as soon as he arrived. Once he had made the transition from home to school by getting involved in an activity, he might then be able to interact with the other children nonaggressively. Future observations would help the teacher to determine whether the intervention strategy had been successful.

Time sampling is thus a useful method for observing children for the following reasons:

1. It takes less time and effort than narrative recording.
2. It is more objective and controlled because the behavior is specified and limited.
3. It allows an observer to collect data on a number of children or a number of behaviors at once.
4. It provides useful information on intervals and frequencies of behavior.
5. It provides quantitative results useful for statistical analysis.

There are of course certain disadvantages as well.

1. It is not an open method and therefore may miss much important behavior.
2. It does not describe the behavior, causes, or results, because it is more concerned with time (when or how frequently the behavior occurs).
3. It does not keep units of behavior intact, because its principal concern is the time interval, not the behavior.
4. It takes the behavior out of its context and therefore may be biased.
5. It is limited to observable behaviors that occur frequently.

6. It usually focuses on one type of behavior (in this case a negative behavior) and thus may give a biased view.

Event Sampling

Event sampling is another method in which the observer waits for and then records a specific preselected behavior. Event sampling is used to study the conditions under which particular behaviors occur or their frequency of occurrence. It may be important to learn what triggers a particular kind of behavior—biting, for instance—in order to find ways to control it. Or the observer may want to find out how many times a certain behavior occurs. Time sampling would be used if time intervals and/or time of day were important. If the behavior occurs at odd times or infrequently, however, event sampling is more appropriate.

The observer must first define the event or "unit of behavior." Then he must determine the setting in which it is likely to occur. The observer takes the most advantageous position to observe the behavior, waits for it to occur, and records it.

Recording can be done in several ways, depending upon the purpose for the observation. If the observer is studying causes or results for certain behaviors, then the so-called ABC analysis is especially useful (Bell & Low, p. 73). It is a narrative description of the entire event, breaking it down into three parts: A = antecedent event, B = behavior, C = consequent event. Each time the event occurs it is recorded; for an example, see the event sampling for Darrell.

If subsequent observations of Darrell show the same sort of sequence as in the event sampling presented, the teacher could interpret this to mean that Darrell does not initiate the kicking, but rather responds to interference with his activities in this inappropriate and harmful manner. Intervention strategies may need to be different with this boy. The teacher wants to help him learn an acceptable way to vent his frustration. In addition, he needs help in getting along with other children and in feeling accepted in the classroom. Until these issues are resolved, he may have to keep his shoes off in the classroom to prevent injury. This in itself may reduce his kicking, since his own uncovered toes will soon teach him how it hurts to kick.

If frequency of occurrence is the main concern, the observer can record with tally marks rather than narrative description. However, this procedure tends to be more useful for research than for practical classroom applications.

The advantages for using event sampling are

1. It keeps the event or behavior intact, making analysis easier.
2. It is more objective than some methods, because the behavior has been defined ahead of time.
3. It is especially helpful in examining infrequent or rarely occurring behaviors.

Event Sampling

Name _Darrell_   Age _3½_

Center _Head Start_   Date _10-5_

Observer _Sue S._   Time _9-12:00_

Behavior: Kicking: Striking out at other children or teacher with right foot, hard enough to make children cry.

Time	Antecedent Event	Behavior	Consequent Event
9:13	Darrell playing alone in block corner; Rob comes in & puts block on Darrell's building	Darrell looks at Rob with frown; stands; pushes at Rob; Rob pushes back; Darrell kicks Rob on leg	Rob cries & runs to teacher
10:05	On playground; Darrell waiting turn in line with others to go on slide; Sally tries to cut in	Darrell kicks Sally hard on leg Darrell kicks teacher	Sally cries; teacher comes & takes Darrell away by arm to talk to him

There are several disadvantages as well, depending on the purpose for the observation.

1. It takes the event out of context and thus may lose other happenings that are important to the interpretation.
2. It is a closed method that looks only for specified behavior and must ignore other important behavior.
3. It misses the richness of the many details that anecdotes, specimen records, or running records provide.

TOOLS FOR OBSERVATION

Rating Scales

Rating scales are tools that indicate the degree to which a person possesses a certain trait or behavior. Each behavior is rated on a continuum that goes from the lowest to the highest level (or vice versa) and is marked off at certain points along a scale. The observer must make a judgment about where on the scale the child's behavior lies. As an observational tool, rating scales work best when particular degrees of behavior are well-defined or well-understood by the observer, and there is a distinct difference between the behavior at the various points on the scale.

These tools are useful in diagnosing a child on a wide range of behavior at one time. The observer watches the child and checks off or circles a point on the scale to indicate the child's current position in regard to behaviors or abilities. Such scales are simple to make: simply state the behavior, draw a line, and mark off a number of points or intervals along the line. Five intervals are often used so that there is a middle, or neutral, position and two intervals on either side of it.

GRAPHIC SCALES

Here is a rating scale for only one behavior. Many similar behaviors could be listed on this same scale.

Graphic Scale
Shares Toys: _____
Always   Often   Sometimes   Seldom   Never

Such scales are called *graphic scales* and can be drawn either horizontally, as shown here, or vertically. Many traits can be listed on one sheet. Graphic scales may be easier to construct than to use. The observer must know children well, be able to interpret their behavior, and be able to make an objective judgment within a limited period of time.

NUMERICAL SCALES

Other rating scales may be *numerical* in form. Two items—attention span and curiosity—are shown in the example here, but altogether there are a total of twelve items on this scale.

Raters observe children for as long as it takes to check off a number for each item, or they can observe on a daily basis and then average their scores. The numbers on the above scale were also represented by words.

1 = Definitely needs help
2 = Could use help
3 = Adequate
4 = Strength

SEMANTIC DIFFERENTIAL

A third type of rating scale sometimes used with children is the *semantic differential*, sometimes called the "Osgood scale" because it was developed

---

Numerical Scale

Attention Span

1. Rarely finishes task, moves rapidly from one to another.
2. Usually needs encouragement to stay with task until complete.
3. Can usually remain with task appropriate to age level until it is finished.
4. Can stay with a chosen activity for very long periods, even returning next day.

Curiosity

1. Shows little or no interest in anything new.
2. Can be intrigued by really exciting things but often uninterested.
3. Actively explores any new things in the room.
4. Interested in new ideas, words, and relationships as well as things.

NOTE: From Hodgden, p. 119

by Charles Osgood (Irwin & Bushnell, p. 209). It uses a seven-point scale with adjectives of opposite meanings (bipolar) at either end. A number of traits should, of course, be included in order to develop a comprehensive profile of the child.

Semantic Differential Scale

Happy └──┴──┴──┴──┴──┘ Sad
Friendly └──┴──┴──┴──┴──┘ Hostile

FORCED CHOICE

A fourth type of rating scale is the *forced choice* scale, where observers must choose one out of the several ranges of behavior listed for each trait (Hodgden, p. 67).

Forced Choice Scale

Ball Catching

Fearful	Usually misses	Often misses	No accommodation	Uses body	Hands only
___	___	___	___	___	___

A different kind of observer error can affect the use of rating scales. Contrary to other types of observation, the use of this tool calls for the observer to make an on-the-spot judgment. It is extremely difficult for such an observer to be totally unbiased and objective. He may be influenced by other things he already knows about the child or his family, or by outside influences completely unrelated to the situation he is observing. For example, one observer persistently gave lower ratings to an overweight child. When asked about it later, the observer admitted a prejudice against overweight children because he had been one himself.

To guard against these tendencies, the observer should rate all of the different children he is observing on the same trait before going on to another trait. To check objectivity, a second rater could observe the same child and compare results.

Rating scales may be used on their own, implemented with other observation methods as a part of the procedure, or filled in later after the observation is completed from data gathered through specimen or running records. As with the other methods, there are several advantages to using rating scales.

1. They are easy to design and less time-consuming to use.
2. They provide a convenient method to observe a large number of traits at one time.
3. They make it possible to measure difficult-to-quantify traits such as "shyness."
4. They can be used by nonspecialist observers.
5. They are easier to score and quantify than most other methods.

The disadvantages also need to be considered before the observer decides to use a rating scale.

1. Rating scales utilize a closed method. They examine specified traits and may overlook other important behavior.
2. They feature the negative as well as the positive side of each trait.
3. Clearly differentiating between each point on the scale is sometimes difficult for both the designer and the observer.
4. It is difficult to eliminate observer bias when judgments must be made quickly on so many different traits.

Checklists

Checklists are lists of specific traits or behaviors arranged in a logical order. The observer must indicate the presence or absence of the behaviors either simultaneous with the observation or upon later reflection. Checklists are especially useful for types of behaviors or traits that can easily and clearly be specified. We tend to see what we look for; thus a checklist can prove to be a valuable tool for focusing our attention when many different items need to be observed. A survey or inventory of a situation can be done more efficiently, for instance, with a checklist than with almost any other observation tool. If the observer needs to know whether a child displays the specified behavior or not, a checklist is the instrument of choice.

Both checklists and rating scales often include large numbers of traits or behaviors. The difference in the two is not necessarily in their appearance but in their use. An observer using a checklist merely checks off the presence of the trait (a blank denotes absence). The observer using a rating scale must make a judgment about the degree to which the trait is present.

Checklists can be used in a number of ways, depending on the purpose for the observation. A different checklist, for instance, can be used for each child in the class, if the results are to be used for individual planning. On the other hand, all of the children's names can be included on the same checklist along with the checklist items, if it is the observer's purpose to make a general survey of the class.

The items on a checklist can simply be checked off, or the date or time when they first appear can be entered to make a more complete record. A different checklist can be used for each observation, or a single checklist can serve in a cumulative manner for the same child all year if dates are recorded for each item. A single checklist can be used by one observer or by several observers who will add to the cumulative data over a period of time.

Finally, information gained from anecdotal records, specimen records, and running records can be transferred to checklists for ease in interpretation. It is much simpler to scan a list of checked behaviors than to read through long paragraphs of wordy description when attempting to interpret observational evidence.

It is obvious that checklists need to be prepared carefully. The items listed should be specified very clearly in objective, nonjudgmental terms. The items should be easily understood by the users; thus, it makes sense to put items through a pretest before actual use as an observation tool. All checklist items should be positive in nature, unlike rating scale items where a range of behavior from positive to negative is necessary.

Checklist items that an observer does not witness are left blank, indicating absence of the particular behavior. If the observer does not have the opportunity to observe certain behaviors, these items should not be left blank, but indicated by some symbol (e.g., N, meaning no opportunity to observe). Some suggestions for developing checklist items include

1. Items should be short, descriptive, understandable.
2. They should be parallel in construction (i.e., word order and verb tense the same for each).

3. They should be objective and nonjudgmental (e.g., not "jumps high" but "jumps over a 1-foot object").
4. They should be positive in nature.
5. They should not be repeated elsewhere in the checklist.
6. They should be representative of children's behavior but not include every behavior.

Overall, the format of the checklist should allow the observer to scan the items at a glance. The *Child Skills Checklist* at the end of this chapter is an example of an observation tool that looks at twelve important areas of child development, breaking down each area into eight specific items. Each item is brief, representative of an important aspect of development, parallel in construction (beginning with a verb), and positive in nature. Together they form the profile of a whole child as he or she works and plays in the environment of an early childhood classroom.

Advantages for using checklists of this nature include

1. They are easy, quick, and efficient to use.
2. They can be used with ease by the nonspecialist observer.
3. They can be used in the presence of the child or later from remembered behaviors.
4. Several observers can gather the same information to check for reliability.
5. These checklists help to focus observation on many behaviors at one time.
6. They are especially useful for curriculum planning for individuals.

At the same time there are disadvantages for using checklists. The observer must weigh one against the other, always keeping in mind his purpose for observing. Checklist disadvantages include

1. They are closed in nature, looking at particular behaviors and not everything that occurs. Thus they may miss behaviors of importance.
2. They are limited to "presence" or "absence" of behavior.
3. They lack information about quality of behavior (how), duration (how long), and description.

CHOOSING THE METHOD FOR OBSERVING AND RECORDING

Table 1 compares the seven methods for observing and recording young children discussed in this chapter. Each has advantages and disadvantages that

TABLE 1. Methods for observing and recording

Method	Purpose	Advantages	Disadvantages
Anecdotal Record: A narrative of descriptive paragraphs, recorded *after behavior occurs*	To detail specific behavior for child's record; for case conferences; to plan for individuals	Open-ended; rich in details; no special observer training	Depends on observer's memory; behavior taken out of context; difficult to code or analyze for research
Running Record: A narrative written in sequence over a specified time, recorded *while behavior is occurring*	To discover cause and effects of behavior; for case conferences; to plan for individual	Open-ended; comprehensive; no special observer training	Time-consuming; difficult to use for more than one child at a time; time-consuming to code and analyze for research
Specimen Record: A detailed narrative written in sequence over a specified time, recorded *while behavior is occurring*	To discover cause and effects of behavior; for child development research	Open-ended; comprehensive and complete; rich in details	Time-consuming to record; time-consuming to code or analyze for research; difficult to observe more than one child at a time
Time Sampling: Tallies or symbols showing the presence or absence of specified behavior during short time periods, recorded *while behavior is occurring*	For behavior modification baseline data; for child development research	Objective and controlled; not time-consuming; efficient for observing more than one child at a time; provides quantitative data for research	Closed; limited to observable behaviors that occur frequently; no description of behavior; takes behavior out of context
Event Sampling: A brief narrative of conditions preceding and following specified behavior, recorded *while behavior is occurring*	For behavior modification input; for child development research	Objective; helpful for in-depth diagnosis of infrequent behavior	Closed; takes event out of context; limited to specified behaviors
Rating Scale: A scale of traits or behaviors with check marks, recorded *before, during, and after behavior occurs*	To judge degree to which child behaves or possesses certain traits; to diagnose behavior or traits; to plan for individuals	Not time-consuming; easy to design; efficient for observing more than one child at a time for many traits; useful for several observers watching same child	Closed; subjective; limited to specified traits or behaviors
Checklist: A list of behaviors with check marks, recorded *before, during, and after behavior occurs*	To determine presence or absence of specified behaviors; to plan for individuals, to give observer an overview of child's development or progress	Efficient for observing more than one child at a time for many behaviors; useful for an individual over a period of time; a good survey or inventory tool; useful for several observers at once; no special training needed	Closed; limited to specified behaviors; no information on quality of behavior

an observer needs to consider before choosing a particular method. The final choice is often based on the purpose for the observation.

A checklist was chosen as the basis for this book because of the unique ability of a checklist to give an observer a good overview of child development. It is a teaching tool as well as an observational tool. The *Child Skills Checklist* at the end of this chapter will thus assist the observer not only in gathering information on specific children, but also in learning the sequences of child growth in the areas of emotional, social, physical, cognitive, language, and creative development.

USING THE CHILD SKILLS CHECKLIST

The *Child Skills Checklist*, around which this book is written, is as much a learning device for the observer as it is a planning tool for helping the child. With sequences of child development as its focus, it presents the areas of emotional, social, physical, cognitive, language, and creative development by dividing each of these aspects into two major categories, and then subdividing each category into eight representative items of development.

Emotional development, for example, is divided into "self-identity" and "emotional development," with a chapter devoted to each of these topics. The observer learns from the chapters some representative behaviors in the sequence of emotional development that can be seen in the early childhood classroom.

Learning for the Observer

As a learning device for the observer, the checklist is best used one section at a time. To understand the sequence of emotional development as it appears in the early childhood classroom, for instance, the observer should first plan to use the self-identity section of the checklist in observing one or two children for enough time to see if all eight items are present. The observer should not only check off the items as they appear, but also record evidence for each item. (See the accompanying example.)

The observer should then read the chapter on self-identity, paying special attention to the items that were not checked. He or she will learn that a three-year-old like Sheila may still not be secure enough in herself to let go of her mother easily when she first comes to the preschool. The observer should not be too concerned when Sheila transfers her clinging to the teacher, for the observer learns that three-year-olds often exhibit such behavior at the beginning of school. The "Helpful Ideas" section after each item in the chapter on self-identity gives suggestions that may assist this child to make the transition from home to school more easily. Since Sheila has been in school for a month and still has difficulty making this transition, she may need special help.

Child Skills Checklist

Child's Name *Sheila, 3*   Date *10-22* Time *9-12:00*
Observer *Connie R.*   Center *Head Start*

Self-Identity

	Item	Evidence	Date
_____	Separates from parents without difficulty	Sheila clings to mother & cries, "Oh, Mommy!"	10/22
_____	Does not cling to classroom staff excessively	Sheila clings to teacher when anything upsetting happens	10/22
__✓__	Makes eye contact with adults	Sheila makes eye contact with teacher & aide	10/22
__✓__	Makes activity choices without teacher's help	Sheila paints, plays with dolls, reads books on her own	10/22
_____	Seeks other children to play with		
__N__	Plays roles confidently in dramatic play		
__✓__	Stands up for own rights	Calls out to teacher: "She ate my orange crayon!"	10/22
__✓__	Displays enthusiasm about doing things for self	Does most activities on own, but watches others carefully	10/22

Using the Entire Checklist

Once the observer is familiar with each of the checklist areas and items, he or she can use the entire checklist with one child to gain a complete overview. To use the checklist most effectively, many observers prefer to make a running record of the child they are observing, transferring the data they have gathered by marking items on the checklist later in the day. In this way they combine the best of both methods of observation: the open-ended advantages of the running record with the focus of a developmental checklist.

In addition they have a record of written evidence for the various checklist items.

A running record for Sheila on 10/22 contains the following:

Sheila and Beth are each coloring on blank papers at a table with box of crayons between them. Beth asks Sheila, "May I borrow your orange?" Sheila says, "No," and covers crayon with hand. Beth grabs her hand, takes crayon with other hand and pops it into her mouth! Sheila says, "That's not fair!" and calls teacher. When teacher comes, Sheila says, "She ate my orange crayon so I can't finish my pumpkin!" Teacher says to Beth, "People shouldn't eat crayons," but teacher is distracted by other events and doesn't follow through on this. Then Sheila goes to book corner and takes book. She carries book around room, looking carefully at what is going on, but not joining in. She whispers to Brian: "Becky painted yesterday and she's going to paint again today. See!" and points to easel. When Brian does not respond, she yells to teacher, "I wanna paint! I wanna paint!" Teacher tells her she can paint when Becky is finished.

From this running record, the observer can continue to fill in the *Child Skills Checklist* for Sheila, checking off items and filling in evidence under "Emotional Development," such as:

 Shows interest/attention in classroom activities
Evidence: Walks around classroom looking carefully at what is going on

and under "Social Play," items such as:

 Plays by self with or without objects
Evidence: Plays with crayons and book alone

 Plays parallel to others constructing or creating something
Evidence: Colors independently but next to another child

Other items that can be checked based on this running record include:

Small Motor Development

 Uses drawing/writing tools with control
Evidence: Draws pumpkin with crayon

Spoken Language

 Speaks in expanded sentences
Evidence: "She ate my orange crayon so I can't finish my pumpkin."

Art Skills

✔ Makes pictorial drawings
   Evidence: Draws a pumpkin

On the other hand, the observer would not check this item:

Self-Identity

_____ Seeks other children to play with
   Evidence: Plays by self; does not seek others

INTERPRETATION OF DATA

Once you have observed a child and recorded data about her in a running record and on the *Child Skills Checklist,* the next step is to interpret the information. Objective observing and recording like this helps make possible a deeper understanding than a lifetime of merely being around children can do. We need to step back from children and look at them impartially and objectively. Only then do we truly see who these children are and how we can help them reach their highest potential. Learning to know and understand a child is a fascinating process.

Interpreting the information you have acquired from your observations takes knowledge and skill. You need to know a great deal about child development, both from reading and studying about children and from actual experience with them, before you can make valid inferences and conclusions based on observations.

This textbook is organized to help you gain such knowledge. Using the *Child Skills Checklist* will focus your attention on important behaviors in each aspect of child development. Reading the chapters that feature each aspect will help you to acquire knowledge of the particular area. Interpretation of the data you acquire will then be more meaningful to you and helpful to the child as you apply it in your individual planning.

Inferences

The first step in interpreting the data you have gathered about the child is to read it through carefully, making inferences where possible, based on the behavior you have observed. An inference is a statement considered to be true—tentatively at least—because it is founded upon information believed to be true. In other words, it is a possible explanation derived from the behavior you have witnessed. In order to make an inference, you must actually have seen and recorded objectively the behavior upon which you are basing the inference.

Looking back at the running record made for Sheila, we might consider making the inferences in the following chart.

Incident	*Faulty Inference*	*Valid Inference*
Sheila would not let Beth borrow her orange crayon.	Sheila does not know how to share.	Sheila was not finished using her orange crayon.
Sheila whispers to Brian that Becky painted yesterday and she's going to paint again today.	Sheila likes to tattle on other children.	Sheila is alert to what Becky did with paint yesterday and today.

After reading carefully the first incident in the running record involving Sheila (that Sheila says "no" when Beth asks to borrow her orange crayon, and then covers the crayon with her hand), we need to ask ourselves what we can infer, if anything, from this. Do the words tell us that Sheila does not know how to share? They do not seem to indicate this. Thus the inference that "Sheila does not know how to share" is probably invalid. We just do not have enough information to make this particular inference. We may want to observe Sheila further to see if she is able to share materials with others before we can infer that she does not know how to share. Does the running record tell us that Sheila was not finished using the orange crayon? Yes. The words say, "She ate my orange crayon so I can't finish my pumpkin." Thus we can infer that Sheila was not finished using the crayon.

The second incident, in which Sheila whispers to Brian that Becky painted yesterday and she's going to paint again today, should be approached in the same way. What, if anything, can we infer from this incident? Does it mean that Sheila likes to tattle on other children? We do not have any indication that this is true; thus, such an inference is faulty. We can infer that Sheila is alert to what Becky did with paint yesterday and now today. That is about all. We may want to infer that Sheila is using such an approach to gain access to an activity she likes, or that Sheila whispers about others in order to get attention, or that Sheila just likes to stir up things in the classroom in this manner—but we truly do not have such information about Sheila, and thus cannot make any of these three latter inferences.

Try making your own inferences from an anecdotal or running record you have made after observing a child. One thing you will learn from such an exercise is the importance of recording with rich detail. You need to learn this skill through practice. There is always something more you can add to an objective record—facial expressions, gestures, reactions of other children. They may be the keys to the inferences you are trying to elicit about a child.

The principal stumbling block in making valid inferences based on recorded observational data is that we try to read more into the data than is actually there. We are used to making judgments continuously about people and situations in our lives. Often they are faulty judgments based on insufficient information, or misinterpreted information. Do not allow yourself to be misled like this when you have the written data before you on child observations. Look at the data and ask yourself the question: "Is there evidence to support my inference?" If there is, then you can make it.

Conclusions

The final step in your interpretation of recorded data about children is to make whatever conclusions you can. A conclusion in this case is a reasoned judgment based on accumulated observational evidence. As with inferences, you cannot make such a judgment unless you can show sufficient evidence. Read through your observational data. Based on what you have recorded, what is it possible to conclude about the child? We can conclude very little from the one running record on Sheila by itself. For instance, we cannot conclude that she is always so alert to other children and activities in the classroom unless future observations show this. It may be that she is really only concerned with painting.

Observing, recording, and interpreting in this careful, objective manner should help you to sort out what children are really like. You may be surprised by what you find.

PLANNING FOR CHILDREN BASED ON OBSERVATIONS

The ultimate reason for observing and recording is not just to learn what children are like, but to help them grow and develop. That is why they have come to your classroom. You can assist them in this goal if your observations have helped you identify their strengths and their areas needing strengthening.

After observing Sheila for only one morning and transferring her observational data from a running record to the *Child Skills Checklist*, we can begin to get a picture of her strengths and which areas need strengthening. From this developmental portrait, we can begin to make plans for Sheila that will help to build on her strengths and speak to her needs—always accentuating the positive.

Learning Prescription

Creating a *learning prescription* for Sheila is the next step in the process of planning for an individual child based on observational data. To create such

---

Learning Prescription

Name ___Sheila_____ Date _10/22_

Areas of Strength and Confidence

1. She makes definite activity choices on her own.
2. She speaks in expanded sentences.
3. She enjoys art (crayons and painting) and displays art skills.

Areas Needing Strengthening

1. To separate from mother more easily.
2. To rely less on adults in classroom.
3. To play with other children.

Activities to Help

1. Arrange a transition activity when Sheila first arrives that she will have to do with another child; for example, Sheila and Becky could clean the rabbit cage and feed the rabbit.
2. Sheila could talk into the cassette tape recorder, telling her story of "the loudest noise I ever heard." She could then be in charge of taping the other children's stories.
3. Sheila and another child could begin painting the large cardboard carton that the class wants to use as a "space ship."

---

a prescription, we look over the *Child Skills Checklist* to find at least three *areas of strength*. Although her checklist is far from complete, it is still possible to identify some real strengths for Sheila: for example, she makes definite activity choices on her own; she also speaks in expanded sentences; and finally, she really enjoys art. There are other areas of strength, such as her ability to stand up for her own rights, but it is easier to work with a learning prescription of three of the most important strengths. (See Appendix B, page 372, for a reproducible copy of a *Learning Prescription* form.)

Then we look for *areas needing strengthening*. We do not call these "weaknesses," a negative term. Words are important, and we should use them carefully. If we talk in terms of negatives, we will think in terms of negatives regarding Sheila and our other children. If we think in terms of areas needing strengthening, we should be able to plan a positive program for Sheila that will help her to continue in her development and improve in areas that need improving. Put yourself in the same position. Wouldn't you prefer to be involved in a training program that would help you to improve in your "areas needing strengthening" rather than a program to overcome your "weaknesses"?

Finally, the learning prescription needs to include specific ideas for helping the child to improve in her areas that need strengthening by drawing upon her strengths. Specific ideas for *activities* can come from your own experience or the ideas listed in the various chapters after every checklist item under the heading "If You Have Not Checked This Item: Some Helpful Ideas." An *Index of Activities* at the end of the book will help you to locate these ideas easily. An initial learning prescription for Sheila might read something like this example.

The teachers in Sheila's class will want to continue their observing and recording to evaluate how these activities help Sheila, as well as the other children, and what other individual plans are needed.

The chapters that follow in this text can serve as guidelines for you in evaluating children's strengths and needs, and then in planning for activities to help individuals or small groups of children with similar needs. The ideas listed under "If You Have Not Checked This Item: Some Helpful Ideas" should prove useful not only for assisting children in areas of their needs, but also in providing the stimulus for your own ideas for activities.

Chapter 14, "Observation of the Whole Child," brings together the twelve separate checklist areas and applies them to a single child. Observers learn how to use the checklist in a classroom situation, how to interpret the results, and finally, how to convert checkmarks into an individual learning prescription. Once you have learned where one child stands developmentally, you can make similar plans for each of the children in your own program.

Child Skills Checklist

Name: _____ Observer: _____

Program: _____ Dates: _____

Directions:
Put a ✔ for items you see the child perform regularly.
Put *N* for items where there is no opportunity to observe.
Leave all other items blank.

Item	Evidence	Date
1. Self-Identity		
_____ Separates from parents without difficulty		
_____ Does not cling to classroom staff excessively		
_____ Makes eye contact with adults		

Item	Evidence	Date
_____ Makes activity choices without teacher's help		
_____ Seeks other children to play with		
_____ Plays roles confidently in dramatic play		
_____ Stands up for own rights		
_____ Displays enthusiasm about doing things for self		
2. Emotional Development		
_____ Allows self to be comforted during stressful time		
_____ Eats, sleeps, toilets without fuss away from home		
_____ Handles sudden changes/ startling situations with control		
_____ Can express anger in words rather than actions		
_____ Allows aggressive behavior to be redirected		
_____ Does not withdraw from others excessively		
_____ Shows interest/attention in classroom activities		
_____ Smiles, seems happy much of the time		
3. Social Play		
_____ Plays by self with or without objects		
_____ Plays by self in pretending-type activities		
_____ Plays parallel to others with or without objects		

Item	Evidence	Date
_____ Plays parallel to others in pretending-type activities		
_____ Plays parallel to others constructing or creating something		
_____ Plays with a group with or without objects		
_____ Plays with a group in pretending-type activities		
_____ Plays with a group constructing or creating something		
4. Prosocial Behavior		
_____ Shows concern for someone in distress		
_____ Shows delight for someone experiencing pleasure		
_____ Shares something with another		
_____ Gives something of his or her own to another		
_____ Takes turns with toys or activities		
_____ Waits for turn without a fuss		
_____ Helps another do a task		
_____ Helps another in need		
5. Large Motor Development		
_____ Walks down steps alternating feet		
_____ Runs with control over speed and direction		
_____ Jumps over obstacle, landing on two feet		

Item	Evidence	Date
_____ Hops forward on one foot		
_____ Climbs up and down climbing equipment with ease		
_____ Moves legs/feet in rhythm to beat		
_____ Claps hands in rhythm to beat		
_____ Beats drum alternating hands in rhythm to beat		
6. Small Motor Development		
_____ Shows hand preference (which is _____)		
_____ Turns with hand easily (knobs, lids, eggbeaters)		
_____ Pours liquid into glass without spilling		
_____ Unfastens and fastens zippers, buttons, Velcro tabs		
_____ Picks up and inserts objects with ease		
_____ Uses drawing/writing tools with control		
_____ Uses scissors with control		
_____ Pounds in nails with control		
7. Cognitive Development: Classification and Seriation		
_____ Recognizes basic geometric shapes		
_____ Recognizes colors		
_____ Recognizes differences in size		
_____ Recognizes differences in musical tones		

Item	Evidence	Date
_____ Reproduces musical tones with voice		
_____ Sorts objects by appearance		
_____ Arranges events in sequence from first to last		
_____ Arranges objects in series according to a rule		
8. Cognitive Development: Number, Time, Space, Memory _____ Counts by rote to ten		
_____ Counts objects to ten		
_____ Knows the daily schedule in sequence		
_____ Knows what happened yesterday		
_____ Can build a block enclosure		
_____ Can locate an object behind or beside something		
_____ Recalls words to song, chant		
_____ Can recollect and act on directions of singing game		
9. Spoken Language _____ Speaks confidently in classroom		
_____ Speaks clearly enough for adults to understand		
_____ Speaks in expanded sentences		
_____ Takes part in conversations with other children		

Item	Evidence	Date
_____ Asks questions with proper word order		
_____ Makes "no" responses with proper word order		
_____ Uses past tense verbs correctly		
_____ Plays with rhyming words		
10. Written Language		
_____ Pretends to write by scribbling horizontally		
_____ Includes features of real letters in scribbling		
_____ Identifies own written name		
_____ Identifies classroom labels		
_____ Knows some alphabet letters		
_____ Prints real letters		
_____ Prints letters of name		
_____ Prints name correctly in linear manner		
11. Art Skills		
_____ Makes random marks or covers paper with color		
_____ Scribbles on paper		
_____ Forms basic shapes		
_____ Makes mandalas		
_____ Makes suns		
_____ Draws human as circle with arms and legs attached		
_____ Draws animals, trees		
_____ Makes pictorial drawings		

Item	Evidence	Date
12. Imagination		
_____ Pretends by replaying familiar routines		
_____ Needs particular props to do pretend play		
_____ Assigns roles or takes assigned roles		
_____ May switch roles without warning		
_____ Uses language for creating and sustaining plot		
_____ Uses exciting, danger-packed themes		
_____ Takes on characteristics and actions related to role		
_____ Uses elaborate and creative themes, ideas, details		

Permission is granted by the publisher to reproduce this checklist for evaluation and record keeping. (See Appendix A, pages 365–371, for reproducible copy of the checklist.)

REFERENCES CITED

Bell, Donald, and **Roberta M. Low.** (1977). *Observing and Recording Children's Behavior.* Richland, WA: Performance Associates.

Hodgden, Laurel (Ed.). (1974). *School Before Six: A Diagnostic Approach.* St. Louis: CEMREL.

Irwin, D. Michelle, and **M. Margaret Bushnell.** (1980). *Observational Strategies for Child Study.* New York: Holt, Rinehart, and Winston.

OTHER SOURCES

Bentzen, Warren R. (1985). *Seeing Young Children: A Guide to Observing and Recording Behavior.* Albany, NY: Delmar Publishers.

Cartwright, Carol A., and **G. Phillip Cartwright.** (1984). *Developing Observation Skills.* New York: McGraw-Hill.

Cohen, Dorothy H., and **Virginia Stern.** (1983). *Observing and Recording the Behavior of Young Children.* New York: Teachers College Press.

Richard, Ann Sherrill. (1980). *Understanding Children Through Observation.* St. Paul: West Publishing.

Touliatos, John, and **Norma H. Compton.** (1983). *Approaches to Child Study.* Minneapolis: Burgess.

LEARNING ACTIVITIES

1. Have two different observers use the *Child Skills Checklist* to observe the same child at the same time period for three days. Compare results. How similar were the observations? In what areas were there differences? In what ways can you improve future observing and recording?

2. Make an anecdotal record of a child after you have observed him/her for an hour. At the same time have another observer make an on-the-spot running record. Compare the two. Which showed more detail? Which was more accurate? Which would be more helpful to you in understanding the child or planning for him? Why?

3. Have two different observers make a running record of the same child for 30 minutes. Compare the results. Which, if any, of the problems mentioned for running records on page 9 turned up? How can you overcome these problems in the future?

4. Make an anecdotal record on a child after you have observed him/her for an hour. What inferences can you make about this child? Upon what specific evidence is each inference based? Can you make any conclusions? Why or why not?

5. Construct a graphic rating scale on five social behaviors of children and use it to observe children in your class. Discuss your results. Did you have any problems making judgments? How can you use the information gained?

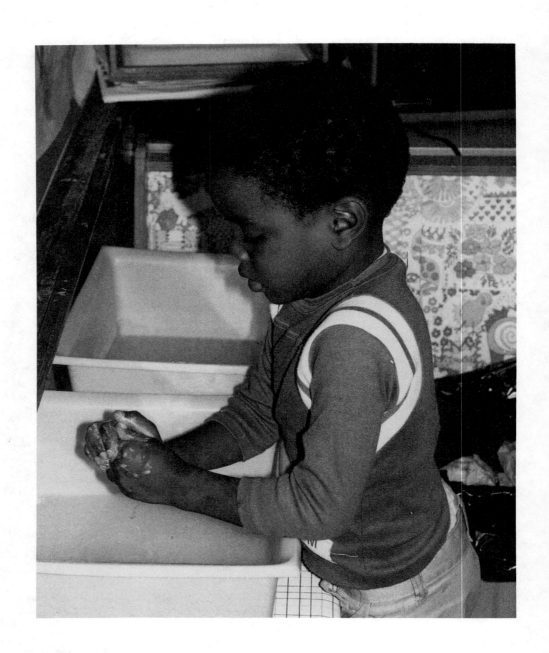

2 Self-Identity

Self-Identity Checklist

☐ Separates from parents without difficulty
☐ Does not cling to classroom staff excessively
☐ Makes eye contact with adults
☐ Makes activity choices without teacher's help
☐ Seeks other children to play with
☐ Plays roles confidently in dramatic play
☐ Stands up for own rights
☐ Displays enthusiasm about doing things for self

F rom the moment of birth, the young human being is engaged in the dynamic process of becoming himself or herself. The child continually develops into a whole person with a temperament, personality, and value system—with a physical, cognitive, language, social, emotional, and creative makeup that is uniquely his or her own. It is a totally engrossing process that will take a lifetime to complete, but its early stages are perhaps its most crucial, for they set the pattern for all that is to follow.

This chapter discusses some of the developmental sequences that are observable in children three to five years of age as they strive to develop in the setting of the child development center or classroom. Although the children carry their own unique packages of genetic traits and home influences, the caregivers they meet and the care they receive at the center will nevertheless have a strong bearing on their future development.

Each item of the *Child Skills Checklist* will be discussed separately in this and subsequent chapters. Each checklist item is positive in nature and should be checked if the observer sees the child performing in the manner described. Suggestions for helping and supporting the child's development in the unchecked items will follow the discussion of the item.

SEPARATES FROM PARENTS ☐ WITHOUT DIFFICULTY

Initial Attachment

Most studies of young children agree that a key ingredient to successful development is a strong initial attachment to a primary caregiver, usually the mother. Without such an attachment, babies may seriously lag in their development and, in some cases, even die. It seems a great paradox, then, to suggest that for successful development to continue, the young human must learn at the same time to separate from the parent. Nevertheless, such is the case. This separation should occur first in the home—not only with the child, but also with the parents, who must encourage the infant to become independent of them, and who must also let go of the infant.

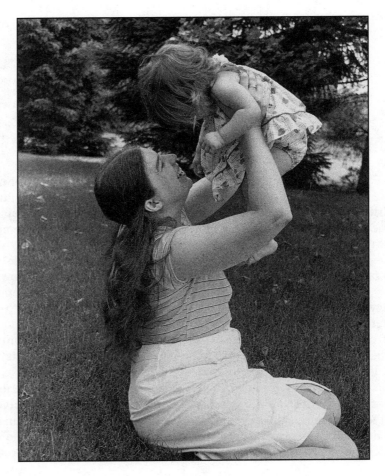

A key ingredient to the young child's emotional development is a strong initial attachment to a primary caregiver, usually the mother.

Many current attachment/separation studies are based on the work of John Bowlby (1969) and Mary Ainsworth (1978), whose work also reflects Jean Piaget's theories of cognitive development.

The first separation of the child from the mother is, of course, the physical one that occurs at birth. Some psychologists believe that much of life thereafter is a striving by the developing being to achieve that perfect state of oneness once again with another human (Kaplan, p. 43).

But in the first few months of life, the baby hardly recognizes itself as a separate being apart from its mother or primary caregiver. When it cries, the mother feeds or changes it. When it gurgles or coos, the mother holds it close or smiles. Little by little, as visual memory develops—and "person permanence" occurs—the infant comes to recognize this primary caregiver as being different from everyone else. The child then strives to be near the caregiver or to bring this person close as often as possible. *Person permanence* means that the infant has developed the ability to hold the memory of the person in the mind when the person is out of sight (Damon, p. 34).

It is necessary, therefore, that this primary caregiver be a consistent one. The formation of a strong attachment becomes complicated if the infant has too many primary caregivers. If the mother works during the day, for example, she should make arrangements to turn over the secondary caregiving arrangements to one consistent person while she is away. She can still function as a primary caregiver when she returns from work, if this is the role she has chosen. If she has turned over the role of primary caregiver to the father or to another person from the beginning, then this should be the consistent person whom the infant can turn to at the end of the day. The baby who has developed person permanence will welcome this person happily when he or she returns.

This is the beginning of the strong initial attachment that is necessary on the part of both infant and caregiver in order for later separation to occur successfully. Such an attachment leads to a sense of security and trust on the part of the infant. The lack of such an attachment often interferes with the child's building trust in future relationships. In fact, the failure to thrive in infancy is frequently the result of the breakdown of this initial attachment relationship (Seagull & Kallen, p. 8).

Both the primary caregiver and the infant play a part in the building of this initial attachment. The adult must respond promptly and in an appropriate manner to the infant's cries—time after time after time. For example, the adult should feed the infant and not spank it when it cries out of hunger. Some adults do not. On the other hand, the infant should also respond appropriately to the caregiver's actions. For example, the infant needs to stop crying when the adult cares for its needs, or to show delight when the adult plays with it or cuddles it. Some babies do not.

It is difficult for the initial attachment to be a strong one when the actions of one or the other (or both) are not satisfactory over a period of time. It takes most of the infant's first year to develop the relationship with a caregiver, in fact (Damon, p. 29). Without such an attachment, however, it is difficult for the infant to develop trust in anyone else, and it becomes doubly difficult for the infant or developing child to separate from the caregiver.

After all, if it cannot trust its primary caregiver, how can it risk trusting anyone? The attachment between the infant and primary caregiver, in fact, serves as a model for future human relationships.

Initial Separation

The initial separation of the infant from its mother or primary caregiver begins when it first recognizes that it is separate from that person. This develops within the first six months of life as the baby recognizes that there is a difference between itself and the caregiver—and later, between itself and others. At this time, its first memories—visual in nature—are occurring. Some psychologists call this the "psychological birth" of the baby (Kaplan, p. 121). It is the first glimmering of self-identity.

Toward the end of the first year, as the infant learns to move about by creeping and finally by its first unsteady steps, an interesting pattern of interaction with the caregiver often emerges. The youngster uses the caregiver as a base from which to explore its environment. It moves out a bit and comes back, moves further and returns, moves out again, and this time may only look back, making the eye contact that will give it the reassurance to continue its exploration.

During this same period or sometimes before, *separation anxiety* also emerges; that is, the infant sets up a strong protest of crying or clinging if the caregiver attempts to leave. This pattern of distress is also exhibited when a stranger appears, making it obvious that the baby recognizes the difference between the caregiver and others.

Thus self-identity develops as the toddler ventures out and scurries back, clings and pushes away, holds on and lets go. But the stronger the initial attachment, the more secure the developing child should feel each time he or she lets go.

In addition, the young human learns who he is by the way other people respond to him (how others seem to be affected by whatever he does). Ideally, this response is mainly positive, so that by the time he enters nursery school, day care, or Head Start, he already will be feeling good about himself. Table 2 summarizes the child's attachment/separation milestones.

School Separation

No matter how good the young child feels about him- or herself, the initial school separation from a parent is often difficult. At three years old, the sense of self is still a bit shaky. Although the child has an identity at home and can hold onto an image of the caregiver even when the caregiver is not present, at school the child is in a strange environment as well. To complicate matters, the parent/caregiver may be experiencing "separation anxiety" too, and the child often senses this.

TABLE 2. Attachment/separation milestones in child development

Attachment

Preattachment
Birth through first eight to twelve weeks
> Responds to people but cannot distinguish one from the other; does not recognize self as separate from primary caregiver.

Person permanence
First months
> Learns to distinguish primary caregiver from others

Attachment to caregiver
First months to second or third year
> Seeks proximity to caregiver; shows separation anxiety when caregiver leaves; shows stranger anxiety when stranger appears—most common at seven months.

Partnership
Second or third year on
> Comes to understand caregiver's point of view and adjusts own behavior accordingly.

Separation

Physical separation from mother
Birth
Psychological birth
First six months
> Recognizes self as separate from mother.

Exploration of physical environment
Last months of first year to second, third years
> Explores first by creeping, then walking; uses caregiver as base to explore and return.

Strengthening of self-identity
Second, third years on
> Gets stronger recognition of self-identity as child and parent let go of one another for more frequent and longer periods of time.

NOTE: Includes information from Damon, p. 33

Each child handles the situation in his or her own way. One may be used to the home of a loving babysitter, and will take this new playroom in stride. Another may cling to her mother and scream whenever the mother attempts to leave. The child used to playing with others may quickly join the group in the block building corner. A shyer child may need the teacher's urging to join in. One fussing, crying child may stop as soon as his mother leaves. Another may withdraw into herself and sit in a corner sucking her thumb.

You as a classroom worker hope that the children will become adjusted to this separation within a few days or weeks. Most of them will. One or two may not. How can you help them develop a strong enough sense of self that they also feel free to let go of their primary caregiver?

If You Have Not Checked This Item: Some Helpful Ideas

One or more of the children in your center may have unchecked self-identity checklist items. Because you are aware that each item represents a step in the developmental sequence of young children, you may be able to lend children support at the outset by arranging your schedule or classroom ahead of time to address their problems. Here are some ideas that may help preschoolers separate from their parents with less difficulty.

■ Make an Early Initial Contact with Parent/Caregiver and Child

If the child and the parent have met you ahead of time, they may feel less reluctant to separate on the day that school begins. For the child, it is better if this meeting takes place close to the time of school opening rather than the spring before. Memories of a brief visit several months before school begins have little meaning for the young child. An immediate follow-up is more effective. If you visit the child's home, you might take a camera with you to record the occasion for later use in the classroom to help the child make an easier transition from home to school.

■ Try Staggered Enrollment

Rather than having all of the children in your class begin school on the same day at the same time, you might consider having half of them begin on the first day, and half the second—or half in the morning and the rest in the afternoon. This will allow staff members to devote more time to the individual children and their parents. In addition, the first day may not be so overwhelming for the children, if only half of the class is present at once.

■ Create a Simple Initial Environment

The more complex the classroom environment, the more overwhelming it is for certain children. You might plan to have the classroom arranged with fewer activity areas for the first weeks and less material on the shelves. As the children settle in and become more secure, you can add activities and materials as needed.

■ Use Transition Materials

Children can make the transition from home to school—can separate more easily from their parents—if there are familiar materials to bridge the gap.

Water is one such material. A water table or basin with an egg beater, funnel, and squeeze bottles may take a child's mind off his parents long enough to get him happily involved in the center. Toy trucks and dolls often have the same effect. Have a special set of little toys you can allow children to take home with them at the end of the day and return again in the morning to make the transition less difficult.

■ Utilize Parent/Caregiver Visits

Allow the parents to stay as long as necessary on the first days or come in for visits from time to time. The shy child may use her parent as a base for exploration in the classroom, venturing away and returning just as she did as a toddler at home. If the separation is a difficult one, have the caregiver return early to pick up the youngster. Little by little, the children should be able to stay longer without their parents.

■ Read a Book

Children like to hear stories about other children who have feelings similar to their own. Try reading a book about separation to children having difficulty in this area. Talk about the story and ask the child or children how they feel. *Dear Daddy* by Philippe Dupasquier (New York: Puffin Books, 1985) is a wonderfully illustrated letter from a little girl to her father, who is a seaman on a merchant ship. The horizontally divided pages show Sophie at home on the lower half of the page, while the top illustrations show what her daddy is doing on the ship at the same time.

■ Show and Foster Acceptance of the Child

Up till now the child's self-identity has evolved from the reactions of her family to her. Now that she is in your classroom, you, your co-workers, and the other children will be adding details to the child's interior picture of herself. These details need to be positive, happy ones. You need to support this process first of all by accepting the child and her family unconditionally. Show your acceptance both verbally and nonverbally. Smile at her frequently. Greet her personally every day. Demonstrate that you enjoy being near her and having her near you. You are the behavior model for the other children as well. If they see that you accept a child no matter what, they will be more likely to do the same.

DOES NOT CLING TO CLASSROOM □
STAFF EXCESSIVELY

The next developmental step for the children in your classroom is to build enough confidence to become involved on their own with the other children and the activities available. Those with a strong sense of self may have no difficulty. Others may not be ready during the first days or weeks. A few may not be ready at all.

Psychologists use the term *significant others* in referring to the particular people who have the most important influence on our lives (Seagull & Kallen, p. 13). For the young child, this usually means his immediate family. Once he enters your classroom, however, you and your co-workers will also become significant others. This means that your reactions toward the child will have an effect on what he thinks about himself. This may reinforce the view of self learned at home, or it may modify that view. If the responses to him are generally positive, then his feelings about himself as a good person are strengthened. The opposite, of course, is also true.

The development of a self-identity is thus a subtle but lengthy process. No one knows for sure how long it takes—probably much of a person's life. The early childhood years are the most crucial because they set the course. That is why it is so important for the young self in its most sensitive, formative period to receive positive responses from the adults around it.

Many children develop a similar kind of attachment to one or more of the adults in the early childhood classroom as they did to their primary caregiver at home. These children need a consistent caregiver here as well, in order to develop trust in this new environment. It is thus important that the staff of an early childhood center be present consistently throughout the year—not merely dropping in and dropping out.

If the teacher must leave, she should try to have the replacement teacher visit the classroom several times before she departs, so that the children may get to know the replacement. The transition will thus be more gradual and generally more acceptable to the children. Otherwise, for certain children, changing teachers will be nearly as traumatic as changing primary caregivers.

The child who looks to the teacher as a caregiver may cling to the classroom adult. He or she may not have the necessary trust in the world, or may not have developed a strong enough sense of self yet to let go in a strange new environment. Three-year-olds, especially, may relate much more comfortably to adults than to other children. After all, much of their lives thus far may have been spent in one-to-one relationships with adults. A classroom of fifteen to twenty children may be totally overwhelming. How can you help such a child?

If You Have Not Checked This Item: Some Helpful Ideas

■ **Display Acceptance**

You must accept the child's clinging behavior, knowing that it is a normal step in the developmental sequence. But you also need to know ways to encourage and support this child when she is ready to move out. If she feels that you accept her presence near you and will not force her to do something she is not ready to do, she is much more likely to move out on her own. Forcing a clinging child away from you before she is ready to go may only make her cling more tightly.

■ Have Child Follow the Adult's Lead

The child who clings to or "shadows" an adult may follow the adult's lead as well. You could lead her to a table and sit down with her to make a puzzle. If she becomes involved with it on her own, you might try moving on to another group of children. Or you could try playing a role in the dramatic play area and inviting the child to accompany you on some pretend errand, or to help you accomplish some pretend task. If the child accepts your efforts to involve her, you can freely leave the activity. If she does not, she may not be ready yet to move out on her own.

■ Observe the Child

You may be able to tell when the time is right by your observations of this child. Does he spend a great deal of time observing the others? Is this looking behavior done from the "protection" of your side, or does he stand in a "safe" spot and watch? If his eyes seem to be more engaged in following the activities of the others rather than keeping track of you, it may be time to help him become involved with them.

■ Ask the Child to Help an Adult or Another Child

The clinging child will sometimes allow herself to become involved in classroom activities as the adult's helper. Ask her to help you get out the paints or the puzzles . . . to dress a doll in the housekeeping area . . . to feed the guinea pig . . . to deliver a message next door. Little by little, she may venture away from you and then return, just as she did with her primary caregiver at home. Or you might ask a second child to join you as a helper. The two of them could then do the same tasks, at which point you could try leaving them on their own.

■ Follow Up on the Child's Interest

One of the most successful techniques for involving the clinging child in classroom activities is to discover what interests him. Your conversations with him may give you a clue. If he is nonverbal, your observations of the things that attract his attention may suggest an activity he could pursue by himself and then later with another child when he feels enough at ease. You might leaf through a magazine with him and ask him to point to the pictures of the things he likes. He or you could cut these out, and he might paste them in a scrapbook to get him started. Or you could use the information you gain about his interests to involve him more directly with similar class-room activities.

If none of these ideas work, you should continue to be patient about his clinging. Do not push. When he feels secure enough in the class-room, he will venture out on his own. The child who never feels secure enough is probably still not mature enough to handle a classroom situation. If he still continues to cling after several weeks in your program, you may want to discuss with the parent the possibility of keeping him at home for another year or placing him in a home-type program with fewer children.

☐ MAKES EYE CONTACT WITH ADULTS

Nonverbal cues are among the most important signals people send out about their feelings. Facial expressions, head position, muscle tension, body carriage—all reveal a person's state of mind regarding himself and those around him. All of us read these expressions subconsciously. Our subconscious minds process this intake and help our conscious minds to make decisions about the people we interact with. We feel that they are friendly, hostile, frightened, or unsure as a result of this constant subconscious processing of visual stimuli.

As teachers of young children, we need to read such nonverbal cues consciously as well, because of the important information they can give us about young children. In addition, we need to be aware of how important such information is to young children. Because they are not fully verbal at ages three and four, young children depend heavily on nonverbal cues from us to make determinations about the people and situations they encounter.

We can say polite words to children and their parents, but if our faces are tense and our eyes give out signals of distaste, the child picks up and responds to these. That is why we say children instinctively know which adults to trust. Children read nonverbal signals exceptionally well, partly because children are nonverbal themselves and partly because they are more visually oriented than most adults.

Eye signals are the most important. Eyes give messages of affection, love, happiness, contentment, and humor. They show pain, frustration, anger, fright, and despair. The way the eyes are partly or wholly open, the position of the eyebrows, the size of the pupils, the number of blinks, the length of a stare—all are indicative of the feelings of a person. Words may not always tell the truth, but the eyes do.

Earlier studies assumed that the size of the pupils of the eye remained constant if the level of light remained the same. Research subsequently has disproved this notion. What research discovered instead was that the pupils increase in size in the presence of pleasant things and become noticeably smaller if people and situations are disagreeable. Eyes also respond to more than visual cues. Laboratory tests have shown that eye pupils change size in response to voices. Loud, harsh, or scolding voices may cause them to shrink. The size of eye pupils is in fact a reliable indicator of a person's feelings (Thompson, p. 90).

Eye contact between people is important. The first encounter with someone's eyes reveals much about the person's feelings concerning himself. Subsequent contact often tells a great deal of how that person feels about you. The first actual eye contact itself is a recognition that you exist in a person's world and that person exists in yours. If he feels uncomfortable about himself or you, he often shifts his gaze. We hope you will not need to do the same.

Preschool children are at an egocentric stage in their development when they enter your classroom. They see things mostly from their own points of view. If you asked one to hide so that you would not be able to see her, she might very well cover her own eyes. From her self-centered point of view, she believes that you cannot see her because she cannot see you. Children who are initially tense or frightened or uneasy in your presence may use this same subterfuge by refusing to make eye contact—if they do not look at you, surely you will not be able to see them—or if they do not look at you, maybe you will not really be there.

Certain cultures and ethnic groups also condition their children not to look adults directly in the eye because they feel it is disrespectful. You need to decide whether your children avoid eye contact because of cultural conditioning or because they are truly uncomfortable with themselves or you. Eventually you will need to have eye contact with all of your children in order for them to recognize the freedom and openness of this new environment—to understand that they are worthy human beings in your sight.

When eye contact finally occurs, it often diffuses tense situations. If you can succeed in getting the shy or frightened child to make eye contact with you, you may be able to dispel his fears without saying a word. He will see in your eyes the friendliness, sense of humor, and enjoyment he can expect from your presence. But you need to know that your eyes cannot fake it. You must truly project to this young developing child that you like him already, no matter what (because you really do).

Research shows that the more a person likes someone, the more he looks at him (Thompson, p. 91). This applies to teachers as well as their children. It is therefore important that you do not pick favorites or reject any of your children, because their sensitivity to nonverbal cues will soon tell them this. You will be looking more frequently at the children you like than at the children you do not like. As a professional, you cannot afford to pick favorites or dislike a child. Of course, it is human to like one person more than another. In your position as a child care worker, however, this is not permissible. You must make a concerted effort to correct your feelings if you find yourself responding like this.

If You Have Not Checked This Item: Some Helpful Ideas

■ **Acceptance**

Many of the same ideas used to help the child who was not checked for the first two items also apply here. This child either is not sure of himself or has not developed basic trust in the people and world around him. Or she may have a disability of some sort. Austistic children seem to avoid eye contact. Some mentally retarded children have difficulty making eye contact with people outside their families.

To help any child develop a self-identity strong enough to make eye contact with strange adults, you, as the strange adult, must show you accept the child unconditionally. Use both verbal and nonverbal cues. Tell him or her how nice it is to have her in your center. Use his name frequently. Exclaim with delight when he accomplishes something, no matter how insignificant.

■ **Make Eye Contact Yourself**

You are the model for behavior in your classroom. If you feel it is important for your children to behave in a certain way, then you need to do the same yourself. Make eye contact with the shy child at all times. When she finally has the confidence to return the look, she needs to see you smiling at her.

■ **Read a Book**

Read to the shy or insecure child a book such as *I Am Eyes Ni Macho*, by Leila Ward (New York: Scholastic, 1987). It is an illustrated story of what an African child sees during the day. You could then ask your child what he or she sees.

■ **Have Patience**

Do not force the issue. You must remember that the child's avoidance of eye contact is not a negative action but a clue to you that he is still not confident enough in your presence to return the look. You need to do all in your power to help him develop that confidence. But sometimes the best thing to do is nothing. Have patience. Forcing will not help. You must have the confidence to know that his refusal to meet your eyes is nothing personal. When he finally feels at ease within himself and within your center, he will return your look.

All children at one time or another avoid looking at a caregiver. They may be embarrassed, ashamed, or feeling foolish about something they have done. But if they can see that you still accept them when they finally confront your gaze, they will be able to return your look with confidence as they continue on their own unique paths of development.

MAKES ACTIVITY CHOICES □
WITHOUT TEACHER'S HELP

One of the next observable indicators of a child's feelings about herself in your classroom is her willingness to make a choice on her own about the activity she wants to engage in. Once she feels confident enough to leave your side, she needs to explore the new environment and try out the various materials and activities on her own. Many children have a strong enough sense of self to go immediately to the activity areas upon first entering the

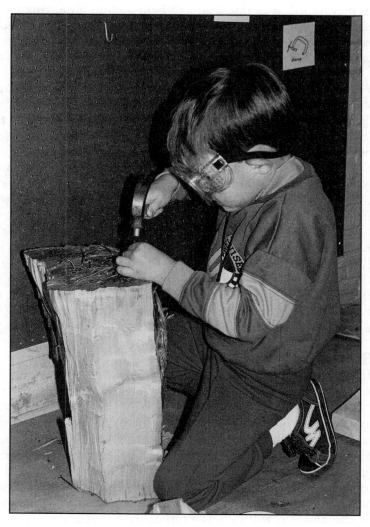

An observable indicator of a child's self-confidence is his willingness to choose an activity without the teacher's help.

room. Others use the adult who accompanies them as a base for their explorations, going into an area and coming back to the person, much as they did during their initial separation from their primary caregiver when they were infants. Some also use the teacher as this base.

Research seems to imply that having a secure base of attachment facilitates exploratory behavior on the part of two-year-olds in center-based day care (Fein & Schwartz, p. 88). Three-, four- and five-year-olds also do better when they have this strong attachment. These attachment findings seem to indicate that, just as within the family, the child who is secure in his relationship with a caregiver will also be secure on his own. Thus, as previously mentioned, it is important to help a child build this relationship initially. It is also important to observe which children are able to become involved with activities independently—and which are not quite ready, possibly because the sense of self-identity in these children is not yet strong enough.

Your goal for children who do not participate independently in activities will be to help these children develop a sense of security with you and within the center. Once they develop this feeling of security, they may take the next step toward self-identity: becoming involved in center activities on their own.

You may need to help the clinging child get started, as mentioned previously. But then you should withdraw. Children need to have every opportunity to express their self-identities on their own. They need to explore the center environment. They need to learn to make their own choices.

It is so tempting for teachers to help them make decisions—and the children will listen. They will even ask for help. They are used to having adults tell them what to do. You must resist the temptation. Invite them to look for themselves. Then support them in their exploration. It is so much simpler for you to make up their minds for them, you may argue. But then they will have lost the opportunity to take the next step in their development as a person. Give them this chance.

If You Have Not Checked This Item:
Some Helpful Ideas

■ Provide an Explorable Environment

For younger children, your environment needs to be simple, with a few activity areas and a small number of items within each. This applies especially to two- and three-year-olds. Some environments are just too complex for these children to be comfortable. Too many things are going on, and the children respond by refusing to explore or get involved. For this age group, you need to simplify your physical environment—at least at the beginning of the year. Later, the children will be ready for additional activities.

Four- and five-year-olds, on the other hand, need the stimulation of complexity, novelty, and variation. This age group tends to be less fearful of new things and more venturesome. For them, a more complex physical environment may encourage rather than discourage exploration.

■ Give Children Time

Once children feel secure with you and your center, they should be able to make activity choices on their own if you give them enough time. Let them wander around at first during the free choice period. Don't force them into an activity before they are ready. Some children need more time than others. Others need to try out many things before they can settle on one.

■ Act as a Base for Children's Exploration

Sit or stand in an area of the room where children can see you—near, but not in any one activity area. Those who still need the security of an adult attachment can make eye contact, receive your smiles of support, and even come over for a moment or so before you encourage them to go off on their own again. The child who is still clinging can explore with her eyes. When she feels secure enough, she will join the others, knowing you are nearby.

■ Read a Book

Hearing a book read about a nursery school classroom and all of the interesting activities it contains may motivate the insecure child to look around his own classroom and be more willing to make activity choices on his own. *Gwenda Turner's Playbook* (New York: Viking Kestrel/Penguin Books, 1985) is a beautifully illustrated picture book of nursery school children engaged in all sorts of fascinating play activities.

SEEKS OTHER CHILDREN TO PLAY WITH ☐

Although this particular item seems to relate more to the child's social rather than emotional development, it actually indicates both. Seeking other children to play with is a part of the progression of the developing self as well as a step on the sequence of socialization.

As the preschool child moves away from the parent to stay by himself in the early childhood classroom, and then, as he moves away from the teacher to make activity choices on his own, his next step in the development of his self-identity should involve joining the other children in play. Yet he often does not join the others—at least not right away. Depending on his previous experience with peers—or lack of it—he may prefer to play on his own at first. In other words, other children do not replace a child's primary or secondary caregivers as objects of attachment. When children finally do seek other children to play with, it is indeed an indication of the development of a stronger self-identity.

Children seem to recognize that other children are like themselves—having a dependence on adult caregivers. From their self-centered perspectives, in fact, children may see peers as competitors for the attention of the caregivers as well as for the use of materials and activities.

Through socialization, they will be finding ways to get along with other children, as well as to share and take turns with materials—and even people—in your center. Through development of self-identity, the children will eventually be seeking contact with others like themselves.

Even as infants and toddlers, children recognize one another and may engage in social behavior. This contact, however, is not at the same level, type, or intensity as their interactions with adults. Infants' and toddlers' striving for attachment does not involve another child. While infants may look at, imitate, and even vocalize with peers, these interactions are few and far between and are not sustained for long periods. With adults, on the other hand, and especially with their mothers, infants' interactions involve touching, holding, and hugging during more instances, for longer periods, and at a more intense emotional level than anything they do with peers. The most frequent initial contact between two infants, in fact, takes place around toys (Damon, p. 59).

By the time the young child has entered your class, he or she has usually had a number of contacts with peers. Again, the interactions are not the same as with adults. Children look to the adult as their base of attachment. They look to their peers as a reflection of themselves. Those children with a strong sense of self will have less difficulty interacting with the other children in your center from the outset. They are indicating by this behavior how far along they are in the development of their self-identities.

Those who need help developing this sense of security within themselves may not seek other children to play with at first. As with the other areas of self-identity, you may need to help the children progress. Do not expect success to occur overnight in this particular area. Some children are just not ready for many days or even weeks to make contact with peers. By looking at and treating each child in your center as an individual, you will begin to elicit clues about each that can help you support their development in this crucial area. As before, you will need to use acceptance and patience whenever a child is slow in moving ahead.

If You Have Not Checked This Item:
Some Helpful Ideas

- **Find a Friend**

For many young children who are used to dealing with a limited number of people at a time, a roomful of lively peers is overwhelming. You may need to help find a friend for the shy child who may need to relate on a one-to-one basis with one other child before she can cope with a group. Choose someone who gets along with others, and ask the two to do an errand for you—perhaps mix paints or play dough, wash the doll clothes, or get out the cots for nap time. Or you might ask the "friend" to show the shy child how to use the saw or how to record her voice on the tape recorder. Make the activities as personal as possible to attract the shy child's interest and get her to focus on the activity or material instead of on her unsure feelings about herself. Once she successfully relates to one other child, she may begin to seek others to play with on her own.

■ Read a Book

Will I Have a Friend? by Miriam Cohen (New York: Collier Books, 1971) is a children's picture book classic about Jim, who worries about finding a friend at nursery school on the first day. Read it to a small group that includes the shy child, and ask the children about their own feelings when they first came to your class. The shy child may be relieved to realize that other children feel the same as she does and that they, like Jim, will also be able to find a friend.

■ Use Small Groups

Young children are better able to relate to peers when in small groups. You can arrange the physical environment of your classroom so that each of the activity areas accommodates only a certain number of children (say, no more than four). Methods to accomplish this include placing four chairs around a table; using masking tape on the floor to divide the block corner into four building areas; and providing only four aprons for water play, two saws or hammers for woodworking, or three pillows in the book area. When you read to the children, read to two or three or four rather than the total group.

■ Use a Material Activity for Two or Three Together

This idea is more often used in European programs to teach children to share, but you might also design or designate a certain material or activity in your classroom as always for use by two or three children together. The use of a saw, for instance, can be set up for three: two to hold the wood and one to saw. You might attach one of your wagons to a trike, so that one child must pedal while one rides. Your job chart of daily chores (which children choose or are assigned to) could require that pairs or teams work together to do the jobs. Can you think of other team enterprises?

PLAYS ROLES CONFIDENTLY □ IN DRAMATIC PLAY

Once the young child has begun playing with others in your center, you need to be cognizant of another indicator of his developing self-identity. Is he able to take on and play a role in the pretend situations that abound in early childhood programs? Can he pretend to be father or brother or baby in the housekeeping corner? Is she a nurse or doctor or famous skater in the dressup area? Can they be a race car driver, helicopter pilot, or crane operator on the playground? When children can play a pretend role with confidence in your center, then they are presenting observable proof that their self-identities have taken on an even more mature aspect.

In order to play a pretend role, children need to be able to see things from a different point of view than their own. Their perspective, in other words, cannot be egocentric. We mentioned how young children cover their eyes and think you cannot see them because they cannot see you. That view is, of course, totally egocentric. At some point, however, three- and four-year-olds seem to be able to step out of themselves and pretend quite realistically to be someone else.

It is not clear whether this ability is stronger or appears sooner in some children because of opportunity, encouragement, and practice at home, or whether certain children are instinctively or temperamentally more imaginative. But no matter what causes the behavior, it indicates that here is a child who has reached a milestone in her development of self-identity.

A child's ability to play a role other than her own says a number of things to the observer.

1. The child can distinguish reality from fantasy (i.e., she knows she is pretending).
2. The child is able to symbolize things (i.e., represent a real person or event in a make-believe manner).
3. The child can see things from another person's perspective.
4. The child has a strong enough sense of self to step out of herself and be someone else.

Until all four of these statements are true for the young child, she is really unable to play make-believe roles.

Once she can perform this behavior, she is able to explore in a wholly new way. She can try out roles. She can see what it is like to be the mother, the older sister, the baby. She can dominate the situation. She can make her father or brother do what she wants them to. This ability is a heady discovery. Of course, in a group situation, she is often dominated or at least controlled to some extent by the others and must remain in an assigned or assumed role. If she plays the role "wrong," she will be reprimanded by those often strict conformists, her peers.

Adults in the early childhood classroom may wonder aloud: "Is this what we want our children to do? Isn't it wrong to encourage fantasizing like this?" Not at all, say child development specialists. This is a natural progression in the young child's development. This fantasizing is the way young children explore concepts about people and events in the world around them. While adults look askance at the "Walter Mitty-type" who seems to live in a world of make-believe, it is not only natural but imperative that our children have the opportunity to use their imaginations playfully in exploring their own world (see Chapter 13, "Imagination").

Besides, this playful use of the imagination is the next step developmentally for the young child in his creation of a strong self-identity. He started as a new human being so attached to his mother that he thought she was a part of him. Then he made the separation in which he not only recognized he was separate from her, but he also realized he could move out from her. Next he developed confidence enough to come to a new environment and allow other adults to be his caregivers. From these adults, he moved out to explore his new environment and interact with his peers. Now he has developed a strong enough sense of himself that he can try out being someone else.

A great deal of power surrounds gaining control over people and situations, even imaginary ones. Up till now, the young child has been virtually powerless in a world controlled by adults. But when she plays a role in dramatic play, she is able to take a stand, be what she wants to be, and make things come out the way she wants them. Her self-identity is thus strengthened as she expands her horizons, gains control over ideas and feelings, and receives immediate feedback from the other players as to how her role affects them.

Also, in playing such pretend roles, the player gets to find out more about himself. The other children's reactions to his role and his own reactions to it help him realize his capabilities and understand his limits. He can explore gender roles more fully—what it is like to be male or female.

Children in our society are treated differently from the moment of birth, it seems, depending on their gender. Now the young pretender can try out being the mother, father, sister, or brother in the family. Because children often play these familiar family roles in a very stereotyped, exaggerated manner—their own interpretation of the way real family members act—the players soon learn which roles are considered the "best" and how the others feel about mothers and fathers, boys and girls.

For a child who did not participate in dramatic play upon first entering your program, now doing so signifies a major step. It means she not only has a strong enough sense of self to try being someone else, but she also now has this unparalleled opportunity to practice her budding interpersonal and communication skills, thus strengthening her self-identity in a manner that was impossible before. Again a paradox exists: once she is able to be someone else, she becomes more of herself.

If You Have Not Checked This Item: Some Helpful Ideas

■ Provide Dramatic Play Material

Have at least one area of your classroom set up for dramatic play. This section can be a family area with child-sized table, chairs, refrigerator, stove, and sink; a bedroom area with doll beds, dresser, mirror, and chest of drawers; a store with shelves of empty food containers and a toy cash register; or any other such setting. If you take your class on a field trip, you should consider setting up a similar pretend area in your room (for them to try out the roles they saw enacted on the trip): a doctor's office, a clinic, a laundromat, a barber or beauty shop.

In addition to life-sized settings and props, you need miniature toys to encourage role-playing as well. Little cars, trucks, people, animals, boats, and planes can be placed strategically in the block corner, at the water table, and with the table blocks. A box full of dramatic play props can be taken out on the playground. Pictures of people in a variety of roles—from family members to community helpers—can be hung at children's eye level around the room to encourage the exploration of roles. Ask the children what kinds of roles they would like to try out and have them help you assemble the props. Books such as Phyllis and Noel Fiarotta's *Be What You Want to Be* are full of ideas for making your own props from discarded material.

■ Allow Time to Pretend

Because the best dramatic play is spontaneous—even though you may have provided the props—you need to set aside a particular time during the day for free choice activities to occur. Often these activities are scheduled at the beginning of the day, but they can take place any time. Allow enough time for children to become involved in their roles. The length may vary from day to day depending upon the children's interests and yours, but free choice activities should be scheduled to occur at the same time every day so that the children can depend upon a set period for pretending and playing roles.

■ Play a Role Yourself

Sometimes the only way to help the nonparticipant to become involved is to play a role yourself. Obviously, if a child is not ready emotionally, your efforts may be wasted. But some children who are ready to play a role may not know how to get started. In that case, you might pretend to be a mother and invite the child to go on a pretend errand with you, ending up in the dramatic play area where the other children are often delighted to see the teacher playing like they are. If the child accepts your lead and becomes involved with the others, you can gradually withdraw.

■ Be an Observer of Pretend Play

It will help you immensely in your understanding of children if you take time out to observe and record the various children's engagement in pretend play. Station yourself unobtrusively in an area of the room where a particular child is playing and record as many details as possible in a running record. Do this for several days if possible. Some of the things to look for can include

1. Theme of the play
2. Role the child is playing
3. Who else is playing and what are their roles
4. Type of interaction with other children
5. Dialog
6. Length of time the child sustains the role

What can you conclude about the child from your observations? Have you learned anything that can help you plan your program differently so that other children will become more easily involved in dramatic play? Could you add props or suggestions to help the children sustain their play? Chapter 13, "Imagination," has additional suggestions.

STANDS UP FOR OWN RIGHTS □

In order for preschool children to stand up for their rights within the classroom, they need to have developed a strong enough self-identity to believe in themselves as individuals with a point of view worth other people's consideration. Thus far in their development of a self-identity, they have been able to make the separation from their parents, not cling to the adult caregiver, make eye contact with classroom adults, choose activities on their own, seek other children to play with, and try out roles confidently in dramatic play because they could see things from another person's point of view. Now the children are progressing further by developing their own points of view worthy of other children's consideration.

What are some of the classroom rights such a self-confident child might insist on? One is the right of possession. If a child is playing with a piece of equipment, he should be able to continue using it unless some previous turn-taking rule is in effect. Many childhood squabbles take place over objects, often because of children's egocentric perspectives. A child feels he should have a toy because he wants it. The fact that another child is playing with it does not count in his mind. The development of mutual respect is difficult among three- and four-year-olds because so many of them lack the ability to understand the other's perspective (Berndt, p. 255). The child who feels his right of possession is worth defending will often refuse to give in.

A child's choice of participation is another personal right often established in early childhood classrooms. If a child opts to join or not join a particular activity, you and the other children need to honor her choice. Use enticements rather than force if you feel the child should be involved when she chooses not to be.

Completing independent projects her own way is a right that self-confident children will defend. If a child is doing a painting, modeling clay, constructing a building, or dressing a doll on her own, she should be able to do it as she sees fit so long as she is not interfering with others. In like manner, others should not be allowed to interfere with her. The child with the strong self-identity will continue in her own manner, disregarding or rejecting the attempts of others to impose their will.

Protecting property is another right that self-confident children will insist on. Toys or games they have brought from home are often the focus of conflict. You need to provide a private space like a cubby for each child to store his possessions. Block buildings are also important to the children who have built them. The child who insists on saving his building may want help in making a sign informing others: "Please Leave Jeffrey's Building Standing."

Children may stand up for their own rights in a number of ways. They may physically prevent another child from doing something or making them do something. They may verbalize their position with the child. They may tell the teacher. Some of their actions may not even be acceptable in a classroom full of children. Use of power or aggression is, of course, not appropriate. You need to help such children find more acceptable means for making their point.

As you observe your children on this particular item, look to see which ones do not allow another child to urge or force unwanted changes on them, and which ones do not back down, or give up a toy or a turn. At the same time, take note of children who always give up or give in to the demands of another. They also need your support in the strengthening of their self-confidence.

If You Have Not Checked This Item:
Some Helpful Ideas

▪ Model Behavior

You need to model the behavior you want your children to follow. Stand firm on decisions you have made. Let your children know why. If you are "wishy-washy" or inconsistent in your treatment of them, they may have trouble standing firm themselves.

▪ Allow Children Choices

One way to help a child learn that her rights can count is to give her a chance to make choices that are important to her. Let her choose a favorite activity to participate in or a toy to take home.

▪ Stand Up for the Child

When it is clear to you that a child's rights have been infringed upon by another child, you should take a stand yourself supporting the child and at the same time letting the others know "why Karen can finish her painting now and Bobby can't," for example.

DISPLAYS ENTHUSIASM ☐
ABOUT DOING THINGS FOR SELF

The lifelong quest to develop an identity is, in the final analysis, a struggle for autonomy. If young children are successful in this quest, they will be able and willing to behave independently in many ways. Louise J. Kaplan's *Oneness and Separateness: From Infant to Individual* describes the importance of the struggle: "In the first three years of life every human being undergoes yet a second birth, in which he is born as a psychological being possessing selfhood and separate identity. The quality of self an infant achieves in those crucial three years will profoundly affect all of his subsequent existence" (p. 15).

Your observations in the area of self-identity will have helped you determine which children in your class are well on the road to developing strong self-identities and which ones are not. The most successful children will be those who can and want to do things for themselves. They will have achieved enough of a self-assurance about their own abilities to be able to try and eventually succeed in doing things on their own. Achieving this competence will then allow them a measure of independence from the adults around them.

What are some of the activities you may observe such children performing independently in your classroom? Here is a partial list.

Dressing and undressing	Painting with brush
Tying or fastening shoes	Mixing paints
Using own cubby	Getting out toys
Toileting	Putting toys away
Washing hands and face	Returning blocks to shelves
Brushing teeth	Dressing dolls
Setting table for eating	Handling hammer, saw
Pouring drink	Cutting with scissors
Dishing out food	Cutting with knife
Handling eating implements	Mixing dough
Eating	Using climbing equipment
Cleaning up after eating	Making puzzles

The adeptness level of three- and four-year-olds in these various activities depends on their own sense of self, the practice they have had at home or elsewhere, and on the encouragement or discouragement the adults around them have offered. This author has noticed that children from low income families are often more adept at accomplishing many of the self-help skills than children from middle and upper income families. We might infer that children in low income families have had to do many self-help activities on their own and thus become more skilled sooner than their middle and upper income counterparts.

In like manner, children who have always had things done for them by the adults around them often give up the struggle for autonomy. You and your co-workers need to beware of the temptation to help the little children in your care more than necessary. Children can do many more things for themselves than we realize. You need to allow time for children to learn to zip up jackets and pour their own drinks. Otherwise, you are denying them an unparalleled opportunity to develop their own independence.

The way adults behave toward children during these formative years can indeed make a difference in children's feelings about themselves and thus in the way they behave. Research regarding gender-stereotyping has found that mothers and fathers treat their young daughters differently from their sons when it comes to independent behavior. Parents often allow and encourage boys to behave independently earlier than girls in such areas as using scissors without adult supervision, crossing the street alone, playing away from home, and riding the bus. When girls ask for help, they often get it, but boys more often receive a negative response. Boys are encouraged to manipulate objects and explore their environments, while girls are more often discouraged. Thus it seems that parents value independence in boys more than in girls (Brooks-Gunn & Matthews, pp. 145–146).

This type of discriminating behavior may, of course, result in girls feeling less capable than boys, and therefore attempting fewer things on their own. Or this behavior may cause girls—and therefore women—to become dependent on men and less willing to risk using their own capabilities.

You and your co-workers need to take special care that stereotyped attitudes about the roles of men and women do not color your behavior toward the boys and girls in your center. As in all areas of development, your goal should be to help each child become all he or she is capable of being. When each shows enthusiasm about doing things independently, you know that he or she is well on the way to developing a strong sense of self-identity.

If You Have Not Checked This Item: Some Helpful Ideas

■ Assess Your Center for "Independent" Possibilities

What can children do on their own in your center? It gives them great satisfaction to accomplish difficult tasks. Walk around your physical area and make a list of things that children can do. Some items that can go on your daily job chart for individuals or teams to choose include

Feeding the rabbit	Taking own attendance
Cleaning the aquarium	Getting out playground equipment

Watering the plants
Scraping carrots for snack
Delivering mail to the office

Sweeping the floor
Sponging off the tables
Getting out cots for nap time

■ Encourage Performance of Self-Help Skills

Teach children how to tie their shoes when their small motor coordination allows them this capability. Or have another child help them get started with buttons or zippers or Velcro tabs. Allow enough time for even the slowest child to perform this task on his own.

■ Help Children Get Started

Sometimes the first step is all a child needs to start her on her way to independence. Sit next to the child who tells you she cannot make the puzzle, and put in a piece yourself. Then ask her to look for the next one. Stay with her until she completes the puzzle if need be. Then ask her to try it again on her own. Give her positive verbal support all the way, but refrain from helping this time.

■ Read a Book

There are many picture books about individual children doing things on their own. Read one of them, such as *I Can Do It by Myself* by Lessie Jones Little and Eloise Greenfield (New York: Thomas Y. Crowell, 1978), to a small group of children. It is about Donny, who has to overcome a number of problems in order to buy his mother a plant for her birthday—all by himself.

■ Be Enthusiastic Yourself

Enthusiasm always scores very high on lists of the competencies of successful teachers. You as a behavior model in your classroom need always to be enthusiastic and positive about everything you do. If children see you acting on your own with vigor, they will be encouraged to do likewise.

OBSERVING, RECORDING, AND INTERPRETING SELF-IDENTITY

Self-identity was chosen as the first topic on the *Child Skills Checklist* because this is the first area of child development a teacher should be concerned with when she meets new children in her center. In order to determine how children feel about themselves in their new environment and which children may need help in making the transition from home to school, you may want to observe and record the behaviors of all of the children in your class at one time.

To do this, use one sheet of paper listing the names of the children down the left side of the paper and the checklist items along the top. Draw lines horizontally and vertically to section off the names and items. Now you can mark the items you have seen each child performing under "Self-Identity." When you find a number of blank spaces for a particular child, you may want to observe this child in more detail, using the entire checklist.

You will then be able to design a learning prescription for the particular child, as was done for Sheila on page 32. The checklist results will tell you which areas of strength and confidence the child displays, as well as which areas needing strengthening may be necessary. Then you can begin planning for the individual by listing several activities to help the child, based on his or her strengths. Such activities can come from your own repertoire or from those suggested in the chapter.

Be sure that observation of such children is an ongoing process in your center. Do a follow-up of children who seem to need special help. Has your learning prescription been helpful? Did the activities you planned really help this child? Share your observations with your classroom team and with the child's parents. Ask them to make similar observations. Include their ideas, as well, in your individual plans for each child.

REFERENCES CITED

Berndt, Thomas J. (1982). "Fairness and Friendship." In Kenneth W. Rubin and Hildy S. Ross (Eds.), *Peer Relationships and Social Skills in Childhood.* New York: Springer-Verlag.

Brooks-Gunn, Jeanne, and **Wendy Schempp Matthews.** (1979). *He and She: How Children Develop Their Sex-Role Identity.* Engelwood Cliffs, NJ: Prentice-Hall.

Damon, William. (1983). *Social and Personality Development: Infancy Through Adolescence.* New York: W. W. Norton.

Fein, Greta, and **Pamela M. Schwartz.** (1982). "Development Theories in Early Education." In Bernard Spodek (Ed.), *Handbook of Research in Early Childhood Education.* New York: The Free Press.

Fiarotta, Phyllis, and **Noel Fiarotta.** (1977). *Be What You Want to Be.* New York: Workman.

Kaplan, Louise J. (1978). *Oneness and Separateness: From Infant to Individual.* New York: Simon and Schuster.

Seagull, Elizabeth A. W., and **David J. Kallen.** (1978). "Normal Social and Emotional Development of the Preschool-Age Child." In Norbert B. Enzer, with Kennith W. Goin (Eds.), *Social and Emotional Development: The Preschooler.* New York: Walker and Co.

Thompson, James J. (1973). *Beyond Words: Nonverbal Communication in the Classroom.* New York: Citation Press.

OTHER SOURCES

Balaban, Nancy. (1985). *Starting School: From Separation to Independence, a Guide for Early Childhood Teachers.* New York: Teachers College Press.

Beaty, Janice J. (1988). *Skills for Preschool Teachers.* Columbus, OH: Merrill Publishing Company.

Briggs, Dorothy Corkille. (1970). *Your Child's Self-Esteem.* Garden City, NY: Doubleday & Company.

LEARNING ACTIVITIES

1. Observe all of the children in your classroom each morning of the first week of school, using the items in the "Self-Identity Checklist" as a screening device as mentioned on pages 67–68. Note which children can separate without difficulty from their parents and which children cannot. Make a written learning prescription for a particular child to help him or her overcome this initial anxiety. Discuss the plan with your supervisor and then implement it. Discuss the results.

2. Choose a child who seems to have difficulty getting involved with other children or activities. Make a running record of everything the child does or says during three different arrival periods. Transfer this information to the *Child Skills Checklist* under "Self-Identity." How do you interpret the evidence you have collected? Can you make any conclusions yet about this child?

3. Meet with one or more parents of children in your classroom. Discuss how children develop their self-identities and give the parents ideas that can be used at home to help strengthen their child's self-concept. Ask them for suggestions about how they would like you to work with their child.

4. Observe a child playing a role in dramatic play for three days. Keep a running record of everything the child does or says. Pay special attention to the things to look for discussed on pages 62–63. Can you make any conclusions about the child's self-identity based on these observations?

5. Choose a child for whom you have checked "displays enthusiasm in regard to doing things for self." Observe this child during the first half hour of class for three days. Which of the other items can you check for this child based on your observations? What is your evidence for each checkmark? What conclusions can you make about this child based on these observations?

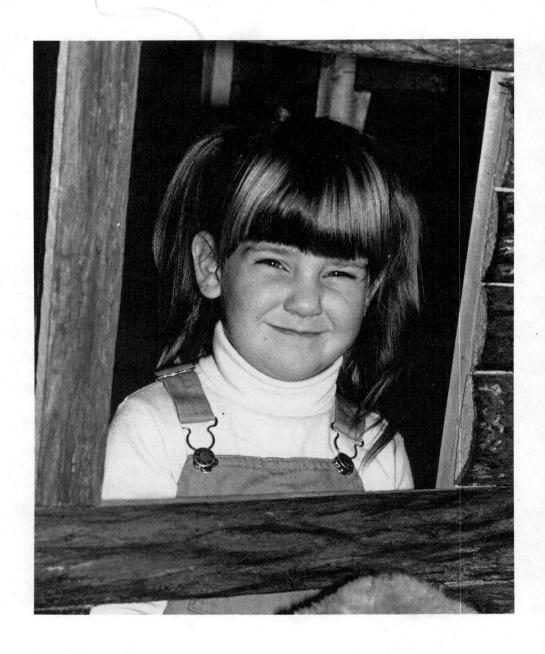

3 Emotional Development

Emotional Development Checklist

- ☐ Allows self to be comforted during stressful time
- ☐ Eats, sleeps, toilets without fuss away from home
- ☐ Handles sudden changes/startling situations with control
- ☐ Can express anger in words rather than actions
- ☐ Allows aggressive behavior to be redirected
- ☐ Does not withdraw from others excessively
- ☐ Shows interest/attention in classroom activities
- ☐ Smiles, seems happy much of the time

T he emotional development of the preschool child is somehow different from other developmental aspects. True, emotional growth happens simultaneously with physical, social, cognitive, language, and creative development and is interdependent upon them. But it seems as if the youngsters do not stay developed, or rather, that they must repeat the same sequences of emotional development over and over until they get it right . . . throughout life.

In some respects this observation is true. Emotional development does have a physical and cognitive basis for its expression, but once the basic human abilities are in place, emotions are much more situational in appearance.

If we agree that emotions are particular reactions to specific stimuli, we can conclude that these reactions may not change much in a developmental sense over a person's lifetime. Many of us get red in the face when we are angry and cry when we are sad, both as infants and as adults. In other words, it is the situation—the stimulus—rather than the development of the child that seems to govern the emotional response.

Actually, emotional development is even more complex. Whereas physical and cognitive development seem to be based on "nature," "nurture," and their interaction—that is, the genetic traits children inherit plus the environment in which they are raised—emotions have three internally interacting dimensions, including

1. The conscious feeling or emotional experience
2. The process in the brain and nervous system
3. The observable expressive patterns or reactions (Izard, p. 4)

71

Obviously, the brain and nervous system, because they are physical, can exhibit inherited traits. But can emotions themselves be inherited and then developed through maturation and surroundings—just like the ability to think? Many psychologists have trouble accepting the idea that emotions are at all biological and based on maturity. However, scientists have to admit that certain emotional responses—separation anxiety, for instance—occur at about the same time and for the same reasons in infants and toddlers around the world. Similarly, other types of emotions seem to trigger universal "fight" or "flight" responses in adults.

Psychologists studying universal responses talk in terms of the functions of emotions (how they help the human species to adapt and survive). These scientists note that certain emotions that trigger necessary survival responses in infants have outlived their usefulness when they occur in older children and adults. The acute distress felt by the infant and expressed in tears or screams when mother leaves the home, for example, has outlived its usefulness if it is a daily occurrence with a four-year-old when mother leaves him at the child care center. While such basic emotions seem to help preserve the self or the species, the higher emotions serve social purposes, and their appropriate responses must be learned.

Thus, we should focus on the response—not the emotion itself—when we speak of emotional development in preschool children. Moreover, what most concerns us is not simply the development, but rather the control of the response. In the areas of physical and mental development, we want young children to grow, mature, and extend their abilities to the utmost. With emotional development, we want children to learn to make appropriate emotional responses, and especially to control negative responses. An emotionally disturbed child is, after all, often one who is out of control.

This chapter examines the observable emotional responses of young children in eight different areas and makes suggestions for improving a child's behavior if the particular item is not demonstrated. Each of the checklist items refers to a particular emotion. It should be noted, however, that the order in which the items are listed is not a developmental sequence, because sequence as such does not seem to be an important factor in emotional development.

Many psychologists recognize either eight or ten basic emotions and their combinations. These are sometimes listed as interest-excitement, enjoyment-joy, surprise-startle, distress-anguish, anger-rage, disgust-revulsion, contempt-scorn, fear-terror, shame/shyness-humiliation, and guilt-remorse (Izard, p. 46). The emotional responses of preschool children seem to be involved principally with the following seven emotions (plus one response): distress, fear, surprise, anger, aggression (a response), shame, interest, and joy.

In order to help children develop emotionally, the preschool teacher should be concerned with promoting positive emotions and helping the child to control negative emotions. Although techniques to accomplish this control may vary, depending upon the emotion and the situation, the following four strategies can be used to control negative emotions:

1. Remove or reduce the cause of the emotion.
2. Diffuse the child's negative reaction by allowing him to "let it out" through crying, talking, or transferring his feelings into nondestructive actions.
3. Offer support, comfort, and ideas for self-control.
4. Model controlling behavior yourself.

Your goal for the child should be the same as in the other aspects of her development: for her to gain self-control. In order to help her acquire this control, you first need to find out where she stands in her present development. Does she exhibit crying, whining, or complaining much of the time? Does she ever smile? Does she show anger or aggression toward others? The *Child Skills Checklist* lists eight representative items of emotional behavior of children three through five years of age in early childhood programs. Observe the children in your class to determine which ones have accomplished the emotional self-control described in the checklist. Children who have not exhibited these checklist behaviors may benefit from the ideas and suggestions discussed in the remainder of the chapter.

ALLOWS SELF TO BE COMFORTED ☐ DURING STRESSFUL TIME

Distress

Children who do not allow themselves to be comforted during stressful times are often exhibiting the emotion known as *distress*. At its lower extreme, distress may result from physical discomfort due to pain, extremes of temperature, or noise; whereas at its upper level, distress may take the form of anguish, grief, or depression due to the loss of a loved one. A basic cause of distress throughout life is physical or psychological separation, especially from a loved one. The child who perceives himself as having been abandoned by an adult, even when this is not true, experiences the same emotion as the child who has actually been abandoned.

Children express distress by crying, whining, or showing a sad face. Sometimes they cling to an adult caregiver. Distressed children may feel uncomfortable, disappointed, lonely, sad, or rejected.

Distress is not the most severe negative emotion found in children; therefore, adults do not always take it seriously. They should. Distress is an indication that all is not well with the child. Failure to reduce the distress or its causes over a period of time tends to break down the child's trust in adults. Furthermore, the child may learn to become unsympathetic to others who are distressed, because that is the way she has been treated.

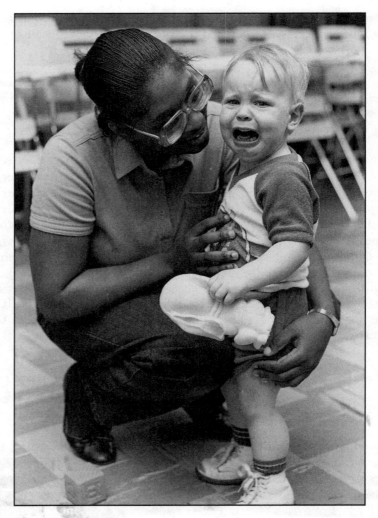

Distress is not the most severe of the negative emotions; yet,
adults should take it seriously in children.

Every human being endures the initial distress of the birth experience, which is not only a physical discomfort but also a separation ordeal in
the extreme. As such, birth is greeted with lusty crying by the distressed
infant. Psychologists feel that distress, whenever it occurs, thus serves as a
warning to others that something is wrong with the person and action
should be taken. Because it is concerned with separation, distress also seems
to serve as a device to keep a group together (Izard, p. 293).

What are the principal causes of distress in the child care center?
For many youngsters, the separation from their primary caregiver is the most
stressful. Discomfort or pain from a physical cause, rejection by peers, dissat-
isfaction with the performance, or lack of a skill are other causes of distress.

A stressful situation in the family—such as the birth of a new baby, a death, a hospitalization, moving, or divorce—may also be carried over into classroom behavior by the child who is disturbed by it.

The Teacher's Role

How can you help? Your principal role in children's emotional development should be to help them master their feelings. You should not be the controlling device yourself, but instead you should help the children find ways to control their feelings from within. Adults are often tempted to take control of an emotional situation. Young children, in fact, look to you to solve the emotional problems that so often are overwhelming. You do children a disservice if you comply. Your role should be that of a facilitator, not a controller. Otherwise, without you, the children will be no better off the next time the emotional situation occurs. As with all other aspects of development, your overall goal for children should be the development of their emotional independence (in other words, their emotional self-control).

Although the particular situation may determine your response, distress most often requires that you first give comfort to the child. She is upset and uncomfortable; she may be whining or crying. You can show your concern through comforting words and actions such as holding or hugging.

Requiring that he stop crying right away is usually not the best way to approach helping a child master his emotions. Venting through tears is, after all, a catharsis. He may feel that you are not sympathetic to his plight if you insist he stop crying. He may, in fact, stop on his own when he hears your comforting words or feels your touch.

Once the child can verbalize, he can begin to take charge of his emotions. He may be able to tell you what happened or how he feels. This is the first step toward self-mastery of emotions. He might even be able to tell you what would make him feel better.

If the situation is too overwhelming for him to stop crying or to verbalize his feelings, your best strategy may be to redirect his attention when the time seems right. If he was injured on one leg, perhaps you can get him to show you the other leg. How does it look? How does he think it feels? Maybe together you can do something to make the injured leg feel like the uninjured one. Distress, then, can often be relieved when you (1) give comfort, (2) redirect attention, and/or (3) help the child to verbalize.

As for mastering distress so that it will not happen again, this is probably not possible and certainly not appropriate. Distress may be relieved and perhaps controlled, but not completely mastered. Nor should we want it to be. Distress is a necessary symptom signaling that all is not well with the individual. In your child care program, you should hope to help relieve—not prevent—distress in a child. If you are successful, then a distraught child will allow herself to be comforted or redirected. But if her sense of self is not strong enough or if the distress is too overwhelming, she may not even allow this. What can you do to help such a child?

If You Have Not Checked This Item: Some Helpful Ideas

■ Hold and Rock

An adult-sized rocking chair can be an important furnishing in your center. Sometimes the best help for a distraught child is to hold and rock him.

■ Have the Child Hold a Huggable Toy

A child is often comforted by holding something soft. That is why toddlers carry "security blankets." Your center should have cuddly stuffed animals or similar toys available, not only for play but also for stressful situations. The child who does not allow you to comfort her may help herself by holding such a toy. Be sure the toy is washable for use by other children.

■ Use a Material with Soothing Properties

Water play or finger painting are activities with soothing qualities. Distressed children can take out their frustrations by moving paint around a surface with their hands or by swishing water, thus transferring their negative energy in a harmless fashion.

■ Have the Child Talk to a Puppet

Again, verbalizing negative feelings is one of the best ways for defusing or controlling them. You could designate one of the puppets in your room as a "feelings" puppet and keep it in a special place for the times when children are feeling sad or upset. They can talk to the puppet about how they feel and ask the puppet how it feels. Your modeling the use of this puppet when upsetting occasions arise will give them a lead to follow.

■ Read a Book

Sometimes distraught children will allow you to read a favorite book to them. Or you could keep particular books for them to look at on their own during troubling times. Here are some books especially suitable for stressful situations.

Feelings

Sometimes I Like to Cry by Elizabeth and Henry Stanton (Chicago: Albert Whitman & Company, 1978) is about a little boy named Joey, who smiles and laughs at his cat, frog, and brother, but sometimes cries when he cuts a finger, is not invited to a party, or experiences the death of his hamster.

Grownups Cry Too by Nancy Hazen (Chapel Hill, NC: Lollipop Power, 1978; in English and Spanish) is narrated by a little boy, who tells about the various stressful times in his life when he and his parents cried.

Moving

Moving Gives Me a Stomach Ache by Heather McKend (Windsor, Ontario: Black Moss Press, 1980) reveals how a boy must pack his toys to move and tries to joke about it because he feels bad. Older children (five- and six-year-olds) would understand the humor better.

Moving Molly by Shirley Hughes (Englewood Cliffs, NJ: Prentice-Hall, 1978) is a much more developed story than the previous one. This book tells about little city-girl Molly, who willingly moves to the country but is lonely until children move in next door.

Death

The Tenth Good Thing About Barney by Judith Viorst (New York: Atheneum, 1971) is about a sad little boy, whose cat, Barney, dies and whose mother tries to comfort him by having him think of ten good things to say about Barney when they bury him in the backyard.

My Grandson Lew by Charlotte Zolotow (New York: Harper & Row, 1974) is a touching story about six-year-old Lewis, who misses his grandfather, who had died earlier. Lewis finally shares memories of his grandfather with his mother.

Nana Upstairs and Nana Downstairs by Tomie de Paola (New York: G. P. Putnam's Sons, 1973) is the story of Tommy, who makes visits to his grandmother and great-grandmother, who live in the same house on different floors. When the great-grandmother dies, Tommy's mother comforts him by telling him that his great-grandmother will come back in his memory whenever he thinks about her.

EATS, SLEEPS, TOILETS WITHOUT ☐ FUSS AWAY FROM HOME

Fear (Anxiety)

Children who have difficulty eating, going to sleep, or going to the toilet in your center generally behave this way because of tension. This tension is most often produced by anxiety, one of the most common expressions of fear.

Fear first appears as an emotion in the second half of an infant's first year of life, according to many psychologists. Somewhere between five and nine months of age, the baby begins to recognize an unfamiliar face and is afraid of it. Before that, his physical and cognitive development have not progressed to the point where he can distinguish between friend and stranger. After that, he recognizes unfamiliar faces as a possible threat . . . until he learns differently.

The emotion fear is thus caused by the presence of something threatening or the absence of safety and security (Izard, p. 356). Fear may result when the possibility of potential harm appears, when a strange person, object, or situation is confronted, or when specific fright-producing elements—such as heights, the dark, thunderstorms, or particular animals such as dogs or snakes—are present. When children or others are afraid, they feel anxious and alarmed. They may tremble, cower, hide, run away, cling to someone, or cry, depending on their degree of fright. They often seek protection.

Fear is in some ways age-related. Young children are generally not afraid of heights, the dark, or animals much before their second year. It is as though they really do not know enough to be frightened before then. As they grow older, children add new fears to their repertory and drop some of the old ones. So fear, like distress, seems to serve as a warning signal for the human species: reduce the threat or seek protection. When this warning feeling persists but is no longer useful to the young human, you as a child care worker need to intervene.

We know, of course, that extreme fear can be paralyzing, but we need to realize that even lesser fears like anxiety produce tension: a tightening up of the body and the mind. Anxiety "is the most constricting of all the emotions" (Izard, p. 365). The anxious person has trouble relaxing or feeling at ease in tense situations or in unfamiliar settings that somehow pose a threat.

For the young child used to the security of home, the early childhood classroom can be such a tense setting at first, no matter how relaxing and nonthreatening you have made it. The child views the setting as a threat for three reasons: (1) the setting is unfamiliar, (2) the child lacks initial trust in the setting and the people there, and (3) the child's mother or caregiver has left her.

Most children display some anxiety when they first experience an early childhood classroom. It is a natural reaction to being left in a strange place. But if they have a strong enough sense of self and sense of trust in the world and the people around them, the children should soon come to feel perfectly at ease in your center. For children who do not achieve this sense of ease, you may need to provide special attention in order to help them overcome their anxiety.

How routine functions of eating, sleeping, and toileting are carried out can often provide the careful observer with clues concerning who is at ease in the classroom and who is not. Because these routines are of such a personal nature and so closely connected with the home and the primary caregiver, eating, sleeping, and toileting are deeply significant to the child. From her earliest memories, she is used to having her mother feed her or help her to feed herself. She expects her mother to tuck her in and kiss her goodnight. She is at ease in using the toilet—a rather formidable piece of equipment for a young child—in her own home, for she has learned it will not flush her away.

Suddenly the child is thrust into a new and unfamiliar environment where these very personal processes are directed by strangers. Even the most secure and experienced young explorer may have moments of anxiety in the beginning. Anxiety produces tension in which muscles actually tighten up, whether or not the tense person is aware of it. Unless the tense child is able to relax, he or she may certainly experience difficulty in eating, falling asleep, or using the toilet.

The anxious child in your classroom may not have difficulty with all three of these acts. One or another may be more meaningful in his life at home and thus cause more problems for him away from home. His difficulty may also have causes other than anxiety. A health problem, for instance, could also cause a disruption in his normal functioning. However, if a child exhibits persistent difficulty in eating, sleeping, or toileting at any time while he is in your care, the cause may be anxiety, and the child may need your help to overcome the negative effects of this emotion.

Eating

Eating is the act most closely connected with the child's mother. From baby-hood when he nursed at his mother's breast or was held close to her while being bottle-fed, the child has not only received life-sustaining nourishment but also comfort and love. It is not surprising, then, that the child makes a connection between food and comfort. Later, as he is weaned from breast or bottle and learns to take solid food, he may perceive this as a happy experience or a battle of wills. By the time he enters your center, the child has had at least three years of experience with the emotional nature of eating. You hope this has been positive. But no matter what, you need to make sure eating is a positive experience for the child in your program.

Once you are aware of the emotional nature of eating and how a child's anxiety can interfere with his eating habits, you will be better prepared to deal with children who refuse to eat. Be sure at the outset that your meals take place in an atmosphere of friendliness and relaxation. Are meals served family-style in your classroom around small group tables? School cafeterias are too large, noisy, impersonal, and rushed for children this young. If you have been assigned to a cafeteria, talk with the supervisor in order to explain the needs of young children and to see whether the food could be carried to your room instead.

Do you eat at the table with the children? It is important in family-style eating that a member of the staff sit at each table to converse informally with the children, answering their questions about the food and assisting them in their own pouring and serving. Help the children take a little of everything. If their portions are too large, they may not even want to begin. But involving them with their own dishing out and passing of the food is a physical step that psychologically connects them with eating.

What about rules concerning food? Mealtime should be pleasant and relaxing. Too many rules about portions, second helpings, and dessert may create tension even in relaxed children. Is withholding of dessert used as a punishment for children who have misbehaved? No matter how food is used in the homes of your children, it should never be used in a punitive manner in your center. All of the food served, including dessert, should be nutritious, appealing, and available to all of the children all of the time.

Are you a good eating model yourself? "Practice what you preach" is a cliché worth repeating when it comes to eating. Your children should see that you take a reasonably sized portion of each food, eat all your food, talk about how good it tastes, ask politely for seconds if this is appropriate, refrain from nagging, and make positive comments about the children who have cleaned their plates.

If You Have Not Checked This Item: Some Helpful Ideas

▪ Refrain from Pressure

Do not use force or pressure to get a reluctant child to eat. Force probably will not work anyway, but more importantly, it will certainly not reduce the anxiety and tension that may be the cause of the refusal to eat in the first place. All attempts to resolve the problem should be positive in nature, aimed at removing or reducing the cause of the negative emotion and helping the child to gain inner control over her reactions. Sometimes patience alone is the only solution. When the child feels at ease in your program, she will eat.

▪ Talk with Parents

Ask parents what they expect of their child and what they hope he or she will gain from your program. Talk about food habits and how the child eats at home. Be aware, however, that the basic problem may not be food, but anxiety and how the child reacts to it. Is the child under pressure at home? How does he react to pressure? How can you and the parents relieve him of this pressure?

▪ Read a Book

Perhaps a lighthearted approach will work. If you think the reluctant eater can deal with food in a playful manner, you might try reading together one of the following books.

Gregory, the Terrible Eater by Mitchell Sharmat (New York: Scholastic Book Services, 1980) is the story of a little goat named Gregory, who will not eat the goat food his mother serves (tin cans, rugs, and bottle caps). Gregory wants only fruits, vegetables, and eggs . . . "Good stuff like that." When junk food gets too much for him, he and his family finally reach a compromise.

Bread and Jam for Frances by Russell Hoban (New York: Scholastic Book Services, 1964) is the classic story of a little girl badger named

Frances, who wants to eat only bread and jam . . . until she finds out that is all her family will serve her.

Sleeping

If the children spend all day in your center, you must provide them with a nap period in the afternoon. For some children, this is a welcome relief from the exuberant activities of the morning. They welcome the chance to rest and will promptly fall asleep. For others, naptime is a time of tossing and turning, whispering and squirming, disturbing other children and the teacher. Some may be children who have outgrown naptime. Others may be so wound up that they need to relax before they can fall asleep. A few may be the anxious children we have been discussing, who cannot fall asleep because of tension.

First of all, you need to prepare all of your children for naptime. They can help to get out the cots or mats. They can choose their own area of the room to sleep in. They need to know when the lights are turned out or the curtains pulled that it is time to close their eyes. You might try playing dreamy music at a low volume on the record player. Or you could read a story in a monotone or whispery voice. You might read a sleep story, such as Margaret Wise Brown's *Goodnight Moon* (New York: Scholastic Book Services, 1947), Robert Kraus' *Good Night Richard Rabbit* (New York: Windmill Books, 1972), or Russell Hoban's *Bedtime for Frances* (New York: Harper & Row, 1960). For some children, rubbing their backs helps them let go and fall asleep. But if you rub backs for some, be sure to do it for all who want it. Children like you to trace their names on their backs with your finger. What if some children still do not fall asleep?

If You Have Not Checked This Item: Some Helpful Ideas

■ Naptime Toys

If after ten or fifteen minutes, certain children show no signs of falling asleep, you may decide to allow them to play quietly on their cots with some sort of "naptime toy," perhaps a tiny car or doll from a basket you pass around to the nonsleepers. Because they do not move from their sleeping quarters, the nonsleepers still have the chance to fall asleep if they want. Some teachers prefer to have a different area where nonsleepers can go to play quietly.

■ Reduce Tension

If some children are still too anxious and tense to allow themselves to fall asleep, you may need to try a variety of methods for reducing tension. Can these children take a teddy bear to bed? Ask them how they can help themselves get sleepy. Will rocking help? What do they do at home? In the end, your acceptance of them as worthy human beings should eventually help them to relax and take a nap if their bodies have the need for it.

Toileting

Children's bathroom habits are as different from one another as their eating habits. Children will probably learn the most about what is expected of them in your center from their peers. But you also need to be aware of what the children expect or need. Do you have a single classroom bathroom or a public-type bathroom with several stalls? Are the children used to being in a bathroom with other children? Can they handle their clothing, clean themselves, and wash their hands alone?

You may need to talk to newcomers in the beginning about what they can expect and ask them what they are used to. You may need to go into the bathroom with them in the beginning to help them and get them used to the equipment.

If parents tell you their children are not using the center facilities or if they begin to have accidents in the classroom, you will want to talk with the youngster about it as gently as possible. Because toilet training—unfortunately—is controlled in some homes through the negative method of shaming, you need to be careful that your concern will not make the child feel ashamed.

Is the child too shy to use the bathroom with other children? You may need to accede to his feelings at first until he is used to your center and his peers.

If You Have Not Checked This Item: Some Helpful Ideas

■ Use Rewards

The behavior-modification concept of giving a reward is always controversial, but for some children it works. An external reward can become an internal behavior if the child plays his part. Try keeping a private chart that adds a check or smiley face each time the child uses the toilet. Once a child is in the habit or has overcome anxiety about using your facilities, the use of the chart should fade away.

■ Display Acceptance

Use every strategy you know to show the child you accept him or her. Nonverbal cues such as smiles or hugs, as well as friendly words, special activities, and jobs or errands make a child feel accepted. Help him to be accepted by the other children as well. Once anxiety about your center and its inhabitants is lessened, a new child should not be so tense about using the bathroom facilities.

■ **Read a Book**

An incredible book about using the toilet is *Toilet Tales* by Andrea Wayne von Konigslow (Toronto, Canada: Annick Press, 1985). This hilariously illustrated story tells why big boys and girls can use the toilet and why animals like elephants, lions, snakes, and beavers cannot. When your children are finished laughing, all the tension about toilets should be gone!

HANDLES SUDDEN CHANGES/STARTLING □ SITUATIONS WITH CONTROL

Surprise (Startle)

Surprise is different from the other emotions in that it lasts only for a moment, although its results may continue for some time with young children. A sudden or unexpected external event causes a reaction of surprise or startle. The event could be a loud noise such as an explosion or clap of thunder at one extreme, or the unexpected appearance of a person at the other extreme. A startled person's mind goes blank for an instant, and his muscles contract quickly. He may even jump if the incident is surprising enough. Depending upon the situation, the person may be shocked, bewildered, confused, or embarrassed because of his reaction. Or he could be delighted.

Although a startle reflex appears in babies a few hours after birth, this reflex does not seem to be the same as the emotion of surprise, which occurs in infants between the fifth and seventh months. By that time, enough cognitive development has occurred to enable the infant to form expectations (Izard, p. 283).

Because everything is new for the child, there will be many startling events in her young life. If most of her surprises are pleasant ones, she will come to view surprises positively. If the opposite is true, surprises may cause the child to cry or exhibit defensive behavior.

Many mothers help to prepare their children for surprises (unintentionally, no doubt) by playing low-key surprise games such as peek-a-boo with them. The surprise is always a pleasant one, of course: the revealing of mother's hidden face. But if the child is scolded or ridiculed too severely at home when he cries or makes a fuss over unexpected happenings, he may become fearful of anything different, whether or not it is sudden.

Research shows that most adults view surprise as pleasant. Their experience has taught them this. Young children, on the other hand, do not necessarily show the same response. Perhaps because their experience is limited or because the occurrence of sudden happenings leaves them overwhelmed, they tend not to greet unexpected things as adults do. Most young children, for instance, do not react happily to surprise birthday parties. Young children are, in fact, more likely to cry or withdraw. It may take some time for the shock to wear off and for them to become their pleasant selves again. Sensitive adults will not impose such startling events on children. Children enjoy the pleasant anticipation of parties rather than startling surprises.

What about the children in your center? How do they respond to the unexpected? They need to be prepared for it in their lives, and they need to be able to control their responses. Like the other emotions, surprise/startle cannot be eliminated, nor should it be. It serves the useful function of preparing an individual to deal with an unexpected event. But if an individual's reaction is one of such alarm as to immobilize her, you need to help her deal with it in a better way.

What are some startling events you might anticipate? Most centers have fire alarms, which they may or may not be able to control. Ask your building supervisor if your children can have a chance to practice a fire drill with the alarm until they are able to do it with ease. Practicing with simulated emergency situations is one of the best ways to learn to deal with real ones.

In addition to practice, your children can learn to handle sudden changes or surprising events by acting the way you do. You need to be calm and collected yourself, modeling the behavior you would like your children to emulate.

Some children go to pieces when they are startled. They may be the ones who have not developed a strong enough sense of self or a sense of trust about the people around them. These children may cry, cling, or withdraw long after the event is past. How can you help them?

If You Have Not Checked This Item: Some Helpful Ideas

▪ Read a Book

Children may be helped to overcome their negative responses if they hear how others like themselves deal with surprises. Books about startling situations should be read not only to groups of children, but also to individuals who have exhibited a poor emotional response to a surprise. Some excellent books with this theme are included here.

Peek-a-Boo! by Janet and Allen Ahlberg (New York: The Viking Press, 1981) is about a baby in his crib, his high chair, his stroller, and so on. While this story may seem to be directed to infants, it is much too complex for any babe-in-arms. A preschooler, instead, should enjoy shouting "peek-a-boo" and looking through the dollar-sized hole in every other page to guess what complicated things the other members of the family are doing.

Maybe a Monster by Martha Alexander (New York: The Dial Press, 1968) is a small-format book in which a little boy narrator builds a trap and a cage to catch a monster and becomes afraid as he thinks about it. The building and the suspense take up all but the ending of the book, when the little boy is surprised to catch a rabbit.

Jim Meets the Thing by Miriam Cohen (New York: Greenwillow Books, 1981) can be reassuring to the many young children who are startled and frightened by the things they see on television. In this story, young Jim seems to be the only one in his class who is scared by the monster movie on TV the night before. But when they play superheroes on the playground at lunch time, only Jim stays calm when a praying mantis bug suddenly lands on Danny.

Drummer Hoff by Barbara and Ed Emberly (Englewood Cliffs, NJ: Prentice-Hall, 1967) may help to diffuse the fear of children frightened by loud noises. A cumulative folktale-like story, this book tells about colorful playing-card soldiers who put an old cannon together piece by piece and fire it off at the end.

Although some teachers have indicated that certain quiet children are frightened even by book experiences, you might ask the children themselves if hearing a book like *Drummer Hoff* will help them to get over their fear of loud noises. Let the children be the ones to say the "ka-a-a-boooom!" at the end.

Storm in the Night by Mary Stolz (New York: Harper & Row, 1988) tells, with wonderful words and illustrations, how Thomas, his grandfather, and his cat named Ringo deal with a thunderstorm that puts out their lights one night.

CAN EXPRESS ANGER IN WORDS ☐ RATHER THAN ACTIONS

Anger

Anger is the negative emotion of most concern not only in the child care center but also in society at large, perhaps because anger has the potential for such destruction. We are very much concerned that people learn to control their anger. Therefore, we begin teaching what to do—or rather what not to do—very early. We are often not very successful. There is, however, a positive approach to controlling anger that can diffuse the anger, so that children do not turn it against others or themselves.

First, we need to look at the emotion itself to understand what it is, what causes it, and what purpose it serves. Anger is the emotion or feeling that results when we are physically or psychologically restrained from doing something, frustrated in our attempts, interrupted, personally insulted, or forced to do something against our will. We feel hurt, disappointed, irritated. We frown, our face gets hot, our blood "boils," our muscles tense, our teeth clench, our eyes stare. At anger's highest level, we feel a rage that threatens to erupt in an explosive manner. At the other extreme, we feel hostility, a cold type of anger.

With anger comes a sense of physical power and a greater self-assurance than with any other negative emotion (Izard, p. 331). The body, in fact, rallies its resources, ready to strike out against the cause of the anger. In primitive man, anger mobilized the body's energy quickly and was important for survival. In modern man, the anger still appears, but its primary purpose has all but vanished.

Here we are, then, ready to turn this rush of physical energy against the "enemy." What should we do with it? This energy must be released or somehow diffused; otherwise, we will turn it against ourselves. Repressed anger has been implicated as one of the causes of skin diseases, ulcers, migraines, hypertension, and certain psychological disorders (Izard, p. 351).

Most parents teach their children from the start not to display anger. When they allow angry feelings to begin to show on their faces, children sense their parents' displeasure. Many children soon learn to conceal or disguise their expression of anger. Others let anger out in acts of aggression. Neither response is satisfactory. Yet many of us carry these responses throughout life.

Instead, we need a positive approach that teaches children from the start what they should do (expression) rather than what they must not do (repression). Anger definitely calls for some sort of release, but children and adults need to "let off steam" harmlessly.

One of the most satisfactory methods used by many preschool teachers coaches children to verbalize their feelings. Verbalizing involves not yelling or name-calling, but expressing in words how one feels about the thing causing anger. This approach has at least two advantages: it gives children an acceptable release for their strong feelings and it puts the children in control. They—not adults—deal with the situation, and solving the problem on their own strengthens the children's sense of self.

Strong feelings such as anger overwhelm and thus frighten young children. A method for learning control from the inside and not being controlled from the outside will help children in the future when adults are not around. The anger emotion calls for action. But if children learn to speak out rather than strike out, they will not have to suffer the guilt or remorse afterwards for an unacceptable act.

Expressing anger in words is not easy in the beginning. It does not come naturally for young children whose communication skills are still limited. It is even more difficult for the child caught up in the throes of an overwhelming emotion who finds it simpler to strike out physically or shout or cry. Yet three-, four- and five-year-olds can learn the response of telling how they feel in words.

How do you teach them? First of all, you have to model this behavior yourself. When you become angry, tell the individual or the group how you feel and why you feel this way: "I feel very upset when I see you dropping the tape recorder on the floor like that! If you break it, no one can enjoy the music any more," or "Paul and Gregory, I am so angry to see you ganging up on Leslie again! Two against one is not fair!"

You must also convey to your children that their actions—not them as individuals—make you angry. You must show you still respect and like the children no matter how angry they get or how upset you feel over their actions. Show the children both verbally and nonverbally that you still accept them as good people.

You also must intervene at every occasion where the children display temper, and you must help them repeatedly to express their feelings in words: "Shirley, tell Rachel how you feel when she takes your book," or "Von, don't hit Tony—tell him how you feel."

Make eye contact with the children. Help them to make eye contact with one another in order to help diffuse their anger. "Von, look Tony in the eyes and tell him."

Teaching children to express anger in words is a time-consuming process. But then, so is all learning. If you believe children must gain inner control over their anger and if you understand they must have some acceptable way to vent their feelings, then you will find it worthwhile to put in the time and effort necessary to divert anger's destructive energy into words. You will know you have been successful when the children begin telling one another: "Don't hit him, Bobby, tell him!"

If You Have Not Checked This Item: Some Helpful Ideas

▪ Talk About Feelings

Have a "feelings" corner in your room with pictures of people looking sad and angry and glad. Ask the child to tell you what he feels when he looks like that. Have a "feelings" hand puppet that the children can hold and talk to about the bad feelings they have.

▪ Read a Book

Read a "feelings" book to a child or small group at any time of the day (not only when tempers are short). Two classics on this topic are described here.

I Was So Mad by Norma Simon (Chicago: Albert Whitman & Company, 1974) lets many different children tell about what makes them mad, how they feel, and what they do about their feelings. They talk about being teased, picked on, or blamed; not being able to do something; having an activity interrupted or ruined; and being forced to do something they did not want to do. The story ends with the words and music to the song one father sings: "There Was a Man and He Was Mad." Your children can learn the song.

The Temper Tantrum Book by Edna Mitchell Preston (New York: Puffin Books, 1976) features a lion, a tiger, an elephant, and other animals, who get upset enough to have a temper tantrum until they can diffuse their anger by expressing in words why they feel furious.

☐ ALLOWS AGGRESSIVE BEHAVIOR TO BE REDIRECTED

Aggression

Aggression is not an emotion but the expression of one, the actions commonly taken by an individual as a result of anger or frustration. The hostile actions or angry words are intended to harm, defeat, or embarrass the person who caused the anger. Aggressive behavior in the classroom most commonly takes the form of hitting, throwing things, name-calling, spitting, biting, kicking, pushing or pulling, physically forcing someone to do something, restraining someone, destroying property, and forcefully taking someone else's possessions or turn.

Young children who have not learned to control their negative emotions often resort to this aggressive behavior. Children who have been neglected or treated harshly sometimes use aggression to strike out at the world around them. Children who have had to fend for themselves among older peers without much adult guidance may have learned aggressiveness as a survival strategy. Other children with highly permissive parents may have learned certain aggressive acts to get their own way: hitting and name-calling, for instance.

Research tells us that boys are more aggressive than girls. Since Helen Dawe's early observational study of the quarrels of preschool children in 1934, all findings everywhere have shown that boys are more aggressive (Brooks-Gunn & Matthews, p. 130). We can blame boys' aggression on genetics—physical development and hormones—but we also need to look at society's expectations for boys and girls. Society expects boys to be more aggressive than girls; thus boys are allowed and even encouraged to be more aggressive. If aggressiveness were considered a feminine trait, then, no doubt, the findings would quickly change.

Is all aggressiveness among children bad? Not according to researcher Wendy Matthews, who found in 1972 that among preschoolers in Paris, the most popular child in play groups was also the most aggressive both physically and verbally, whether or not the child was a boy or girl. Aggressive children were the leaders, using forceful behavior to keep their followers in line (Brooks-Gunn & Matthews, p. 131). This type of forceful behavior, however, is not the same as aggression due to anger and frustration.

How, then, can a preschool teacher help children control their unwanted aggressive behavior? Putting negative feelings into words, of course, helps achieve inner control. But if their actions are already aggressive, the children need to be redirected into a less destructive activity.

Children who strike out aggressively could be redirected to hit a ball of clay, hit a nail with a hammer, punch a pillow, kick a ball, hit a tether ball, throw a beanbag at a target, or use rhythm band instruments. Activities that calm over-wrought children include finger painting, water play, working with play dough, mixing dough, and listening to music or a story.

If You Have Not Checked This Item: Some Helpful Ideas

■ Hold the Child on Your Lap

Sometimes you must physically restrain a child from hurting someone else. Because you are bigger, you can hold the child so she cannot hit or kick until she calms down enough to control herself. Hold the child on you lap, restraining her from using her arms. If she kicks as well, you may need to remove her shoes. This child is totally out of control and needs your help to restore herself to normalcy. Do not lose control yourself. Children are afraid of their own overwhelming emotions. They need you to remain calm and to prevent them from doing damage. Ask the child if she feels calm enough for you to let her get up. If she cannot tell you, she is not ready yet.

■ Read a Book

When the right time comes, some children who use aggression to solve problems may want to listen to a book about others who do the same.

The Grouchy Ladybug by Eric Carle (New York: Thomas Y. Crowell, 1977) is a time/counting book about a ladybug who challenges one after another of the animals all around the world to a fight. When each agrees, the ladybug flies off, telling them they are not big enough. Finally the whale, without knowing it, slaps some sense into the grouchy ladybug.

No Fighting, No Biting! by Else Holmelund Minark (New York: Harper & Row, 1958) is a classic book that contains stories about two little children and their older cousin Joan, who will not let the younger cousins sit with her while they continue to fight and pinch. Additional stories focus on two little alligators, who also fight and bite.

DOES NOT WITHDRAW FROM OTHERS EXCESSIVELY ☐

Shame (Shyness)

As you observe the children in your classroom at the beginning of the year, you may note that certain ones seem to stay by themselves. They may stand apart or sit apart. If you try to get them involved, they may lower or avert their eyes, turn their heads, or even put a thumb in their mouths. They seem to want to shrink into invisibleness. They seem, in fact, to be exhibiting all of the indications of painful shyness.

Shyness is one of the least studied of the negative emotions. Yet nearly all humans experience shyness at one time or another. Early childhood is a common time for such an occurrence. Shyness results from a heightened degree of self-awareness, in which the individual feels exposed, helpless, incompetent, and somehow shameful about it all.

As with so many of our feelings about ourselves, shyness seems to come from a combination of inherited traits plus first year experiences (Izard, p. 405). The earliest "shame" feelings that an infant experiences occur when he first recognizes the face of a stranger around the age of five to seven months. Previously, he has been fascinated with the human face. It has been a stimulus for excitement and joy. He wants contact with it. He wants some kind of interaction.

Then something occurs within the cognitive development of the infant that allows him to discriminate one face from another. Suddenly, when a stranger appears, the infant realizes he is not looking at a familiar friendly countenance. He no longer responds joyfully, but instead, seems to realize his mistake and thus suffers his first embarrassment. He may cry, become red in the face, or try to get away. If the child has a series of negative experiences with strangers at this time, he may learn that he is subject to shame whenever he meets a stranger (Izard, p. 395). Highly sensitive children exhibit such embarrassment whether or not their experiences have been negative.

In addition, something else is happening within the child. He is becoming aware of himself as a separate being. This awareness has to happen before embarrassment—and therefore shyness—is able to occur. The shame (shyness) emotion is, after all, the feeling of exposure of self, of extreme self-consciousness, in which the person feels that all eyes are on him and he is uncomfortably out of place. According to research, these feelings occur most frequently in large groups, in new situations, and with strangers (Izard, p. 399).

Is it any wonder then that certain children exhibit this emotion in your classroom, especially at the beginning of the year? These children may be the sensitive ones or the ones whose parents have used shaming as a method of discipline. Or they may be children who have not yet developed a strong enough sense of self to be comfortable among strangers. Shyness can be emotionally crippling to a child. It can prevent her from enjoying the best of herself and of others in your center. You need to find a way, using the utmost tact and sensitivity yourself, in order to help the shy child.

Children have no need to feel ashamed. They often do so because they are not able to live up to their expectations of themselves. They look around at other people and see themselves as a shameful example of what they would like to be. To help them change this inaccurate perception, you need to let them know—in many ways—how good they really are. Tell them verbally, show them nonverbally, and involve them actively in important duties and projects. You need to engage the children in activities where they will find out for themselves how worthy they are. But never at any time should you use shaming or ridicule as a method of discipline or scolding (e.g., "Ronny, look what you did to the paints! How could you be so clumsy!").

The shame emotion does have a use in human development. Shame is the emotion—and a very powerful one—that keeps us from acting shamefully among others, so that we do not bring ridicule down on our heads. Rules for behavior (such as polite manners) are one result of the shame emotion. People who lack a sense of shame may commit such shameful acts as incest or child abuse. On the other hand, people who are overcome with an irrational sense of shame may also be emotionally crippled by it.

Some young children have this irrational feeling of shame. Because shame results from a real or perceived put-down of the self, and not just from an act the self has performed, there is real danger in allowing the child to feel that he is not good. If you do nothing to help the child correct this negative perception of himself, he may come to believe it. He may express his belief by withdrawing from others excessively. Thus you must make a concerted effort to correct the situation.

If You Have Not Checked This Item: Some Helpful Ideas

■ Focus on the Child's Strengths

Because the shame/shyness emotion expresses the feeling that a child has not accepted herself, you can best help a shy child by finding ways for her to feel good about herself. Is she wearing a brightly colored dress? Maybe she could cut out pictures from a magazine of other dresses the same pretty color as hers. Or have her look at her pretty hand (she may be too sensitive to look at her face in a mirror at first). Could she trace around her fingers, color the hand, and then cut it out? Perhaps she will allow you to display it on the classroom wall.

■ Do Not Dwell on Her Shyness

Reading books about shy children may not be a good idea. Shy children are already painfully aware of how they feel. To point out this shyness by reading a book about it may only make it worse.

■ Pair with Another Child

If one other child accepts her, the shy child may find it easier to accept herself and become involved with the others. You may need to take the initiative in this case, asking another child to work with the shy child on a puzzle or to go on an errand for you together.

■ Talk with Parents

Does the child exhibit this same behavior at home? Maybe not. Many children act completely differently at home from at school. This may mean that it is in your classroom where the child feels self-conscious and thus exhibits shyness. In that case, continue your activities to show acceptance and to help her accept herself. But if the parents admit that the child behaves the same at home, you may want to discuss tactfully with them the methods of discipline they are using. If shaming or ridiculing are involved, perhaps the parents could learn another way. You might consider having a parents meeting, where a speaker or film discusses the discipline issue.

☐ SHOWS INTEREST/ATTENTION IN CLASSROOM ACTIVITIES

Interest (Excitement)

Interest is the most frequent and pervasive positive emotion that human beings possess. Children show interest by directing their eyes toward an object or person that catches their attention and then exploring it with their eyes and other senses, if possible. Interested people are alert, active, self-confident, and curious. Interest is the motivator for much of children's learning, as well as for their development of creativity and intelligence. Thus, it is crucial for the growing child to have his interest stimulated by the interesting people, objects, and ideas in his environment.

Psychologists believe that change or novelty is the basis for the interest emotion. The novelty of an object first attracts the person's attention. Once he is aroused and curious, he should be motivated to find out more about the object, thus increasing his knowledge, skill, and understanding. Interest, in other words, is the impulse to know, which then sustains our attention in the things about which we are curious. Excitement is the most intense form of interest.

For an infant to perceive an object, she must first pay attention to it over a period of time. It is the emotion of interest that keeps her attention. Without this emotion, she may become passive, dull, and apathetic, with little initiative or movement. The final result may be developmental lags or even retardation.

The interest emotion appears very early in an infant's life. Interest is evident in the attention she shows to the human face; eyes rivet to her mother's face and turn to follow it. Objects such as rattles, bottles, mobiles, and her own fingers and toes are fascinating fields for exploration with her eyes and then her mouth. Later she shifts from external exploration to manipulation. What will objects do when you kick them, throw them, drop them?

When he throws his cereal dish on the floor, the child is not being naughty, only normal. He finds out about his world this way. Acts like this against physical objects obviously teach the child many additional things about the feelings of the people around him. If the family is strict or harsh or punitive about his actions, such exploration motivated by interest will become inhibited. If the child is punished too many times, he may cease exploring altogether, which poses dire consequences for his future development. On the other hand, encouragement to explore, play with things, and be curious will stretch his mind, senses, and physical skills.

Poverty frequently interferes with the development of strong interests because the variety of objects or activities available in the child's environment is often limited. In cases where the parents must also spend much of their energy struggling to survive, they may have little or no time to interact with their youngsters. The parents may, in fact, actively discourage them from exploratory endeavors. If, in addition, negative emotions dominate the atmosphere, interest quickly fades away.

Thus, it is important for you to know which children in your classroom have retained their native curiosity and which have not. The interest and attention individual children pay to classroom activities may give you a clue. But you need to remember that interest is stimulated by novelty and change, so a truer test might be to set up a new activity area and observe which children notice it, who plays in it, and for how long. Because interests by now are very much individualized and personalized, what interests one child will not necessarily cause a flicker of attention in another. For this reason, you must provide a wide range of activities and materials for your group. Remember also to add something new once in a while.

The basic interest emotion also affects attention span. Children must first be attracted to an activity through interest, which is activated by change or novelty. If they find it interesting, they are likely to pay more attention to it; in other words, they are more apt to give their attention longer to the activity. Although we know that age and maturity have a great deal to do with how long a child's interest can be held (i.e., the older, the longer), we can also increase the attention span by providing highly attractive materials and activities. Because children must attend in order to learn, the length of the attention span is crucial in every learning situation. Teachers thus need to know what kinds of things are attractive to children three, four, and five years old.

If You Have Not Checked This Item: Some Helpful Ideas

■ Focus on the Self

Although children's interests are widely varied, all humans, and especially egocentric youngsters, have a basic interest in themselves. Think of something new and different about the child who shows little interest in center activities. Make it some kind of question, problem, or challenge that is intriguing and fun. Then turn the child loose with it. For instance, have a Slappy Shoe Contest with a "winner" every day. The child who shows little interest can start by being your first "winner." Have him make some kind of paper crown or design that he can tape to the top of his shoes. At some time during the day, have him slap out a rhythm with his shoe that you tape record. Play the tape. Let other children try to copy it. Let him choose who is the one who will be the Mr. or Ms. Slappy Shoe winner tomorrow.

Is this novel enough? It may sound strange, but it is not when you remember how much children love shoes. Can you think of other things about the children—their clothing, hair, pets, or favorite foods or songs—that can be turned into a similar activity? Start with the children who seem to show little interest and go from there.

▪ Arouse Curiosity

Children love mysteries. Have a mystery guest (an adult dressed in a costume and mask) visit the classroom. Let children guess who it is. Or bring a big stuffed animal in a bag and let the children guess what it is. Give them hints about what it eats and the noises it makes. Maybe the slow-to-respond child would like to think of a name for it.

▪ Read a Book

Read a book about a mystery. Steven Kellogg has written several small-sized picture books involving mysteries; other authors offer mysteries for this age group in full-sized books.

The Mystery of the Magic Green Ball by Steven Kellogg (New York: Dial Press, 1978) is the story of Timmy, who loses his big green ball in the woods, and the Mystery Gypsy Fortune Teller, who finds it but refuses to give it back until Timmy uses some magic himself.

The Mystery of the Flying Orange Pumpkin by Steven Kellogg (New York: Dial Press, 1980) is a startling but hilarious escapade about a pumpkin the children grow in a garden that comes to be owned by a scrooge-type character. When the "scrooge" refuses to let the children have their pumpkin for Halloween, three "ghosts" make it rise out of the field and fly away, and then they involve him in a party to get it back.

The Mystery of the Missing Red Mitten by Steven Kellogg (New York: Dial Press, 1974) is another small-sized book about a little girl who loses her mitten in the snow and after a long search finds it as the heart of the snowman she has built.

The Vanishing Pumpkin by Tony Johnston (New York: G. P. Putnam's Sons, 1983) is a full-sized book about a 700-year-old woman and an 800-year-old man whose Halloween pumpkin has been stolen; they must confront a ghoul, a rapscallion, a varmint, and a wizard before finding it. This book is just the thing to tickle the fancy of a bored-acting child. Can he make up his own mystery afterwards and tell it to a tape recorder?

The Spooky Old Tree by Stan and Jan Berenstain (New York: Random House, 1978) features the exploits of three small bears who explore the mysteries of a spooky old tree. As the bears journey through the tree, the reader is invited to guess whether the bears will dare to go up the twisting stairs, into a spooky hall, and over a scary sleeping bear.

■ **Start with Something Simple
That the Children Like**

Do the children like apples? How many things can you do with an apple? The book *Apple Pigs* by Ruth Orbach (New York: Philomel Books, 1976) might get them started when they hear the zany story in rhyme about the family so overwhelmed with apples that they invite an entire zoo in to help consume them. Directions are given for making "apple pigs."

SMILES, SEEMS HAPPY MUCH OF THE TIME □

Joy (Enjoyment)

Joy, the most positive of the emotions, is also the most elusive. Seek it and you may not find it. Try to experience it directly, and it may escape you. But live a normal life and it will appear spontaneously. Joy does not occur so much on its own as it does as a by-product of something else: a pleasant experience, a happy thought, a good friendship. In other words, this emotion is indicative of a child's feeling good about himself, others, and life in general. The absence of joy tells us that the child is not feeling good about these

Joy is the most positive of the emotions.

things. We need to observe the children carefully to see where they stand in regard to this important indicator of inner feelings, and we need to take positive action if this emotion is missing.

Joy is the feeling of happiness that may precede or follow a pleasant experience: sensory pleasure such as a hug, a kiss, or a back rub; or psychological pleasure such as the remembrance of good times or the anticipation of seeing a loved one or of having fun with friends. People express joy with smiles, laughter, the lighting up of eyes, increased heart beats, inner feelings of confidence, a sense of well-being, or a glow. The emotion itself is fleeting, but the good feeling it creates may color the child's actions and responses for many hours.

As with the other emotions, the capacity for joy is inherited and different for each individual (Izard, p. 239). Its development, however, depends greatly on how the mother or primary caregiver responds to joy in the infant. A person cannot teach another person to be happy, but she can influence the occurrence of happiness by creating a pleasant environment in the first place and then responding positively when joy occurs.

A baby may smile during the first days of life. At first, the baby smiles in revery or dreams; then the infant smiles during waking hours when a pleasant, high-pitched voice talks to it; and finally, by the fifth week, the infant smiles at the sight of a friendly face coming close (Izard, p. 239). The first smile, in fact, is almost a spontaneous reflex, coming two-to-twelve hours after birth. But the elicited smile, which comes as a result of a voice, occurs soon afterwards, within the first week. By the second or third month, if he has been responded to pleasantly by his caregivers, the infant will smile spontaneously without seeing or hearing anyone. But the human face is the single most effective stimulus to smiling (Izard, p. 248).

Laughter has its own developmental sequence: it first occurs between five and nine weeks of age, usually in response to patty-cake-type games or tickling. Scientists believe the motor development of the child has some relationship to the development of laughter. Both laughter and smiling, however, can be stimulated by the same expressions of joy on the part of another.

Situations that discourage or prevent the emotion of joy from occurring include poor physical health, conditions of fatigue or boredom, harsh treatment or neglect, conditions of poverty that limit a child's possibilities, and the lack of joy on the part of caregivers.

Recognition of a familiar person, object, or situation helps stimulate or encourage the expression of joy. Whereas change and novelty seem to stimulate the emotion of interest, familiarity and being comfortable with things set the stage for joy. Keep this in mind in your child care center. A little change is challenging. Too much change is overwhelming for the young child. He or she needs a stable schedule of daily events that can be depended on and a physical arrangement of materials that does not change too drastically overnight. Then the child can look forward with joy to coming to the center every day.

If You Have Not Checked This Item: Some Helpful Ideas

■ Talk to Parents

Children who express no joy probably are not very happy. You will need to converse with their parents in a sensitive manner, trying to elicit how the child reacts at home, whether there are any particular problems or pressures presently affecting him, and what his basic personality is like. Is the child basically happy? What are his favorite things: foods, colors, toys, activities? What makes him laugh? Perhaps you can use some of these favorites as a focus for an activity to make him feel good.

■ Read a Book

You cannot teach a child to be happy, but you can help him experience joy and therefore stimulate him to want more of it. Maybe a humorous book will tickle his funny bone enough to open his life to joy. The first two books that follow have words. The others are wordless. He needs to make up his own. Read them on a one-to-one basis with a child, or with no more than two or three others if you want individual participation.

TABLE 3. Childhood emotions in the classroom

Emotion	Common Cause	Possible Results
Distress	Separation from loved one; abandonment	Crying; whining; clinging
Fear (anxiety)	Presence of threat; absence of safety	Tightening of muscles; refusal to eat, fall asleep, go to toilet
Surprise	Loud noise; unexpected appearance or event	Crying; withdrawing; clinging
Anger	Physical or psychological restraint; interruption; insult	Red face; loud words or screaming; physical aggression
*Aggression	Anger; frustration	Hitting; throwing; biting; kicking; pushing
Shame (shyness)	Heightened self-consciousness; exposure	Red face; crying; withdrawal
Interest (excitement)	Change; novelty	Looking at something; exploration with senses; wide eyes
Joy (enjoyment)	A pleasant experience; happy thoughts; friendship	Smiling; laughing; lighting up of eyes; talking happily

*NOTE: Not a true emotion

What Do You Do with a Kangaroo? by Mercer Mayer (New York: Scholastic Book Services, 1973) is the question faced by a little girl when a kangaroo, opossum, llama, raccoon, large baby moose, Bengal tiger, and a camel invade her house and make themselves at home one by one whether she wants them there or not. The little girl tries throwing them out but ends up with the whole menagerie in bed.

Squeeze a Sneeze by Bill Morrison (Boston: Houghton Mifflin, 1977) is a hilarious rhyming game with words like pickle, tickle, and alleycat matched up with zany pictures to illustrate the nonsensical rhymes.

Ah-Choo by Mercer Mayer (New York: Dial Press, 1976) is a comical wordless picture book in which Elephant sneezes and trouble begins. The rhino policeman doesn't think it is very funny when Mr. Elephant sneezes down the jail and then ah-choos his way into his girl friend's heart. Your children will have to make up their own words to suit the pictures.

A Boy, a Dog and a Frog by Mercer Mayer (New York: Dial Press, 1967) is a classic picture story of the boy and dog who fail to catch the frog they want as a pet, so the frog catches them. This is the first of several books with the same characters.

▪ Be a Joyful Person

Children and others feel joy when they meet a person who thinks they are delightful and wants to be around them. Make yourself that kind of person.

OBSERVING, RECORDING, AND INTERPRETING EMOTIONAL DEVELOPMENT

In order to understand and interpret the emotional growth of individual children, it is helpful to fill out the emotional development section of the *Child Skills Checklist* for specific children. Using data gathered during observations, the teacher filled out this section of the checklist for Sheila, the child discussed in Chapter 1, as follows:

Emotional Development Checklist

___✓___ Allows self to be comforted during stressful time
Evidence: Lets teacher calm her down when Beth takes her crayon

___✓___ Eats, sleeps, toilets without fuss away from home
Evidence: Always does these things with ease on own

_____ Handles sudden changes/startling situations with control
Evidence: Cries or runs to teacher when upsetting things happen (when paint spills)

___✓___ Can express anger in words rather than actions
Evidence: When Beth takes her crayon she says to Beth: "That's not fair!"

_____ ✓ _____ Allows aggressive behavior to be redirected
Evidence: Does not use aggressive behavior, but allows teacher to involve her in other activities when she complains too much

_____ Does not withdraw from others excessively
Evidence: Does not play with other children

_____ ✓ _____ Shows interest/attention in classroom activities
Evidence: Goes around room trying out everything; spends much time with art activities

_____ Smiles, seems happy much of the time
Evidence: Rarely smiles; does not give evidence of being happy

Sheila shows confidence in her use of language, as well as in her eating, sleeping, and toileting away from home without a fuss. This seems to indicate that she is at ease in the classroom setting. However, she does not seem to be comfortable with the other children, since she does not play with them yet and runs to the teacher whenever anything upsetting happens. The other important indicator is the fact that she does not smile or seem happy. Perhaps Sheila does not display happiness because she is ill-at-ease with the other children.

These observations were made at the beginning of the school year before all of the children were used to each other and to the center. Some of the activities listed under "If You Have Not Checked This Item: Some Helpful Ideas" may help Sheila to feel more comfortable with the others. The fact that Sheila goes around the room trying out everything is a sign that she will eventually want to get involved in everything. Perhaps Sheila can do an art activity with another child. Her teacher may want to pair Sheila with a child who is already at ease and can help Sheila feel more at home in the center.

REFERENCES CITED

Brooks-Gunn, Jeanne, and **Wendy Schempp Matthews.** (1979). *He and She: How Children Develop Their Sex-Role Identity.* Englewood Cliffs, NJ: Prentice-Hall.

Izard, Carroll E. (1977). *Human Emotions.* New York: Plenum Press.

OTHER SOURCES

Beaty, Janice J. (1988). *Skills for Preschool Teachers.* Columbus, OH: Merrill Publishing Company.

Candland, Douglas K., Joseph P. Fell, Ernest Keen, Alan I. Leshner, Robert Plutchin, and **Roger M. Tarpy.** (1977). *Emotion.* Monterey, CA: Brooks/Cole Publishing Company.

Cherry, Clare. (1983). *Please Don't Sit on the Kids: Alternatives to Punitive Discipline*. Belmont, CA: Pitman Learning.

Enzer, Norbert B. (Ed.), with **Kennith W. Goin.** (1978). *Social and Emotional Development: The Preschooler*. New York: Walker and Company.

Kersey, Katharine. (1986). *Helping Your Child Handle Stress*. Washington, DC: Acropolis Books.

Kvols-Riedler, Bill, and **Kathy Kvols-Riedler.** (1979). *Redirecting Children's Misbehavior: A Guide for Cooperation Between Children and Adults*. Boulder, CO: R.D.I.C. Publications.

Marion, Marian. (1987). *Guidance of Young Children*. Columbus, OH: Merrill Publishing Company.

LEARNING ACTIVITIES

1. Observe the children in your classroom for a week in the eight areas of emotional control. Which children exhibit behavior that seems to show emotional control? Which ones have not yet learned inner control? How can you help them? Write out and discuss a plan with your supervisor.

2. Choose a child who has trouble allowing his/her aggressive behavior to be redirected. Observe the child for three mornings, making a time sampling of his behavior. Use a behavior modification idea (discussed in Chapter 1) to see if you can reduce the number of times this negative behavior occurs. What are the results of your follow-up observation?

3. Choose a child who has trouble either eating, sleeping, or toileting in your center. Observe him/her, making a running record on three different days. What other indications of tension do you find? What suggestions do you have for alleviating the tension?

4. Work with one of the children in your classroom who has difficulty expressing his/her anger in words. What actions can you take to help the child? Observe and record the results.

5. Choose a child for whom you have checked "smiles, seems happy much of the time." Observe this child on three different days. Which of the other items can you check based on your observations? What is your evidence for each check mark? What conclusions can you make about this child based on these observations? Do you need any additional evidence in order for you to make conclusions?

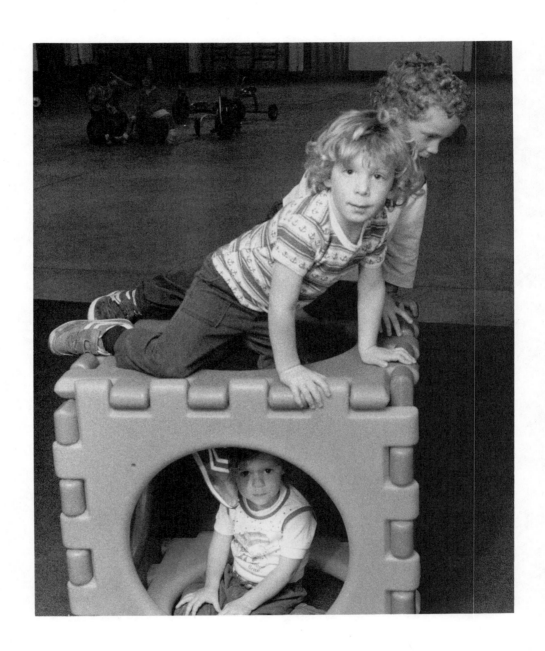

4 Social Play

Social Play Checklist

☐ Plays by self with or without objects
☐ Plays by self in pretending-type activity
☐ Plays parallel to others with or without objects
☐ Plays parallel to others in pretending-type activity
☐ Plays parallel to others constructing or creating something
☐ Plays with a group with or without objects
☐ Plays with a group in pretending-type activity
☐ Plays with a group constructing or creating something

T he social development of the preschool child is revealed in how he or she gets along with peers. Often we think of social actions as manners and politeness, but in the study of young children, social actions refer to how children learn to get along with their peers. Getting along for this age group rarely involves manners and usually is not very polite. Young children, in fact, frequently struggle to develop social skills.

They start out completely self-centered, which no doubt stems from a survival mechanism in infancy. Chapter 2 discussed how infants do not even recognize themselves as different from their mothers in the beginning. Then, little by little, the infants begin to discover their own self-identities. By the time they arrive in your classroom, the children have begun to know themselves as individuals but mainly in relation to their adult caregivers. If the children already have developed strong self-identities, they should do well away from home. They will be able to let go of their primary caregiver more easily and will be more willing to try new things and to experience new people. If the children have siblings at home, they will have learned to respond and react to children as well.

Peers in the early childhood classroom, however, pose a different problem for the young child. Many, if not most, three- and four-year-olds simply have not developed the social skills for making friends or getting along with others. These children focus on themselves. Everything has been done for them up to this time. Even if a new baby has replaced them as the youngest in the family, they still struggle to be first in the eyes of their parents.

This egocentric point of view does not serve them well in the world at large because sooner or later they must learn to deal with others and be treated as part of a group. They may have been enrolled in your program to learn precisely this. The purpose of many preschools, especially nursery schools, is to provide primary socialization for preschoolers.

What do these preschoolers need to learn? If socialization is not concerned with politeness and manners, then what social actions are involved in the early childhood classroom? A few aspects include

1. Learning to make contact with another child
2. Learning to interact with peers, to give and take
3. Learning to get along with peers, to interact in harmony
4. Learning to make friends
5. Learning to take turns, to wait for a turn
6. Learning to share with others
7. Learning to show concern for others
8. Learning to show respect for others' rights

Preschoolers' success in developing these skills, either on their own or with your help, may make the difference in how they get along for much of the rest of their lives.

This chapter is particularly concerned with the young child's ability to make contact, interact, and get along with peers. In order to determine where each of your children stands in the development of these skills, you need to be aware of behaviors that indicate his or her level of development. Because children engage in play—often together—and because play is an observable activity in the preschool classroom, we will focus on observing social play in this chapter.

EARLY RESEARCH

Many early childhood specialists have been interested in determining how children develop the skills to get along with one another. Social play has been the focus of such research since Mildred Parten first looked at "Social Participation Among Pre-School Children" in the late 1920s and published her findings in 1932. She found that social participation among preschoolers could be categorized and that the categories correlated closely with age and maturity.

Parten identified six behavior categories that have since served as a basis for determining children's social skills level in several different fields of study. Her categories include

1. *Unoccupied behavior:* The child does not participate in the play around him. He stays in one spot, follows the teacher or wanders around.
2. *Onlooker behavior:* The child spends much time watching what other children are doing and may even talk to them, but he does not join or interact with them physically.

   3. *Solitary independent play:* The child engages in play activities, but he plays on his own and not with others or with their toys.
   4. *Parallel activity:* The child plays independently, but he plays next to other children and often uses their toys or materials.
   5. *Associative play:* The child plays with other children using the same materials and even talks with them, but he acts on his own and does not subordinate his interests to those of the group.
   6. *Cooperative play:* The child plays in a group that has organized itself to do a particular thing and whose members have taken on different roles. (Parten, pp. 248–251)

Since 1932, a number of other researchers have tried to replicate Parten's study with varying results. Nevertheless, early childhood practitioners like to use Parten's categories when observing children at play because these behaviors really can be seen in the play interactions of young children. Since Parten's day, however, a great deal of new information about the development of young children has surfaced, especially through the work of Jean Piaget and the cognitive psychologists. Today we acknowledge that these early play categories are indeed a valuable beginning point for gathering observational data about a young child's social development, but we also need to incorporate more up-to-date information.

RECENT STUDIES

Sara Smilansky's work, published in 1968, supported the notion originated by Piaget that a child's play is influenced by cognitive development. Since we now recognize that most development is interactive, this idea cannot be disregarded. Smilansky elaborated on the play categories described by Piaget and labeled them.

   1. *Functional play:* Doing simple repetitive muscle movements with or without objects
   2. *Constructive play:* Manipulating objects to construct or create something
   3. *Dramatic play:* Pretending or using the imagination in play; role-playing
   4. *Games with rules:* Accepting prearranged rules and playing by them (Smilansky, pp. 5–7)

We view these categories as age-related, with functional play the first to appear in infancy and games with rules appearing last around age six or seven. Smilansky's work points out the importance of considering cognitive development when we look at the levels of children's play. But how does Smilansky's work relate to Parten's familiar categories? Should we give them up?

Kenneth H. Rubin and his associates have been working on this problem since the mid-1970s. His studies have been successful in combining Parten's and Smilansky's categories for observing the relationship between social and cognitive play. For example, when observing children exhibiting solitary play, he looked for one of Smilansky's four categories: functional, constructive, dramatic, or games. The same four Smilansky categories were also used for parallel play and group play (a combination of associative and cooperative play) (Rubin, 1977, p. 18). The results of Rubin's studies have done much to clarify the developmental levels of children's play in the light of our new knowledge about children.

A modified version (see Table 4) of the Rubin-Parten-Smilansky play categories is used in the *Child Skills Checklist* and discussed in this chapter as we consider observing the level of a child's social play in the preschool classroom. In the *Child Skills Checklist*, Rubin-Parten's solitary play is called "plays by self." Parallel play is called "plays parallel to others." Group play is called "plays with a group."

Only the first three of Smilansky's categories are used: functional, constructive, and dramatic. The category of *games* is omitted here because games with rules are played more frequently by children older than preschoolers. In the *Child Skills Checklist, functional* is called "with or without objects," *constructive* is called "constructing or creating something," and *dramatic* is called "in pretending-type activities."

Rubin's further research has found that constructive and dramatic play seem to emerge at the same time in children's social play development (Rubin, 1985, p. 89). However, the *Child Skills Checklist* has chosen to list

TABLE 4. Social play categories in early childhood

	Solitary Play	**Parallel Play**	**Group Play**
Functional Play	Child plays by self with or without objects.	Child plays parallel to others with or without objects.	Child plays with a group with or without objects.
Constructive Play	Child plays by self constructing or creating something.	Child plays parallel to others constructing or creating something.	Child plays with a group constructing or creating something.
Dramatic Play	Child plays by self in pretending-type activity.	Child plays parallel to others in pretending-type activity.	Child plays with a group in pretending-type activity.

dramatic play first before constructive, as they seem to be seen more frequently by other observers in this order. Moreover, the checklist omits the category of constructing or creating something (constructive) under "plays by self" (solitary play) because this particular activity does not seem to fit the continuum of social play development. Once young children have developed manipulative and art skills, they like to return to solitary play in order to create or construct art or craft projects on their own. Even children who have progressed in their social development from solitary play to group play often prefer to do an art project in a solitary manner. This is no reflection on their level of social play development, and thus the solitary-constructive category is best omitted from the checklist.

SOCIAL PLAY DEVELOPMENT

The development of social play is very much age-related, and it can thus be observed by the preschool child care worker in a particular sequence as children progress from solitary play through parallel play to group play. "Age-related development" thus signifies that the child's social skill level depends upon his cognitive, language, and emotional maturity. It also means that the older a child is, the more experience he has probably had with social contacts.

Observers have noted that infants first begin to imitate one another in play toward the end of their first year. Early in their second year, they already are engaging in peer play whenever they have the opportunity (Smith, p. 132). Often two-year-olds begin peer play by playing alongside another toddler in a parallel manner. If they interact with an age mate, it is only with one. Two-year-olds do not seem to be able to handle more than one playmate at a time. A threesome does not last long for children of this age.

Three-year-olds, as they become more mature and experienced, are able to play with more than one other child at the same time. As they become less egocentric and more able to understand another child's point of view, three-year-olds have more success with social play. Using more mature language, listening to their play partners, and adjusting their behavior to the situation all support such play.

The trick for many children in your center, you will note, is to gain access to play that is already in progress. Sociologists call these maneuvers *access rituals*. Children new to the group may try different strategies to get involved: [1] The youngest children may use nonverbal appeals such as smiles or gestures of interest as they stand nearby and watch, hoping a player will take note and invite or allow them in; [2] Other children may walk around and watch, or stand and watch, waiting for an opportunity to insert themselves; [3] They may engage in similar play parallel to the original players, hoping to join the original players if their own parallel play is accepted;

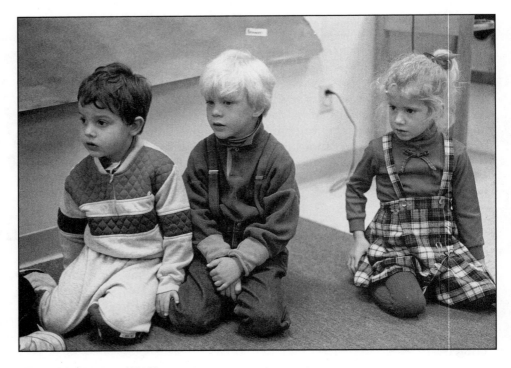

The trick for many children in your center is to gain access
to play that is already in progress.

4. They may intrude in a disruptive manner, claiming that the space or the
toys are their own; and **5.** The oldest preschoolers often use words, asking
"Can I play?" or "What are you doing?" to gain access.

The most successful strategy for a child's gaining access to ongoing
play seems to be to engage in parallel play. The least successful strategy is to
be disruptive (Smith, p. 130). Researchers have noted that parallel play
among preschoolers decreases as group play increases. Still, parallel play
seems to be the principal mode of social play for three- and four-year-olds in
most centers.

■ PLAYS BY SELF WITH OR WITHOUT OBJECTS

The first two checklist items under "Social Play" relate to Parten's "solitary
play" category. This is the type of play the young child engages in at first. It
is the least mature form of play. Children, when they first come into your
center, will often be seen playing by themselves. Part of this particular play
mode results from the strangeness of the situation and a lack of self-
confidence, but now we recognize that their level of cognitive development
also governs their ability to play with others. This development level is age-
related and can be observed by the type of solitary play chosen. Thus, we not

only need to look at solitary play itself, but also at the particular kind of solitary play the child engages in.

*The first level of solitary play is the functional level, in which the child makes simple, often repetitive movements, sometimes with an object and sometimes without. Most children begin here when they are unfamiliar with objects or situations. This manipulative kind of play helps the child to see what she or an object can do.

In block play the functional level usually consists of picking up a block, putting it down, pounding with it, or filling and dumping containers. Very young children, such as two-year-olds, start here. Older children who are unused to playing with blocks also begin by manipulating them in this way. But, very quickly, the mature child progresses through the sequence and soon stacks towers, builds roads, and constructs buildings. The older child thus needs practice with the materials rather than cognitive maturity.

Observations have also revealed that children from low income families spend more time doing this first-level functional play. We can make several possible inferences: [1] These children indeed may be less socially and cognitively mature than their middle-class peers; [2] Children from low income families may have fewer play materials in their homes and thus may not have had an opportunity to learn to play with these things; or (3) The play materials in the program may be unfamiliar to these children, who thus must spend more time in a solitary manner, manipulating these materials to see how they work or what they can do (Rubin, p. 19).

Whatever is the case, we need to provide a wide range of learning materials to encourage children to become involved with these materials on their own, and then we need to give the children the time to play with these toys.

If You Have Not Checked This Item: Some Helpful Ideas

All eight of the checklist items of solitary, parallel, and group play are, of course, descriptive, rather than judgmental. We are interested in observing individual children on each item to try to discover the child's level of social skills. Our observations may or may not reveal a child's developmental level. Thus, we must be careful not to judge a child negatively if we do not check a certain item. The items themselves are neither negative nor positive. They merely describe behavior. What we infer from the checkmarks or lack of them will be more meaningful if we also look at the recorded evidence on which the checkmarks are based.

■ Help But Do Not Pressure the Child

You first must help—but not pressure—the child to becoming engaged with an activity on her own, and later, you can help her to become involved with the other children. You might try sitting at a table with the child and helping her to get started with a puzzle, a pegboard, or some other table game. Once the child is involved, you should unobtrusively extract yourself and let her complete the game on her own. Put another puzzle or game on the table beside the first so that the child can continue her activity.

▪ Introduce Another Child

Another time, when she seems to be working comfortably on her own, you might try to introduce another child to the activity.

▪ In Some Instances, Leave the Child Alone

On the other hand, you may not have checked the "plays by self" item because the child is an onlooker rather than a participant. Some children who are new to a program begin by watching. They even may talk to the participants in an activity, but still not be engaged physically. Watching is often the first step toward group participation. If the child seems engaged in watching, it may be best to leave him alone. He may join the others once he is at ease in the center.

▪ Suggest Parallel Play

If, after some time has elapsed, the child still has not joined in with the others or even done much solitary playing, you may want to suggest that she build a building next to Carolyn's or dress a doll like Susan's. Friendly support—not pressure—works best. And, for some children, patience on your part is the only answer.

☐ PLAYS BY SELF IN PRETENDING-TYPE ACTIVITY

This second checklist item in the solitary play series is, like the first item, one of the least mature forms of social play. But children who have not yet experienced parallel or group imaginative play may move toward these activities by first playing alone in a pretending-type activity.

"Plays by self in pretending-type activity" refers to the child who pretends as he or she plays alone. He may be moving a toy truck or race car along the floor and pretending to be the driver, while making motor sounds and giving directions. She may be the nurse or doctor giving the baby doll a shot as she plays alone in the housekeeping corner. He may be building a garage for his car and talking to himself about what he is doing.

Most dramatic play in preschool programs occurs in group situations, as you might guess. But some dramatic play seems to take place in solitary situations like the ones just described. Often this solitary play is a temporary practice situation or a holdover from home if the child is used to playing alone. The child will have opportunities to join others; or rather, they will probably be joining her if her pretending sounds interesting to someone. Then you will see whether she is ready for group play. She may not be, and she may rebuff the joiner.

Some observers have found that the self-talk of solitary pretend players is less mature than that heard in group dramatic play. Perhaps the child plays alone for this reason. Her language level may not equal group conversation levels. On the other hand, group language experiences may improve her own vocal production.

If you check this item of solitary dramatic play for a child, you should recognize that it is not a negative finding. Instead, this item is a step on the ladder of socialization. When the child is ready, she will take the next step.

If You Have Not Checked This Item: Some Helpful Ideas

Your principal concern for those you have not checked should be children who are unoccupied or merely watching others. The watchers are the ones who need to be engaged in a group activity eventually. Yet not every child engages in solitary dramatic play first. On the other hand, it may be a helpful first step for some children who do not seem to know how to pretend.

▪ Give the Child a Pretending Toy

Give one of the children who is not occupied in play a hand puppet and try to engage her in pretending. You may want to wear a puppet yourself to get her started. Try the same thing with a toy person, animal, or vehicle.

▪ Read a Book

Choose a book based on solitary pretend play, such as *Mashed Potato Mountain* by Laurel Dee Gugler (Windsor, Ontario, Canada: Black Moss Press, 1988), in which Jamie fantasizes that his meal of potatoes is a mountain, the gravy is a river, and the broccoli is a forest. Full-page illustrations place a miniature Jamie in the middle of his fantasy.

In *Martin's Hats* by Joan W. Blos (New York: Mulberry Books, 1984), Martin engages in imaginative play when he puts on an explorer's hat, a party hat, an engineer's cap, a chef's hat, a police cap, and a firefighter's hat, among others. You will want a collection of similar hats in your dramatic play corner to motivate your nonplayers to become involved in pretending.

In *Regards to the Man in the Moon* by Ezra Jack Keats (New York: Collier Books, 1981), solitary player Louie uses his imagination to involve himself and finally the jeering neighborhood kids in a trip to outer space. This book could be the stimulus for any number of your own children to build a rocket ship to the moon.

☐ PLAYS PARALLEL TO OTHERS WITH OR WITHOUT OBJECTS

Parallel play is a fascinating phenomenon. If you are unfamiliar with this type of play, you have to see it to believe it. Parallel play often involves two children who seem to be playing together. As you get close enough to witness what is going on, you find that each child is actually playing a different game from a different point of view. If language is involved, the two children seem to be talking to themselves rather than each other.

At other times, parallel play is done by one child who plays parallel to a group of children. The group often pays no attention to the outsider, but goes on with its own group play. The outside child continues to play his game as well, perhaps using this method as an access ritual (see p. 107) so that the group will eventually accept him.

The first level of parallel play involves functional actions: the children play near one another and merely manipulate objects or materials. This first level is the least mature of the three levels. You might observe it with two or more children at the water table, swishing their hands around or picking up and dropping the water toys without much purpose to their actions. The same type of play might occur at the woodworking bench, the sand table, the housekeeping corner, or the block area.

Rather than build with the blocks, two or more children may only take them off the shelves or push them around the floor aimlessly. This type of play can eventually evolve into parallel constructive play, in which the children begin building or making something.

This first level of parallel play is seen more frequently among children from low income families than among those from middle income homes (Rubin, 1977, p. 18). Again, these children may be less mature or may have had less practice with the materials and the play situation.

All kinds of parallel play go on in the preschool setting, regardless of the children's background. More parallel play occurs with younger than older children. Parallel play, as previously mentioned, seems to enable young children to learn to play cooperatively with others in an early childhood center. This statement makes a great deal of sense when you consider that your center houses a large group of highly egocentric children who are strangers for the most part. They come together in a physical setting full of toys and activities just for them. How are they to deal with such a setting?

They begin by trying out things on their own. Then they play side by side, using the same materials but playing different games. Finally, the children begin to cooperate, to interchange ideas, and to come together to play as a group with self-assigned roles and tasks. Once children have learned to play cooperatively, they may abandon parallel play altogether. Thus, a blank on a child's checklist for "Plays parallel to others with or without objects" and a checkmark for "Plays with a group" probably means that the child has progressed in his development of social play beyond the parallel play stage.

If You Have Not Checked This Item: Some Helpful Ideas

■ **Provide a Physical Setup That Fosters Group Activities**

Set up your room so that two, three, or four children can play together in activities. Put that number of chairs at the tables with games or materials for the children to use together during the free choice period. Put your easels side by side so that children can paint in a parallel manner and can begin an interchange of looks and words.

■ **Invite the Child to Join Group Activity**

Your checklist observation will tell you which children have not started parallel or group play. Invite these children to join a table, work area, or science activity. These children may only manipulate the materials at first, but at least they will be close to another child and can begin by imitation to learn how to play.

PLAYS PARALLEL TO OTHERS IN PRETENDING-TYPE ACTIVITY ☐

The next level of parallel play involves dramatic or imaginative play with more than one person, but each person plays his own independent game. The children can be pretending in the block area, the dramatic play area, at the water table, on the climbing equipment . . . anywhere and everywhere in the classroom and on the playground. Sometimes it is obvious that they are parallel playing. Jeff and Joe, for instance, have buildings next to each other and are pretending that one is a hospital and the other a house. This is not cooperative group play because they do not interchange anything, neither blocks nor words.

Sometimes the observer needs to look very closely at the pretend play to determine whether it is parallel or cooperative. Paul and John, for example, are actually playing with the same building, but are having little to do with one another. John is building a garage for his race car, and Paul is playing with a figure of a person in his house.

Sometimes several children will be engaged in cooperative dramatic play, and one child will join them as a parallel player, who does not interact at all but who plays his own self-imposed role next to theirs. Parten originally called this "associative play," but recent researchers have found it so difficult to discriminate from cooperative play that they call any pretending done in a group, "group play." This categorizing is up to the observer. If you have solid evidence that a child is truly doing his own pretending on the periphery of a group, then this parallel play item should be checked.

Observe children carefully on the playground, and you may see a great deal of parallel pretend play. Often children from other classes use the playground at the same time, so the same equipment will be used by children who do not know one another. One child may pretend that the slide is a space shuttle launch pad, while another child may simultaneously use the slide as "an amusement park ride." The area under the slide or climber is another favorite site for pretend play. Usually groups of children use this area together for a hut or house of some kind. But sometimes two children will pretend different uses for the area at the same time.

Pretend play of this parallel nature occurs more often among children who have not yet developed the social skills to interact with a cooperative play group. But parallel play is a step in the right direction—almost like a practicing of the roles the child will take when she finally joins the group.

Some children from low income families have difficulty joining group dramatic play and thus play in a parallel manner like this. Researchers feel that children who have not joined a group in pretend play have not yet developed the social skills necessary for the give and take that cooperative dramatic play requires (Rosen, p. 926).

If children have not done any pretend play at all, it may mean they are not at the cognitive development level to be able to see things from another point of view. After all, in order to be a jet pilot, a child has to step out of his role as a four-year-old. Again, we see that all development is interrelated. To develop socially, children must also develop cognitively.

Can they be taught to see things from another point of view, or must we wait until they are developmentally ready? Questions about child development frequently involve the issue of *readiness*. We really do not know precisely when each child reaches certain developmental levels. Even if we did, should we wait around to find out if a child is "ready"? That used to be the style. We would give the child readiness tests or readiness games until he was "ready to learn," whatever that meant.

Now we know it is best just to plunge in, ready or not. The child will learn whatever his developmental level and his own motivation will grant him. Classroom teachers and aides must realize that there are individual differences in child development and accept children at whatever developmental level or learning stage they have reached. Teachers and aides must then choose developmentally appropriate materials to promote success among developing children.

Why, then, do we use the *Child Skills Checklist?* Why not just plunge in blindly? Because helping a child in the best possible manner requires that we know all we can about a child's level of development and his areas needing strengthening. If learning to get along with others is important in his life—and it is—then we need to determine where he stands in regard to this skill, in order to help him proceed from there. Building on skills he already possesses is one of the most successful approaches we can use. The checklist will help us to determine what skills those are.

If You Have Not Checked This Item: Some Helpful Ideas

You should be especially concerned with children who are not involved in pretending-type activities either parallel to or with other children.

■ Give the Child a Puppet

With hand puppets, the wearer must take a role other than his own. Let a child first play with hand puppets alone. Then you can wear another puppet and engage the solitary player in a pretend dialog. Once the child gets the idea, turn your puppet over to another child and tell the first child something like: "The brown bear here, who calls herself Grouchy, doesn't know where bears can find anything to eat in this room. Can your puppet, Pretty Boy, help her?"

■ Bring in Two New Stuffed Animals

Children enjoy using stuffed animals both as pretend people and pretend pets. Invite two children who have not exhibited much pretending to take care of your two stuffed animals for the morning. Then someone else can have a chance. To get the children started, tell them what the animals' names are and what the animals like to do. Ask the children if they will help the animals do what it is you have said they like to do. Seeing you pretending like this may encourage the children to try pretending.

PLAYS PARALLEL TO OTHERS □
CONSTRUCTING OR CREATING SOMETHING

Playing parallel to others constructing or creating something is probably the most popular type of play in an early childhood center. Many activities—especially art activities—place children parallel to one another doing similar constructive projects on their own. With most art activities, children sit next to each other at tables, making collages, molding clay or play dough, or cutting and pasting. The children may sit together in the reading corner looking at separate books. Two children may pound nails in tiles at the woodworking bench. Three or four youngsters may play at the water table, each filling his own container. Two or more may build their own buildings parallel to one another in the block building area.

      The physical arrangement of the center is most responsible for this type of play. Most centers are organized into activity areas where several children at a time can play with the equipment. This arrangement brings the children together in a parallel manner to work and play on their own with the same materials.

As they mature, the children may want to combine their materials to create something together, but this activity is a long way down the road for most preschool children.

If You Have Not Checked This Item: Some Helpful Ideas

If you have not checked this item for a particular child, it means that the child is not participating in the principal classroom activities. Hopefully, all of your children would spend some of their time working parallel to others in an activity area of their choice. Even children who have progressed beyond the parallel play stage enjoy creating their own things next to a friend. If some children are not involved in parallel construction or creation, you might try one of the following activities:

■ Try Finger Painting for Two

Set up a small table where two can sit side by side, and put out finger paints to be shared. Invite one of your reluctant participants and one other child to paint. Do not force the reluctant child. Perhaps you could first involve him in a solitary manner and then ask him if another child could work next to him.

■ Try Tape Recording for Two

You will need two cassette tape recorders for this activity. Two recorders are invaluable because they provide an opportunity for two people to play individually with the same materials in a parallel manner. Tape recording is personal and fun. Even the shy child can talk as softly as she wants as long as she holds the mike up close. She can say anything about herself she wants: her name, the names of her brothers or sisters or pets, her favorite foods, or where she lives. Then comes the fun of listening to what she has spoken. Two children can record at the same table if they each talk into their own microphones. They may eventually also want to talk into each other's mikes.

☐ PLAYS WITH A GROUP WITH OR WITHOUT OBJECTS

The final three items under "Social Play" involve cooperative group activities, the highest level of social play. This category also has the same three areas: functional, dramatic, and constructive play. Playing in a group with or without objects describes the functional behavior of preschoolers who first come together to play. They mill around or try things out rather than participating in a purposeful activity. This milling around also represents the kind of group play performed by toddlers. This play is the least mature of the three types of group play and also the type least engaged in by three- and four-year-olds.

An example of this functional type of play can be seen when several children come into the housekeeping area and handle the materials without putting them to use. One teacher set up her dramatic play area with doctors' props after her class had visited a clinic. Several children came into the area to play when they first saw the new materials. At first, the children picked up and looked at the various items, playing with the objects in a nonsensical manner. One boy shouted into the stethoscope that was around another child's neck, as if it were a telephone. A girl dumped out the contents of the doctor's bag onto a table and picked up and examined the contents, object by object. Another girl tried to retrieve these objects and return them to the bag. No real pretending happened at all in the beginning. The children merely explored the objects together in a playful manner.

Children come together to play with one another quite early in life. Two- and three-year-olds will search out each other for group play, as mentioned previously. The younger the child, the less structured the play. Functional group play for two-year-olds in the toddler center often revolves around running, climbing over things, and chasing, with lots of squealing and giggling. Two-year-olds may do silly things with objects, such as using the toy broom to sweep the doll bed instead of the floor. Once someone starts this sort of action, everyone has to have a turn. A follow-the-leader type of activity is very common at this age. Members of this sort of play group come and go; some lose interest and other children join.

Children from low income families tend to engage in more functional group play of this type than in the higher level dramatic play, according to some researchers (Rubin, 1977, p. 19). This finding seems to be based principally on the low socioeconomic status of the children and not their race, according to Catherine Rosen. She found that black middle income children demonstrated as much dramatic play as their white counterparts, whereas poor children of both races did significantly less group dramatic play (Rosen, p. 926). Again, this finding may signify that poor children are less mature in social, cognitive, or language development, or that poor children have had less practice in group dramatic play, or that all four of these situations exist.

As a classroom caregiver, you must structure your program so that all children have the opportunity, time, and encouragement to engage in group free play activities.

If You Have Not Checked This Item: Some Helpful Ideas

■ Provide Group Materials

Children will play with whatever materials are available. If you have puzzles for one, then one child will sit down and play. If you want children to develop social skills, then you need to provide materials for small groups of children. Have four stethoscopes in your dramatic play area and you will encourage four different children to come together in doctor play. Do the same with four basters or four egg beaters at the water table. The children may merely experiment with the materials at first in functional play style, but the opportunity to learn group dramatic play exists.

■ Arrange Classroom for Small Groups

Young children work best in small rather than large groups. Three or four children together is a comfortable group size. It was earlier noted that two-year-olds cannot play for long with more than one other person. Large groups are just too overwhelming for egocentric children of preschool age. Such individuals simply get lost.

Move your furniture around to divide large spaces into areas for small groups of children. Break up a large central area with room dividers. Pull bookshelves away from the walls, and use them as dividers for your ac-

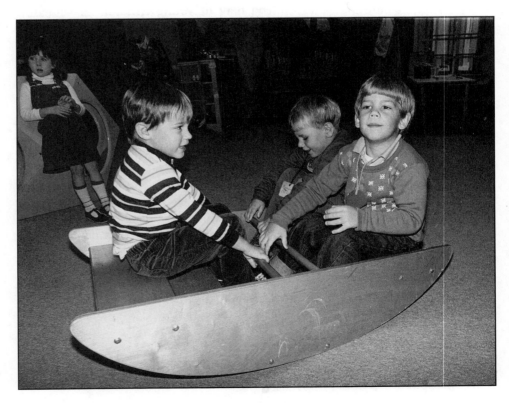

If you want children to develop social skills, you need to provide materials for small groups of children.

tivity areas. Move your classroom tables away from a large central area, and place each of them in a different smaller area. You can help to manage the size of the groups by this type of arrangement. Place four chairs at a table, put four aprons at the water play area, or divide the block area into four building spaces with masking tape on the floor to suggest the size of the groups that will play there.

PLAYS WITH A GROUP IN □ PRETENDING-TYPE ACTIVITY

Most centers provide a place for group dramatic play, the taking of spontaneous roles in imaginary group situations that are made up by the children during free play. Rubin found that these situations mainly involved house, store, doctor, firefighter, and vehicle play (1977, p. 21). And as with the solitary and parallel pretending activities, children from low income families do not engage in group pretending as much as middle income children. A checkmark for a child for this item is an indication of his or her social maturity.

A clear sequence of pretend play in young children has emerged over the past twenty years of research. By age two, children can pretend and often play with imaginary objects. The more complex sociodramatic play with several children taking different roles cannot happen until children can articulate verbally, which occurs between two and four years of age. Three- and four-year-old children, probably influenced by the preschool environment, are at the height of their concentration on other children. At this same age, children engage in group dramatic play most frequently. Such play gradually becomes more complex with five-year-olds in kindergarten until about age six, when the frequency of group dramatic play begins to decline. By age seven, games-with-rules are more prominent, and dramatic play seems to disappear altogether (Smilansky, pp. 10–11).

Thus, the early childhood classroom needs to take advantage of this recognized sequence of children's activities and to provide the materials, equipment, space, and time to allow and encourage children to engage in group pretend play. Chapter 13 discusses the development of a child's imagination and the themes he or she chooses when making up roles and situations in group dramatic play.

In this chapter, we are concerned with a child's social skills. If she is immature, she may not have developed the access skills to enter the group play in the first place. She also must be able to

1. Carry on a conversation
2. Maintain eye contact when speaking
3. Listen to and watch other speakers
4. Adjust own conversation content in order to be understood (Smith, pp. 135–136)

In addition, the child must be able to pretend, take a role, take turns, and show respect for others' roles . . . all within a playful framework. Given such a complex agenda for three-, four-, and five-year-olds, it is little wonder that not all children are successful at it.

Being successful at group dramatic play helps young children to practice and learn the social skills necessary to be successful in life. Some of the skills a child learns through group dramatic play include

1. Adjusting her actions to the requirements of her role and the group
2. Being tolerant of others and their needs
3. Not always expecting to have her own way
4. Making appropriate responses to others
5. Helping others and receiving help from them

In other words, engaging in group pretend play helps to transform a preschool child from an egocentric being who is the center of all attention into a socialized human being who recognizes the existence of others' points of view and can respond appropriately.

If You Have Not Checked This Item: Some Helpful Ideas

■ Read a Book

Some children want to join a dramatic play group but don't know how to go about it. Other children are rejected when they try to join their peers or older children in play. Read the book *I'll Be the Horse If You'll Play with Me* by Martha Alexander (New York: Dial Press, 1975) to any of your children, either players or nonplayers. Then talk about the topic of how someone can join a dramatic play group. This book addresses the problem of little sister Bonnie, who wants to play with big brother Oliver but always gets the worst of the situation.

■ Provide Appropriate Props as Field Trip Follow-up

You will be taking your children on field trips to stores, farms, fire stations, hospitals, laundromats, parks, zoos, pet shops, and construction sites. Upon your return, you will want to provide a variety of ways for children to represent and talk about this experience. An excellent activity involves providing props for them to play the roles seen at the field trip site. Many teachers make up a prop box after every field trip, filled with paraphernalia to be used in pretending the different roles. They label the outside of the box with a picture and words the children soon recognize. Then the children are free to take such boxes from the shelf and play with the equipment during free choice period. If children have shown an interest in the field trip, they are more likely to become involved with pretend play afterwards.

A trip to the post office, for instance, could produce a prop box with stamps (cancelled postage stamps or stickers of some sort), a stamp pad and stamper, envelopes, a mail bag (tote bag), a mail carrier's hat, and a picture book about a mail carrier. Phyllis and Noel Fiarotta's *Be What You Want to Be!* (New York: Workman, 1977) gives dozens of suggestions for making your own props out of discarded materials.

■ Change Your Dramatic Play Area from Time to Time

Everyone is stimulated by change. If you have had housekeeping equipment in your dramatic play area for a number of weeks, try converting the area to something else, perhaps a store or a beauty/barber shop. Talk with the children and have them help to stock it with empty or discarded items from home.

■ Put New Accessory Items in the Block Area

Group pretend play takes place in areas other than the dramatic play corner. Children can do their follow-up pretending after a field trip in the block corner as well. Mount pictures of the field trip site at eye level on the wall to give children seated on the floor ideas for creating new kinds of buildings. Add appropriate accessories to the shelves within the block area as well. If you have been to a construction site, put out little trucks, figures of people, string (for ropes and wires), plastic tubing, even stones if you want to be very realistic. Accessories can also be put at the sand or water table, although pretending in these areas is more often solitary or parallel than group play.

■ Help the Shy Child Get Involved

You may need to take a role yourself in order to help the shy child get involved in the playing. She may not have the access skills to enter an engaged group. You both can pretend to be visitors going to the store, doctor's office, or home. Let her carry something to give to the other players: pretend money, a ticket, or a box of something to exchange. Once she is involved in the play, you can leave.

PLAYS WITH A GROUP CONSTRUCTING □ OR CREATING SOMETHING

A more mature group play level for preschoolers involves a group of children coming together to construct or create something. In order to participate in such a creative venture, the players need language, cognitive, social, and creative skills. The children must express themselves verbally, accept assigned tasks, take turns and wait for turns, respect others' rights, and adjust their behavior to the needs of the group.

The children also need physical skills. Large and small motor coordination are important for success in building a hut, painting a cardboard playhouse, or constructing a block city.

Just as important are the materials provided. One of Rubin's studies ranked the ten most frequently observed preschool activities:

1. Cutting, pasting, and art construction
2. Painting and crayoning
3. Play dough
4. House, store, doctor, fire fighter play
5. Vehicles
6. Sand and water
7. Blocks
8. Science
9. Books
10. Puzzles (Rubin, 1977, p. 21)

Some of these observed activities tended to be nonsocial, while others almost always were group-oriented. Children doing painting and crayoning, play dough, sand and water, or puzzle activities usually worked either in a solitary manner or in parallel play with others. These findings seem to tell us that if we want our children to learn social skills, we need to provide more materials which will encourage small group activities.

Rubin found that gender differences affect group play as well. While boys more frequently engaged in vehicle and block play (which are both potentially social activities), girls engaged in more cutting and pasting, painting, and crayoning activities (which are nonsocial). If we want our girls to learn the give and take of group interchange during this important early development period, we need to provide them with the opportunity to learn about group interaction.

Although free play should allow for children's free choice of activities, you may need to steer individuals toward certain materials and equipment in order to give the children the chance to explore a wide range of activities and to learn the skills of getting along in groups.

Most social interactions occur in house play, vehicle play, and, surprisingly, reading activities, Rubin found (Rubin, 1977, p. 22). The first two activities involve dramatic group play, but reading is considered to be constructive play, the type of activity that teaches skills for getting along in groups. Teachers frequently encourage group interchange before, during, or after the reading of stories. This interchange helps children to take turns, to wait their turn, and to listen to what others have to say. From such activities can come the creation of group stories recorded on an experience chart or a tape recorder.

Teachers need to be aware of the opportunities available in their programs to encourage small group interaction. We tend not to think in these terms. We look at the activities in our classrooms as providing good experiences for children in general, not for children in solitary, parallel, and group play. Yet if we want to promote the social development of children, we need to provide youngsters with opportunities for learning and practicing social skills.

If You Have Not Checked This Item: Some Helpful Ideas

■ Provide Group Construction Materials

Put out two or three hand puppets on a table along with a tape recorder and blank cassette tape. Suggest that two or three children record a story that their puppets would like to tell. Show the children how to record if they do not already know. The puppets can make up the story as they go along. Expect a lot of laughter on your tape! When one group is done, another can have a turn.

Put two chairs side by side at a small table along with some fingerpaint, and suggest that two children fingerpaint on the table surface making a painting together (or on one large paper if you want to make cleanup easier). Cleaning up together can also be a valuable team experience.

Outside on the playground, provide two or three buckets of water and paintbrushes for children to "paint" the side of the building or a fence.

■ Have Partners Help

Whenever possible in your classroom, have one child help another to make something or to cooperate on a project. For instance, have one child draw around another's hand, foot, or stretched-out body for a self-concept art project.

■ Utilize Cooperative Projects

Have group scrapbooks for a variety of purposes. All the children with pets can make a scrapbook together, cutting and pasting pictures of animals, birds, and fish from old catalogs. All the children with baby brothers or sisters can make a baby scrapbook with pictures cut from maternity advertising catalogs or old magazines featuring families or babies. Groups of children can make a scrapbook of their favorite foods by cutting and pasting them from magazines. You do not need to purchase real scrapbooks if your budget is low. Any kind of paper can be stapled together. You will need to label the covers with a title and the children's names. Put the scrapbooks in the book corner for everyone to use.

OBSERVING, RECORDING, AND INTERPRETING SOCIAL PLAY

When four-year-old Lionel entered the classroom as a new child in January, he seemed to have a great deal of trouble interacting peacefully with the other children. By the end of the third week, he still had not joined any of the group games. The staff members decided to make a running record of Lionel during the free play period for several days and then transfer the results to the *Child Skills Checklist*. Here is a typical example of the running record made on Lionel:

> Lionel gets two little cars from box in block corner and sits on floor in corner moving cars around, one in each hand. Makes car noises with voice. Plays by himself with cars for five minutes. Moves closer to block building that two other boys are constructing. Lionel tries to drive his cars up wall of building. Boys push him away. Waits for a minute, then tries to drive car up wall of building again. Boys push him away. Lionel crashes one car into building & knocks down wall. One of boys grabs Lionel's car & throws it. The other boy pushes Lionel away. Lionel cries. Teacher comes over & talks with all three. Lionel lowers head & does not respond. Boys say, "He was trying to knock down our building with his cars" and "We don't want him to play with us."

Social Play Checklist

✓ **Plays by self with or without objects**
Evidence: Plays by self but usually in pretending activity

✓ **Plays by self in pretending-type activity**
Evidence: Yes. He likes to pretend with cars or miniature people or animals.

✓ **Plays parallel to others with or without objects**
Evidence: He often moves close to other children when he plays; he usually pretends.

✓ **Plays parallel to others in pretending-type activity**
Evidence: Plays with cars next to boys' block structure

✓ **Plays parallel to others constructing or creating something**
Evidence: Does art activities and puzzles on his own but always parallel to another child

_____ Plays with a group with or without objects

_____ Plays with a group in pretending-type activity

_____ Plays with a group constructing or creating something

When the staff members reviewed the running records and checklist information recorded for Lionel, they concluded that he knew where to find the materials and toys in the classroom and how to use them. They also felt that Lionel wanted to join the other children in group activities because he always played so close to the others, but that his methods for gaining access to a group (i.e., driving his car up the block building wall and crashing his car into the wall) were not acceptable. The staff decided to try to pair Lionel with Adrian, a mature player, who might help Lionel get acquainted with the others and gain access to their play. They asked Lionel and Adrian to build a block garage for the little cars. Eventually two other boys joined them in this activity.

By using observing and recording in this manner, individual children can be assisted in their development of social play skills.

REFERENCES CITED

Parten, Mildred B. (1932). "Social Participation Among Pre-School Children." *Journal of Abnormal and Social Psychology, 27,* 243–269.

Rosen, Catherine Elkin. (1974). "The Effects of Sociodramatic Play on Problem-Solving Behavior Among Culturally Disadvantaged Preschool Children." *Child Development, 45,* 920–927.

Rubin, Kenneth H. (1977). "Play Behaviors of Young Children." *Young Children,* 32(9), 16–24.

_____. (1985). "Play, Peer Interaction, and Social Development." In Catherine Caldwell Brown and Allen W. Gottfried (Eds.), *Play Interactions.* Johnson & Johnson Baby Products Company.

Smilansky, Sara. (1968). *The Effects of Sociodramatic Play on Disadvantaged Preschool Children.* New York: John Wiley & Sons.

Smith, Charles A. (1982). *Promoting the Social Development of Young Children: Strategies and Activities.* Palo Alto, CA: Mayfield Publishing Company.

OTHER SOURCES

Beaty, Janice J. (1988). *Skills for Preschool Teachers.* Columbus: Merrill Publishing Company.

Johnson, James E., James F. Christie, and **Thomas D. Yawkey.** (1987). *Play and Early Childhood Development.* Glenview, IL: Scott, Foresman and Company.

Rubin, Kenneth H. (1982). "Social and Social-Cognitive Developmental Characteristics of Young Isolate, Normal, and Sociable Children." In Kenneth H. Rubin and Hildy S. Ross (Eds.), *Peer Relationships and Social Skills in Childhood.* New York: Springer-Verlag.

LEARNING ACTIVITIES

1. Use the third section of the *Child Skills Checklist* ("Social Play") as a screening tool to observe all of the children in your classroom. Which ones engage mainly in solitary play? In parallel play? In group play? Are there any who are unoccupied or onlookers?

2. Choose a child whom you have observed engaging in solitary play. Do a running record of the child on three different days to determine the kind of solitary play performed. How could you involve the child in the next level of play? Should you do it? Why or why not?

3. Choose a child whom you have observed engaging mainly in parallel play. What kind of play does the child do? How can you help the child get involved in the next level of play? Use one of the suggested activities and record the results.

4. Choose a child whom you have not seen doing group pretend play. Use one of the activities from the chapter with the child. Discuss the results.

5. Choose a child whom you have not seen engaging in any parallel or group activity. Why do you think the child does not participate in these activities? What particular social skills does the child need to learn? How can you help the child? Try out an activity, and discuss the results.

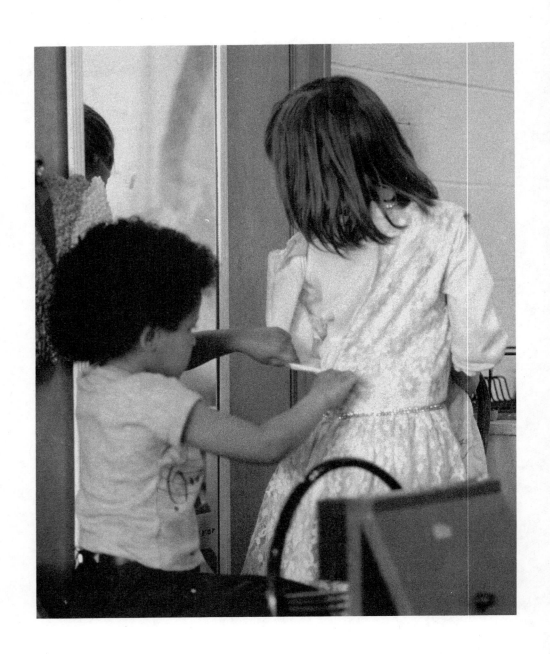

5 Prosocial Behavior

Prosocial Behavior Checklist

- ☐ Shows concern for someone in distress
- ☐ Shows delight for someone experiencing pleasure
- ☐ Shares something with another
- ☐ Gives something of his/her own to another
- ☐ Takes turns with toys or activities
- ☐ Waits for turn without a fuss
- ☐ Helps another do a task
- ☐ Helps another in need

A second area of young children's social development that is of great concern to early childhood caregivers is the positive aspect of moral development, better known today as *prosocial behavior.* It includes behaviors such as empathy, in which children express compassion by consoling or comforting someone in distress or by affirming a person's good fortune; generosity, in which children share or give a possession to someone; turn-taking, in which they share a turn or wait for a turn; and caregiving, in which they help someone to complete a task or help another person in need.

These are some of the characteristics that help people to get along in society, that motivate people to interact with one another, and that help to make us human. Young children are not in the world alone. They are part of a family, a clan of relatives, a neighborhood, a community, a country, and a world of similar beings. To be an integrated member of the "human tribe," the young child needs to learn the tribe's rules of behavior from the beginning.

This learning, you may argue, should happen in the home, and it certainly does, whether or not parents realize they are teaching their children social behavior. Children absorb everything that happens around them: what mom does when the baby cries, what dad does when someone upsets him, and what family members do when they disagree. Every emotional situation presents the young human with forceful patterns of behavior he can model. We know only too tragically that child abusers often come from families of child abusers.

Prosocial behavior can be modeled as well. Both the home and the school should be aware of the powerful lessons taught by behavior modeling, which the child absorbs so readily, especially in emotional situations. The actions of adults in emotional situations can be used to demonstrate the prosocial feelings of caring, sharing, and consoling, too.

Behavior also is taught by methods other than example both in the home and the preschool. Formal—often restrictive—rules for proper behavior have been drummed into children from time immemorial. Children are scolded or punished when they behave in an unacceptable manner. They cry, sulk, or slink away, and they may try to behave correctly next time. But just as often, they stick out a tongue in defiance and grumble, "try and make me!"

There is a better, easier way. Many early childhood specialists these days are turning their focus on the so-called prosocial behaviors in a search for ways to raise more humane members of the race. Not only does the learning of prosocial behaviors promise positive results, but it also offers more satisfying responses for both the child and the caregiver. Those who have tried the positive approach claim it is more effective than the negative method and that as children learn prosocial ways to behave, negative behaviors seem to fade away.

Empathy, sharing, generosity, turn-taking, and helping—how do you teach these behaviors, anyway? They sound so elusive. Are not some children just "good" naturally?

If children seem to be good, they probably have maturity and a good "home start." Now you can add to that maturity and home influence by the way you treat children in the early childhood classroom and by the way you model behavior yourself, for starters. But first, as with other areas of development, you should know where each of the children already stands concerning his or her development of prosocial behaviors. You will need to observe every child on the eight checklist items and then make plans for the individual support or activities you will provide.

Each of the checklist items in this chapter is an observable behavior that shows if the child possesses a particular prosocial capacity.

☐ SHOWS CONCERN FOR SOMEONE IN DISTRESS

Empathy

Empathy is the capacity to feel as someone else does. A person with empathy is able to understand another person's emotional response to a situation and to respond in the same way, in other words "to feel for him." Empathy is a step beyond mere sympathy in which one person can respond emotionally to another but from his own perspective. The empathic person responds from the other person's perspective and participates in his feelings.

Some psychologists believe empathy is the basis for all prosocial behavior. Until a child has this capacity, she will be unable to behave naturally in a helping, sharing, compassionate manner. Obviously, the child can be forced to perform prosocially whether or not she understands what she is doing. But this forced performance is not empathy. Forced behavior has little to do with the prosocial skills of our concern. Behavior must be natural and spontaneous in order to show that children possess empathy.

Are children born with empathy, or do they learn it? Probably a little of both. Researchers have determined that capacities such as empathy have at least two different aspects that must be considered (Damon, p. 129). Empathy has an affective side which is the emotional response to another's distress or joy and a cognitive side that allows the child to see things from another person's perspective.

Until this cognitive development has occurred (as discussed in Chapter 2), the child will have difficulty expressing empathic concern for others because he is still too egocentric to be able to see things from another person's point of view. Because they lack this empathy, infants and toddlers often mishandle their animal pets. The youngsters have no idea that pulling a puppy's ear or squeezing a kitten might hurt. These actions do not hurt the children, so why should the pulling or squeezing hurt their pet? This egocentric point of view eventually changes with cognitive maturity and experience, but until a child can view things from another's perspective, he will have difficulty showing empathic compassion for another's distress.

When does this change take place? It happens gradually, of course, as does all development. Yet, some part of the human capacity to respond to distress must be built in, for even infants one day old will become upset and will cry when a nearby baby starts crying. Somewhere between one and two years of age, the cognitive change takes place. Toddlers, although they may not act appropriately, begin to show genuine concern for others. These youngsters have been observed giving up their favorite stuffed animal to an older sibling who is crying. They feel comforted by the animal, so why not give it to another in distress. The act of giving demonstrates their developing capacity for empathy.

From two to around six years of age, children begin to react more appropriately to the distress of others around them. The ages of the children in your class fall within this range. You will be observing them to determine which ones show concern for another child in distress. Distress may be displayed by someone crying or screaming. It also could be less dramatically disclosed by a child who puts her head down on a table, goes into a corner, or leaves the room after an upsetting incident.

You will note that some children immediately come to the side of the upset child. Others do not. The children who display this empathic concern, of course, may be special friends of the upset child. On the other hand, highly sensitive children who have no particular friendship with the child also will come close. Some youngsters just stand by the side of the distressed child and look at him or her, or look for the teacher. Others actively console the child, touching or speaking to him or her.

If a teacher causes the distress, a similar thing may happen. A child being reprimanded or scolded often will attract a circle of observers. In this case, you will have more difficulty determining empathic behavior because some of the observers are more concerned for themselves and how the teacher feels about them. Others are simply curious. Before you check this item for them, watch who comforts the child after the teacher leaves. The children who comfort the child are not necessarily taking the distressed child's side against the teacher. If they stay with the child after the teacher leaves, they more likely have true compassion for the child.

The classroom worker should know that family life and cultural background have a definite influence on empathic response in children. If families stress prosocial behavior, their children will exhibit it more than children from families who do not teach or demonstrate it.

Some cultures stress consideration of group members more than others. Communal-type cultures, such as the Native American, Pacific Island, or Asian cultures, often stress concern for group members more than the American culture does. Our culture seems to stress competition among individuals more often than cooperation. The individual is glorified in our society, sometimes at the expense of the group.

On the other hand, even individual animals are shown concern in our culture, which is not always true in communal cultures. Communal cultures tend not to treat the individual as more important than the group. As a child caregiver in the multiethnic, multicultural society that makes up America, you need to be aware of such differences.

Research has shown that community size and the role of women also influence a child's prosocial inclinations. Children from a rural rather than urban setting, from a small rather than a large city, or from a society where women have an important economic function outside the home are more inclined to show concern for others (Damon, p. 132). If the mother works outside the home, the children must take on responsibilities at an early age. Learning helping and caretaking tasks so early obviously inclines children toward prosocial behavior. Thus, the teacher must know something about the individual child's background in order to make a more accurate assessment of the child's behavior.

If you have not checked this item for many of your children, do not be alarmed. Showing concern for someone in distress is one of the more difficult prosocial behaviors for preschoolers to learn. Distressful situations that happen to others upset onlookers too. Before the onlookers can respond, they often need to overcome their own anxieties. They thus are more apt to step back and let the adult show the concern. You, however, can involve your children in this humane act.

If You Have Not Checked This Item: Some Helpful Ideas

■ Model Empathic Behavior in the Classroom

You must serve as a model for the children. When something distressful happens to someone, you should show your own concern by going to the person;

touching, hugging, or holding the person, if this is appropriate; talking to the child; and giving the youngster the time and space to feel better again.

A second way to model this behavior is through your actions in distressful situations that happen outside the classroom. If someone is hurt or dies, if a tragic event is shown on television, or if something upsetting happens within their families, then you must let the children know you are concerned too.

■ Help the Children to Show Their Own Concern

Talk to the children both privately and in the group about distressful happenings that have occurred. Encourage the children to ask questions about things they do not understand. Show the youngsters that it is all right to cry and express emotions openly. When a class member is in the hospital, have the class make and send a card.

When children are pretending in dramatic play about people or pets being hurt, listen to see if the youngsters express compassionate feelings even in pretend. You can model a concerned role in pretending too, by expressing your own sympathy when one of the players is pretending to be hurt.

■ Read a Book

Maybe a Band-Aid Will Help by Anna Grossnickle Hines (New York: E. P. Dutton, 1984) is a beautifully illustrated first person narrative of little Sarah's concern and help for her doll, Abigail, when its leg comes off.

Don't Worry I'll Find You by Anna Grossnickle Hines (New York: E. P. Dutton, 1986) is a follow-up story about Sarah and Abigail, both of whom get lost when they go shopping in the mall. Sarah's concern for her doll and Mama's concern for Sarah are cleverly demonstrated.

I Have a Sister My Sister Is Deaf by Jeanne Whitehouse Peterson (New York: Harper & Row, 1977) is a first person narrative by a young girl about her younger sister, who is deaf. The girl tells all the things her sister can—and cannot—do in a manner showing great concern and sensitivity.

SHOWS DELIGHT FOR SOMEONE □ EXPERIENCING PLEASURE

Empathy

Why are we humans always more aware of the bad things than the good? Is it because negative emotions are stronger or more upsetting to us, or because they occur more frequently? Whatever the reason, we seem to give negative emotions more of our attention. Giving negative emotions more attention in the presence of young children can be harmful. We are behavior models for the children, and if the youngsters see us showing more concern over the negative than the positive emotions, children may get the notion that bad is more important to us than good.

If we want children to learn a full range of empathic responses, then we ourselves need to be aware of and respond to the delightful things that happen to the people around us. How many gratifying things have happened to the children and adults in your classroom recently? Could any of the following be counted?

> A new baby arrived at Sandra's house.
> Richie got new sneakers.
> Jeffrey found the mitten he lost.
> Ken and Donnie finally finished their huge block building.
> The bus driver won a lottery.
> The teacher's assistant passed her CDA.
> Michelle got a new dress.
> Rhonda's grandmother is visiting her.

How would you have responded to these happenings? As a behavior model, you need to show the children that you care deeply about their successes as well as their troubles. Hug the children, exclaim over them, shake their hands, and laugh and dance around the room if this is appropriate. When children do the same to show their delight in someone else's success, make a point of thanking them for showing someone their pleasure. Celebrate happy occasions. Make your center one that rejoices in the good fortunes of its members.

We do not need to be like some newspapers that feature only bad news. Look for the good things that happen to individuals, and help your children to share in the other person's pleasure by showing him they are happy for him.

Researchers looking at prosocial behavior in preschoolers report that friendly behaviors occur more frequently than aggressive behaviors among peers in the group; friendly interactions, in fact, increase at a faster rate than aggressive behavior during the preschool years, especially among the older children (Moore, p. 76).

If You have Not Checked This Item: Some Helpful Ideas

■ **Look for Reasons to Rejoice About an Individual's Happiness**

Make a list of the good things that have happened to people in your center. Make sure you model the prosocial behavior of rejoicing with the person yourself. Then invite individual children to do the same. They could make a congratulatory phone call to the person. They could take the person a flower or a finger painting. They could invite an outside person to the classroom and sing a song for the person.

▪ Talk About Successes During Circle Time

Ask children to report on the nice things that have happened to people they know during group time. Start a ritual of going up to one of the children in the circle and shaking his or her hand in congratulations for anything positive that has happened to him or her or in his or her family.

SHARES SOMETHING WITH ANOTHER ☐

Generosity

Sharing and helping may be the easiest prosocial behaviors for young children to learn because these behaviors occur most frequently in the early childhood classroom, which is understandable when you consider the many opportunities children in a group have to learn to share materials with one another. Sharing also is easier to do than some of the other prosocial acts because the child suffers only a temporary loss. The youngster must give up something, but only temporarily.

Again, the child's ability to perform such an action depends upon her cognitive maturity as well as the lessons she has learned from those around her. The younger the child, the more inclined she is to consider the toy she is playing with as her personal possession, whether it is or not. Children still retaining this egocentric view also will try to take the toys they want away from others, and they will be upset if the others do not comply. The fact that these egocentric children want the toy makes it theirs, according to their reasoning.

William Damon's study of the development of a child's sense of justice involved findings about what children considered to be fair in sharing or dividing up candy. The younger children (ages four and five) gave themselves more candy than the older children gave to themselves. A scale that Damon derived to indicate children's levels of positive justice showed children age four and under justifying their choices simply on the basis of their wishes: that they should get something because they want it.

Children at the second level of the scale (ages four and five) justified their actions on the basis of their size, gender, or whatever characteristic would get them the most candy. The next level of children (ages five through seven) preferred to share equally in order to prevent squabbles. Thus older children must realize that preserving the peace is more important than getting an extra piece of candy (Damon, p. 136).

In order to prevent squabbles, early childhood teachers need to establish rules governing property rights at the outset. When children first enter the classroom, they are confronted with a treasure house of materials to enjoy. The youngsters need to understand that these materials belong to the center, not to specific children. Individuals can use the materials, but the items must be shared, which means letting other children use the items either at the same time (as with paints) or one after another.

Nevertheless, some squabbles over equipment can be expected. The primary way young children learn rules is to test them out. Who gets the favorite toy first? Favorites are often trikes and eggbeaters. Some teachers feel it is best to have several of the favorites in order to avoid problems. Other teachers believe that such problems afford good opportunities for children to learn how to share and take turns.

Researchers find that older children are more likely to share than younger ones. Sharing with peers, in fact, increases dramatically between the ages of four and twelve (Damon, p. 128). If a toy belongs to the center, young children are more likely to share the item than if it belongs to them personally. Most teachers ask children to keep toys from home in their cubbies. The youngsters can show the toys to the class at circle time, but afterwards, the toys must be put away until it is time to go home.

Because sharing is such an important prosocial skill in the preschool center, everyone must spend time helping individuals to learn the skill. You may want to start by observing the prosocial behavior of every child in your class to see which children already know how to share and which ones may need help in learning this skill. Some children will share toys, food, and turns when asked by another child, but many still need the teacher to make the request.

If You Have Not Checked This Item: Some Helpful Ideas

▪ Model Sharing Yourself

Sharing is one of children's behaviors that is definitely influenced by adult modeling behavior. Adults often ask children to share with their peers, but how often do adults ask a child to share with them? Try it. Set up a situation where a child who has had difficulty in sharing must share a seat, a piece of equipment, or an activity with you. For example, invite him to paint at your table. Then, set out one jar of paint that the two of you must share. Verbalize as you work on your painting. Let the child know he is doing well in sharing the paints.

▪ Use Group Toys

Encourage a small group of two, three, or four children to construct a building using one set of Lego building blocks. Have several children work on a large puzzle together. Have one child hold the wood while another saws at the woodworking table. Tie a wagon to the trike, and let one child pedal while another rides in the wagon.

■ **Set Up a Food-Sharing Experience**

Bring in one apple, one orange, or one melon for each small group at your snack tables. Discuss with the children how they can share the piece of fruit. Let them help you divide it equally.

■ **Read a Book**

Sharing by Taro Gomi (South San Francisco: Heian International, 1981) is a simply illustrated book about two little girls who find ways to share an apple, colored paper, a ribbon, toys, and the love for their cat.

GIVES SOMETHING OF ☐
HIS/HER OWN TO ANOTHER

Generosity

A great deal of research has been done on this aspect of prosocial behavior, perhaps because researchers find it easy to measure whether or not children are willing to give one of their possessions to someone else. Most studies show that as children increase in age their generosity also increases. What is not so clear is the reason for it.

We assume that as children become cognitively more mature, they will be less concerned with themselves as the center of everything and more aware of others and their needs. We also expect that as children grow older, they will have more experiences with social customs through the teachings of their family, friends, school, and church. In other words, the children will have learned how society expects them to behave.

Other things also affect young children's giving. Length of ownership is one. Children seem more willing to give up a possession they have had awhile than something they have just obtained (Smith, p. 210). Perhaps the novelty eventually wears off.

The item they are giving also makes a difference. It may be a toy, an item of food, a piece of candy, or money. Whether they have more of the same also makes a difference. Reasons for the giving have a bearing too. Is the item given out of friendship, because someone asks, because someone has a need, or because an adult suggests that it might be a nice thing to do? Older children are more apt to respond to adult suggestions or pressure.

Children are more likely to share a favorite toy rather than to give it up totally. Formal occasions for giving such as birthdays or religious holidays teach children about giving. The child's egocentric nature often shows itself when he or she wants to give mom a toy truck or doll for her birthday.

Teaching generosity, however, is tricky in our society. We send children mixed messages. We tell children that it is a good idea to give to people in need, but then the youngsters see us turn away charity solicitors at our front doors. Children hear us refuse to lend a lawn mower or power tool to a neighbor who has a need. "Let him buy his own," the adults say, or "Let him work as hard as we did to buy this one."

Ours is a very material-possession-oriented culture. Children learn this from television and adults' responses to the television messages. Children witness how strongly we feel about our cars, stereos, and microwave ovens. It is an interesting commentary on our values to see families with fewer material possessions being much more generous with them.

Not all cultures value personal material possessions so highly. People of many Pacific Islands, for instance, teach their children from the start that giving is more important than possessing. These people practice what they preach by simply giving a possession to a neighbor or relative who admires or has need of it. These people feel that they are enhanced by the person's accepting something from them.

Nevertheless, as preschool teachers we need to be aware of how this prosocial behavior works with children in our classroom, regardless of our society's confusion over the issue. Use the *Child Skills Checklist* to determine which children will give a possession to someone else. Are these the same children you have checked on the other prosocial behaviors? What other characteristics do these children share? Do they come from families where they have been given a great deal of responsibility? Prosocial behavior such as generosity is often more evident in such children. Are they children who seem more mature in all areas of development? We know that generosity increases with age and maturity.

If You Have Not Checked This Item: Some Helpful Ideas

▪ Be a Model of Generosity

Let children see you give up something of yours to someone in need: an item of clothing, a book, food, or money. How do you feel about this? In our society, we are often reluctant as adults to begin this kind of giving ourselves. Will it get out of hand? Will people take advantage of us? How genuine is your own generosity? We have been conditioned to acquire material possessions and guard against losing them.

▪ Articulate Generosity

When situations arise where giving is appropriate, talk to your children about it. Maybe they could donate some money or services to help someone in need.

▪ Read a Book

Louie by Ezra Jack Keats (New York: Scholastic Book Services, 1975) tells about the little nonverbal boy Louie, who says his first words at a puppet show put on by neighborhood children when he becomes entranced by the doll puppet Gussie. Louie grabs Gussie at the end of the show, but the children convince him to give her up as she has to go to her own home. Later Louie's mother tells him someone has left him a note, which tells him to follow a long green string. At the end of the string, he finds Gussie waiting for him. The children evidently had a change of heart when they saw someone who needed the puppet more than they did. Ask your children how they feel about this. Would they have done the same thing?

Tico and the Golden Wings by Leo Lionni (New York: Pantheon Books, 1964) tells a folktale-like story of a little bird in India that is born without wings. The bird Tico is wingless until a wishingbird grants his wish and gives him a pair of golden wings. But Tico learns that he can never be happy until he gives away all of the golden feathers, one by one, to people in need.

In *Jamaica's Find* by Juanita Havill (Boston: Houghton Mifflin Company, 1986), little girl Jamaica finds a stuffed dog in the park and takes it home for her own. Her family helps her to see that another girl like herself might have lost it. Jamaica returns the dog to the park lost-and-found, by chance finds the girl who lost it, and then shares the girl's delight over the recovery of her favorite toy.

TAKES TURNS WITH TOYS OR ACTIVITIES ☐
WAITS FOR TURN WITHOUT A FUSS ☐

Generosity

These two items reflect a different aspect of generosity: alternating the use of toys, equipment, or activities with other children and taking turns with patience. Opportunities for learning and practicing these prosocial behaviors occur much more frequently in the early childhood classroom than occasions for giving. In order to maintain a smoothly running program, you must help children learn at the outset how to take turns and wait for their turn in the group situation.

Those with brothers and sisters at home may have learned this already, although it is sometimes the inappropriate behavior they learn, such as the biggest or strongest gets the first turn. Research has also shown that authoritarian parents do not necessarily help children to learn this prosocial behavior. When parents strictly control their children's actions, the children have less motivation and fewer opportunities to develop moral reasoning and turn-taking on their own (Eisenberg, p. 854).

In order to grow from an egocentric being, whose only concern is satisfying his own wants, to someone who understands the wants of others, the young child must learn to see things from another person's perspective. To do this, the child needs the freedom to be able to function on his own in an open environment. His parents can support this development best by helping him to understand the views of others and by encouraging him to participate in decision making about his own behavior. Following the dictates of authoritarian parents gives the child little opportunity to develop these skills.

For the young child, warm, supportive mothering also makes a difference in the development of prosocial behaviors. As children move into elementary school, the best support they can have at home is a nonauthoritarian mother who allows and encourages her children to act on their own.

In the preschool, however, the children must learn to take turns and wait for turns. You can help the children the most by setting up the environment so that it speaks to these needs. Arrange activity areas for three, four, or five children at the most, and put signs or symbols for these numbers in every area. Children can then regulate their own numbers during free play. Let children take tags to hang on hooks or pegboards, tickets to put in pockets mounted on the wall, or their pictures covered with clear contact paper to hang in the area where they want to work.

Many centers start the day with a circle time. The teacher lets the class know what activities are available, and the children choose activities by taking tags. If a child finishes playing in her chosen area before free choice

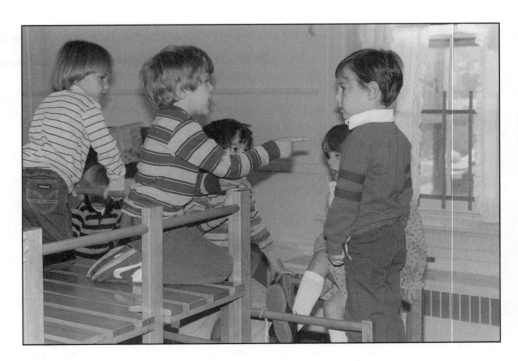

Children can regulate their own numbers during free play if the environment is arranged so that they understand its use.

time is over, then another child can pick up the tag and take his own turn. This is how children learn about taking turns and waiting their turn.

Nevertheless, the teacher must let the children learn about turn-taking on their own. Directing individuals into particular areas is the same as the authoritarian parent telling his or her children what do to. If we want children to develop prosocial behaviors, we must not short-circuit the process. In order for children to learn the social interactions necessary, they must be allowed to experiment with turn-taking on their own.

Giving children this freedom takes forbearance on the part of the preschool staff. It is so much easier for adults to make choices for the children. After all, children take so long to make up their minds. But we must remember the purpose for the free choice period in the first place: to allow children to learn how to make their own decisions based on their own interests and needs and how to deal with the consequences of their choices. Through freedom of choice, children also learn that another child may have the same choice as theirs and that they may have to wait their turn before their choice is available.

Children also learn by using timing tools such as a kitchen timer or three-minute hourglass when several children want turns using favorite toys or equipment. One child can hold the timer while another uses the toy for three minutes. When it is the next child's turn, the child after her gets to hold the timer. Some children enjoy controlling the timer as much as playing with the toy!

If You Have Not Checked This Item: Some Helpful Ideas

- **Have Children Practice Turn-Taking in Dramatic Play**

Set up a particular play area such as a beauty shop or barber shop and put out two or three chairs for the customers. Then the children will have to wait their turn just as in real life. Or set up a bakery shop or other facility where people must take tickets to be waited on. Have tickets available for the children to take. Perhaps one child could be the ticket taker. Set up a traffic light in the classroom for the children to use in their big truck play. The light can be a cardboard milk carton with holes cut out and covered with clear food wrapping paper colored red, yellow, and green. Not only will children learn safety rules, but they also will realize that cars and people must wait their turns before using the road at a street crossing.

- **Bring in a Special Plaything or Activity to Teach Turn-Taking**

Introduce a new toy at circle time and have the children help to set up the rules for playing with it, such as the number of people who can use the toy at one time and for how long. The children may want to use the kitchen timer you have provided to keep track of the time. One child will surely want to keep the time. The teacher can also help children sign up for turns on a chart.

■ Read a Book

Everybody Takes Turn by Dorothy Corey (Chicago: Albert Whitman & Company, 1980) is a book of similar pictures on two pages showing first one child, then another taking turns. A simple line of text tells whose turn it is.

☐ HELPS ANOTHER DO A TASK

Caregiving

Along with sharing, this is by far the most common prosocial behavior exhibited in the preschool classroom, possibly because it is much less of a cognitive act. Children simply assist someone in doing a task. They may be asked or they may volunteer to help when they see that a peer or the teacher needs help with something. The children do not need to understand or to intellectualize about what is happening. They do not need to take another person's perspective. They just need to lend a hand, so to speak. Most children have already learned this activity at home, and they soon realize that the early childhood classroom also expects children to help out.

Research shows that this behavior may occur three times more often than any other prosocial act. Even so, helping others do a task is not all that frequent in proportion to other behaviors. Seeking help occurs about six times more frequently than giving help among three-year-olds (Moore, p. 77). But as children grow and develop through the early childhood years, helping behavior increases. Whereas slightly more than half of the youngest children assessed in one study (three-year-olds) gave some form of help, 100 percent of children nine and ten years old gave help (Smith, p. 216).

The youngest preschoolers, nevertheless, may have some problems with helping. They may not know when to help or how much help to give. Sometimes children overdo their help, becoming bossy and not knowing when to stop. At other times, children do not do enough and simply stand around watching before the task is finished. The best way for them to learn the cues for appropriateness in such social behavior is to plunge in and try it. Other children are not shy about telling peers what they are doing wrong.

You, on the other hand, need to set up activities that require children to give assistance. Setting tables for snack and lunch, getting out cots or mats for naptime, getting out paints and mixing them, filling the water table, feeding the animal pets, and helping with cleanup are a few of the activities that promote helping. These tasks are multiple learning situations for cognitive concepts as well as learning when and how to help.

Children may have favorite chores as well as chores they try to avoid. Making up a "helpers" chart gives every child a chance at every chore. Let the children help design the chart. It can contain pictures as well as titles for every job. Children can hang their name tags on it daily at circle time or once a week. New jobs can be added from time to time as needed. Use your creativity to invent the jobs. A few jobs you may want to include are

> *Mail carrier:* delivers notes to office
> *Zoo keeper:* takes care of pets
> *Aquarium attendant:* feeds fish
> *Door attendant:* opens and closes door
> *Chef:* helps prepare snack
> *Waiter/Waitress:* sets tables
> *Gardener:* waters plants

You cannot expect young children to do all the work in the classroom. Picking up the block corner is a case in point. One or two children can easily empty the shelves in building a complicated construction. Putting all the blocks back in proper order during cleanup time may be an overwhelming chore for two. A teacher should get down on the floor with them and lend her assistance, just as the children help her from time to time.

If children are not helping at all, you need to engage them in chores. Chores do not need to be drudgery. Children enjoy doing grownup things. Youngsters have no idea that pickup is any less interesting than getting toys out, unless adults make pickup seem less glamorous. In fact, you should make cleanup in your room a fun thing to do.

If You Have Not Checked This Item: Some Helpful Ideas

■ Invite a Helper to Your Class on a Weekly Basis

Anyone engaged in an occupation is a helper. Perhaps a different parent could visit the classroom on a weekly basis to talk to the children about how he or she helps.

One class created a new job on their helpers chart each week after the helper had visited. Sometimes the children had to stretch their imaginations. After a telephone lineman visited the room, they finally decided to add the job of telephone attendant, in which one child every day would be allowed to answer the classroom phone.

■ Use Games for Pickup and Cleanup

Block shelves fill up much easier when they are hungry monsters waiting to be fed by the children or when children do pickup to music, trying to finish before the record is over. Long blocks can be bulldozers pushing the blocks or toys over to the shelves. Have your children help you think up other pretend games at cleanup time.

▪ Read a Book

Herman the Helper by Robert Kraus (New York: Windmill Books, 1974) tells the colorful underwater story of Herman, the little octopus who helped his mother, father, brothers, sisters, friends, enemies, and finally himself.

☐ HELPS ANOTHER IN NEED
Caregiving

This particular behavior is perhaps the most difficult of the prosocial skills for young children to attain. Helping another in need is an extension of showing concern for someone in distress. Whereas showing concern involves compassion, a psychological support, helping another in need involves care-

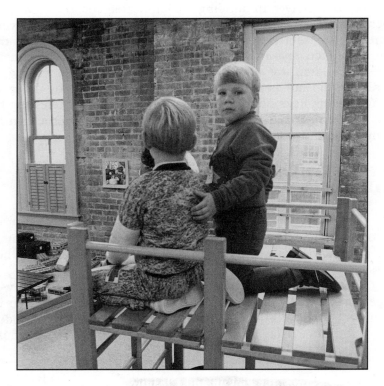

The prosocial skill of helping may consist of giving affection, positive attention, reassurance, or protection.

taking or giving nurturance, a physical act of giving help. The help may consist of giving affection (a hug, a touch), positive attention (getting help, giving help), reassurance (verbalizing support), or protection (standing by, physical protection).

For young children, giving these things is difficult because the youngsters must first overcome their own anxiety caused by the stressful situation. Then they must have an understanding of how to act. In emergency situations even adults are often confused and have difficulty knowing what to do.

Even very young children have been observed taking action when another child or person is in distress, but the instances are rare compared to other prosocial acts. Toddlers have been seen giving their bottles or cuddly toys to siblings who cry in distress. Giving something to the victim seems to be the main response of young children. They more often seek help than give it, however. In addition, those who seek help in the preschool more often approach adults than peers, although older preschoolers are beginning to turn to their companions for help.

Crying and uttering distressful sounds are supposed to trigger an empathic response in others, according to psychologists. Scientists look to the animal world and note the intricacies of response in many species. Have we humans lost much of this seemingly instinctive concern? We read in the news or see on television the instances of adults ignoring victims who call for help. Much of this inattention seems to be a defensive reaction on the part of people who not only do not want to get involved in the trouble but also feel they might be victimized themselves.

Can helping be taught to children? Studies show that children can learn helping behaviors in pretend or symbolic situations, but when the real thing occurs, they still may not respond. Children with nurturant caregivers give more help and express more sympathy. So it seems that modeling behavior does promote prosocial helping (Yarrow, Scott, & Waxler, p. 254).

What kinds of situations calling for help might occur in the classroom? Injury is one situation. Children or adults may fall and hurt themselves, cut themselves, burn themselves. Losing something is another situation that requires help. Children may lose mittens, money, toys. Accidental damage also necessitates assistance. Children may spill paint on themselves, fall in the mud, or spill milk or other food. They may drop and break a dish, a record, or a toy.

How can children help? Depending upon the situation, they could go for help if an adult is not in the immediate vicinity. They could comfort the victim by talking or touching. They could help pick up spilled things, look for lost things, or give information to help the adult solve the problem.

Children are more likely to give help to others when with someone. Teachers should take advantage of this by involving the children in helping situations whenever possible, rather than doing all the helping themselves. When children are involved on their own, teachers should step back and allow the youngsters to do what they can.

If You Have Not Checked This Item: Some Helpful Ideas

▪ Discuss Helping with the Children

When helping behavior occurs, spend time in small and large groups talking to children about it. Sometimes television events seen by children are good discussions items.

▪ Read a Book

Swimmy by Leo Lionni (New York: Knopf/Pantheon, 1963), a favorite of children, is about the little black fish named Swimmy, who helps a school of little fish to swim unafraid like the biggest fish in the sea.

Now One Foot, Now the Other by Tomie de Paola (New York: G. P. Putnam's Sons, 1981) is a touching story of Bobby and his Grandfather Bob, who has a stroke. Bobby never gives up hope that his grandfather will recover—even after his parents do—and finally finds a way to help him walk and talk again, just as his grandfather did for him when he was little.

101 Things to Do with a Baby by Jan Omerod (New York: Viking Penguin, 1984) is a clever book with 101 illustrations of a girl helping out with her baby brother: everything from "say good morning" to "take him for a slow stroll."

I'll Protect You from the Jungle Beasts by Martha Alexander (New York: Dial Press, 1973) is a dream tale about a little boy out in the woods who is protecting his teddy bear from scary noises that in turn frighten the boy himself, until his teddy bear comes to his rescue.

▪ When You Model Helping Behavior, Talk About It

You will help children all year long. Talk about what you are doing with the children, and help them find ways to assist you.

▪ Encourage Children to Help One Another

If a child needs a shoe tied or a coat zipped, ask another child to help.

OBSERVING, RECORDING, AND INTERPRETING PROSOCIAL BEHAVIOR

Sandra is a four-year-old who rarely performs any of the prosocial behaviors on the checklist unless forced to by the teachers (for example, sharing a toy or waiting for her turn); thus, this section of her checklist has no checks recorded on it. The teachers have also noted that she seems immature in the area of social skills and has played only by herself, not parallel to the others or with a group. The teachers have concluded that Sandra may not have developed the ability to see things from a perspective other than her own. Therefore, she has little or no empathy for others who need help or who are in distress. A suggestion to help Sandra develop empathy is to give her two hand puppets: one with a band-aid on its arm and the other a helper. Ask her to find out what happened to the injured puppet. If she likes this kind of play, she may be willing to branch out and play puppets with a second child.

REFERENCES CITED

Damon, William. (1983). *Social and Personality Development.* New York: W. W. Norton & Company.

Eisenberg, Nancy, Randy Lennon, and **Karlsson Roth.** (1983). "Prosocial Development: A Longitudinal Study." *Developmental Psychology, 19*(6), 846–855.

Moore, Shirley G. (1982). "Prosocial Behavior in the Early Years: Parent and Peer Influences." In Bernard Spodek (Ed.), *Handbook of Research in Early Childhood Education.* New York: The Free Press.

Smith, Charles A. (1982). *Promoting Social Development of Young Children: Strategies and Activities.* Palo Alto, CA: Mayfield Publishing Company.

Yarrow, Marian Radke, Phyllis M. Scott, and **Carolyn Zahn Waxler.** (1973). "Learning Concern for Others." *Developmental Psychology, 8*(2), 240–260.

OTHER SOURCES

Edwards, Carolyn Pope. (1986). *Promoting Social and Moral Development in Young Children.* New York: Teachers College Press.

Lickona, Thomas. (1983). *Raising Good Children.* New York: Bantam Books.

Webb, Roger A. (Ed.). (1977). *Social Development in Childhood: Day Care Programs and Research.* Baltimore: The Johns Hopkins University Press.

LEARNING ACTIVITIES

1. Use the prosocial behavior section of the *Child Skills Checklist* as a screening tool to observe all of the children in your classroom. Which ones demonstrate the most prosocial behavior? Do they also have friends in the class? Which children show few prosocial skills? How do these children get along with the other children in general?

2. Choose a child who exhibits few of the prosocial skills. Do a running record of the child on three different days to determine how he or she works and plays with the others. Do an activity with the child to help him or her share, take turns, or help. Record the results.

3. Choose a child who is a good helper and try to involve him or her in getting another child to participate in helping. Discuss the results.

4. Try two of the ideas under "If You Have Not Checked This Item . . . " with a child who shows few prosocial skills. Discuss the results.

5. Read one of the children's books from this chapter with a group of children, or do an activity with the group to promote prosocial skills. Discuss the results.

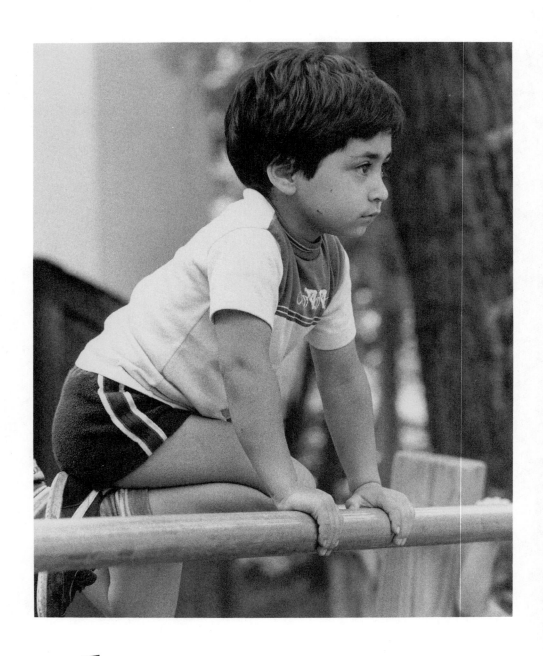

6 Large Motor Development

Large Motor Checklist

- ☐ Walks down steps alternating feet
- ☐ Runs with control over speed and direction
- ☐ Jumps over obstacle, landing on two feet
- ☐ Hops forward on one foot
- ☐ Climbs up and down climbing equipment with ease
- ☐ Moves legs/feet in rhythm to beat
- ☐ Claps hands in rhythm to beat
- ☐ Beats drum alternating hands in rhythm to beat

P hysical development for young children involves two important areas of motor coordination: movements controlled by the large, or gross, muscles and those controlled by the small, or fine, muscles. This chapter will focus on large motor development, involving movements of the whole body, legs, and arms.

Because motor development is so obvious and visible an aspect of children's growth, we sometimes take it for granted. Of course children will grow bigger, stronger, and able to perform more complicated motor tasks as they increase in age. But do all children develop these abilities? What about the awkward child who seems to trip over his own feet? What about the child who never can keep up with the others? Is the "accident-prone" child overly eager or underdeveloped? How can we tell, and can we do anything to help such children?

Yes, children do develop physically in a predictable sequence of skills that can be observed, although there are individual differences in this growth as well as developmental lags in some children. And, yes, there is something we can do to help.

First, we need to become familiar with the entire sequence of normal large motor development. We need to know its origins, patterns, and range for individuals. Then we need to apply this knowledge to the children in order to determine whether they are developing predictably within the normal range or whether they may need special help. Finally, we should assemble a repertoire of activities to help the child who is lagging behind in this development.

MOTOR DEVELOPMENT IN INFANCY

The infant uses motor skills as tools to explore first himself and then the world around him. His initial movements are reflective or involuntary. He sucks when his mouth touches something. He jumps at a loud noise.

Soon after his birth, however, three types of rudimentary movement abilities appear. The nonlocomotor or stability skills involve developing control of the head, neck, and trunk, and eventually the ability to sit and stand. Manipulative skills involve reaching for, grasping, and releasing. And locomotor skills involve creeping, crawling, and eventually walking (Gallahue, pp. 5–6).

Muscular maturation follows both a predictable sequence and a direction. Large muscle coordination develops before small muscle synchronization. In other words, the infant or young child develops arm movement control before finger control. Development is also cephalo-caudal in direction: that is, it begins at the head and progresses to the feet. Control of head and upper trunk occurs in the infant before control of legs and feet. Development also occurs in another direction: from close to the trunk out to the extremities, a pattern called proximo-distal (Allen & Goetz, p. 130).

Many of the infant's first movements are random. She lies on her back in a bassinet or crib and kicks with her legs or waves with her arms. Should she happen to strike a mobile or rattle with either arms or legs, she will usually try to repeat the movement to cause the same interesting sound and touch effect. In repeating the movement over and over, she begins to gain control over her muscles, so that the movement eventually becomes voluntary and controlled.

The rate of development occurs in a predictable sequence and is related closely to the maturation of the central nervous system, the integrating agent. Even though an infant's motor skills cannot develop until the neuromuscular system is ready, a rich environment filled with stimulating sights, sounds, and people motivates the child to initiate and to practice movements.

Are we saying that the environment and the infant's experience with it can improve motor development? Yes, when the required maturation level has been reached. If there had not been a mobile in the baby's bassinet, she would not have struck it with her arm and then would not have continued to practice this movement. Even if her neuromuscular system were not mature enough for her to control this movement, the mobile's presence might still keep her trying until the proper maturity had developed.

Fraiberg's work with blind infants shows the importance of such environmental factors in the development of motor skills. The blind babies developed trunk control and sitting stability within the same time range as sighted children. Blind babies even could support themselves on hands and knees. But they never learned to creep. They lacked the visual stimuli the sighted babies had to motivate them to move across the floor. Their caregivers had to find other means to stimulate them to attempt locomotion (Fraiberg, in Schickedanz, Schickedanz, & Forsythe, p. 146).

This is one of several studies that has proved the importance of sensory stimuli, especially sight, sound, and touch, in the development of large motor skills. We also know that caring adults must interact with infants from the beginning: adults must encourage, support, and praise children for the accomplishment of motor skills, as adults do in all aspects of children's development.

Because such encouragement tends to happen almost automatically in most families, we seem to think infants and young children develop these skills on their own with little support from adults or the environment. A look at infants and children in institutions where little or no human or material support was offered proves otherwise. Hunt and several other American psychologists visited orphanages in Iran where the infant-caregiver ratio was 40 to 3, where many of the two-year-olds could not sit up, and where most of those in their fourth year could not yet walk alone (Pines, p. 59). The quality of early child care does indeed make a difference!

The range for mastery of a particular skill varies from about one month to four-to-six months in young children. Developmental delays may result when early reflexive movements somehow fail to become integrated into higher level voluntary movements (Allen & Goetz, p. 131). Birth defects, handicapping conditions, certain illnesses or injuries, or neglect may cause this lack of integration. Children whose early movement patterns have not become integrated into voluntary responses either do not learn the higher level skills or learn to compensate in some atypical manner.

Large motor skills, then, play an important part in the infant's learning first about himself by moving his body parts and then about his world by responding physically to the people and materials around him. His environment plays an important part, as well, in stimulating this development. He gains more and more independence through the movements he is able to master, and when he finally walks, the world is his to explore.

The eight items under "Large Motor Development" on the *Child Skills Checklist* are neither a complete list of large motor skills nor a sequence of skills, although one skill may precede the other. Instead, these eight items represent a sample of important motor behaviors that children should have acquired by age five.

It is important to screen all the children in your class at the outset using this or a similar list of skills in order to identify children needing special help. Knowing that large motor development precedes small motor growth, you should help all of your children to be prepared in this first area in order to be successful in the small motor tasks expected of them in the reading and writing soon to come.

☐ WALKS DOWN STEPS ALTERNATING FEET

One-Year-Olds

Walking is the skill that separates the infant from the toddler. It occurs at around the end of the first year or beginning of the second year. The child finally is able to move around in an upright position unaided by people or furniture. This movement gives him a freedom he can scarcely comprehend. Now he can investigate in a twinkling all those intriguing items in the room that seemed so far away. Moreover, he is able to see things from a different perspective altogether: upright.

Try it yourself. Get down on your hands and knees and look around you. What do you see? Baseboards, table and chair legs, people's shoes. (No wonder shoes are so important to young children!) See something of interest across the room? Try crawling over to it. By the time you arrive you may have lost much of your interest in the object you sought. Think what walking upright must mean to the child. Suddenly he has a freedom he never knew existed. He can go anywhere on his own that is not blocked off. His eye level reaches a wholly new order of things that, in turn, stimulates increased practice of his new skill.

Beginning walkers are not independent all at once. They still move cautiously and appreciate a helping hand. They do not have the stamina of older children. But they are on their way. They walk with such a wide stance that some child care workers call them "waddlers," and older, more balanced walkers "toddlers." The children's wide stance helps them balance and offsets their top-heavy trunk. As their legs grow longer and their balance improves, they will not have to waddle to move forward without falling. They use their arms to balance themselves, but they do not swing their arms as mature walkers do.

Two-Year-Olds

Two-year-olds, on the other hand, do not need to pay so much attention to balance and can concentrate more on toddling along. They still monitor their walking to some extent and may stop for obstacles, but a quick stop seldom brings them down on their seats like it did when they were age one. Beginning two-year-olds should be able to walk upstairs alone by placing both feet on a step, and they love to do it. By age two-and-a-half, they desperately strive for independence in their locomotion (remember the "terrible two's"?), but they still need supervision because of their disregard for safety. Older two-year-olds may be able to alternate feet going upstairs, but they still walk down two feet on a step.

Three-Year-Olds

Most three-year-olds walk in an adult fashion. Their trunk is no longer top-heavy, and they have mastered walking to the extent that they no longer need to watch their feet or balance with their arms. They swing their arms as they walk, just like adults. They still may fall occasionally on uneven ground, but they are not so far from the ground that falling hurts too much. Now they can walk upstairs alternating feet unaided, although most three-year-olds put two feet on a step coming down. The balance of some children at this age is good enough to allow them to walk a straight line, one foot in front of the other.

Although growth occurs in a predictable chronological sequence, it seems to happen in spurts. The body almost seems to need a stop to assimilate all the development that has occurred before going forward again. This "assimilation stop" often happens at the half-year age. Children who walked and ran smoothly at three may seem to have a "relapse" at three-and-a-half. They suddenly act uncertain with their large motor skills and may even seek the hand of an adult as they walk along. This happens especially going up or down stairs. They may have good days when everything about their bodies seems to work well and bad days when they stumble and fall (Caplan, p. 177).

Four-Year-Olds

Four-year-olds have control of their bodies and take great pleasure in using them. Children age four walk confidently in many ways: forward, backward, sideways, tiptoeing, or striding along. They are able to walk a circular line for the first time without losing their balance. Most can walk both up and down stairs alternating their feet. Although their skipping is not at all perfected (most can do it only with one foot), some start to rollerskate.

Four is an age of great exuberance and expansiveness. If you do not provide enough walking, running, and climbing activities in your center, four-year-olds may make their own. They definitely need an opportunity to practice their large motor skills both inside and outside of the classroom.

Five-Year-Olds

Five-year-olds are at the adult stage in walking. This is another period of great growth when children spurt up as much as two or three inches in a year. Much of this growth occurs in the legs, which lengthen more quickly than the other body parts. Boys may be a bit taller and heavier than girls, but they are about a year behind them in physiological development (Caplan, p. 237).

Children of this age can walk a straight line for about ten feet without stepping off it. Most can skip with alternating feet now. Even the less active children now can walk down stairs alternating feet. Five-year-olds

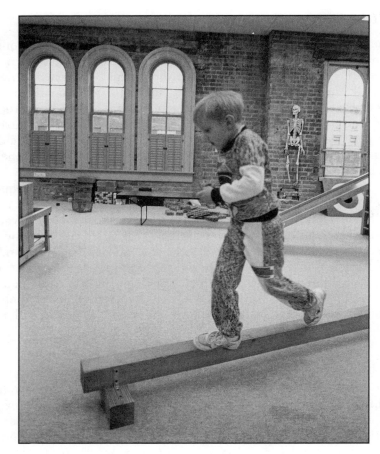

Children age four walk confidently in many ways.

are less expansive and more controlled than four-year-olds in all of their actions, but children age five still love to use their large motor abilities in play.

If You Have Not Checked This Item:
Some Helpful Ideas

■ **Practice Walking**

Studies show that children between the ages of two and six demonstrate observable improvement in basic motor patterns after repeated performance with adult encouragement. Instruction in the movement does not seem to help, but practice does (Flinchum, p. 28).

Play follow-the-leader in the classroom and outside with yourself as the leader who sets the pace. Do all kinds of walking motions, and be sure everyone has a chance to copy you before you change to the next movement: march, shuffle, stride, giant-step, tiptoe, bunny hop, skate.

Set up a walking-hopping-sliding trail in your classroom or large motor room with contact footprints stuck to the floor in various patterns of movement that involve both one foot and two.

■ Practice Step Climbing

If your room is at ground level in a building with a second story, make it a practice to take children up and down the stairs every day. If you have no stairs, go for a field trip to a building that has stairs, or get a rocking-boat-steps piece of large motor equipment to practice on. Some playground equipment also has stairs, but ladders are not the same.

■ Play Charades

Have two or three children demonstrate how an animal walks, and let the others guess what animal it is.

RUNS WITH CONTROL □
OVER SPEED AND DIRECTION

Running may be the large motor skill you think of when you consider young children. They seem to be perpetual motion machines. For some children, this is their principal method of movement. For others, their running is somehow awkward, and they spend much less time doing it than the rest of your children.

What should you expect of the two-, three-, four-, and five-year-old children in your program? As with walking, you will need to know the whole range of development for this skill before you can decide where each of your children stands and how you best can help.

Two-Year-Olds

Running involves moving forward with some rapidity by placing one foot in front of the other, in which there is a brief period of no contact with the running surface. Although one-year-olds move quite rapidly in a hurried sort of walk (which some may call a run), they maintain contact with the surface at all times. The true unsupported run does not usually occur until sometime between the second and third year (Gallahue, p. 25).

A two-year-old's running is not as smooth as it will be at three. A two-year-old still has short legs and a top-heavy trunk. He runs rather stiffly and has trouble with turning corners and with coming to a quick halt. This difficulty does not stop him from using this newfound skill, however. Two-year-olds in the classroom seem like a lively bunch of young puppies scampering here and there with much squealing and giggling. Because they cannot control their stops easily, they are forever bumping into things or each other and falling. They quickly pick themselves up and are off again without a backward glance.

Teachers should provide time and space in the classroom not only for allowing two-year-olds to practice running, but also for giving these human dynamos a chance to let off steam. Otherwise, you may have great difficulty controlling these children for any length of time.

Three-Year-Olds

Running is much smoother for three-year-olds. Their body proportions have grown and changed from a top-heavy appearance. Their legs are now longer and more coordinated in their movements. They have more control over starting and stopping than two-year-olds, but they still have not mastered this skill completely. Since their large motor skills are so much more automatic, they can abandon themselves to the pure enjoyment of running.

Then, at about age three-and-a-half, many children go through an awkward stage where some of the smoothness of their large motor movements seems to disappear, as previously noted. Teachers need to be aware of these "disequilibrium" times in order to support the child during his "bad days," knowing he will return to his smoothness of motion sometime soon.

Such children should not be confused with the truly awkward child. Cratty's studies have found most so-called "awkward" children are boys who seem to show a developmental delay in motor coordination. They exhibit an exaggerated awkward behavior. Some of this behavior may be the result of "learned helplessness," obtained possibly from parents who overreact to their every little problem (Cratty, 1982, p. 36). On the other hand, the physical awkwardness of these boys may be more in the eye of the beholder, especially if a teacher compares them with the best-coordinated boys in the class.

A wide range of individual differences exists in physical development, as in every other aspect of development. Some children simply will never be highly coordinated. Others may grow up to be professional athletes. The sensitive teacher needs to work with each child, encouraging and supporting him to accomplish all he is capable of. Pressure and ridicule have no place in the early childhood classroom. The teacher needs to find interesting motor activities in which the awkward child can succeed and to avoid those activities that pit one child against another in competition.

Can awkward children be helped? Whether they can be assisted seems to depend upon their age and the severity of their problem (Cratty, 1982, p. 37). Providing a wide range of interesting motor activities that are fun to participate in seems the best answer. Three-year-olds are at an ideal age to begin such a program. And because some so-called awkward children are simply beginners in the skill development, it is useless to label them as abnormal. Children are children; they are all different in looks, likes, and abilities. Each of them needs your special affection and support as he or she progresses through the sometimes rocky road of physical development.

You need to be aware of these ages and stages as they apply to your children, nevertheless. Take time to visit this year's class next year, and you may see some surprises. This year's awkward boy may be the best runner around. The sedentary girl who would never join in may be the leader of the physical activities. A year makes such a difference in the development of young children.

Four-Year-Olds

Expansive four-year-olds are good runners. Their movements are strong, efficient, and speedy. They can start and stop without difficulty, and they like to zoom around corners. They seem to know what their bodies can do and to enjoy putting them through their paces. Give them space and time to run.

Some four-year-olds are labeled "hyperactive" because they never seem to stop. Be careful of such labels. Only a doctor can diagnose this condition of hyperkinesis. Some children are just more active than others, often wearing out parents and teachers in the process. The age of four—with its characteristic exuberance and surplus energy—is the period when parents of such children worry most about hyperactivity. Surely, these parents reason, there is a way to slow down these superactive children. Maybe, they think, the doctor will put the children on drugs.

Using drugs to combat so-called hyperactivity is a very serious decision to make for such young children in our overmedicated, drug-dependent society. Really active children probably always have been that way, but as four-year-olds, their activity seems exaggerated. You may want more than one medical opinion before deciding what to do. True hyperactivity is sometimes difficult to distinguish from the normal surplus energy of an active four-year-old.

Five-Year-Olds

As mentioned before, five-year-olds seem to spurt up in height, mostly in their legs. They are more mature runners than four-year-olds and many love to join in games that test their abilities. Their speed and control have increased, and they seldom fall when running across uneven surfaces, as four-year-olds sometimes do. Their running games, like the rest of their actions, are usually not as noisy and out-of-bounds as those of four-year-olds.

If You Have Not Checked This Item: Some Helpful Ideas

■ Use Simple Running Games

Preschool running games should not be competitive. The awkward child may give up trying if he or she is always last. Instead, simple circle games may serve the same purpose. Old classics like "Duck, Duck, Goose" are still favorites of three- and four-year-olds as they walk around the outside of the circle and tap someone who then chases them around to the empty space.

No one wins or loses. Games with rules are often too complicated for preschoolers, but they learn to make the right responses in simple games like this and enjoy the running it affords.

■ Employ Directed Running

You can make up all kinds of inside and outside running activities. For instance, one child at a time can run to the tree and back until all have had a turn. Make the activity more complicated by having them follow a second direction: run to the tree, run around it once, and then run back.

■ Have the Children Run to Music

Have children run to music in the large motor area. Have them run fast or slow, loudly or quietly, according to the music.

■ Involve the Children in Running to Chants

Young children need to run. If you do not have the inside space or the weather outside is bad, have them run and hop in place to a simple chant you have made up, like

> I'm a kangaroo-roo-roo
> See me run-run-run
> Have some fun-fun-fun
> In the sun-sun-sun
> Watch me hop-hop-hop
> Never stop-stop-stop
> Then I run-run-run
> In the sun-sun-sun

■ Try Imaginative Running

Let the children pretend to be cowboys riding their horses or jet planes going down the runway. Have them pretend to be animals that run, such as deer or dogs. Put up pictures of animals that run, and have the children imitate them.

☐ JUMPS OVER OBSTACLE, LANDING ON TWO FEET

Jumping is a skill that involves taking off with one or two feet and landing on both feet. Jumping is sometimes confused with leaping, which involves taking off on one foot and landing on the other, or hopping, which is done all on the same foot. The checklist item mentions "landing on two feet" so that observers will not confuse jumping with leaping or hopping. The obstacle to jump over can be anything—a mark or masking tape on the floor, a block, a toy, a stick, a low barrier, a book, a rug, a box—any item the child perceives as something to be jumped over.

Jumping as a large motor skill, however, can be done in place with the child springing up and landing in the same spot, jumping forward and landing on both feet, jumping from the floor or ground over an obstacle, or jumping from a height such as a step or a chair and landing on the floor.

Two-Year-Olds

Real jumping is not performed by children much before age two. They have to develop some proficiency in walking and running before they can attempt jumping. Their first try at around age one-and-a-half may be a sort of hesitation on the bottom step of the stairs and then a bouncing step off with one foot. By age two, they actually may make their first real jump off the bottom step with two feet.

Also, sometimes between ages two and two-and-a-half, many children make their first jumps off the ground with two feet. This takes strength in their lower extremities, which occurs last in children due to the cephalocaudal direction of development.

Three-Year-Olds

Some children become quite proficient jumpers by age three, but many do not, and we should not expect them to. They must have developed the strength first and then must be encouraged to practice the skill. (Most parents do not encourage their children to jump off steps or from furniture!)

Three-year-olds, though, are becoming more long-legged and coordinated. If they are not too heavy, most probably will be able to do some jumping with practice. In jumping over an obstacle, most children start by leading with one foot. Springing up with both feet simultaneously is more difficult, but possible for some.

Four-Year-Olds

Four-year-olds are much more proficient jumpers, and by age four-and-a-half, most can accomplish any type of jumping: up, down, forward, or over. They may not be able to do a sequence of different actions, though, such as hopping, skipping, and jumping, although they perform some or all of these actions separately. One study showed only 42 percent of preschool children jump well by age three, whereas 72 percent jump well by age four-and-a-half (Zaichkowsky, Zaichkowsky, & Martineck, p. 39).

Four-year-olds can jump higher up in the air and farther down from higher elevations. The second step from the bottom of the stairs is now their big challenge, one you may want to redirect because of its potential for injury.

Five-Year-Olds

Five-year-olds, of course, are long, high, far jumpers, if they have had practice. Maturity is important, but just as necessary is practice of the skill along with encouragement and praise from adult caregivers. If children have been ridiculed because of their awkwardness or lack of physical accomplishment in the past, you may have to spend much of your time helping them improve their self-image.

They may not want to try because they have performed so poorly in the past. This may have been due to undeveloped muscular strength and/or coordination, lack of practice, or a half-year "relapse" stage. Now they need to try again to prove to themselves that they really can have physical skills. Have them jump over a line on the floor. If they succeed, draw two parallel lines (or use masking tape). As they become successful, let them separate the tape to wider and wider positions. They can do this on their own in a corner of the room if they do not want an audience in the beginning. Most five-year-olds soon will feel secure enough to jump anywhere.

This is the age when jumping rope first appears. Girls may try to make it their exclusive sport, but teachers can be the rope turners so that every class member who wants to participate can have a turn. Again, do not force the awkward child. Before you introduce a jump rope to five-year-olds, be sure to check out the jumping skills of all of your children individually, so that no one will be embarrassed in front of peers if he or she tries to jump rope and fails. This failure sometimes happens, and it may prevent a child, especially a boy, from ever putting himself in such an embarrassing situation again, which means he may not participate in group sports in school.

Competition has no place in the early childhood large motor program, but neither do total group activities that play up the weaknesses or inabilities of individual children. Total group games such as jump rope seem like such innocent fun, but they are not for the awkward child. It is better to let three children at a time play with a small jump rope than to insist that all children have a turn on a big jump rope if one of those children will be embarrassed by lack of ability. Your observing and recording the large motor abilities of individual children will help you to decide what new activities to introduce.

If You Have Not Checked This Item: Some Helpful Ideas

- **Work with Individual Children Who Show Poor Skills**

If children are age four or five and still cannot jump, you should try an activity such as jumping over lines, as mentioned under "Five-Year-Olds." If children are three or younger, you do not need to be so concerned, since jumping may not be well developed yet.

■ Chair Jumping

Have a "chair jumping day" when individuals or small groups get to jump from one of the small chairs in the room, and you measure their jumps. Keep a record of each child's jumps on a chart or notebook so individuals can see how well they do each week. Do not measure the results against the others in the class; otherwise, it becomes a competition. Let each child try three jumps, for instance, and have a different child be the measurer for each jumper.

You might want to measure with sticks you have color-coded to certain lengths, a yard stick, or a piece of string you mark off and later measure against a ruler. Whether or not you want to record in inches, centimeters, or merely red sticks will be up to you and the cognitive developmental level of your children. You do not need to be absolutely exact with the youngest children. They will be delighted to find they jumped for two red sticks and a blue stick the first time and three red sticks the second time.

It is probably good to have a special chair that you cover with contact paper to keep the seat from being scratched. Let the children know that this is the only "jumping chair," and put it away when not in use.

■ Try Concept Jumping

When children are learning the concepts *up, down, over, forward,* and *in place,* you might try having the youngsters act out the motions by jumping. Ask the others to guess what kind of jump a child made. Or let one child call out a concept and another child try to demonstrate it by jumping it.

■ Utilize Jumping Animals

Put pictures of jumping (leaping or hopping) animals on the walls at the children's eye level, and have the children try to imitate the animals: kangaroo, kangaroo rat, frog, toad, rabbit, deer, and Mexican jumping bean, for example.

Have a "Mexican Jumping Bean Day" at your preschool, when children can squat down on the floor completely covered over with cloth squares they have colored (such as old sheets or rice sacks). Play Mexican music and have them listen for a *ting* you will make on a triangle or a click on a castenet. At that sound, have your human "beans" pop up in a jump and quickly settle back down till the next signal. Or you can call out the names of the children one by one for them to jump. This activity works especially well if the children have seen real jumping beans and know what they do.

■ Read a Book

That Grand Master Jumping Teacher Bernard, Meets Jerome the Great Jumping Glump by David McPhail (New York: Frederick Warne, 1982) is a fanciful story about Bernard, who was a good jumper even before he was born, and about Jerome, whom Bernard teaches to jump higher than the sky. Your children will enjoy Jerome's jumping contest with Gerald the kangaroo.

☐ HOPS FORWARD ON ONE FOOT

Hopping is the large motor "bounding" skill in which the child takes off and lands on the same foot. Jumping uses both feet together, while leaping uses alternating feet to take off and land. A child can hop in place or hop forward for one or more steps. This checklist item asks you to identify the children in your class who can hop forward (obviously on one foot because they are hopping).

Children need balancing skills before they can hop. They also need the leg length and strength in order to do jumping. This means that not many will be truly hopping before three years of age, and maybe not until three-and-a-half. In fact, hopping for most children is not well developed before the age of four.

There are large individual differences in this skill, just as there are in other areas of development, but the largest difference of all is in gender. Four- and five-year-old girls almost always hop more and better than boys. At first, we may reason that, of course, girls are a bit more physically mature than boys of this same age. Still, someone else may argue that boys generally have a greater proportion of body muscle tissue throughout their lives than girls.

The truth seems to lie instead in the differences in opportunities and encouragement for hopping between girls and boys. Hopping is a girl's skill in our society. Games such as hop scotch and jump rope, which appear among five- and six-year-olds, are examples. These games are played principally by girls, not boys. Challenge a boy to play hop scotch, and he soon finds that girls his age are much more skilled hoppers, just as girls are better jump rope jumpers.

There is no reason why a boy could not also become skilled at hopping if he practiced. But until some new hopping challenge appears that appeals to boys, this improvement probably will not occur. Check the children in your class. How do the boys compare with the girls? Ask the children about the hopping games they play. Preschool children who play few or no hopping games will probably have great difficulty doing any hopping whether they are boys or girls.

If You Have Not Checked This Item: Some Helpful Ideas

■ **Create a Hopping Trail**

Make a hopping-tiptoeing-walking trail in your classroom or large motor room with cutout contact paper footprints that show a sequence of hopping steps on one foot, walking steps with both feet, hopping on the other foot, tiptoeing, and jumping.

■ Hop to Music

Find a bouncy but slow record, and let children try to hop and jump to it. Most four-year-olds will not be able to do more than four or five hops at a time, but the children can change to jumping and then back again for more hopping practice.

■ Hop to Drum Beats

Let children make different movements to different drum beats you play. A one-thump beat can mean to walk, a two-thump beat can signify to hop, and a quick-time beat can indicate to run. See if they can follow your rhythm. Do not change your beat too quickly, since most children are really beginners when it comes to moving to rhythm.

CLIMBS UP AND DOWN CLIMBING □ EQUIPMENT WITH EASE

Climbing involves use of the arms as well as the legs. It is, in fact, an out-growth of creeping. Most children begin climbing as soon as they can creep over to an item of furniture and pull themselves up. If they are allowed, they will creep up the stairs. They will try to creep down, too, and soon find out that a backward descent is the only kind that works!

Most two-year-olds are avid climbers. Once they walk upright and are able to see the world from that new perspective, they want to see more. Climbing is their method to see farther. Parents of two-year-olds are soon putting away all breakables. Some late two-year-olds will even try climbing to the top of a jungle gym, although they cannot climb down.

Many three- and four-year-olds enjoy climbing on all sorts of things: jungle gyms, ladders, ladder climbers, dome climbers, slides, rope climbers, trees, rocks, poles, and drain pipes. By the time they are in your program, children this age should be able to climb down as well as up with ease.

Although it takes some bravery in addition to muscle strength and coordination to be a successful climber, many of your children will be able to accomplish this skill if they have the opportunity. You should consider pro-viding climbing equipment and climbing possibilities both inside and outside your classroom.

Safety factors, of course, should be considered. Since falling is the main concern with climbing, be sure that floor or ground surfaces are cush-ioned. Padding can be used inside. Sand or wood chips are preferable to grass or hard surfaces outside.

Not all children will attempt to climb. Do not force the reluctant ones. You can encourage them and help children if they try to climb, but if they refuse, they should not be forced to try. Not all children will want to accomplish climbing skills, which is perfectly acceptable. Children have as much right to their own personal choices and interests as adults. Were you a climber when you were four?

If You Have Not Checked This Item: Some Helpful Ideas

▪ Provide a New Piece of Climbing Equipment

A packing crate (with splintery edges sanded down) is often a tempting piece of climbing equipment than can be used either inside or outside. Ladder steps can be fastened to the outside of the crate if necessary, or children may use a step stool to climb up the crate. Cargo netting is also an excellent piece of climbing equipment. Fasten it to a classroom wall with padding underneath or to a horizontal bar outside on the playground.

▪ Build a Loft

Lofts not only give preschool children extra space for various new activities, but lofts also provide a new perspective on the activities below. Some lofts use ladders to reach their tops, while others use steps or stairs. Some have several means of entrance and exit. Even nonclimbers often learn to manage all of the methods of access because being up in the loft is such fun.

▪ Have a Multiple-Access Slide

A multiple-access slide is perhaps the most valuable piece of large motor equipment you can purchase if your center can afford only one piece of equipment. Children are motivated to learn to climb in order to get to the platform at the top of the slide. There are usually steps, bars, or ladders to help children reach the top, and the youngsters soon know how to use them all. If you have space inside, an indoor multiple-access slide can serve as a loft as well as a large motor device.

▪ Make an Obstacle Course

Use planks, sawhorses, barrels, ladders, and boxes to create an obstacle course for climbing. Rearrange them frequently. Children can climb up, over, and under.

☐ MOVES LEGS/FEET IN RHYTHM TO BEAT

The acquisition of musical skills by preschool children crosses several areas of development, including physical, cognitive, language, and creative. But because music itself involves both rhythm and sound, we will look first at

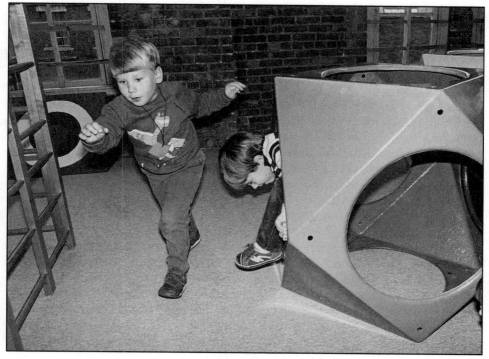

Use classroom equipment to make an obstacle course for
children to follow.

young children's development of rhythm, partly a large motor ability. In
Chapter 8, we will consider musical sound, partly a cognitive ability; and in
Chapter 9, we will consider musical memory, another cognitive skill.

All of us humans are rhythmical beings, whether or not we recognize the fact. Rhythm, in fact, is the essence of life: witness the beating of
our hearts and the breathing of our lungs. It is not so surprising to find,
therefore, that even infants can make rhythmical responses with arms,
hands, legs, and feet. These claps, kicks, or wavings seem to be triggered by
internal stimuli and not by external sounds or motions, although Cratty
mentions that in cultures where dance is important, infants too young to
stand have been observed picking up the beat of nearby adult dancers with
their own bodies and limbs (Cratty, 1986, p. 257).

Nevertheless, the first voluntary rhythmical movements of young
children are stimulated by sounds rather than visual cues. As with other
physical development, young children's rhythmic development proceeds in
an observable sequence. First their arms and hands and later their legs and
feet can move to a regular and rather slow rhythmic beat. Next, young children are able to replicate movement to an irregular beat. Finally, children can
learn to follow sound cues of different intensities. Horizontal movements
are acquired before up and down movements of the arms. Children learn to

control the rhythmic movement of one leg or one arm before they develop the ability to move both limbs rhythmically.

But regardless of development, most young children love to dance and sing. They will make attempts to imitate any rhythmic activity around them. Young children also will follow their own internal rhythms with moving and singing on their own. If we want children to continue the natural development of their musical abilities, the next move is ours. Adults who notice young children moving rhythmically must compliment them, encourage them to continue their creative movements, and call the attention of others to the children's accomplishments.

Children very quickly pick up on the values of the adults around them. If the adults show interest in children's dancing, the youngsters will continue to dance. On the other hand, if adults disregard this action or reprimand children for moving around so much, the children will stop.

You need to provide the stimulus in your program for young children to move rhythmically. That means you must praise them for any impromptu creative moving they do. Then you must schedule creative movement activities in the daily life of your classroom. Be creative yourself, and think of the curriculum areas that might include creative movement. An excellent book to follow is *Feeling Strong, Feeling Free: Movement Exploration for Young Children* by Molly Sullivan.

Creative Movement/Dancing

An entire class of preschool children can gain tremendously from creative movement and dance activities if the activities are led by a sensitive teacher and held in a creative environment. A drum, tom-tom, tambourine, or simply hand-clapping may be used for the beat, but the teacher must be sensitive enough to pick up the pulse or rhythm of the group, instead of imposing a rhythm on them. Records or tapes can be used as well; but again, the teacher needs to rely on the group rhythm, which is usually different—often slower—than that of a record.

The environment should be attractive, orderly, and comfortable. If a gymnasium is used, it should be uncluttered. If the preschool classroom is large enough, clear a space for expansive movements. Preschoolers need to be able to run, leap, and gallop.

The teacher should be the leader—a sensitive and creative leader. If a child does not want to participate, the sensitive leader can take her hand and swing it gently to the music. The teacher should be prepared, as well, with a series of simple movement activities for the children to try. Children do not like the ambiguity of directions like "Do whatever you want to do" or "Move any way you want to the music." Such statements lead only to confusion.

Instead, you should lead the children into creative movement activities through the stimulus of a steady, rhythmic beat. They need to master the basic locomotor movements of walking, running, crawling, leaping, and galloping to music or to a beat. They also should master some of the nonlocomotor movements, such as swinging, swaying, rocking, bending, and stretching.

Use a drum or tap on a tambourine to set the beat for movement. First have the children tap their feet to the beat. Then have them move across the room to the beat. Change the beat, making it faster or slower, louder or softer. Whatever you do with rhythm, make it fun and do not expect perfection.

The short attention span of preschoolers makes it necessary to keep the sessions short (about twenty minutes) and include a variety of movements and dance activities. Young children like activities that take place on the floor, so be sure to include "snake" and "worm" dances, where they can wriggle and crawl. Four-year-olds especially love to run. You will want to include a "jet plane zoom" or a "race car rally," where children can run to music or a beat.

You could do a follow-the-leader activity in a line where you as leader set the pace. You can march, tramp, slide along, trip along on tiptoes, or walk in cadence calling out a beat ("One, two, buckle your shoe; three, four, shut the door). Use music as well as a drum to help children move their legs and feet to the beat. Put on a record with a strong beat, and have the children move around the room keeping time. You may want to wind down your session with a slow record. Choose an appropriate tune for a "monster shuffle" or a "dinosaur clump." Children are usually happily exhausted after such a creative movement session.

If You Have Not Checked This Item: Some Helpful Ideas

▪ Use a Tape Recorder

Children may want to create some "foot music" of their own. Have them sit while an individual child taps out a rhythm with his or her feet. Record it. Play it back, and let the other children try to imitate this rhythm.

Children may want to tape-record other rhythms they hear. Have them listen for rhythms in the classroom. Can they hear the bubbling of the aquarium, the dripping of water from a faucet, the tapping of typewriter keys in the office down the hall? If you tape-record such sounds and play them back, children may be able to stand and move their feet to these rhythms.

▪ Walk to Music

Play records or pieces of music with different rhythms, and have your children try to walk around the room keeping time with the beat. Then have them walk to the rhythm of your drum beats or a clicker. Speed up the tempo. Slow it down. Make it syncopated.

■ **Use a Rock Record**

Rock music is characterized by its strong beat. Bring in several rock records with a beat, and let children move or dance to them in the classroom.

■ **Walk to Chants or Poems**

Read some of the animal verses from Clare Cherry's *Creative Movement for the Developing Child* (Belmont, CA: Fearon, 1971), and have the children imitate the way the particular animals walk. Bring in animal pictures, and discuss how they walk. Let the children make up simple verses about rabbits hopping or deer moving silently through the trees. Let the children demonstrate these movements.

■ **Read a Book**

Read a story about dancing or movement, and then put on a record or tape that seems appropriate for children's dancing. *The Paper Crane* by Molly Bang (New York: Mulberry Books, 1985) is about a poor Japanese traveler who pays the restaurant owner for his meal with a paper crane (bird) that he creates by folding a paper napkin. When he claps his hands, the bird comes to life and dances. Illustrations show the bird dancing. Your children could dance, too, to Japanese music.

Where the Wild Things Are by Maurice Sendak (New York: Harper & Row, 1963) is the classic story about Max, who sails away in fantasy to an island where the wild things are. Midway through the book, Max and the Things join in a "wild rumpus." Your children could perform this dance to appropriate music in your classroom.

☐ CLAPS HANDS IN RHYTHM TO BEAT

Most preschool children have participated in hand-clapping activities from infancy. They have imitated mother doing pat-a-cake; they have imitated others around them who acknowledged a person or performance by clapping. Now, in this item, they are asked to perform a musical activity with their hands: clapping to a beat.

As discussed in the previous item, rhythm is a natural part of all of us. Our heart goes on beating whether or not we think about it. Our fingers may tap out a rhythm automatically. But can preschool children clap their hands in rhythm to a beat created outside of their body? They can if their physical skills have developed normally and they have had practice clapping in rhythm.

The developmental sequence of head-to-foot and trunk-to-extremities also applies to the physical maturity necessary for children to perform rhythmic movements. In other words, arm control in children occurs before hand control, and hand control occurs before finger control. A second sequence of development begins with control of one arm and hand independent of the other (as in waving); next comes the simultaneous use of both arms and hands (as in clapping); finally comes alternate movements of the two arms and hands (as in drumming).

Although the clapping ability appears early in a child's development, the ability to clap with control comes later. Two-year-old children, for instance, enjoy clapping, but they usually cannot clap in a pattern without a great deal of help and practice. The concept of clapping in a rhythm or clapping out the syllables of a name is beyond most of them.

Three-, four-, and five-year-old children also may have some difficulty at first in following a clapping pattern. Nevertheless, most of them can learn to clap the syllables of words or names and enjoy repeating the activity (Moomaw, p. 44).

Once they have reached this maturity, children need to have practice in order to follow external rhythms. The creative movement activities discussed previously should have given the children practice in moving their feet and bodies to rhythm. During those activities, they heard you, the teacher, providing the beat with your hands. Now it is their turn.

When you sing songs or play records in your classroom, give the children practice clapping to the rhythm. Or use familiar folksongs to practice clapping on different beats. For instance, in "Paw Paw Patch," children can clap on every other beat at first.

> *Where*, oh, *where* is *sweet* little *Susy?*
> *Where*, oh, *where* is *sweet* little *Susy?*
> *Where*, oh, *where* is *sweet* little *Susy?*
> *Way* down *yonder* in the *paw* paw *patch.*

When children are able to follow this regular rhythm without difficulty, let them try to clap on every beat. Nursery rhymes and jump rope rhymes also are excellent for clapping practice. Let children follow the irregular rhythm of

> Rain, rain, go away,
> Come again another day,
> Jill and Betsy want to play.
> > *Or*
> One for the money,
> Two for the show,
> Three to get ready,
> And four to go!

If You Have Not Checked This Item: Some Helpful Ideas

■ **Try Name Clapping**

Focusing on a child's name is the surest way to interest a young egocentric child in almost any activity. At circle time or small group time, you can introduce "name clapping": clapping out the syllables in each child's name as the children say the name aloud. Make the activity more interesting by adding other words, such as "hello" or "my name is . . ." Now the children can chant and clap

Hel-lo-Bob-bie
My-name-is-San-dra
Hel-lo-Ver-on-i-ca

Finally, as the children become more adept, add their last names to this clapping activity.

My-name-is-Mel-is-sa-Brad-ley

■ Use a Tape Recorder

Children may want their own clapped rhythms recorded on the tape recorder and then played back for others in the group to try to imitate. Have each child say his or her name and then clap out a rhythm.

■ Read a Book

Mother Goose books, nursery rhyme books, and books containing jump rope rhymes can be used for clapping in unison. *The Lady with the Alligator Purse*, adapted by Nadine Bernard (Boston: Little, Brown and Company, 1988), is a hilariously illustrated version of this well-known jump rope rhyme. Children will enjoy the pictures, the rhyming words, and the rhythm. Let them clap in unison when you read the book a second time.

Books with a rhythmic refrain also give children practice clapping in unison. *Tikki Tikki Tembo*, retold by Arlene Mosel (New York: Holt, Rinehart and Winston, 1968), is a folktale based on a little Chinese boy's impossibly long name: "Tikki tikki tembo-no sa rembo-chari bari ruchi-pip peri pembo." You will be repeating the name so many times as you read the story that soon your children can help you by clapping it out with great gusto as you read.

☐ BEATS DRUM ALTERNATING HANDS IN RHYTHM TO BEAT

Moving the two arms and hands alternately in a vertical motion, such as beating on a drum, indicates a more mature development of a child's arm and hand control than does clapping the hands together. Young children enjoy beating on drums, pans, wooden blocks, and almost anything that will make a noise. For beaters they use their hands (fingers, palms, knuckles, fists), drumsticks, mallets, building sticks, ladles, or anything else they can pound with. Now, in this item, you are observing children to see whether they can use both hands alternately to beat out a rhythm.

The developmental sequence of drumming with the hands follows that of clapping. But children will have more success in beating a drum in a particular rhythm if they first have had many clapping experiences. When your children demonstrate that they can clap in rhythm, it is time to introduce the drum.

Instruments used in preschool programs fall into the same categories as those used by professionals: sound makers, rhythm, melody, and harmony instruments. Sound makers are pots, pans, glasses, seed pods, stones, and cans with seeds. Rhythm instruments include rhythm sticks, tone blocks, coconut shells, bells, triangles, gongs, cymbals, tambourines, sand blocks, rattles, maracas, and drums, to name a few. Melody instruments include xylophone, marimba, tone bells, tonette, flutophone, and ocharina. Harmony instruments include autoharp, harmonica, guitar, ukelele, banjo, mandolin, accordion, and piano.

Rhythm instruments like the drum need to be taken seriously in the preschool; that is, a drum is not a toy but a real instrument and should be treated as such. Perhaps because teachers do not understand that rhythm instruments are serious instruments used in real bands and orchestras, they allow children to treat these items as toys. Instead, each rhythm instrument should be introduced to children separately with directions on how to use it properly. In this way, children get the most from the experience: they learn how to use the instrument, to appreciate the sound it makes, and to practice the physical skills the instrument affords them.

Unfortunately, rhythm instruments are often used in "rhythm bands" in the preschool classroom, with all of the instruments played at once as the children march around to music. The youngsters, of course, may have fun with such an activity, but it adds little to their enjoyment of music, their skill development, or their appreciation for the instrument they hold. Instead, children tend to bang as loudly as they can all at once, creating a cacophony of sound—noise—that drowns out the sounds of the individual instruments, the music, and the rhythm they are supposed to be following.

Drums come in all sizes and shapes. Commercial drums are usually wooden or plastic with a skin or plastic head over one or both ends. Have several drums and drumsticks available in your classroom. Take time to introduce their use to the children, rather than merely putting the instruments on a shelf. Talk to the children about the drums. Demonstrate what each one sounds like and how it can be beaten. Let the children try them out. Then have the children sing a song while you clap out the beat. Next, have the children clap the beat as they sing. Finally, let them try beating the drums to accompany the song. They can use drumsticks or their hands. Pass the drums around until everyone has a chance.

Be sure to follow up this drumming activity for several days in order to give the children practice. You can use different songs, records with different rhythms, and a variety of activities. Some children may want to beat the drums while the others march around the room.

If You Have Not Checked This Item: Some Helpful Ideas

▪ Use Drums in Clapping Activities

Drums can be used alone or with clapping for any of the activities described under the previous checklist item on clapping.

▪ Send Messages

Children enjoy sending drumbeat messages. If they have learned to clap out names by syllables, they will be able to send drum messages the same way. Let them try sending their names ("My-name-is-Ran-dy") with drumbeats. Can the other children guess what they are saying on the drum?

▪ Make Your Own Drums

Making drums is an activity for the teacher, not the children, in the preschool. Various types of drums can be made, depending on the material. Use large cans, ice cream containers, oatmeal boxes, round plastic containers, plastic bleach bottles, coffee cans, margarine cans, or wooden or metal buckets for the body. For the head, use animal parchment (from repair departments of music stores), inner tube rubber, goatskin, heavy plastic, or canvas. Remove one or both ends of the can or container. Cut one or two circular head pieces larger than the container opening. Punch holes around the edge of the drum head material about two inches apart. Soak the parchment or goatskin in water for half an hour. For a double-headed drum, place the drum head circles on both ends of the drum body and lace them tightly together on the sides with a cord; or, for a single-headed drum, place the material on the open end and tack it to the container.

To make drumsticks, glue small rubber balls on the ends of sticks such as pencils, building sticks, or wooden dowels; wrap cloth around the ends of wooden ladles; or insert sticks into spools and wrap cloth around the spools.

OBSERVING, RECORDING, AND INTERPRETING LARGE MOTOR DEVELOPMENT

It is important at the beginning of the year to screen all of your children using the large motor development section of the *Child Skills Checklist*. List the name of each child along the left side of a lined sheet of paper. At the top indicate the eight items of the checklist. Draw vertical lines separating the eight items. Check off the large motor skills you observe for each child. For children who have few checkmarks, you may want to do an in-depth observation on each of the items.

For Lionel, the boy mentioned on the "Social Play Checklist" at the end of Chapter 4, the following information was gathered:

Large Motor Development Checklist

_____ Walks down steps alternating feet
  Evidence: Holds onto rail and puts two feet on each when descending stairs
_____ Runs with control over speed and direction
  Evidence: Does not run often
___*N*___ Jumps over obstacle, landing on two feet
___*N*___ Hops forward on one foot
___*N*___ Climbs up and down climbing equipment with ease
___*N*___ Moves legs and feet in rhythm to beat
___✓___ Claps hands in rhythm to beat
  Evidence: Claps in time to records
___✓___ Beats drum alternating hands in rhythm to beat
  Evidence: Likes to use drum during rhythm activities

The observational data gathered for Lionel were helpful to the classroom staff. They could see that Lionel spent more time in sedentary activities. He seemed more at ease sitting and playing than running around in large motor activities. During a parent conference, the teachers learned that Lionel lives in a large apartment building and has little opportunity to run outside and play. However, the staff was also concerned with the fact that the program itself offered few large motor experiences for the children. The *N* designation, meaning "no opportunity to observe," was listed for most of the children because the program does not have a playground, gymnasium, or indoor climbing equipment. Children are taken for walks, weather permitting, and are allowed to run around on the lawn outside the building. But it is obvious that additional large motor activities need to be provided.

Because Lionel and many of the other children showed skills and interest in rhythm activities, the classroom team plans to incorporate creative movement and dance activities at one end of the large classroom on a daily basis. As children become accustomed to moving to music and drumbeats, the teachers plan to take the children outside on the lawn for more expansive creative movement exercises.

TABLE 5. Large motor skills

Age	Walking	Running	Jumping	Climbing
Eight months–one year	Walks in a wide stance like a waddle			Climbs onto furniture and up stairs as an outgrowth of creeping
One–two years	Walks in a toddle and uses arms for balance (arms are not swung)	Moves rapidly in a hurried walk, in contact with surface	Uses bouncing step off bottom step of stairs with one foot	Tries climbing up anything climbable
Two–three years	Walks upstairs two feet on a step	Runs stiffly, has difficulty turning corners and stopping quickly	Jumps off bottom step with both feet	Tries climbing to top of equipment, although cannot climb down
Three–four years	Walks with arms swinging; walks upstairs alternating feet; walks downstairs two feet on step	Runs more smoothly, has more control over starting and stopping	Springs up off floor with both feet in some cases, jumps over object leading with one foot	Climbs up and down ladders, jungle gyms, slides, and trees
Four–five years	Walks up and down stairs alternating feet; walks circular line; skips with one foot	Displays strong, speedy running; turns corners, starts and stops easily	Jumps up, down, and forward	Climbs up and down ladders, jungle gyms, slides, and trees
Five–six years	Walks as an adult, skips alternating feet	Shows mature running, falls seldom, displays increased speed and control	Jumps long, high, and far; jumps rope	Displays mature climbing in adult manner

REFERENCES CITED

Allen, K. Eileen, and **Elizabeth M. Goetz.** (1982). *Early Childhood Education: Special Problems, Special Solutions.* Rockville, MD: Aspen.

Caplan, Theresa, and **Frank Caplan.** (1983). *The Early Childhood Years; The 2 to 6 Year Old.* New York: Putnam Publishing Group.

Cherry, Clare. (1971). *Creative Movement for the Developing Child.* Belmont, CA: Fearon.

Cratty, Bryant J. (1982). "Motor Development in Early Childhood: Critical Issues for Researchers in the 1980's." In Bernard Spodek (Ed.), *Handbook of Research in Early Childhood Education.* New York: Free Press.

———. (1986). *Perceptual and Motor Development in Infants and Children.* Englewood Cliffs, NJ: Prentice-Hall.

Flinchum, Betty M. (1975). *Motor Development in Early Childhood: A Guide for Movement Education with Ages 2 to 6.* St. Louis: C. V. Mosby Company.

Fraiberg, S. (1975). "Intervention in Infancy: A Program for Blind Infants." In B. Z. Friedlander, G. M. Sterritt, and G. E. Kird (Eds.), *Exceptional Infant: Volume 1.* New York: Brunner/Mazel.

Gallahue, David L. (1982). *Developmental Movement Experiences for Children.* New York: John Wiley & Sons.

Moomaw, Sally. (1984). *Discovering Music in Early Childhood.* Boston: Allyn and Bacon.

Pines, Maya. (1979). "A Head Start in the Nursery." *Psychology Today, 13*(4), 56–68.

Schickedanz, Judith A., David I. Schickedanz, and **Peggy D. Forsythe.** (1982). *Toward Understanding Children.* Boston: Little, Brown and Company.

Sullivan, Molly. (1982). *Feeling Strong, Feeling Free: Movement Exploration for Young Children.* Washington, DC: National Association for the Education of Young Children.

Zaichkowsky, Leonard D., Linda B. Zaichkowsky, and **Thomas J. Martineck.** (1980). *Growth and Development: The Child and Physical Activity.* St. Louis: C. V. Mosby Company.

OTHER SOURCES

Ames, Louise Bates, and **Frances I. Ilg.** (1976). *Your Three Year Old: Friend or Enemy.* New York: Dell Publishing Company.

———. (1976). *Your Four Year Old: Wild and Wonderful.* New York: Dell Publishing Company.

———. (1979). *Your Five Year Old: Sunny and Serene.* New York: Dell Publishing Company.

Beaty, Janice J. (1988). *Skills for Preschool Teachers.* Columbus, OH: Merrill Publishing Company.

Greenberg, Marvin. (1979). *Your Children Need Music.* Englewood Cliffs, NJ: Prentice-Hall.

Haines, Joan E., and **Linda L. Gerber.** (1988). *Leading Young Children to Music.* Columbus, OH: Merrill Publishing Company.

Torbert, Marianne. (1980). *Follow Me, a Handbook of Movement Activities for Children.* Englewood Cliffs, NJ: Prentice-Hall.

LEARNING ACTIVITIES

1. Use the fifth section of the *Child Skills Checklist* as a screening tool to observe all of the children in your classroom for large motor development. Which children are the most physically accomplished? Which need the most help? What are their ages?

2. Choose a child who seems to need a great deal of help in large motor development. Do a running record on three different days to determine what the child can do physically. Do an activity with the child to promote a skill he or she needs help with. Record the results.

3. How do the girls and boys of the same age in your program compare with one another in each of the large motor checklist items? How do you explain any differences or similarities? Can you make any conclusions about gender differences based on your observations?

4. Choose a child who needs help in moving to rhythm. Involve the child using one or more of the rhythm ideas from the text. Discuss the results.

5. Have a staff member involve children in a new large motor game while you observe and record. Discuss your results as compared with the original screening you did. What conclusions can you draw?

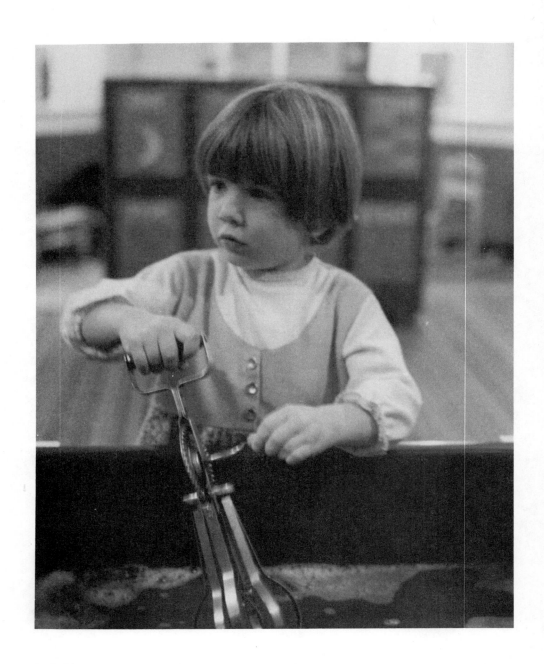

7 Small Motor Development

Small Motor Development Checklist

- [ ] Shows hand preference (which is _____)
- [ ] Turns with hand easily (knobs, lids, eggbeaters)
- [ ] Pours liquid into glass without spilling
- [ ] Unfastens and fastens zippers, buttons, Velcro tabs
- [ ] Picks up and inserts objects with ease
- [ ] Uses drawing/writing tools with control
- [ ] Uses scissors with control
- [ ] Pounds in nails with control

S mall motor development involves the fine muscles that control the extremities. In the case of young children, we are especially concerned with control, coordination, and dexterity in using the hands and fingers. Although this development occurs simultaneously in children along with large motor development, the muscles near the trunk (proximo) mature before the muscles of the extremities (distal) that control the wrists and hands.

Thus, it is important for the young child to practice use of the large muscles before he or she becomes involved in small motor activities to any extent. Delays in developing large motor coordination may very well have a negative effect on the development of small motor skills. But once small motor involvement is possible for the child, preschool caregivers should encourage him to engage in all types of manipulative activities so that he can learn and practice the skills needed to use his hands and fingers with control and dexterity.

REFLEXES

Surely infants and toddlers use their hands and fingers without much previous experience, you may counter. Why, then, do three-, four-, and five-year-olds have a different situation? The difference is important. It involves voluntary versus involuntary movements. Infants move their arms, hands, and fingers through reflexes, not voluntary movements. These involuntary movements are assimilated by the nervous system as it matures in order for the child to be able to control her movements in a voluntary manner. As these initial reflexes disappear, the child must purposefully learn to replace them by using and controlling her hands and fingers in a voluntary manner.

A very large number of reflexes are present in the infant. They include the Moro, or startle, reflex, in which the infant throws out his arms with a jerk and lets out a cry; the rooting reflex, in which the infant turns his head and opens his mouth when touched on the side of the cheek; the sucking reflex, in which the infant sucks if his lips or mouth are touched; the walking reflex, in which the infant makes stepping movements when held in an upright position on a surface; and the swimming reflex, in which the infant makes swimming movements when held in the water with his head supported. Many more reflexes exist (Zaichkowsky, Zaichkowsky, & Martineck, p. 37).

The reflex most connected with small motor hand skills is the grasping reflex, or palmar grasp, in which the baby clamps her fingers around anything put in her palm. This grasp is so strong in the beginning that it will support the infant's weight and can be used to lift the baby entirely off the surface on which she is lying. It is difficult, in fact, for the infant to let go. You may have to pry her fingers apart.

Involuntary responses such as this have their origin in the lower brain stem and spinal cord, and they eventually come under the control of the higher brain centers of the nervous system as the child matures. This higher part of the brain inhibits these initial reflexes after they have finished their task of aiding the survival of the helpless newborn, and the higher brain center then allows voluntary movements to replace them.

The initial reflexes fade away within their own recognized time-table, depending on individual differences, of course. Rooting and sucking usually disappear after three months, walking and swimming after five months, and Moro—the last to go—usually leaves after nine months. When such reflexes persist after their allotted time, it may be an indication of brain impairment (Zaichkowsky, Zaichkowsky, & Martineck, p. 37).

The grasping reflex lasts until about nine months. Thus, infants cannot start to control hand and finger actions voluntarily before this. Infants may reach for things (but not very accurately) before age six months; then, letting go is the infants' main problem. They can grasp an object easily but find it extremely difficult to let go. Even year-old children may struggle to release an object voluntarily, and some do not gain control of "letting go" before a year-and-a-half of age.

READINESS

We understand that like the large motor skills, voluntary small motor skills do not just happen; they must be learned naturally and then practiced by young children. But is there a certain time period when particular skills can be learned best? Again we face the problem of readiness. When is the child's neuromuscular system mature enough for him to control his movements and perform certain actions? Should we wait until he is ready? Not necessarily. As with large motor skills, we should encourage children to use their small muscles as soon as they can. Because each child's development is different, this time period may differ for each.

All of us carry within us a biological time clock that we have inherited. For some of us, small motor development occurs in "textbook fashion," just as the charts for average physical growth indicate. For others, this development happens just a bit behind or ahead of the charts. This staggered individual development will exist in all of the children in your program. Each child has his or her own built-in biological clock. But you do not know what time it is for the child except in general terms, and neither does the child. Since everyone's development occurs in a particular sequence, the best we can do is to assess the child's development and then provide him or her with appropriate activities, materials, and encouragement.

Is there a critical moment when small motor skills must be learned or it will be too late? Not really, except in broad general terms. The best time to learn a small motor skill seems to be when the skill is changing most rapidly (Zaichkowsky, Zaichkowsky, & Martineck, p. 36), but because this is not easy to determine, it is best to offer many different types of activities for all of your children and to help them get involved with those activities that offer both success and challenge.

In order to know where your children stand in their small motor development at the outset, you may want to screen them using the eight small motor checklist items. These items are observable behaviors that demonstrate acknowledged small motor skills of young children in the areas of rotation, manipulation, and dexterity, as well as handedness.

SHOWS HAND PREFERENCE □
(WHICH IS _____)

Many but not all of your children will have developed a hand preference by age three. You may want to take note of this preference, but you should not be concerned about it. A great deal of interest and controversy—as well as incomplete understanding—surrounds the development of handedness, or *lateral dominance* as it is called. Lateral dominance also includes the development of a foot preference and eye preference. These preferences may or may not be the same as the hand preference.

Infants tend to use both hands in the beginning. This is due to reflexive rather than voluntary movements. As the neuromuscular system matures enough for voluntary movements to occur, the infant may begin to show a preference for one hand. In the beginning, this preference may not be very strong, and because involuntary movements do not disappear all at once, the infant may use both hands for many months.

This seems to be the case at age one. By age two, the child may begin to prefer using one hand over the other. By age two-and-a-half, about 58 percent of American children have established a dominant hand, and by age three, about 70 percent have established dominance. This percentage does not increase much until age eight-and-a-half. By age eleven, 94 percent have established a preferred hand, and the remaining children are ambidextrous, having a mixed dominance (Zaichkowsky, Zaichkowsky, & Martineck, p. 75).

Not all of the world is the same. Hand preference development in Japanese children is similar to that of American children until about age two-and-a-half. But between then and age four-and-a-half, its development is much slower. Only 50 percent of Japanese children establish hand dominance by age four-and-a-half (Zaichkowsky, Zaichkowsky, & Martineck, p. 75).

This is an important finding because we know that children develop in the same sequence and within the same timetable around the world. Differences, therefore, must be due to cultural influences . . . in other words, the child's environment. In America, we are particularly concerned with handedness, and many parents go out of their way to make sure their child develops right-handedness. They put emphasis on the right hand by handing things to his right hand or having him use his right hand to eat, hold, or throw. They give him praise and positive feedback when he is successful.

Such practice accompanied by feedback and positive reinforcement is, of course, the best way to develop any motor skill. Evidently, the Japanese are not so concerned with hand dominance at an early age and have allowed their children to develop it naturally. In the end, parental influence seems to make little difference, because 90 percent of the human race eventually uses the right hand for small motor activities. More boys, by the way, are left-handed or ambidextrous than girls.

Foot dominance is somehow different. Even infants often show a clear-cut preference for one foot over the other. By age five, 94 percent have developed foot dominance.

Our concern over handedness has always centered around children's ability in learning to read and write. Will lefties have more trouble? Will children with mixed dominance have learning problems? Should you try to change a child's hand preference from left to right? The answers are not all that clear. A great deal of controversy exists regarding the relationship between perceptual-motor development and learning disabilities. There is still so much we do not know about human development.

The best advice at the moment, it seems, advocates helping young children develop small motor dexterity, no matter what their hand preference. Children need to succeed. A strong hand preference may help them perform small motor tasks with dexterity. If you know what that preference is for each of your children, you can help them to develop it with practice and positive feedback.

If You Have Not Checked This Item: Some Helpful Ideas

- **Do Not Make a Fuss**

You may want to know if the child has established handedness and with which hand, but keep your efforts at a low key. Encourage the child to use whichever hand he prefers, so that he will become more skillful in using it.

TURNS WITH HAND EASILY □ (KNOBS, LIDS, EGGBEATERS)

Twisting or turning movements done with the wrist, hand, and fingers by rotating the wrist and/or forearm take several different forms. The child may enclose a doorknob with her hand and try to twist and then pull it to open the door. Depending upon the size and stiffness of the knob and door, she may or may not succeed at first. Or she may not be tall enough to make her small motor skills work effectively. Turning a key in a lock involves this same type of motion.

Another form of small motor rotating involves vertical turning at the wrist or rotating the forearm while the fingers are gripping an implement, a cranking type of movement. Eggbeaters, food mills, and can openers use this motion. Still another type of small motor rotating uses the fingers to twist a nut onto a bolt, turn a screw into a hole, or twist a lid onto or off a jar or bottle.

Children at an early age can accomplish this motor skill. Two-and-a-half and three-year-olds, for instance, can turn a doorknob if they can reach it. They love to screw and unscrew lids or tops on jars and bottles. Have the children's parents collect empty plastic bottles and containers of all sizes along with their screw top lids, and keep the items in a box in the manipulative area of the classroom for the children to practice on.

Small motor control is far from perfect, especially with the younger children; things have a way of slipping out of their fingers from time to time. Thus, it is important to use only unbreakable containers such as plastic—never glass—in the classroom.

This same hand-rotating skill is used by three-year-olds and older children as they try to put together a puzzle. Whereas two-year-olds will often try to jam a puzzle piece into place and will give up if it does not fit, older children will rotate the piece to try to match the shape of the hole.

Watch how your children put puzzles together. Obviously, perceptual awareness is also at work in this instance, but children first need the small motor rotating skill in order to use their shape recognition ability. Puzzles of differing complexities should be an item on your shelves of manipulative materials. These puzzles offer excellent practice for finger dexterity and eye-hand coordination, as well as the cognitive concepts of matching, shapes, and part-to-whole relationships.

Three-year-olds can turn an eggbeater, and they do love to do it. Be sure to have more than one eggbeater at your water table, since the eggbeater is usually a favorite implement and the focus of many squabbles if only one is available. Children like to try turning food mills and can openers as well, but sometimes youngsters do not have the strength to succeed if the items to be ground or opened are too difficult.

Research has found that objects of differing shapes and objects that permit the child to modify them are more interesting to children than objects that are rigid and unchangeable. Novelty is also an important quality in encouraging children to handle and manipulate objects. When the novelty wears off, children are less interested in playing with the items. Teachers should respond to such findings by including a variety of items in the manipulative area and by changing them from time to time (Cratty, p. 214).

If You Have Not Checked This Item: Some Helpful Ideas

■ Have a Collection of Food Utensils for Play

Visit a hardware store having a large assortment of food preparation utensils, and stock up on all kinds of grinding, squeezing, and cranking types of implements. Better still, visit a flea market, and buy the same things second-hand. Some of the old-fashioned hand tools of great-grandma's kitchen will make a big hit in your classroom. Keep the items in your housekeeping area, near the water table, or on your manipulative shelves, and watch what your children do with them.

■ Make a Nuts-and-Bolts Board

Fasten bolts of differing sizes to a sanded-down board, and give children a box of nuts to screw onto the bolts. The children will need to use their size-sorting as well as small motor skills.

■ Get Sample Doorknobs

Ask a building supply company for sample doorknobs, door locks, bolts, or other similar items when it no longer uses the particular model on display. Another source for doorknobs and other hardware might be companies that regularly deal with used building materials, such as wreckers and demolition firms.

■ Collect Old Locks and Keys

Have a box of old locks and keys for children to experiment with. The youngsters will need persistence as well as motor skills to match up and make the locks and keys work.

■ **Try an Orange Squeezer**

Bring in an orange squeezer that works by hand, and let your children take turns twisting half an orange on it to make juice.

POURS LIQUID INTO GLASS □ WITHOUT SPILLING

Two-year-olds are able to hold a glass of milk, at first with two hands and then with one. Most parents are not really concerned that their children do more than this sort of holding. Pouring tends to be an adult activity that mothers do for their children. Many nursery school teachers and day-care personnel feel the same way. Why should children learn to pour? Won't they just make a mess if they spill? Isn't it much quicker and more efficient if the adults in the classroom do the pouring?

Children should learn to pour not simply as a helping activity but also to acquire and practice small motor coordination. Pouring is an excellent real activity that children can participate in, and that is both helpful to others and, more importantly, helpful for their own small muscle development.

Long ago, Maria Montessori, the renowned Italian early childhood educator, recognized the value of pouring by including all sorts of pouring activities in her "daily living exercises," which taught children small motor skills such as eye-hand coordination. Today, Montessori children still learn by pouring rice before they finally pour liquids successfully from small pitchers.

The size of the pitcher is the key to successful pouring. Put a small pitcher on each of your children's snack or lunch tables, and let the youngsters help themselves to juice or milk. If they should spill, they can help clean up with a soft sponge, another good small motor exercise.

Allowing children to pour may not be as efficient as having an adult pour the drinks, but you need to think about the purpose for your program. Is it to take care of a group of children, or is it to help young children develop their own skills and learn to take care of themselves? Young children take a great deal of pride in being able to do adult-type tasks. Performing these tasks not only makes them feel grown up but also gives them a real sense of self-worth and accomplishment.

There will be accidents. Spills are part of the price our children pay for the complicated task of growing up. Remember the problem of releasing the grip, in which children actually have to learn how to let go because some traces of the palmar grasp reflex may still remain? And if they do not have their minds on what they are doing, they may release their grip without meaning to. Again, make spilling a learning experience, not an embarrassment. They will enjoy squeezing out the cleanup sponge.

Three-year-olds may need to use both hands for pouring. If the pitcher is small enough, four- and five-year-olds can often handle it with one hand.

If You Have Not Checked This Item: Some Helpful Ideas

■ Have Pouring Implements in Your Water Table

Have several sizes and types of plastic pitchers in your water table. Some can be large with lids on the top; some can be small and open at the top. All should have handles. Children can do much of their initial pouring practice here without worrying about spilling.

■ Use Pouring Implements on Your Food Table

Have small plastic or ceramic pitchers that the children can use to serve themselves. You can fill these small-sized containers as they empty. Again, the flea market is a good source for interesting pouring implements such as vinegar cruets and small metal pitchers.

☐ UNFASTENS AND FASTENS ZIPPERS, BUTTONS, VELCRO TABS

Unfastening and fastening zippers, buttons, and Velcro tabs are other self-help skills we want children to accomplish not only in order to take care of themselves, but also to help them develop small motor dexterity. Young children want to do things for themselves. Often they have trouble accomplishing unfastening and fastening because their motor coordination has not developed sufficiently. Just as often, however, their difficulty has to do with a lack of practice because the adults around them do everything for them.

It is interesting to note that economically disadvantaged children frequently develop small motor dexterity before middle income children do. Economically disadvantaged children often have more practice. In fact, preschoolers in many large one-parent families are expected to help dress themselves when the working mother has her hands full getting herself ready for work every morning, the baby ready for the sitter, and breakfast for everybody before she has to leave.

If mothers and fathers do all the buttoning and fastening of clothing for their preschoolers, the children miss an excellent opportunity for learning how to do it on their own. They may even resist when the preschool teacher encourages them to try, wanting the teacher to perform the same function as their mothers.

Three-year-olds are able to unbutton first—always an easier task—but many can also button large buttons on clothing if given the chance to practice. Most three-year-olds also can fasten regular snaps but may have trouble with the heavy-duty jeans-type snap. Even four-year-olds seldom have the finger strength necessary to make these heavy-duty snaps work.

Four-year-olds should be able to button and unbutton clothing with little difficulty. They can unzip zippers, but they often need help getting started with jacket zippers that come apart completely.

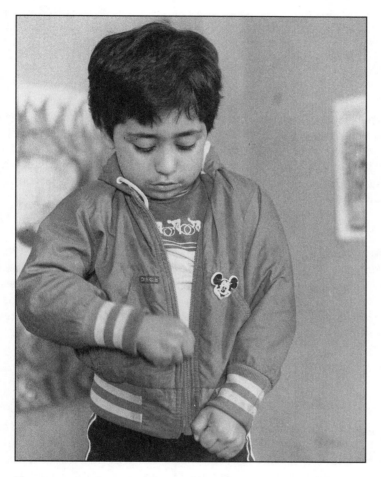

Four-year-olds can undo zippers with ease but sometimes need help in getting started with zipping up jackets.

Many shoes and articles of clothing are now fastened with Velcro-type fasteners. This seems to be the easiest fastener for children to handle. A Velcro tab fastener is pulled apart by gripping the end between the thumb and forefinger and pulling; it is fastened merely by pushing the side with the tiny hooks against the backing side. Preschoolers have the strength and coordination to do this with ease.

If You Have Not Checked This Item: Some Helpful Ideas

■ Use Buttoning/Zipping Boards

Make or purchase several boards that will help your children acquire and practice these skills. If you make your own boards, have only one skill practiced on each board: buttoning on one, zipping on another, snaps on yet another. Have these boards available in the manipulative area of your classroom.

■ Talk with Parents

Talk with parents about the importance of their child's development of small motor coordination. Let them know the kinds of activities their children will be doing in your class. Suggest some of the activities the children could be doing at home, such as self-help skills like dressing themselves—including buttoning, zipping, and snapping clothing—or helping to dress younger members of the family.

■ Read a Book

I Love My Baby Sister (Most of the Time) by Elaine Edelman (New York: Viking Penguin, 1984) is a first-person story by a little girl who tells about the things her baby sister can do, as well as the things the girl does to help her sister, such as showing her how to dress herself. Self-help skills are featured with intriguing illustrations. Your children should be motivated to talk about their own experiences along this line.

☐ PICKS UP AND INSERTS OBJECTS WITH EASE

Manipulative Materials

Picking up and inserting objects is the small motor skill most frequently promoted in the early childhood classroom. This skill involves manipulation of items by gripping them between thumb and fingers and inserting or placing them somewhere else. Using puzzles, pegboards, and stacking toys; lacing; sewing; weaving; stringing beads; and sorting small items—all call for this skill. Playing with Lego building blocks, Tinkertoys educational toys, geoboards, formboards, bristleboards, and many plastic table games also calls for the presence of picking-up and inserting skills.

All classrooms should have a permanent space for manipulative activity of this sort, with shelves at children's level equipped with many materials for easy selection and return. There should be a table in the area next to the shelves as well as floor space for playing with the larger toys.

The selection of materials should cover a wide range of children's abilities, as well. Wooden puzzles, for example, should include simple, single pictures with pieces showing an entire part of the picture for beginners, as well as more complicated pictures with many pieces for older or more experienced children.

Teachers should plan to check all of the manipulative materials at least once a week to be sure all the parts and pieces are there. If some pieces are missing, either replace the pieces or remove the material. It does not help beginners to try to make puzzles or play games with pieces missing; many beginners soon give up.

It is not necessary to put out all of the manipulative materials that the program owns at once. Add a few new ones to the area every month, and remove some of the old ones. Remember that the novelty of materials motivates children to use them. Save some of the more complicated table toys for challenging the experienced children later in the year. If you have a limited supply of materials, consider trading with other programs.

Children's Skills

You will want to know which children visit the manipulative area during your free play period. Use the "Small Motor Development Checklist" as a screening device to help you to find out. Are children avoiding the area because they are not comfortable with small motor skills? Do mainly boys avoid the manipulative materials?

Once you know which individuals avoid manipulative activities, you will be able to sit down at a table with a single child and challenge him or her to make a puzzle with you, stack blocks, or sort shapes into a form-board. If you are keeping file card records of each child, you can add this information to his or her card. You or your co-workers may need to spend time every day with children who need extra practice with small motor skills. You may need to encourage these children to complete some of the small motor activities on their own.

Gender Differences

Our society seems to encourage girls to engage in small motor activities more than boys. Even the women's movement has not changed the way many parents raise their children. Boys are still encouraged to run outside and climb trees or play ball. Girls are given manipulative-type toys for their play. Partly as a result, many girls are more dextrous with their fingers, while boys are more skillful in large motor activities such as running and throwing.

In the end, all children need to be skillful and at ease with both large and small motor activities. Once involved with formal education, both genders will need to handle writing tools and reading activities. Girls who are more skillful with finger dexterity and eye-hand coordination have an edge over boys in writing and reading at present. Is this skill imbalance perhaps the reason that more boys than girls have problems in learning to read?

If You Have Not Checked This Item: Some Helpful Ideas

▪ Use Bead-Stringing

Put out all kinds of materials for both boys and girls to use in making necklaces. Have macaroni and all sorts of pasta shapes available. The children can color them first by painting. Bring in little sea shells with holes drilled in them (hobby shops may do this), as well as acorns and horse chestnuts in the fall, plastic or wooden beads, and any other small items you can find. Save tops from plastic bottles and tops of magic markers; punch holes in them and use them for stringing necklaces and bracelets.

▪ Make a Geoboard

Make a one-foot-square wooden board of some thickness and pound in headless nails over the surface of the board in rows one inch apart. Allow the nails to protrude above the surface about an inch. Let the children string colored rubber bands over the tops of the nails, making all kinds of designs. Older children can try to copy design cards you have made, as well. Make foot-square cardboard cards with dots for the nails in the exact arrangement as the geoboard. On each card, draw the outline of a shape such as a red square, a blue triangle, or a yellow rectangle; let the children try to copy each pattern with similarly colored rubber bands on the geoboard. These designs must be simple for three- and four-year-olds, since their copying skills are still at an early level. Kindergarten children will have an easier time copying geoboard designs. If this play becomes a favorite activity, you will want more than one geoboard.

▪ Make Pegboards

Ask a building supply company for scraps of pegboard it normally would throw away. You can cut the scraps to child-sized shapes and sand down the edges. The pegboards do not have to be squares. Triangular pegboards are just as useful and appealing. Get boxes of colored golf tees for pegs, and let the children use the tees in the same way the colored rubber bands are used on the geoboards. You may want to make simple designs on paper or cardboard for the children to copy on their pegboards, as well. Graph paper is helpful if you do not want to spend time measuring spaces.

▪ Have Parents Help

Have a parent "Board-Making Bee" to help stock your classroom as well as to make enough extra boards to take home for their children to play with. You can almost always attract parents to come to your program to help like this if they know they will be making educational games they can also take home. Besides helping their children both at home and at school, the parents themselves can be learning the importance of small motor activities for their children. Too often adults tend to look upon all children's activities as play, an unimportant entertainment. Parents need to be aware that play is essential to their children's physical, mental, and social development as human beings. Such parent group activities may change parents' outlook.

■ Read a Book

The Balancing Girl by Berniece Rabe (New York: E. P. Dutton, 1981) is the story of Margaret, a handicapped girl in leg braces and a wheelchair, who nevertheless is a whiz at manipulating books, blocks, and dominoes. A domino maze, her outstanding creation, not only helps the school carnival succeed but also reconciles her problems with Tommy, her chief competitor. Be sure to have at least one set of dominoes on hand after reading this story.

USES DRAWING/WRITING □ TOOLS WITH CONTROL

Preschool programs for two-, three-, and four-year-olds should not be concerned with "teaching" children how to draw pictures or write words. Some of your older children may—and probably will—progress to this stage of development and be able to do some pictorial drawing and word-writing naturally. Do not expect all of your children to reach this more advanced stage. Instead, you should provide children with opportunities to use writing and drawing implements of all kinds to encourage development of their small motor finger strength and dexterity and of their eye-hand coordination.

The first time preschoolers use crayons, pencils, or magic markers, they usually hold them in the so-called *power grip*, with all of the fingers clamped fist-like around the implement. This does not give them much control over the marks they will make since the entire hand, wrist, and arm are involved in the movements, rather than just the fingers. As their motor skills develop and they have the chance to practice, they will eventually switch to the *precision grip*, holding the implement between the thumb and fingers.

Young children go through predictable stages in their development of writing skills. Cratty has noted that the earliest stage is a grasp in which only the pencil touches the page, with the arm and hand unsupported in the air. Next, the little finger and elbow side of the hand are rested on the page of paper, but the hand and fingers are moved as one unit. Finally, children learn to use their hand and fingers separately, with the hand as an anchor on the paper and the fingers moving the pencil. The final stage, however, may not be reached until between five to seven years of age (Cratty, p. 244).

Watch the children to see which are using a mature grip on their writing implement and which still seem to prefer the fist clench. Ask their parents what writing or coloring tools they have at home. Some children, because they have no materials, may not have had the practice like others. You may want to send home a few crayons and paper for those who need more drawing and writing practice.

Are your children using these tools with their preferred hand? Children often pick up an implement with either hand and start to use it whether or not the hand works well. For those whose handedness you have already identified, you might have them try switching hands if they are crayoning with the nondominant hand.

The stubby fingers of preschoolers sometimes have more success gripping a thick tool, although some youngsters prefer regular pencils and crayons. Magic markers are already thick and easy for them to use. Easel paintbrushes are thick enough but usually too long for them to control readily. You may need to cut off a few inches of the handle and sand it smooth. Day-care supply houses have finally got the message and are coming out with properly proportioned paintbrushes for preschoolers. (Art and writing skills for preschoolers will be discussed more fully in Chapters 11 and 12.)

If You Have Not Checked This Item: Some Helpful Ideas

▪ Use Coloring Books

Coloring books are quite controversial with preschool program people. There is great concern that these stilted, stereotyped pictures will substitute in the classroom for creative art. It seems we have missed the point. Coloring books have little to do with art, but they have a great deal to do with small motor skills. Coloring books should be kept on the shelves with manipulative materials. Children love to fill in the outline pictures with various colors. At first, children merely scribble over them with one color. As they gain control of the crayons, the youngsters work more carefully using different colors. Finally, the children are able to stay within the lines, a very satisfying accomplishment for the child struggling to control the use of his fingers.

Using coloring books, in fact, is an excellent prewriting activity for young children if the books contain simple pictures with large spaces. Children can color in the pictures, trying to stay within the lines, or they can trace over the outlines of the pictures with a crayon or magic marker.

▪ Have a Writing Table

Place a small table in your library corner. Have primary pencils, regular pencils, magic markers, ball-point pens, crayons, and notebook or tablet paper of various sizes to scribble on. Let the children pretend they are writing.

■ **Read a Book**

We Are Best Friends by Aliki Brandenberg (New York: Greenwillow Books, 1982) is the story of Robert, whose best friend Peter moves away. The two boys write letters to one another and finally make new friends. Your children may want to write a letter—with your help—to someone who has moved away.

USES SCISSORS WITH CONTROL ☐

Learning to cut with scissors takes a great deal of coordination and practice. Children who have had practice with this activity at home may be way ahead of those who have not, regardless of age. Sometimes the scissors themselves make it difficult for youngsters to learn how to use them. The blunt scissors found in many preschools are often dull and difficult to manipulate even by adults. Try the scissors yourself, and loosen and sharpen them before giving them to the children. Really good scissors cost money, but they are a worthwhile investment when you consider what fine practice they give children in developing strength in their hands and coordination in their fingers.

For children who have not learned to cut, you can help them in several ways. Show them how to hold the scissors with their favored hand. As with crayons, children sometimes pick up scissors with either hand, but they will not have much success if they are trying to use the nondominant hand. Hold a narrow strip of paper stretched taut between your two hands for the child to cut in two. Once she can do this cutting without difficulty, get another child to hold the paper, and let each take a turn holding and cutting. Give them a task of cutting all the yellow strips into small pieces.

On another day, show the child how to hold the strip of paper in her own hand and cut with the other hand. She needs to keep her scissors in her dominant hand. Let her practice on different kinds of paper, including construction paper, typing paper, and pages from magazines. Finally, draw a line on a sheet of paper, and let the child practice cutting along a line. Be sure to have at least one pair of left-handed scissors.

Most four-year-olds can cut along a straight line without difficulty, but many have trouble turning corners and following a curved line. Children need practice of all kinds in cutting. Whenever you are preparing art materials for the children to use, especially cutouts that need to be pasted, try to involve the children in helping to do the cutting.

If You Have Not Checked This Item:
Some Helpful Ideas

■ **Use Wrapping Paper Ribbons**

Let children practice cutting wrapping paper ribbons into confetti. Ribbons have more body than ordinary paper and so cut easier. Save the confetti for a celebration.

■ Read a Book

Let's Make Rabbits by Leo Lionni (New York: Pantheon Books, 1982) is a simple story about a talking pencil and a pair of scissors who get together and decide to make rabbits. The pencil draws a rabbit, the scissors cuts out a collage rabbit, and the two rabbits immediately become best friends. The teacher can trace the circular pieces that make up the rabbit and help the children cut out their own collage rabbits.

The Trip by Ezra Jack Keats (New York: Scholastic Book Services, 1978) tells the story of the inner city boy, Louie, who moves to a new neighborhood where he does not know anybody, so he creates his own world in a shoe box peep show. Directions for making the peep show appear on the last page. Although making the peep show is too complicated for most young children to do on their own, teachers can prepare some of the materials and ask children to help with the cutting and pasting.

☐ POUNDS IN NAILS WITH CONTROL

Holding a nail and pounding it with a hammer held in the opposite hand is the most complicated small motor skill thus far discussed. Many children will not be able to do it well until they are older and more coordinated. Even adults often have difficulty. Try it yourself and find out.

Handedness makes a difference. So does arm and wrist strength. The small toy hammers in play sets should not be used. They are not heavy or strong enough to have much effect other than frustrating the pounder. A small adult hammer is better.

Both boys and girls should be encouraged to pound. It is an excellent activity to develop small motor strength and coordination. If you do not have a carpenter's bench in your room, you can set up a woodworking area by hanging tools on the wall from a pegboard and using several tree stumps as pounding surfaces. Often building supply companies will provide you with wood scraps.

To get children interested in this or any activity area in your classroom, simply go into the area yourself and begin pounding something. Pounding always attracts attention, and soon children will want to do the same thing the teacher is doing. Again, you should check to make sure they are holding the hammer in their favored hand. You can easily control the safety factor by limiting the number of hammers or tree stumps available for pounding.

If You Have Not Checked This Item: Some Helpful Ideas

■ Use Soft Materials

Do not start your pounding activities with wood. Children need to acquire the skill before they will be able to drive a nail through wood. Start with a

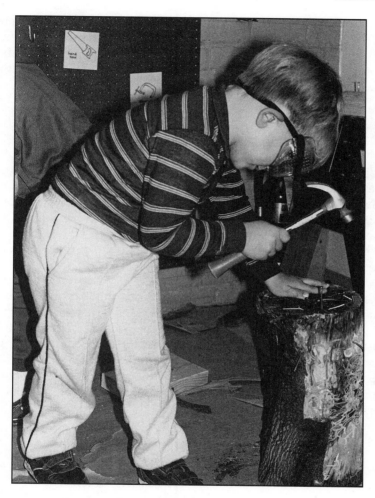

Holding a nail and pounding it with a hammer held in the opposite hand is a complicated small motor skill.

softer material such as fiberboard, ceiling tiles, or foamboard. Children also love to pound nails through the holes in Tinkertoy educational toys.

■ Use Large-Headed Nails

The children should use large-headed nails at first. Most tacks are too short for the pounder to hold, but roofing nails or upholstering tacks are large and long enough to work well.

■ Read a Book

Tool Book by Gail Gibbons (New York: Holiday House, 1982) is a simple but effective introduction to tools for your children. Tools are categorized by their function and illustrated with careful, colorful drawings showing their use. Be sure to bring to class real tools like the ones shown when you read this book.

Building a House by Byron Barton (New York: Penguin Books, 1981) shows carpenters, masons, plumbers, electricians, and painters putting together a house.

OBSERVING, RECORDING, AND INTERPRETING SMALL MOTOR DEVELOPMENT

As you did with the large motor development checklist items, you should also screen your entire class on the eight small motor development checklist items. Make a similar chart with the children's names on one side and the eight items across the top. Check off the accomplishments for all of your children based on your observations. Then you can see by just a glance at the blanks which of the children may need special help in order to accomplish small motor skills.

Observe each of these children who need special help separately during the free choice period, recording their actions in a running record. Later you can transfer this information onto the entire checklist for an individual by checking off items and writing in evidence. Finally, you should make an individualized learning prescription for each child needing special help. The activities you choose to help the child in the areas needing strengthening should be based on his or her areas of strength and confidence. For instance, Lionel, the new boy discussed at the end of Chapters 4 and 6, had a "Small Motor Development Checklist" as follows:

Small Motor Development Checklist

___✓___ Shows hand preference (which is __Left__)

___✓___ Turns with hand easily (knobs, lids, eggbeaters)
Evidence: Plays with water table toys easily

___✓___ Pours liquid into glass without spilling
Evidence: Pours own milk at lunch

___✓___ Unfastens and fastens zippers, buttons, Velcro tabs
Evidence: Dresses and undresses self with ease

___✓___ Picks up and inserts objects with ease
Evidence: Makes puzzles with ease

_____ Uses drawing/writing tools with control

_____ Uses scissors with control

___N___ Pounds in nails with control

Using the information gained on the "Social Play Checklist" and "Large Motor Development Checklist" as well, the staff put together a learning prescription for Lionel.

Learning Prescription

Name *Lionel*   Date *10-14*

Areas of Strength and Confidence

1. Does manipulative activities well by self
2. Does well with music and rhythm activities
3. Has good small motor coordination

Areas Needing Strengthening

1. Needs to develop large motor skills
2. Needs to learn to play with others
3. Needs to develop small motor skills of writing, drawing, cutting

Activities to Help

1. Bring in a pair of left-handed scissors and have Lionel cut out pictures of cars from magazines to make a car scrapbook with one of the other boys
2. Bring in hammer, nails, and tree stump; ask Lionel to help another child with pounding nails to make a rhythm instrument shaker
3. Have Lionel and other children paint the rhythm instruments they make

Because Lionel shows the ability to make puzzles and to fasten and unfasten zippers and buttons, the staff felt he could use his small motor skills to work with another child in a class project. He likes art activities such as play dough and fingerpainting, but he does not use paint brushes, writing tools, or scissors. Could this be because he is left-handed? We will provide him with left-handed scissors and give him support in the activity of cutting out pictures of cars for the class scrapbook. We have not had a woodworking bench, but Lionel says he has helped his grandfather pound nails. Perhaps he and other children could make rhythm instruments from wood, paint them, and then use them in a rhythm activity (Lionel excels at rhythm). Using things Lionel likes to do and is good at doing may help him get involved with the other children.

REFERENCES CITED

Cratty, Bryant J. (1986). *Perceptual and Motor Development in Infants and Children.* Englewood Cliffs, NJ: Prentice-Hall.

Zaichkowsky, Leonard D., Linda B. Zaichkowsky, and **Thomas J. Martineck.** (1980) *Growth and Development: The Child and Physical Activity.* St. Louis: C. V. Mosby Company.

OTHER SOURCES

Beaty, Janice J. (1988). *Skills for Preschool Teachers.* Columbus, OH: Merrill Publishing Company.

Caplan, Theresa, and **Frank Caplan.** (1983). *The Early Childhood Years: The 2 to 6 Year Old.* New York: Putnam Publishing Group.

Dunn, M. L. (1979). *Pre-Scissors Skills.* Tucson, AZ: Communication Skill Builders.

Schickedanz, Judith, David I. Schickedanz, and **Peggy D. Forsythe.** (1982). *Toward Understanding Children.* Boston: Little, Brown and Company.

Thompson, David. (1981). *Easy Woodstuff for Kids.* Mt. Rainier, MD: Gryphon House.

LEARNING ACTIVITIES

1. Use the sixth section of the *Child Skills Checklist,* "Small Motor Development," as a screening tool to observe all of the children in your classroom. Pay special attention to which hand each seems to favor. Also note which ones spend time in small motor activities and which do not.

2. Compare the children in your classroom on their checklist results in both large and small motor development. Do you see any relationships?

3. Choose a child who seems to need a great deal of help with small motor skills. Do a running record of him or her on three different days, concentrating on small motor skills. Do a learning activity with the child based on the results.

4. How do the girls and boys of the same age compare with one another in small motor skills? What conclusions can you make based on your observations?

5. Put out a new small motor activity for the children to use. Observe and record the results. What conclusions can you draw?

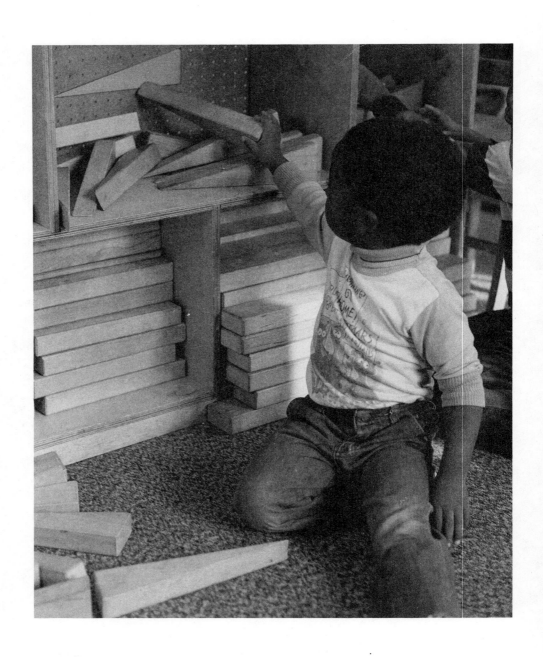

8 Cognitive Development: Classification & Seriation

Cognitive Development: Classification and Seriation Checklist

☐ Recognizes basic geometric shapes
☐ Recognizes colors
☐ Recognizes differences in size
☐ Recognizes differences in musical tones
☐ Reproduces musical tones with voice
☐ Sorts objects by appearance
☐ Arranges events in sequence from first to last
☐ Arranges objects in series according to a rule

C ognitive development of preschool children is concerned with how they develop their thinking abilities. We are only at the beginning of our understanding of how this takes place. The work of researchers like Swiss psychologist Jean Piaget in his investigation of how knowledge is created (see Table 6) and psycholinguist Noam Chomsky in his exploration of how language is acquired has given us new insights into how children think as well as how their thinking evolves.

The use of the computer and the work on artificial intelligence to program the computer to work like the human brain have added even more understanding of how the brain works and of its unimagined complexity. The technological advances in time-lapse photography, videotaping, and other laboratory observation methods of infants and children have given us entirely different perspectives on child development. Still, we are only at the gates, the mere frontiers of understanding about intellectual ability and how it develops.

What we do know is something quite startling to those unfamiliar with recent findings: that *children create their own knowledge*. Using the physical and mental tools they are born with, children interact with their environment to make sense of it, and in so doing, they construct their own mental images of their world. The brain seems to be preprogrammed to take in information about objects and their relationship to one another. What do things look, feel, taste, sound, and smell like? What can they do? How are they like one another? How are they different? What happens if you touch, push, or throw them?

TABLE 6. Piaget's stages of cognitive development

Sensorimotor Stage (Birth to age 2)

Child thinks in visual patterns (schemata).

Child uses senses to explore objects (i.e., looks, listens, smells, tastes, and manipulates).

Child learns to recall physical features of an object.

Child associates objects with actions and events but does not use objects to symbolize actions and events (e.g., rolls a ball but does not use ball as a pretend car).

Child develops object permanence (comes to realize an object is still there even when out of sight).

Preoperational Stage (Age 2 to 7)

Child acquires symbolic thought (uses mental images and words to represent actions and events not present).

Child uses objects to symbolize actions and events (e.g., pretends a block is a car).

Child learns to anticipate effect of one action on another (e.g., realizes pouring milk from pitcher to glass will make level of milk decrease in pitcher as it rises in glass).

Child is deceived by appearances (e.g., believes a tall, thin container holding a cup of water contains more than a short, wide container holding a cup of water).

Child is concerned with final products (focuses on the way things look at a particular moment, "figurative knowledge," and not on changes of things or how things got that way, "operational knowledge"), and he cannot seem to reverse his thinking.

Concrete-Operational Stage (Age 7 to 11)

Child's thoughts can deal with changes of things and how they got that way.

Child is able to reverse his thinking (has ability to see in his mind how things looked before and after a change took place).

Child has gone beyond how things look at a particular moment and begins to understand how things relate to one another (e.g., knows that the number two can be larger than one, yet, at the same time, smaller than three).

Formal-Operational Stage (Age 11 +)

Child begins to think about thinking.

Child thinks in abstract terms without needing concrete objects.

Child can hypothesize about things.

NOTE: Information from Forman (pp. 69–93) included

USING PLAY

Another startling finding, for those new to the field, involves the method that children use to create this knowledge: they do it by playing around with things, people, and ideas. Most people think of play as something recreational, something we do for enjoyment, and something rather inconsequential. For adults, this definition of play may be true, but for infants and young children, play is a way of trying out and finding out. Children fool around with toys, clothing, their hands and feet, sounds, words, and other people. Youngsters use their senses of taste, touch, sound, sight, and smell in a playful manner with anything and everything they can get their hands (or feet) on in order to find out what an object is, what it feels like, what it sounds like, and what you can do with it. The fact of the matter is that child's play is practice in learning to think.

From the time he is born, the human infant pursues such information with a single-minded determination. At first, everything goes into the mouth. Then the infant bangs objects against the side of the crib to see what they sound like, to see what they will do, and to find out what will happen. The toddler has an extra advantage. He has expanded his field of exploration by learning to walk. Suddenly the world's objects are his to touch, pick up, shake, throw, taste, and take apart. He uses his senses to play with his world in order to find out what it is about. And as soon as he can talk, he plays with words and word sounds as well.

All of the information extracted through this playful exploration of the environment is filed away in predetermined patterns in the brain, to be used to direct or adjust the child's behavior as he continues to respond to the stimuli around him. We now know that this knowledge is organized by the brain in predictable patterns from a very early age. Some of these patterns may even be inherited. Recent highly sophisticated research with two- and three-year-olds has convinced psychologists that children may be born with the ability to make distinctions between animate and inanimate things and to understand cause and effect (Pines, 1983, p. 48).

Nevertheless, if the child does not have the opportunity to explore his environment—if his environment is uninteresting or sterile, or if his caregivers are harsh, controlling, or neglectful—he may not develop his intellect to the same extent as children without these handicaps. We mentioned in Chapter 6 the apathetic children in the Iranian orphanages who could hardly walk at age four. Yet when Dr. Hunt trained their caregivers to use vocal play with newly arrived infants, an overwhelming change took place in them. Not only did these youngsters learn to walk and talk on schedule, but even their appearance and their facial features also changed for the better (Pines, 1979, p. 63).

ASSESSING DEVELOPMENT

How have your children fared in the construction of their own knowledge? They need to have built up mental representations of objects, ways to differentiate things by their appearance and by their sound, ways of telling what kinds of things are alike, and ways to decide how things fit together as a part of a sequence or series. These are the types of patterns or concepts the brain forms in organizing the data it takes in.

You will need to assess each of your children by observing his or her ability to accomplish the eight checklist items at the head of this chapter. The first six of these items refer to classification skills the child needs to know, and the last two items involve skills for arranging things in a series.

You should plan activities or playful exploration periods for children to use in order to continue developing their intelligence.

☐ RECOGNIZES BASIC GEOMETRIC SHAPES

The development of thinking begins with the infant's seeing, hearing, and feeling things in her environment: her mother's face, the nurse's face, and her bottle or mother's breast. Her brain takes in these important visual perceptions and stores them in particular schemes or patterns that are mental representations for the objects and events she experiences. Her brain seems to be preprogrammed to pay attention to certain things in her environment and to ignore the rest.

Research has shown, for instance, that she looks longer at the human face than at anything else around her (Schickedanz, Schickedanz, & Forsythe, p. 152). The infant seems, in fact, to prefer visual stimuli that have a contour configuration. She is beginning her construction of knowledge.

The first aspect of this knowledge is called *figurative knowing* because it deals with shapes and configurations, as well as the patterns of movements, tastes, smells, and so on (Saunders & Bingham-Newman, p. 117). The infant will have to recognize these objects and shapes again and again. She will need to respond to her caregivers, bottle, rattle, and other environmental objects in an appropriate manner. Perceptual recognition, then, is the earliest form of the infant's store of knowledge.

As the young child learns new things (as he or she acquires new mental constructions), an interesting phenomenon occurs. He seems to store his new knowledge in previously constructed categories that are very general in nature. For instance, not long after he learns that his own specific four-legged animal pet is a *doggie*, he categorizes all four-legged creatures—even cats and teddy bears—as *doggies*. In other words, his brain overgeneralizes. As it matures, the brain will eventually have to learn more discriminating features and develop new categories for a variety of different animals. This refinement seems to take place especially between the ages of two and four.

The first checklist item on shape is concerned with this refinement in perceptal recognition. In order to think, the child needs to know and discriminate among basic shapes of things. The checklist starts with geometric shapes because the concept of shape is one of the first concepts to emerge in the child's cognitive development. He needs to distinguish between a circle, a square, a rectangle, and a triangle, not in order to do geometry, but to be able to categorize mentally and to distinguish among the objects in his environment.

Adults are often surprised to learn that young children overgeneralize about shapes, too. At first, children view all enclosed figures as being the same. In other words, youngsters think that a circle and a square are the same. They have difficulty distinguishing one shape from another. They need to learn the special features of the shape that distinguish it from a similar shape. Surely they can look at a circle and a square and see the difference, you may think. But the point is that they cannot do so in the beginning. The brain evidently processes this visual input all in one category. They have to create new categories by learning the differences between shapes.

This learning takes place not just by a teacher's telling the child, "This is a square" or "This is a circle," but more effectively by the child's playing or exploring with all of his senses about what makes one shape a circle or another a square. Seeing pictures of the various shapes is helpful, but it is too abstract as the only method for young children to learn. Youngsters need hands-on activities with three-dimensional materials as well.

Your program should provide the children with many such experiences. Since the children learn these classification skills through the senses, you should give the youngsters all kinds of sensory play opportunities. Play with dough, for instance, allows children to make dough balls, which the youngsters flatten into circles with their hands or roll flat with a rolling pin and cut into circular cookies. Sensory learning involves taste, touch, smell, and sight in this instance. Clay and play dough provide similar experiences.

Block building is an excellent medium for creating squares, rectangles, and triangles. In the beginning, you will need to provide a vocabulary of new terms that apply to the shapes the children are making. Can the children build a triangle, one of the most difficult shapes? Their triangles may be rather rounded in the beginning, because corners are hard for the children to deal with. The brain seems to use the circular shape as the model for its overgeneralizations. Put masking tape on the floor in the shapes of squares, rectangles, and triangles, and let children try to build these shapes with their blocks.

The diagonal line is the last to appear in children's learning. For this reason, triangles and diamonds are very difficult for children to copy. See Chapter 9 on space and Chapter 12 on art skills for further discussion of shapes.

If You Have Not Checked This Item: Some Helpful Ideas

■ **Start with One Shape at a Time**

Children need to focus their attention on one concept before expanding it to include other aspects. The circle is good to begin with because children are used to the roundness or ovalness of the human face. They need to experience examples of all kinds of circles. Let the youngsters find out how many circles they can discover in the classroom. Did they find the wheels on toy vehicles, the casters on the doll bed or office chair, or the mark on the table made by a wet glass?

How long should you concentrate on this shape before including a second shape in their explorations? It depends on your children and their interest. Be sure every child has a chance to have enough sensory involvement with circles so that he or she can internalize it. The internalization may take several weeks, depending on the age and experience of your children. Bring in a collection of things that contains some circular shapes, and let each child try to sort out the circles. Include items such as bottle tops, coasters, jar lids, and rings. Then have the children try sorting blindfolded. Can they sort circles by feel alone? If some children are frightened by having a blindfold tied over their eyes, let them shut or hold a hand over their eyes.

■ Have the Children Make Their Own Circles

Use circle-making activities that involve molding clay, shaping dough, finger painting, cutting out circles, cutting out jack-o-lantern tops, stamping circular shapes on paper, and tracing around circular objects. When the children finally have a strong sense of circleness, introduce the square as the next shape.

■ Read a Book

Wheels Go Round by Yvonne Hooker (New York: Grosset & Dunlap, 1981) is an interesting cardboard book with large colorful pictures of vehicles and their wheels. From steamrollers to go-carts, vehicles with wheels that are cut out appear on every other page of the book, with each set of wheels becoming increasingly smaller. On the page opposite is a four-sentence rhyming description of the vehicle. Children will enjoy feeling the roundness of the cutout wheels and may want to trace the wheels on paper.

Round in a Circle by Yvonne Hooker (New York: Grosset & Dunlap, 1982) follows a similar cardboard book format with squares, circles, and triangles cut out of every other page from things like an artist's easel, a television, a balloon, and a teepee.

Tatum's Favorite Shape by Dorothy Thole (New York: Scholastic Book Services, 1977) is the story of little Tatum, who has trouble in school keeping straight the different shapes until his mother plays a shape-finding game with him at home.

☐ RECOGNIZES COLORS

Another way the brain classifies things is by color. Research shows that infants as young as four to six months of age begin discriminating colors (Richardson et al., p. 123). Children develop color perception shortly after shape recognition, although they seem to talk about colors first. More reference is made to color than shape by adults, and children quickly pick up this fact. Your children may, in fact, be able to name many colors just as they name numbers, without truly knowing what the name means. Just because a child tells you he knows red does not mean that he really does know the color. Ask the child the color of his shirt or her dress. Ask the youngster to find red in the classroom.

Color, like shape, is a type of visual perception the child's brain uses to help classify and sort out the world. Although the child sees colors from the beginning, she now needs to put names to the different ones.

Again, concentrating on a single color at first and then adding other colors is best. Basic colors such as red, yellow, green, and blue, plus black and white, are usually easier for children to recognize at first. However, you must take advantage of seasonal colors as well. Orange should certainly be a part of your classroom during the Halloween season.

Allow children to play with sorting colors as they do with sorting blocks. Give them things like poker chips or golf tees, and let the children see if they can find all the reds. Some children will be able to sort out all of the items by color, but do not expect everyone to be so accurate at first. Let the children experiment with the look and texture of "redness" in all of its shades as they mix red and white paint. Give the children plenty of time to experience one color before you focus on another.

As your group begins its investigation of other colors, you can add colors one by one to the easel. Have color lotto cards, colored plastic blocks, and many other table games featuring colors. Be sure to bring in many different items of the color you are exploring. If you have bilingual children, be sure everyone learns color names in both languages.

Handicapped children can learn color concepts along with all of the other youngsters. Set up your activities so that children with physical and mental disabilities can participate. If you keep concept games in the manipulative area, be sure the shelves are low enough for everyone to reach.

If You Have Not Checked This Item:
Some Helpful Ideas

■ Let the Children Mix Colors

Let children have the fun of mixing colors. Put out squeeze bottles of food coloring, spoons for stirring, and plastic cups or muffin tins full of water. You may want to use only one or two colors at first, or you may want to let children discover how mixing blue and yellow together makes green, since this is such a dramatic change. At another time, use cups of predissolved colors, medicine droppers, and muffin tin cups full of clear water.

There are many different ways for children to play with colors. The youngsters can finger paint with the color you are focusing on. When the children add a new color to their repertory, add the same one to the finger paint table.

■ Cut or Tear Colored Paper

Colored construction paper can be used in many ways. When children have learned two or three colors, let them cut up pieces of construction paper of these three colors for a sorting activity or for making collages. Do not confuse children by combining shape and color activities when they are first learning color concepts.

■ Play Concept Games

Children love to play any game that focuses on them. A game that asks them to identify the color of their clothing makes an excellent transition between activities: "The boy with the blue and white sneakers may go to lunch; the girl with the red and white top may go next; all the children with brown pants may go."

■ Read a Book

Many picture books feature colors. One of the most simple, yet dramatic is Leo Lionni's classic *Little Blue and Little Yellow* (New York: Astor-Honor, 1959), in which a little blue circle and little yellow circle want to play together but are not allowed to by their blue family and yellow family. When the two circles finally do come together, a dramatic change takes place: they, of course, become green. Cornell University Early Childhood Specialist Sue McCord has added a most effective method for demonstrating the blue-yellow change—she reads the story at naptime with the room darkened and two flashlights covered with blue and yellow cellophane playing on the ceiling as the children watch from their cots. The yellow circle and blue circle on the ceiling turn just as green as paint when they finally come together.

Another classic is Margaret Wise Brown's *The Color Kittens*, reissued by Golden Books (New York: Golden Press, 1977), about Brush and Hush, two kitten painters who have all of the colors in the world except green and spend the story trying to find green.

Other favorite books featuring colors include the following:

Carle, Eric. *The Mixed-up Chameleon*. 2d ed. New York: Harper & Row, 1984.

Ehlert, Lois. *Planting a Rainbow*. San Diego: Harcourt Brace Jovanovich, 1988.

Feczko, Kathy. *Umbrella Parade*. Mahwah, NJ: Troll Associates, 1985.

Freeman, Don. *A Rainbow of My Own*. New York: Puffin Books, 1978.

Hoban, Tana. *Is It Red? Is It Yellow? Is It Blue?* New York: Greenwillow Books, 1978.

Kellogg, Steven. *The Mystery of the Flying Orange Pumpkin*. New York: Dial Press, 1980.

———. *The Mystery of the Magic Green Ball*. New York: Dial Press, 1978.

———. *The Mystery of the Missing Red Mitten*. New York: Dial Press, 1974.

Robinson, Deborah. *Anthony's Hat*. New York: Scholastic, 1976.
Stinson, Kathy. *Red Is Best*. Toronto, Canada: Annick Press, 1983.

■ **Create Book Activities**

Besides reading these books to your children, think about other fun activities that can extend the book experience while helping the children learn colors. Deborah Robinson's *Anthony's Hat*, for example, can be played as a game. The book features little Anthony, who gets a beautiful black hat for his birthday. When Anthony wears it outside to show his friends, however, a number of different items drop on the hat and turn it different colors, unbeknownst to Anthony. One child in your classroom can sit in a chair with a hat on and his eyes covered while another child drops a colored cloth or item of clothing over the hat. The first then can guess what color his or her hat is now.

If you purchase paperback books, you can cut up a duplicate copy of *Anthony's Hat*, mount the pictures on cardboard with a sandpaper backing, and let the children use the pictures to retell the story on a flannelboard.

RECOGNIZES DIFFERENCES IN SIZE ☐

As the young child constructs his own knowledge by interacting with the objects and people in his environment, his brain seems to pay special attention to the relationships between things. Size is one of those relationships. Is it big? Is it small? Is it bigger or smaller than something else? The property of size, like the properties of shape and color, is an essential understanding the child needs in order to make sense of his world.

There are various orders of size, usually thought of in terms of opposites: big-little, large-small, tall-short, long-short, wide-narrow, thick-thin, and deep-shallow. Direct comparison of objects based on one of these aspects seems to be the best way for young children to learn size.

Natural Curiosity

The children already should be making sensory explorations of objects in the classroom. Are they? We know that infants are born investigators. They are not only predisposed to explore their surroundings with their senses, but they seem to be driven by some inner urge to try out, get hold of, and get into everything that is within reach. We call this *natural curiosity* when its results are positive. However, we say other less pleasant things about it when infants, toddlers, and preschoolers get into things that they should not touch.

All investigations by children are part of the same natural urge to find out. We should cultivate this drive in children, for it is their principal motivation for learning. Some parents encourage this exploration, but some do not. You can see parental influence—or lack of it—in the behavior of your preschoolers. Some children seem to have retained their natural curiosity; others have not, maybe because their original investigations were stopped by their parents.

Rather than stop such investigations, some parents realize it is better to "child proof" the house by putting dangerous and breakable items away, covering electrical outlets, and blocking off stairs and cupboards. The child can then explore without negative consequences for anyone.

If children, on the other hand, have been constantly scolded, punished physically, or restrained from exploring their environment, many eventually give up. You may have to talk with their parents about how children learn and how to work with the children in trying to reactivate their natural curiosity.

Bring in some new, interesting, but unknown item, and watch to see which of your children try to find out about it. For instance, seal an onion in a box covered with colored wrapping paper and punctured with several holes. Put it on a display table in your classroom with a sign reading: "Guess what's inside!" Then observe and record which of your children are curious enough to try to find out.

They will have to ask what the sign says. You can tell them, but do not give them any other hints. Does anyone shake the box, smell it, or try to see through the holes? Does anyone ask another child or another classroom worker?

Let the children individually tell their guesses to the tape recorder, saying why they think they are correct and giving their names. Later at circle time, you can play the tape, discuss it, and then open the box to see if anyone guessed its contents correctly.

This activity can help you in two ways: first, you can determine who are the curious children and which ones never seem to notice or do not have the courage to make a guess; second, it should motivate your children to do sensory exploration. It may even remotivate those who seem to have lost their natural curiosity.

Repeat this activity every few days for several weeks, and see if it makes a difference in your children's sensory exploring abilities, their guessing abilities, and their interest in new things. In addition, you should take the lead in modeling the behavior you want your children to exhibit. When you yourself come to something new, explore it with your senses and make your own educated guesses. Shapes, colors, and now sizes are some of the properties you and your children should be focusing on.

Comparisons

Comparing one object with another is one of the best ways to investigate the properties of something new or different. This is, in fact, how the brain works. It takes in and evaluates data about the new object on the basis of what the brain has previously processed about a similar object.

When you are first using comparisons with your children and are focusing on the concept of size, be sure to use objects which are alike in all of their properties except size. This is not the time to use differently colored or differently shaped items. Instead, first try using two similar objects, one that is large and one that is small.

Using Opposites

Making a direct comparison of two objects that are similar in every aspect except size is one of the best methods for helping children learn the concept of size. Use things such as two apples (a big and little one), two cups, two blocks, two books, or two dolls. Be sure to talk in positive terms ("This one is big. This one is little"), rather than negative terms ("This one is not big"), which may only confuse the child. Also be sure the children are making comparisons of the two objects themselves and not their position in space. Some children look at two similar objects and say that the closest one is biggest because it looks bigger than a more distant object.

Use the size opposites *big* and *small* in all sorts of comparisons in your classroom before you move on to another aspect of size such as *tall* and *short*. Children's brains seem to overgeneralize with many of the size opposites, equating *big* with *tall*. That may be the reason they believe that a tall thin container of liquid has more in it than a short wide container, although both contain the same amount in Piaget's classic experiment. In other words, *tall* means *big* or *more* to most young children.

Use the words for size opposites whenever you can in the classroom: "Look, Alice has built a tall building, and Bonnie has made a short one," or "Who can find a thick pencil? Who can find a thin one?"

If You Have Not Checked This Item: Some Helpful Ideas

■ Play Size Transition Games

When you are waiting with the children for lunch to be served, for the bus to come, or for something special to happen, it is a good idea to have a repertory of brief transition games, fingerplays, or stories to tell. This time provides an excellent opportunity for concept games such as these: "The girl wearing the skirt with wide stripes may stand up" or "The boy wearing the T-shirt with narrow stripes may stand up." Or play a guessing game with your fingers. Hold your hands behind your back, and ask your children to guess which hand has a big finger held up and which has a little finger held up. Then show them. Can one of your children then be the leader of this game?

■ Read a Book

Some children's books feature size. A favorite one is Steven Kellogg's *Much Bigger than Martin* (New York: Dial Press, 1976), in which Martin's little brother fantasizes about what it would be like to be much bigger than his brother. The illustrations are hilarious.

Fast-Slow High-Low, a Book of Opposites by Peter Spier, (Garden City, NY: Doubleday & Company, 1972) is a wordless picture book with one set of opposites on each double page. The book is illustrated by many pairs of similar but opposite objects or people. The many examples may be confusing to children who are just at the beginning of their understanding of differences, but it is a good book for most kindergarten children. You may want to pick out only certain pages to use at a time: big-small, long-short, deep-shallow, tall-short, or wide-narrow.

☐ RECOGNIZES DIFFERENCES IN MUSICAL TONES

Music for young children—indeed for all of us—is a language. It is a natural means for communicating our feelings and our ideas. This language uses musical sounds (tones) and rhythm (beat) for its expression. In Chapter 5's discussion of large motor moving of feet, clapping of hands, and beating of drums, we considered the rhythm part of music. Here we will consider the sound. Musical tones have several different aspects, including intensity (loud-soft), duration (length-shortness), pitch (high-low), and quality (timbre). For preschool children, the most important aspects of musical tones are loudness-softness and highness-lowness. The concepts of loud-soft and high-low should fit in easily with activities about sizes and opposites that the children are already pursuing.

Young children recognize musical sounds very early in their development. Even infants respond to music by turning their heads in the direction of the sound or clapping their hands to music. If bells or tone-producing mobiles are accessible, infants will hit them again and again to repeat the sound. Toddlers continue this tone-producing activity by hitting toy instruments such as xylophones or by rolling jingling toys across the floor with great gusto. Toddlers will also try to imitate the singing they hear around them by humming or chanting.

Thus, preschool teachers need to include all sorts of musical experiences in the curriculum in order for young children to continue their development of the language of music. Teachers and children should sing songs, chant chants, do musical fingerplays, play records and tapes, play simple instruments, listen to guest instrument-players, and explore sounds and sound making in every way possible. Not only should teachers model an interest in music, but most especially, they should make music fun for children. Teachers can make music a pleasurable experience for both children and themselves if they develop an understanding of what music really is, why it is attractive to human beings, and how its attractiveness can be preserved.

Young children have a tremendous interest in sounds and sound making. They are surrounded with sounds from the very beginning. Their natural curiosity motivates children to explore new sounds to find out what they are. Children do this playfully by imitating the sounds they hear and then by inventing their own sounds. Some of their sounds are pleasant to the ear; some are pure noise. We wonder how they can possibly stand the noise. But we must remember two things: (1) that sounds of all kinds are the raw materials of music and (2) that people like sounds best when they are the sound makers.

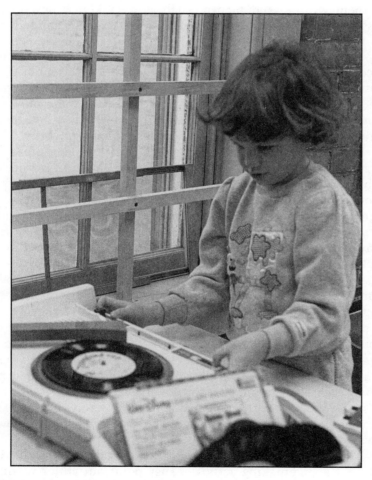

Young children have a tremendous interest in musical sounds and sound making.

Thus, the preschool teacher's role is to provide opportunities and direction in helping young children convert their enthusiastic sound making into music making. For example, set up a sound table in your science corner with various types of sound-making objects from time to time. When you are exploring the concept of loud-soft with the children, have the table set up with shakers (sealed boxes, jars, bandage boxes, margarine cups, and other plastic containers filled with materials that make loud or soft noises when shaken). The materials inside could be pennies, pebbles, beans, rice, paper clips, sand, rock salt, or table salt. Children can try to identify which of the containers makes the loudest noise and which the softest. Then they can shake the containers to the beat of the music that you play.

Another time have a variety of empty glass containers and let children tap them with a "soft tapper" such as a Tinkertoy building stick or paintbrush. A "hard tapper" could be made of metal, but children must tap gently so the glass does not break.

Have children explore only one aspect of sound at a time. When they are concentrating on loud and soft sounds, try to use sounds that are all on the same pitch. Otherwise, children may confuse *loud* with *high*, or *soft* with *low*. Have them beat drums loudly and softly. Let them blow a whistle loudly, then softly. Can they chant a nursery rhyme loudly and then softly? Let them choose whether to sing a favorite song loudly or softly.

Is it fun for the children to perform like this? Pleasure, not perfection, always should be your goal with developing children. Do not force reluctant children to participate. If the activity is interesting enough, they will want to join. These musical sound activities can be done with the total class, a small group, or individuals. We sometimes think that music must be performed with everyone at one time. Instead, let the type of activity determine how many children should be involved. Chanting calls for a group, but sound-makers on a table are for individuals.

When children are thoroughly familiar with the concept of loud and soft musical tones, you can introduce high and low sounds. Your sound table can then display glass containers filled with water of varying amounts. Children can experiment by tapping to find out which glasses sound high and which sound low. Melody and harmony instruments can also be used to demonstrate high and low sounds. Let individuals tap on a xylophone or blow on a tonette or harmonica. (Be sure to wipe clean the mouth instruments after each use to prevent spread of germs.) Montessori materials include "sound tablets" with graduated sounds like a xylophone. The high-instrument players also might stand high (on a chair), while the low-instrument players sit low (on the floor).

These musical concepts involve auditory discrimination. It is possible that your sound-making activities may point out children who do not discriminate loud-soft or high-low because of a possible hearing impairment. If you think that this is the case, arrange with a child's parents for a professional hearing examination.

If You Have Not Checked This Item:
Some Helpful Ideas

■ Listen to Sounds in the Environment

Children can listen for animal sounds and try to determine whether they are loud or soft, high or low. Have them listen to birds, dogs, squirrels, or a guinea pig. Other interesting environmental sounds are car and truck horns, bicycle bells, church bells, squealing brakes, and sirens. Tape-record these sounds, and play them back for later discussion.

■ Play Sound Games

Have children demonstrate with their voices a sound they know, and let other children try to guess what it is. Examples include a buzzing bee, zooming jet plane, racing car, dripping faucet, blowing wind, pouring rain, mooing cow, and growling bear. Another time, have children demonstrate only soft sounds or only high sounds.

■ Do a Whistling Activity

Can anyone in your class whistle? Let them try. Then read them Ezra Jack Keats' classic story, *Whistle for Willie* (New York: Viking Press, 1964), in which Peter learns, after many attempts, to whistle for his dog, Willie. Can you yourself whistle? You will need to when you read this book! Talk about whistles with your children. Listen for factory whistles and train whistles. Tape-record them. Bring in whistles for the children to blow. A familiar type is the referee's whistle. Can anyone's grandfather make a "willow whistle"?

■ Read a Book

Music, Music for Everyone by Vera B. Williams (New York: Greenwillow Books, 1984) is a heartwarming story about four neighborhood girls who played accordion, violin, flute, and drums. Their own enjoyment of music helped them share it with others by forming a neighborhood band. Although the story features children older than preschoolers, the lively action and colorful illustrations will hold the attention of younger children, too.

REPRODUCES MUSICAL TONES WITH VOICE ☐

Young children's first sound maker is their own voice, and they soon recognize its importance in communicating their wants and needs. Because they learn how to use things through playful exploration, infants and young children are soon playing around with the sounds their voices can make. Some of the sounds are crying or laughing; some are speech sounds; and some finally become musical sounds or singing.

Children learn to sing very early if they are around adults who sing. Some mothers sing nursery songs to babies, make up tunes and words as they bathe or dress their youngsters, and sing lullabies when they put their children to bed at night. Preschool and nursery school teachers can continue this beneficial tradition of communicating to children through song. They can sing greeting songs in the morning to individuals or the group; they can sing directions at transition times; they can play concept games with children through songs.

Children who are comfortable with the give and take of "song-versation" between themselves and an adult soon may be answering your song questions with song replies of their own. The traditional fingerplay song "Where Is Thumbkin?" (tune: "Are You Sleeping?") asks the whereabouts of a child's thumb and the other fingers one by one. It is up to the child to answer in song: "Here I am, Here I am."

The voices of toddlers do not have much range. In other words, it is difficult for children from one-and-a-half to two-and-a-half years old to sing very high or very low. Preschoolers, on the other hand, not only have greater vocal range but also the ability to discriminate musical sounds and match them with their own voices. The belief that young children have high singing voices is a myth. Their voices average around middle C to an octave above. Thus, songs for young children should be sung in this middle range.

Many preschool teachers depend upon records and tapes for the music in their programs. Children enjoy almost any kind of music, but they truly show their appreciation for an adult who takes the time and effort to sing with them on her own and who teaches them new songs to sing on their own. After all, it is the music maker who enjoys music the most.

When should you and the children sing in the classroom? Any time! It is better to sing when you are happy, when you are feeling good, or when the children are busy at other activities than during a formal music period. If you wait for a formal period before singing, that period is probably the only time vocal music will be heard in your classroom. On the other hand, if you sing when you feel like it, vocal music may set a happy tone for the whole day, month, and even year!

If You Have Not Checked This Item: Some Helpful Ideas

■ **Make Up a Simple Song for Children to Sing**

If you do not know any new songs, take old traditional tunes, and make up new words. You may know these tunes:

"Row, Row, Row Your Boat"
"Three Blind Mice"
"Here We Go Round the Mulberry Bush"
"Twinkle, Twinkle, Little Star"
"Are You Sleeping?"

"Do You Know the Muffin Man?"
"A Tisket, a Tasket"
"London Bridge"
"Ring Around the Rosy"
"Ten Little Indians"
"Sing a Song of Sixpence"
"This Old Man"
"Mary Had a Little Lamb"

A change in the weather, a happy occasion, or a visitor may inspire you to make up new words to an old tune like "Sing a Song of Sixpence."

> Come with us together,
> We'll all go down the hall;
> Someone's here to see us,
> And he is very tall;
> He has some news to tell us,
> And it's a nice surprise;
> So keep your ears wide opened up,
> And do not close your eyes!

■ Make Comb Harmonicas

Provide combs and squares of wax paper for every child. Have them fold the wax paper over the comb, put the comb between their lips, and hum. Once they have mastered the skill, have them hum a simple tune. They can hum individual songs or all hum together on a song the class knows.

SORTS OBJECTS BY APPEARANCE □

Once they have begun to notice the similar properties of objects, children can begin to group or classify the objects. This ability is necessary in cognitive development in order for the brain to sort out and process the wealth of incoming data obtained through the sensory activities of the child. Sorting objects and materials gives children practice in this skill and involves identifying the similarities of objects as well as understanding their relationships (i.e., which items belong together because of their similarities). The more we learn about young children's development of thinking abilities, the more we realize that thinking is concerned primarily with information processing and retrieval.

Piaget and other researchers have noted that children progress through a sequence of sorting skills and that each skill is more complex than the previous one. The earliest sorting skill to appear is simple classification, which many two- and most three-year-olds can do. Children doing simple classification can sort or group objects that actually belong together in the real world. For example, they can group together all of the toy animals that live on the farm in one set and all of the toy animals that live in the zoo in another set if the youngsters have had the appropriate experiences concerning such animals. This activity is not quite true classification because it is based on associations between the animals and their homes rather than likenesses or differences between the animals.

Another type of simple classification in which young children place things that belong together into a group involves putting all of the toy trucks, cars, and motorcycles together in a group because "you can drive them," putting the proper hats on all of the dolls, or putting all of the blocks together because they make a house.

Less verbal children seem to do as well in simple classification tasks as verbal children (Richardson et al., p. 181). These simple classification tasks do involve real classification skills. In order to perform them, children need to understand the rule for sorting and to follow it with consistency. In addition, the youngsters must discriminate likenesses and differences based on function or some other rule in order to place objects in the correct group. The main difference between this kind of sorting and real classification is that simple classification is based on something other than appearances only, and the groups formed are not true classes.

A more mature type of classification that many three-year-olds and most four- and five-year-olds can do involves classifying objects into separate sets based on a common characteristic like color, for instance. You can ask the children to place all the red blocks in one set and all the blue blocks in another.

The problem most young children have in doing this kind of sorting involves consistency. They have difficulty keeping in mind the rule upon which the sorting is based. They will often start sorting objects on the basis of color but will switch in the middle of the task to some other property, like shape, and will even switch again before they are finished.

Children need to practice with all kinds of sorting games, activities, and collections, and the youngsters love this practice. Give a child a box of mixed buttons, and let the individual sort it out in any way he or she chooses. Talk with the child afterwards, and ask how he or she decided on which buttons to put in each pile. Look around your classroom for other objects to sort, things such as dress-up clothing, blocks, and eating utensils.

By age five, children with experience can sort objects into intersecting sets based on more than one characteristic, using color as well as size, for instance.

If You Have Not Checked This Item: Some Helpful Ideas

■ **Use Block Sorting**

Have children help sort out a certain size of the unit blocks during clean-up time before putting them back on the shelves. This activity will give you an indication of which children can and cannot sort objects based on appearances. Make the activity a game, though, and not a task.

■ Play with Lotto Cards

Make or purchase simple lotto cards that the children can match. You can mount different colored construction paper onto cardboard, cover it with clear contact paper, and cut it into playing card size. Have at least four cards for each color. Mix the cards up, and let the children try to sort them out.

Get several duplicate catalogs from companies such as car dealers, and cut up the catalogs, mounting four similar car pictures on each set of four cards.

■ Make Collection-Sorting Games

Take a shoe box, three empty margarine cups that have a hole cut in the top of them, and a collection of three kinds of seeds. You can use three varieties of beans, three sizes of paper clips, or any other similar collection. Let the child dump the collection into the top of the shoe box and sort it piece by piece into the margarine cups. This activity provides good small motor practice as well.

ARRANGES EVENTS IN SEQUENCE □
FROM FIRST TO LAST

In observing children to determine their cognitive development, we have been concentrating thus far on the classification aspects of what is known as logico-mathematical knowledge. Children display three aspects of this knowledge:

1. *Classification abilities:* The ability to understand particular characteristics or properties of objects and the ability to group things into classes with common properties.
2. *Seriation abilities:* The ability to understand "more than" or "less than" and the ability to arrange things systematically in a sequence or a series based on a particular rule or order.
3. *Number abilities:* The ability to understand the meaning and use of numbers, and the ability to apply them in counting and ordering. (Saunders & Bingham-Newman, p. 120)

The last two checklist items here in Chapter 8 involve seriation abilities in children, while the first two items in Chapter 9 deal with number abilities. All of these aspects are part of a child's *operative knowing,* the system of knowledge she has constructed about her world through the organization of her perceptual experiences.

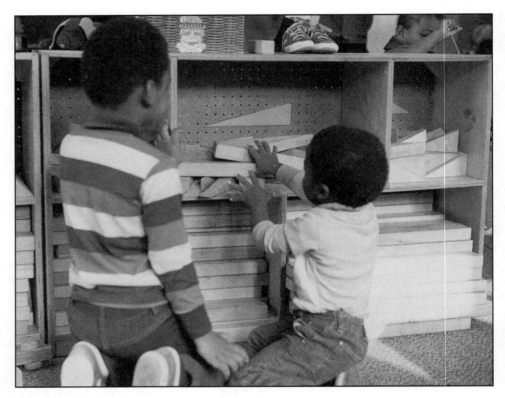

Have children sort out blocks by shape during pickup.

In order to arrange events in a sequence, the child first has to recognize their properties and relationships. How are they alike? How different? What is the common thread that creates their relationship to one another? The child must then understand order, that something comes first, something happens next, and something occurs last. Her practice in sorting things by appearances should help her to note both properties and relationships among events as well.

But just as the young child often changes the rule she is using as she sorts a number of things, she also displays inconsistency in arranging events in a sequence. It is as if the immature mind cannot hold for long the rule upon which the sequencing is based.

Cards with action pictures frequently are used in sequence games. The cards show sequences of an action from beginning to end, with one part of the sequence on each card. For example, one set of cards may have pictures of a pencil lying on a desk, rolling off the desk, falling through the air, hitting the floor, and lying on the floor. Three- and four-year-olds often arrange only the first and last cards correctly. Another card set may show a baseball being thrown, going straight through the air, being hit by a bat, looping through the air, and being caught by a person with a baseball glove.

Such sequence cards really are not appropriate for preschoolers, since games with rules are beyond many of them at their developmental level and since many of the cards depict events that are unclear and difficult even for adults to arrange. Some preschoolers will be able to arrange three easily understood sequence cards in their proper order. Kindergarteners, with their increased maturity, are more successful. When asked to tell about a series of events in the order they occur, many young children can do so correctly if the events are familiar. If the sequence is too long and complicated, however, the best most preschoolers can do is to identify the correct beginning and ending.

Ask your children to relate their favorite stories that you are familiar with. Do the youngsters get the plot sequence in the right order? Ask them to tell you what they would do in a fast food restaurant in order to get something to eat. Did they include all the essential steps?

If You Have Not Checked This Item: Some Helpful Ideas

■ Use an Instant Print Camera

Children learn best from their own actions. Take a series of three photos of a child performing an action: for instance, bringing in a birthday cake, blowing out the candles and eating the cake; or building a block house, standing by the completed house, and knocking it down. Cover the photos with clear contact paper for protection, and put the sets in envelopes for the children to play with. If youngsters understand number sequence, you can number the pictures on the back for the children to check on their accuracy.

■ Use an Illustrated Recipe Chart in Cooking

Use a large chart with each step in the process numbered and illustrated in sequence. You can use drawn outlines of measuring cups and spoons or mount actual three-dimensional plastic utensils (cut in half) on cardboard. Discuss each step with the children as they do it. Ask them which comes next, and then what.

You may discover that some of the preschoolers' problems with sequencing can be explained by their incomplete understanding of a particular process. For instance, children who had completed all of the steps in the recipe chart for making a birthday cake and were ready to put it in the oven were asked, "What should we do next?" Some said, "Eat it," others thought that candles should be put on, but nobody understood that the next step was to bake it!

■ Make Your Own Sequence Cards

Coloring books often show simple drawings of people or animals in a sequence. You can cut out each drawing and mount them separately on cardboard for use in your table games area. Comic books, of course, show pictures in a sequence. If you find any that are simple enough or appropriate for preschoolers, you can also cut and mount sequence pictures from comics in sets. In addition, you can buy duplicate paperback storybooks from which you can cut out and mount sets of three sequence cards from the favorite stories.

■ Make a Pictorial Daily Schedule

Draw or paste pictures to illustrate the time blocks of your daily schedule in the order they occur. Display this pictorial schedule prominently, and discuss it with the children whenever the need arises, using questions such as "What do we do first today?" and "What comes next?"

☐ ARRANGES OBJECTS IN SERIES ACCORDING TO A RULE

The final item involving seriation asks us to observe children to see if they can arrange objects in a series based on a certain rule (e.g., from the biggest to the smallest, from the tallest to the shortest, from the hardest to the softest, or from the loudest to the quietest). Children's previous activities with opposites should prepare them for identifying the extreme differences in objects and events.

Young children are usually able to arrange items in a series if they are provided with cues. Montessori size cylinders, for instance, can be arranged in a board containing a series of graded holes. Children try to fit the cylinders from large to small in the increasingly smaller holes. They match the size of each cylinder with the size of each hole by trying out which cylinders fit or do not fit. Once they have learned the concept, many children are able to line up the cylinders in the proper order without cues from the board.

Stacking blocks, boxes, and rings work on the same principle of arranging items in a series from the largest to the smallest. Even toddlers soon learn that the smallest ring will not go down all the way on the stacking column. They find that they have to put the largest ring on first or one ring will be left over, and they will need to start over again to find their mistake. The point is that children play these learning games on their own and come to discover the concept of sequencing through play.

It is true, though, that three- and four-year-olds have difficulty forming a consistent series from a large number of items when no cues exist, just as they have trouble in sorting out large collections or arranging a large number of action cards into the proper sequence. Although young children are able to compare two items on the basis of size, as soon as several other graded items are added, the youngsters have difficulty arranging the items in the proper order.

Most preschoolers understand the concept of bigger and smaller, but when this concept is applied to a series, the complexity of the many comparisons seems to confuse the youngsters. How can an object that is bigger than one item at the same time be smaller than the item that precedes it?

You may find that you have not checked this particular checklist item for any but the most mature children. This finding is to be expected with three- and four-year-olds. Five-year-olds, on the other hand, usually are more successful. You may decide to add a number of new series games and activities to your manipulative or science/math areas in order to promote this skill. Be sure the new materials provide enough cues for your children to be successful. Most of all, be sure these activities are fun to do.

If You Have Not Checked This Item: Some Helpful Ideas

▪ Arrange Children

Have groups of three children at a time arrange themselves from tallest to shortest. Mix up the children so that the shortest child in one group may not be the shortest in another group.

▪ Read a Book

The traditional classic stories of *Goldilocks and the Three Bears*, *The Three Little Pigs*, and *The Three Billy Goats Gruff* all feature a graduated series of characters, from the smallest to the biggest, along with their graduated series of furniture, cereal bowls, houses, and even noises. Children love these stories and will want to say aloud the repetitious dialog or sounds as you read or tell the stories. The youngsters may want to act out the stories as well.

You can cut out the pictures of the three characters from extra paperback copies of each of these books. Then you can mount the cutouts on sandpaper and use them with your flannelboard activities. Can your children arrange the characters in proper order from smallest to biggest?

OBSERVING, RECORDING, AND INTERPRETING COGNITIVE DEVELOPMENT

In order to include all of the aspects of a child's cognitive development, you will need to observe and record the items from both this chapter and Chapter 9 (number, time, space, and memory) before you design a learning prescription for a particular child.

REFERENCES CITED

Cowan, Philip A. (1978). *Piaget with Feeling: Cognitive, Social and Emotional Dimensions*. New York: Holt, Rinehart and Winston.

Pines, Maya. (September 1979). "Head Start in the Nursery." *Psychology Today,* 13(4), 56–68.

———. (November 1983). "Can A Rock Walk?" *Psychology Today,* 17(11), 46–54.

Richardson, Lloyd I., Kathy L. Goodman, Nancy Noftsinger Hartman, and **Henri C. LePique.** (1980). *A Mathematics Activity Curriculum for Early Childhood and Special Education.* New York: Macmillan Publishing Company.

Saunders, Ruth, and **Ann M. Bingham-Newman.** (1984). *Piagetian Perspective for Preschools: A Thinking Book for Teachers.* Englewood Cliffs, NJ: Prentice-Hall.

Schickedanz, Judith A., David I. Schickedanz, and **Peggy D. Forsythe.** (1982). *Toward Understanding Children.* Boston: Little, Brown, and Company.

OTHER SOURCES

Beaty, Janice J. (1988). *Skills for Preschool Teachers.* Columbus, OH: Merrill Publishing Company.

Bybee, Rodger W., and **Robert B. Sund.** (1982). *Piaget for Educators.* Columbus, OH: Merrill Publishing Company.

Forman, George E., and **David S. Kuschner.** (1983). *The Child's Construction of Knowledge: Piaget for Teaching Children.* Washington, DC: National Association for the Education of Young Children.

Greenberg, Marvin. (1979). *Your Children Need Music.* Englewood Cliffs, NJ: Prentice-Hall.

Moomaw, Sally. (1984). *Discovering Music in Early Childhood.* Boston: Allyn and Bacon.

Osborn, Janie Dyson, and **D. Keith Osborn.** (1983). *Cognition in Early Childhood.* Athens, GA: Education Associates.

Siegler, Robert S. (1986). *Children's Thinking.* Englewood Cliffs, NJ: Prentice-Hall.

LEARNING ACTIVITIES

1. Use section seven of the *Child Skills Checklist* on cognitive development as a screening tool to observe all of the children in your classroom. For which of your children did you check most of the items? How did these children do on other areas of the checklist (e.g., in small motor development)?

2. Choose a child who did not have many checks in the area of cognitive development. Observe him or her on three different days, making a running record to help you get a more detailed picture of the child's cognitive skills. Plan an activity to help this child, and record the results when you use it.

3. What are the ages of the children who had the most checks on the checklist? What are the ages of the children with the fewest checks? What are the children's backgrounds? Can you make any inferences about cognitive development based on this information?

4. Choose a child who needs practice in discriminating likeness and difference, and set up activities for him or her to practice this skill, or play some appropriate games with the child. Record the results.

5. Read one of the children's books from this chapter with a child you have identified as needing help in a particular area. Discuss the results.

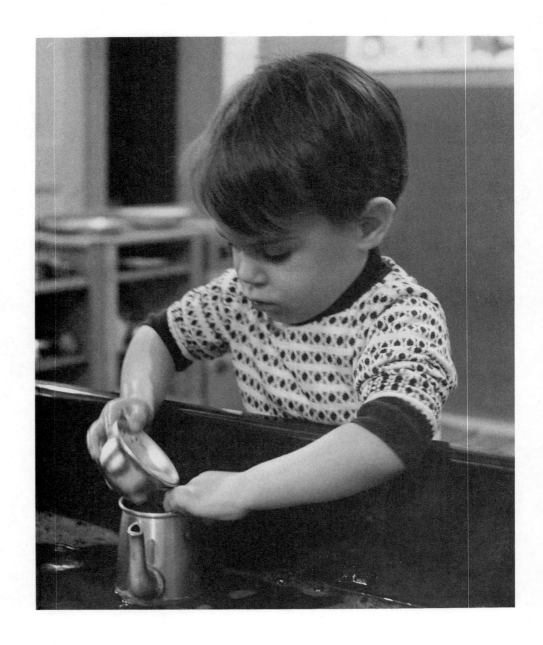

9 Cognitive Development: Number, Time, Space, Memory

Cognitive Development: Number, Time, Space, Memory Checklist

☐ Counts by rote to ten
☐ Counts objects to ten
☐ Knows the daily schedule in sequence
☐ Knows what happened yesterday
☐ Can build a block enclosure
☐ Can locate an object behind or beside something
☐ Recalls words to song, chant
☐ Can recollect and act on directions of a singing game

T his second chapter on children's cognitive development continues the discussion begun in Chapter 8 but deals with several different aspects: children's learning to understand the concepts of number, time, and space, as well as the development of memory. There are two checklist items devoted to each of these aspects. Observers will need to watch and listen to children as they work and play naturally in the classroom, displaying evidence of their cognitive development.

As with all of the checklist items, those in the area of cognitive development are not a test of children's abilities under research conditions, but a listing of behaviors that are possible for children to accomplish in the normal classroom environment. As you interact with the children, watch for these behaviors to be performed spontaneously by individuals. If there is no opportunity to see the behaviors performed, the observer needs to record *N* rather than leaving the item blank.

COUNTS BY ROTE TO TEN ☐

Learning the concept of number is important for young humans to accomplish. They will be dealing most of their lives with the numbers involving size, distance, amount, time, temperature, cost, money, and measurement. As their minds quest to create their own knowledge, the children will be going through a predetermined sequence of development, internalizing the information gained from their sensory interactions with the world around them.

Even two-year-olds display a rudimentary knowledge of numbers when they hold up two fingers to show you their age and count aloud "one, two." This counting is more of a parrot-type response and not a true understanding of "two years." Some two-year-olds and most three- and four-year-olds are able to count by rote to at least ten.

This rote counting does not mean that the children understand the concept of number in the beginning. Often, in fact, children do not get the sequence correct in their counting, or they may even leave out a number or two. These mix-ups and omissions are understandable since the children are performing a memory task, not a concept task. Their counting is really chanting, as in a nursery rhyme. If you ask them, you will find that the children really do not know the meaning of each word. In fact, their chanting of numbers seems more like one long word instead of ten separate ones: "onetwothreefourfivesixseveneightnineten."

This type of counting is due in part to the children's limited language experience. In order to understand the meaning of each number word, the child must form a mental image of it. You cannot expect this mental image formation in two-year-olds. By age three, some children will have formed mental images of certain numbers because of their sensory experience with these numbers in their environment. It is therefore important for parents and other adults to use numbers frequently in the children's everyday living and to involve children in the use of numbers with activities such as measuring, weighing, counting out items, counting out money, and playing games involving the counting of moves.

With infants and toddlers, the chanting of numbers and the singing of number rhymes such as "one, two, buckle my shoe" are an important prelude to the understanding of number concepts. But before children of any age can be expected to know the meaning of each number, they must first accomplish several of the developmental skills discussed in Chapter 8, which are dependent on both maturity and practice.

The children will need to be able to place objects in a series and to understand that the objects are more or less than one another. The youngsters will need to know the answers to questions such as "how many?" Of course, they will also need to know the names of the numbers. Some of these skills are just beginning in the preschool classroom, but many children will not fully grasp the concepts of seriation and number much before the age of seven, or second grade (Cowan, p. 181).

For children who can count to ten rapidly but have no real understanding of numbers or of what counting really means, try having them count to seven or to nine. The children will have to slow down and think about what they are doing. They may not be able to stop at a number other than ten at first. Play games with individuals or small groups, asking each to count to a number other than ten that you will call out. Make such games exciting. Children who have not learned to count will soon be picking up this skill in order to play the game.

If You Have Not Checked This Item: Some Helpful Ideas

▪ Play Number Chanting Games

Say or sing chants such as "One little, two little, three little Indians," using fingers or even children who jump up, sit down, or perform some other action.

▪ Chant Backwards

Use number chants in all sorts of ways. Children love to count down 10–9–8–7–6–5–4–3–2–1–0 before the missile or space shuttle blasts off. Have them make models in their woodworking area or with clay, or ask them to bring in toy space ships.

▪ Read a Book

1, 2, 3 to the Zoo by Eric Carle (New York: Philomel Books, 1968) is a wordless picture book with a number symbol on each double spread page and a large colorful illustration of animals in a train car on the way to the zoo. Although the numbers show one-to-one correspondence with the animals, the book is principally a counting book because there are no words.

Moja Means One: Swahili Counting Book by Muriel and Tom Feelings (New York: Dial Press, 1971) gives the numbers from one through ten in regular number symbols, but with the number name in the Swahili language on each double page. One sentence of text describes the African scene or custom portrayed. Children enjoy learning new names for things.

Ten, Nine, Eight by Molly Bang (New York: Greenwillow Books, 1983) is a simple counting book showing a little black girl and her father as they count down the objects in her bedroom before she goes to sleep.

COUNTS OBJECTS TO TEN ☐

Three-, four-, and five-year-olds can master simple one-to-one correspondence, which is what we are asking them to do when they count objects. Learning that a number stands for an object is their next step in the sequence of learning number concepts. At first, youngsters try to rush through their counting chant without actually including all of the objects. The children are more concerned with saying all of the numbers than with making sure each number represents an object. When the youngsters finally understand the concept behind the task, they will learn to do it accurately.

Start with fewer items than ten in the beginning, just as you did with number chanting. Then the children will learn to stop before they get to ten. Also have the children touch each item as they count. If they skip one, have them try again. Or have them hand you an item as they count it.

Learning to do sorting, as discussed in Chapter 8, is good preparation for counting things. Putting a cup with a saucer or a hat on a doll helps them understand one-to-one correspondence. Now they must apply their learning to numbers. They learn by their sensory actions that the number *one* represents the first object, that *two* represents the second, and so on. This learning is a first step. Nevertheless, counting in a progression is still not the same as understanding one-to-one correspondence.

Children may be able to count a row of ten children and still may not be able to choose four of them. Once they are able to count up to ten objects in a progression, the youngsters will need practice in picking out a particular number of items, such as three dolls, five blocks, or seven dominoes. Phrase your questions or directions to give the children practice with both activities. "How many red markers are there?" asks them to count in a progression. "Bring me eight napkins" takes them one step further in their development of number concepts.

Recording Numbers

To support your children's number activities, you must record their counting. You should not use number symbols at first, but instead use familiar pictures or shapes to represent the numbers. For example, keep an attendance chart with all of the children's names, and mark a symbol for each child present. Then the children can count the symbols. Put signs in each activity area with a particular number of stick figures to represent the number of children allowed in the area at once. Have a certain number of hooks on the wall and name tags to hang on them in each area. Check from time to time with the children in the area, having them count how many participants are there and whether this is the proper number.

Use charts and bar graphs at appropriate times to record numbers. Hang a calendar chart near the guinea pig's cage, and record the number of carrots he eats every day by pasting or drawing carrot symbols. Record how tall each child's seeds grow every week by posting a chart with the child's name and having him or her measure the height with a ruler. The child can count and record the height after his or her name each week. Or use a bar graph that can be colored in up to the height the plant has grown.

Later in the year when the children have shown that they understand one-to-one correspondence, you may want to use real number symbols along with the picture symbols. Numbers alone are often too abstract for many of the children at the beginning of the year.

If You Have Not Checked This Item: Some Helpful Ideas

■ Have Children Count One Another

Any activity is more meaningful to a young child if it involves him and his peers directly. Have children help you take attendance in the morning by going around and counting how many children are present. Have the counters touch each child. Give the counters help if they need it with numbers above ten.

■ Have Many Counting Materials

Fill your manipulative or science/math area with counting materials or games. Use egg cartons for children to fill the sections with items and count how many there are. Use buttons, seeds, dominoes, spools, paper clips, and macaroni as items to fill the sections.

■ Read a Book

One Bright Monday Morning by Arline and Joseph Baum (New York: Knopf Pantheon, 1962) is a cumulative counting book of the objects seen by children on the way to school on each day of the week.

One Snail and Me by Emilie Warren McLeod (Boston: Little, Brown, and Company, 1961) is a hilarious cumulative counting book with each page showing another odd menagerie of animals that a little girl has with her in the bathtub. Humorous illustrations and rollicking rhymes help children to count groups of animals from one to ten.

Bunches and Bunches of Bunnies by Louise Mathews (New York: Scholastic, 1978) shows several sets of rabbits on one page, the total number on the next page, and a rhyming text that multiplies the sets to get the total number. Although the multiplication is certainly inappropriate for young children, they can ignore it (or learn from it if they can) and still have fun counting the groups of bunnies in comical antics.

■ Have Children Set the Table

Let the children set the table for meals and snacks. They will need a set number of eating utensils, plates, cups, and napkins for each table. This real task is an especially useful activity for teaching one-to-one correspondence.

KNOWS THE DAILY SCHEDULE IN SEQUENCE □

Understanding Time

Time is the next cognitive concept we need to look for in young children. Three-, four-, and five-year-olds are only at the beginning of their temporal understanding. We need to provide them with simple activities involving time, but we cannot expect them to develop a mature understanding of so abstract a concept during the preschool years and kindergarten.

Time comprehension has a number of different aspects: (1) the ability to understand what comes *before* and what comes *after*; (2) the ability to describe past events; (3) the ability to anticipate and plan for future events; (4) the ability to describe the order or sequence of things; (5) the ability to understand the passage of time and how it is measured (with clocks, calendars); and (6) the understanding of units of time (seconds, minutes, hours, days, weeks, months, years, and centuries).

The child's ability to arrange things in a sequence or series based on a particular rule or order was discussed in Chapter 8 under seriation abilities. This knowledge that events may occur in a particular order with something happening first, something next, and something last generally precedes a child's understanding of time intervals.

Because young children are still egocentric, looking at everything exclusively from their own point of view, they do not perceive time as adults do. To young children, time occurs because they are there. For example, "snack time" and "nap time" do not happen unless they participate. They learn to understand the movement of the hands on the clock only very superficially, that two hands pointing straight up means lunch time. Calendars likewise have little meaning for young children, although they can repeat the names of the days of the week.

Time is a very abstract concept. It is not something you can see. Even adults realize that the passage of time seems uneven in different circumstances. If we are occupied, time goes quickly; if we are bored, time seems to drag. For young children, the present moment is the most important. Children's comprehension of past and future is limited to periods of time not too distant from the present.

Time is one of the basic organizing dimensions of the child's experience (Cowan, p. 126), and as such, time needs to be considered an important part of the child's cognitive development. Although the young child will not develop a mature perception of time while in your classroom, you need to be aware of each child's present development in this area in order to provide activities and support for its continued growth.

Using the Daily Schedule

Since children learn best from things and events that involve them directly, using the daily schedule to help them understand the concept of time is a good place to begin. First of all, you must have a daily schedule that is clear and consistent. The activity periods can be of various lengths so long as they follow one another in the same order daily. A brief transition activity between each period helps children to understand that the next period is about to begin.

A full-day's program might consist of

A.M.	P.M.
Arrival	Nap time
Morning circle	Free choice
Free choice	Snack
Snack	Afternoon circle
Outdoor play	Departure
Toilet	
Story	
Lunch	

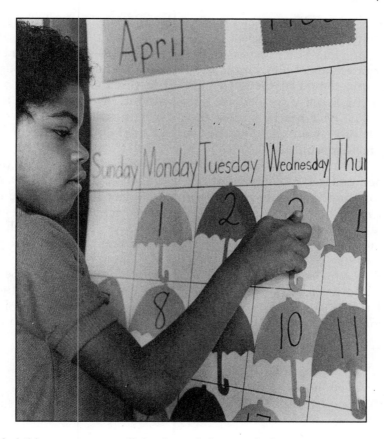

Preschool children can count off the days of the month, but a
true understanding of time comes later.

If you follow this same schedule consistently day after day, children not only feel secure about what will happen, but they also come to an
understanding about the sequence of things. The ability to represent mentally and to remember the order of events is essential in the young child's
development of the concept of time. Even if your morning free choice period
varies in length from day to day, the children will still know that it comes
after morning circle and is followed by snack time.

The morning circle time is essential in bringing about awareness
of this sequence, in helping children to make choices and to plan for future
activities, and in giving them an awareness of time in general. The checklist
observer should attend the morning circle in order to hear which children
give appropriate answers to the teachers' questions about the activities to
follow and which children do not seem to understand time intervals.

Although many teachers do calendar activities at this time as well,
they need to be aware of children's superficial understanding of calendars

and clocks. We really cannot expect children to understand these abstract concepts much before age seven.

But four-year-olds are aware of established sequences and become upset if things are not done in the regular order. If one of your periods is to be omitted, this should be made clear at circle time. On the other hand, the length of the activity periods can vary without anyone seeming to notice. Teachers who have had to shorten their day by several hours report that the children hardly notice the difference so long as the activities follow one another in regular sequence.

Giving children advance notice that a period is coming to a close is another method for helping them to understand the passage of time. "Five more minutes before cleanup time" may not have the same meaning for young children as it does for adults—since children still do not completely understand "minutes"—but youngsters do know that this signal means the free choice period is almost over and that they must soon help to clean up.

Having some kind of transition between each activity period also helps a child to order the day mentally. When everyone has finally arrived and it is time for morning circle, you could give a transition signal by playing a chord or song on the piano, or singing a transition song such as

Good morning to you, Come sit in our group,
Good morning to you, Come sit in our group,
Good morning everybody, Good morning everybody,
Good morning to you. Come sit in our group.
(Tune: "Happy Birthday")

When circle time is finished, you could play a concept game as a transition to send the children to their activities: "All the children with red on may go to their activity area." Free choice period usually ends with cleanup. When children are finished with that, they go to the snack table on their own. The transition from snack to outdoor play could be a song that will send them to get their outdoor clothes on.

We're waiting to go out, We're waiting to go out,
We're waiting to go out, We're waiting to go out,
Jill and Joe and Rodney too, All the girls at table one,
Get ready to go out. Get ready to go out.
(Tune: "The Farmer in the Dell")

When they come in from outdoor play, the youngsters already know that they go to the bathroom and wash their hands after hanging up their coats. From the bathroom, they generally go over to the library corner where one of the teachers will be waiting with a book to read. The transition activity to lunch could involve something from the story you have just read.

Harry, the Dirty Dog is looking for a hungry boy or girl to go to the lunch table. Everyone, close your eyes and wait for Harry to tap you on the head.

Activities such as these help the children to establish a meaningful order to the day. This order is more than an explanation in words, for the children must interact with their environment in order to construct mentally the concept of daily time sequences.

An afternoon circle time is important to help the children internalize these activities and to help you realize their understanding of the things they have been doing. Now is the time to discuss what the children liked best about the day. Ask things like "What did you make today that you can tell us about?" or "What did you choose to do during free choice in the morning?" Just as the morning circle asked them to look at the daily schedule and make plans for the future, so the afternoon circle asks them to look back at the past and think about what they have accomplished. Checklist observers need to be present at this group meeting as well in order to determine who really understands the daily schedule and can remember past events.

If You Have Not Checked This Item: Some Helpful Ideas

▪ Play a Time Game

Since children learn best by doing/playing and especially by doing something that involves themselves, you might play a time game with them that involves children pretending to be your various activity periods. For instance, you could have one child represent each of the morning periods: arrival, morning circle, free choice, snack, outdoor play, story time, and lunch. Put a sign on each child. The sign could have both words and a symbol: a handshake for arrival, a circle for morning circle, blocks for free choice, a glass of juice for snack, a swing for outdoor play, a book for story time, and a plate for lunch. Then let the children try to arrange themselves in the order they occur. To get the children started, ask them, "Which child should come first? Which one next?" Do the same for afternoon activities.

▪ Make a Pictorial Daily Schedule

Draw or paste pictures to illustrate the time blocks of your daily schedule in the sequence they occur. Display this pictorial schedule prominently, and discuss it with the children.

▪ Play Before and After Games

Make up brief transition questions that you ask the children while they are waiting for something else to happen; for example, you could ask them,

"Does lunch come before nap or after nap?" or "Does snack come before out-door play or after outdoor play?" Have them make up similar questions of their own.

■ Read a Book

Going Shopping by Sarah Garland (New York: Viking Penguin, 1986) shows a mother, baby, girl, and dog getting into the family car, driving to the super-market, shopping for groceries, checking out the groceries, getting back into the car, driving home, and getting out of the car with the bags of groceries. After reading the story, see which of your children can reconstruct the se-quence of events.

The following stories take place in a nursery school and show chil-dren engaged in a sequence of activities. After reading the books, you could discuss the order of the activities and how they compare with the activities in the children's own school.

Cohen, Miriam. *Best Friends.* New York: Collier Books, 1971.
———. *Will I Have a Friend?* New York: Collier Books, 1967.
Rockwell, Harlow. *My Nursery School.* New York: Greenwillow
Books, 1976; Puffin Books, 1984.

☐ KNOWS WHAT HAPPENED YESTERDAY

One of the problems young children must face in learning time concepts is recognizing the fact that while they are involved in a present event, the memory of the preceding events has already disappeared. Thus, the past may exist for a young child only vaguely. We all know that as we mature recollec-tions of the distant past fade away and are stored in the recesses of the brain, not to appear again unless tapped by something like hypnosis or jogged into life by some trigger event. For young children, memories of even the recent past may slip away unless they learn to be aware of them.

Just as all development is interrelated, so the formation of the cog-nitive concept of time is dependent for young children on the development of both language and memory. Children first of all need to understand the vocabulary of time words: before, after, during, next, today, yesterday, tomor-row, next time, while, and soon. This understanding does not occur over-night. Psychologist Margaret Donaldson, in fact, believes that "we have tended both to underestimate children's competence as thinkers and to over-estimate their understanding of language" (Donaldson, p. 60).

Recent studies are showing that while children seem astonishingly adept at making original spontaneous utterances, the youngsters' under-standing of what is said to them is not always that clear. The first words they learn, in fact, are naming words or nouns, then action words or verbs. Prepo-sitions and adverbs that show place, order, and time are much farther down the scale of words young children understand or use. It takes much longer for these seemingly less important words to become a part of the young child's vocabulary.

For children to conceptualize the past, they must first learn what *before, after, yesterday,* and *tomorrow* mean. Children learn these terms as they learn everything: through actual experiences. Your circle-time discussions will help the children to focus on the good experiences they had the day before and the good things they can look forward to tomorrow. As such concepts become meaningful to the children, they will incorporate these time terms into their vocabularies as well.

Although most of their distant past already may be gone, they will be able to bring to mind the recent past if it is focused on as a part of their life in your center. In addition, memory and recall (to be discussed later in this chapter) play a part in their ability to "know what happened yesterday."

If You Have Not Checked This Item:
Some Helpful Ideas

▪ Play "Yesterday-Today-Tomorrow" Games

Afternoon circle time is a good time to play games that involve events that happened yesterday, today, or will happen tomorrow. Make three signs, one for each of these days, with a stick figure of a person with hands on hips representing *today,* with hand pointing backward (left) representing *yesterday,* and with hand pointing forward (right) representing *tomorrow.* Then ask the children questions about activities that actually happened: "Which day did we get new fish?" or "Which day was Bobbie's birthday?" or "On which day will we go to visit the farm?" Let children hold up the proper sign when they guess the correct day.

▪ Read a Book

One Bright Monday Morning by Arlene and Joseph Baum (New York: Knopf Pantheon, 1962) is a counting book using the days of the week. As you read it, you can stop after each page and ask the children, "What happened yesterday?"

The Mysterious Tadpole by Steven Kellogg (New York: Dial Press, 1977) is a story involving days and the calendar as everyone waits for the mysterious tadpole to turn into a frog. Stop and talk about time sequences, what happened yesterday, and what might happen tomorrow as you read this story.

CAN BUILD A BLOCK ENCLOSURE ☐

Understanding Space

Space, like time, is another of the basic organizing dimensions of the young child's experience. Like the other basic dimensions, it has several aspects:

(1) enclosure, (2) position of things, (3) closeness of things, (4) distance between things, (5) location of things, (6) order of things, and (7) shapes and sizes, including body parts and body in space. The concept of space answers the question "where?" about things and is one of the three dimensions, along with number and time, that eventually merge to make up the basis for logical thought (Osborn & Osborn, p. 115).

Also like time, space is an abstract concept that young children cannot represent mentally until they experience enclosure. As with the other knowledge they create, the idea of space comes from their sensory exploration of things. Children see objects and perceive objects as being close to or far away from other things.

But in the beginning, the infant's only experience with space involves the nearness of objects. When the object is out of sight, it is literally out of mind for her until she develops so-called *object permanence* at about age eight months. Before that time, she will not continue to search for an object that is out of her range of vision or one that has been hidden. She acts as though the object she cannot see is no longer there, as if it has disappeared completely or no longer exists.

With experience and maturity, she comes to understand that objects in her environment are still there even though out of her sight. Yet even with object permanence, most young children cannot perceive objects from any point of view other than their own. Nor can children imagine how an object will look if its position in their space is changed.

Because space is not perceived readily by a youngster unless it is enclosed, checklist observers are asked first to look for this aspect of space perception in assessing a child's cognitive development in this dimension.

Using Block Building

One of the most effective activities for developing cognitive concepts about space involves playing with "unit blocks," those deceptively simple and plain wooden units, half units, double units, quadruple units, cylinders, curves, triangles, ramps, pillars, floorboards, and switches that were invented before World War I by Carolyn Pratt for use by her children in the experimental City and Country School in New York City (Winsor, p. 3).

Unit blocks are found today in almost every nursery school and in many kindergartens throughout the country. Children learn to sort and categorize during cleanup by putting the blocks back on the shelves having the correct cut out block shape. The block-building corner is a favorite area for children's play during free choice period. The youngsters build houses, farms, towers, hospitals, and anything else their imaginations can invent. Adults rarely think of block building as a primary activity for children to develop such an abstract cognitive concept as space.

Adults often have trouble thinking this way because they often have trouble keeping in mind how children learn: (1) by constructing their own knowledge through sensory interactions with things in their environment, and (2) through free play with such materials. Abstract concepts can come to life in children's minds when such versatile yet defined playthings as unit blocks represent these concepts.

Harriet Johnson, another pioneer early childhood specialist who worked with Carolyn Pratt and later founded the nursery school that became the demonstration school for the Bank Street College of Education, spent years observing children's use of building blocks. She eventually published her findings in the 1933 classic study, "The Art of Block Building" (Johnson, pp. 9–24). She found that children go through predictable stages in learning to use blocks, based on their maturity and experience, when they are given the freedom to use blocks naturally without adult interference. Sound familiar? Her observational data give strong support to much current research on child development.

Her block-building stages serve us well today in our observation of children's cognitive development. What better way to determine if children understand spatial concepts and relationships than by watching how the youngsters use unit blocks? If the first understanding that children can grasp about space comes only when they can enclose it, their block creations offer a fine way to witness whether they have mastered this concept.

The children Johnson worked with ranged from two to six years in age and varied in their experience with blocks. She found that the older children with no experience still progressed through the same stages as the younger ones, but with greater speed. An amended version of her stages includes

1. Carrying, filling, dumping
2. Stacking and lining
3. Bridging
4. Enclosures
5. Patterns
6. Representation

Two-year-olds or older children with no block-building experience begin by massing the blocks together, carrying them around, filling up containers (or toy trucks) with them, and dumping them out—over and over—but not building. This manipulative action is typical of the novice child's approach to most new activities: getting the feel of the blocks, the heft of them, the way you can move them around, but not using them for their purpose (which he has not figured out yet), then repeating the activity again and again. It is a pattern the child will use throughout his natural development of block-building skills if he is given the freedom to proceed on his own.

Somewhere between the ages of two and three, real building begins. The first real building stage is either stacking blocks up into a tower or lining them up in a row. Some children do one activity first; some do the other. Some combine the tower and the row. Some learn to straighten their blocks neatly so that their towers will not fall. Others pay little attention to either vertical or horizontal alignment. When they have mastered this first attempt, they tend to repeat it again and again before moving on to the next stage (Johnson, pp. 11–12).

Eventually, the children are faced with the problem of bridging, or using a horizontal block to span the space between two parallel vertical blocks. If the youngsters are working without the help of a teacher or peers (and they should be), it may take a great deal of time to resolve this building problem. The children's concepts of size and distance are still somewhat hazy at this age, and they often make many trials and errors before they can get the right size block. The other solution to the bridging problem, of course, is to move the two upright blocks closer together so that the horizontal bridging block will fit. Some children discover one solution but never the other.

Even when peers at higher levels are building nearby, the novice builder usually does not try to copy their methods. Block building, like art, is a very personal and satisfying expression of a child's individual creativity. What someone else is doing matters very little. For that reason, teachers should let children build on their own. The youngsters will learn cognitive concepts only by struggling with building problems and finding solutions on their own. Once children have learned to bridge, they can incorporate this skill into their own personal building styles over and over.

Next comes enclosures, for many children, although some master the problem of enclosing or encircling a floor space horizontally with block walls or fences before they learn to bridge.

Adults find it difficult to understand why children have trouble making an enclosure. A child will start out correctly by making two walls to enclose the corral for her toy horse, but she will somehow be unable to turn the corner for the third wall, and thus the wall goes on and on. She seems to know what she wants to do but is unable to do it. It is frustrating indeed, something like an adult standing before the bathroom mirror and trying to cut her own hair! The child needs your support—but not your help—in arriving at her own solution and achieving her own understanding of space and how to manipulate the objects in it.

Many three- and even four-year-olds make incomplete enclosures for a long time before they perceive how to close the gap. Their enclosures tend to have some rounded corners, as well, for children still have difficulty at this age either constructing or drawing a square (see Chapter 8 on geometric shapes). But once they have mastered the problem of completing an enclosure, they incorporate this too into their block-building repertory.

A few children begin naming their enclosures when they start to build, but most youngsters do this after they have finished the enclosures. It may be a "garage for my car," a "house for my doll," or a "house for the guinea pig." These buildings may not have been in their minds as they started to build, but they know that adults and peers want them to name things, so these names sound reasonable.

Whether the name is reasonable depends upon whether the toy car, doll, or guinea pig fits into the building. You will have an additional opportunity to observe the children's conception of space and size when you see whether the object fits its enclosure. Often it does not. Children sometimes try to force a toy car into a block building without seeming to realize that the object is too big and will not fit. Why can't children see that it does not fit, we wonder? Their mental structures still have gaps, still overgeneralize, still are not refined enough to handle such details. Children need more practice as well as maturity. Playing with blocks on their own will help to correct these deficiencies.

With skill in towers, rows, bridging, and enclosures, children are ready to build in patterns—decorative, repetitive, often geometric—building either horizontally or vertically and incorporating the entire repertory of building they have developed over the years. Four- and five-year-olds use the same building styles they began with at ages two and three, but in a more sophisticated and complex manner. If you thought that block building is simple children's play, you know now that it is neither simple nor play as adults know it. Perhaps you will want to record with an instant print camera the children's stages of building over the year or two they are with you.

The final stage, as with art, is representative building. Children start by building a structure and then giving it a name such as school, playground, house, store, or fire station. Eventually they learn to name the building first and then build it according to their own inner design. Most early efforts at representation do not look much like the building they name. But practiced builders eventually are able to represent a wide range of structures. The play of these practiced builders now becomes less solitary or parallel and more of a group effort, as discussed in Chapter 4. Once children have mastered the skill of building with unit blocks, they are usually ready to contribute to another child's building or invite other children to help them. At this point, they often want their structures to remain standing at the end of the period in order to play with them later. You may have to enlarge your block-building area if you have many such skilled builders.

Keep magazine pictures of houses, stores, bridges, roads, barns, and office buildings mounted in your block-building area at the child's eye level when seated on the floor. Where can you mount pictures when block shelves are in the way? Pull the shelves away from the walls and use them as room dividers for your building area. Then pictures can be mounted on the walls. Take photos of completed buildings and their creators, and mount the photos attractively in the same area to motivate further building.

If You Have Not Checked This Item: Some Helpful Ideas

■ Have a Special Building Day

If boys tend to dominate the block-building area, try having a special building day for girls only. Is this idea too sexist for you? If so, try having a special building day for all the children wearing red (or blue or sneakers or some other distinctive feature). If one child never seems to build, perhaps you could choose the feature from that child's clothing to help him or her get interested.

■ Build Things Seen on a Field Trip

Take your instant print camera along on your next field trip, and take photos of structures that children might want to represent in blocks when they return to the center: highways, bridges, towers, office buildings, stores, barns, and houses. Mount the pictures in the block area, and watch what happens.

■ Supply Pictures to Motivate Building

Make photocopies of illustrations from a book that features buildings, and mount the copies in the block area to motivate building. The children will not copy the buildings pictured as adults see them, but from their own inner view of what buildings in the pictures should look like.

■ Read a Book

The Trip by Ezra Jack Keats (New York: Scholastic Book Services, 1978) shows the inner city boy Louie taking a fantasy trip through the towers of mid-Manhattan.

Anno's Counting Book by Mitsumasa Anno (New York: Philomel Books, 1982) shows an interesting house with cutaway rooms and windows with people appearing and disappearing. It may be too difficult for preschoolers to use for counting, but perhaps it could motivate their building.

Nothing Ever Happens on My Block by Ellen Raskin (New York: Scholastic Book Services, 1966) shows a little boy sitting on the curb in front of a block of houses in which all kinds of wild things are happening, but he does not notice all the excitement because his back is turned.

If your children like these stories, those who can may want to try building the structures.

☐ CAN LOCATE AN OBJECT BEHIND OR BESIDE SOMETHING

The second checklist item that demonstrates your children's understanding of space asks whether they can locate an object that is behind or beside something. To respond accurately, they need to have constructed mental images of the position of things, the closeness of things, the distance between things, as well as the meaning of the spatial prepositions being used. This checklist item provides an especially good example of the interrelatedness of child development.

Children must have developed physically enough to be able to make sensory explorations of the objects in the environment. Youngsters need the mental maturity to convert this perceptual knowledge into cognitive concepts. Children need the language development and experience to put words to these concepts. Preschoolers and kindergarteners are only at the beginning of such a synthesis, but your program is in an excellent position to help them create this knowledge.

Here are some of the prepositions children need to know in order to understand spatial relationships:

behind	by the side of	down	above	in
back of	next to	under	up	inside
beside	in front of	underneath	up above	into
alongside	between	below	on	out
at the side of	in between	over	on top of	outside
				out of

It must be an overwhelming chore for youngsters to make sense of so many seemingly "unimportant" words. As mentioned earlier, children first learn nouns, or naming words. These nouns are much easier to learn because children hear them over and over in the abbreviated sentences used around them when they are first learning to speak. Nouns can be seen, touched, and experienced in many ways. Next come verbs, the action words. These words too are used frequently in children's presence to describe what is happening to the noun.

Prepositions, however, are much more abstract. They do not represent a thing, but a location, which means that children must first learn the concept of location in space by experiencing the concept. Then the youngsters pick up a few of the location words, but the children's understanding of these words during the preschool years is still limited and incomplete. One of the difficulties may be that these words are so much alike. *Behind* and *beside* even sound alike. Children tend to learn one or two words for the same location, but they do not realize that there are still other words with the same meaning. For instance, *under, underneath,* and *below* can all mean the same thing. Most young children have trouble with such synonyms.

An interesting study of preschool children's understanding of the words *on, next to, in, underneath, behind, over, outside of, below, between, in front of, above, beside, inside, under,* and *out of* was carried out by Holzman and her students in the form of a game. Each child was asked to put the Cookie Monster doll in a certain location involving a small red box inside a large one-shelved blue box. Twenty percent of the children made errors on the words *underneath, below, over,* and *under* (Holzman, p. 120).

The concepts of *inside* and *outside* evolve from the child's understanding of enclosure or surrounding. Observe to find out how many of your children who can make an enclosure can also understand the location of *beside*. What about the other children?

Because a child's awareness of space and location grows out of his awareness of his own body in space, he will need to move physically around

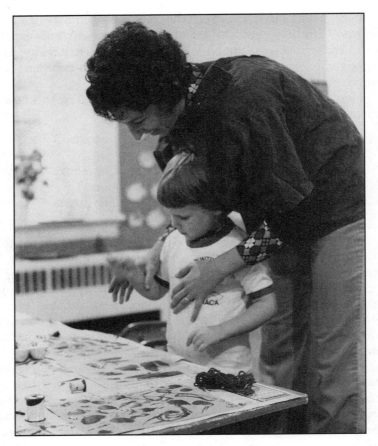

Preschool children demonstrate an understanding of space if
they can locate an object behind or beside something.

your classroom in order to determine the locations of *behind* and *beside*.
The child's perceptual awareness of space develops more rapidly than the
more abstract concepts involving space. But if the child has many meaningful sensory experiences with space in your classroom, his mental construction of spatial location will eventually be created.

If You Have Not Checked This Item:
Some Helpful Ideas

■ Play Location Games

"Where is the fish?" is a cumulative game that children enjoy. Play it during
circle time by asking the children "Where is the fish?" Have one child go to
the location of the fish (or whatever), point to it, and respond, "The fish is in
the fishbowl." Then ask, "Where is the fishbowl?" Another child must go to

the fishbowl, touch it, and say, "The fishbowl is on the table" (or wherever). This can continue as long as there is interest. Be sure the children answer in sentences containing a location preposition.

Unlike the concept of enclosure, which children learn best on their own, youngsters need more help understanding location prepositions. You should take the lead in games and questions.

■ **Read a Book**

Use books to help children understand location words through locate-the-animal activities.

Find the Cat by Elaine Livermore (Boston: Houghton Mifflin, 1973) should be used with one or two children at a time, since they must look closely at complex line drawings in order to find the cat. After the children have put a finger on the cat, ask them to tell you in words where it is located. This is a good whole-part game as well, for some of the pictures show only the cat's tail or head.

But Where Is the Green Parrot? by Thomas and Wanda Lacharias (New York: Delacorte Press, 1968) can be used in the same way. In this book, the reader is challenged to find the green parrot hidden on pages with a brightly colored train, house, toy chest, garden, and circus.

One Snail and Me by Emilie Warren McLeod (Boston: Little, Brown, and Company, 1961) is another book full of humorous animal antics. Children can be asked things like "Where are the turtles?" (The turtles are on the rim of the tub, not in it.) "Where is the duck?" (Sometimes the duck is in the water, but other times it is on the girl's head, on the whale's back, or on top of another duck.)

RECALLS WORDS TO SONG, CHANT □

Developing Memory

Memory, the last of the cognitive abilities to be discussed, is an integration of all of the others. It is the process of storing information in the brain for future use and of retrieving that information later. Memory depends not only upon the child's development of classification and seriation abilities, as well as number, time, and space concepts, but memory also rests upon the child's previous experiences. The more a child experiences, the richer his memory banks become.

Children and adults do not necessarily remember things in a pure form, so to speak, but instead experiences are enriched by being built upon. In other words, every experience a person has changes every previous experience by building on it. For this reason, it is essential for children to participate in numerous activities of every possible variety in your program.

The most basic experiences in the beginning, as we have reiterated, are perceptual: the sensory experiences of seeing, hearing, feeling, tasting, and smelling. The richness of perceptual learning will determine the meaningfulness of future experiences. According to Spitzer, "the most important single determinant of what we remember is the meaningfulness of the information" (Spitzer, p. 64). This statement may be one of the most important ones you will read in this text. Think about how this statement might affect what you do in your program.

If information must be meaningful to the child in order to be remembered, we need to provide all kinds of activities the child will participate in because he or she finds them interesting, enjoyable, exciting, worthwhile, or fun. Then we must give the child the freedom to explore the activity on his or her own. The activities must be experiences the child chooses because he or she wants to try them and not because he or she is directed to them by an adult. It is no wonder that children have made spontaneous play their particular process for learning, and it is no wonder children have difficulty remembering information that has little meaning for them or is dull or boring.

Why haven't adults made play the basis for their own learning throughout life? It is because the basis for learning shifts during the early elementary years from perceptual experiencing to language. As language facility increases, verbal functions take over the role of the senses and become the principal basis for learning. We should not forget, though, that the meaningfulness of verbal information is still the most important determinant of our ability to remember.

Due to the cumulative effect of past experiences—that is, even verbal experiences have to be built on the child's earlier perceptual experience—it is the child with the richest perceptual experiences who can develop the richest language and verbal memory.

Developing Recognition and Recall

Memory has three different aspects: recognition, recall (both discussed here), and recollection (discussed under the next checklist item). Recognition is the most basic of the three processes. It is the simple knowing that an object has been met with previously. The infant uses this form of memory to make sense of his world. As he experiences his environment over and over again, he begins to recognize its forms and ingredients. By about eight months of age, his recognition of objects has developed to the point that he knows they exist even when he cannot see them. The more experiences he has, the more material his memory has to build on in the future. Recognition seems to be the primary mechanism for remembering until about age two (Spitzer, p. 65).

At about age two, recall comes into play more and more. This is the memory process by which pieces of information are retrieved from the memory banks of the brain for use by the child. Recall is more abstract than recognition; recall does not depend upon an outside object, person, or event to trigger memory. Children who show understanding of the time concepts of past and future have the ability to recall this information. Until this process has developed, youngsters really cannot remember much of the past and have difficulty anticipating the future.

Recall is necessary in order for the child to learn language. Many of his early attempts involve imitating the words of others, which he files in his memory and then recalls at the appropriate time in his speaking.

Recalling Songs and Chants

Observers using the *Child Skills Checklist* are asked to listen to whether children in your program recall the words to a song or a chant. Singing and chanting are excellent methods for practicing recall abilities. Such activities give children perceptual memory cues, making an appropriate bridge between sensory and language learning. For example, songs and chants are rhythmic. Children can tap their toes, clap their hands, or beat out a rhythm while they sing in unison or listen to a record. Songs and chants are also usually in rhyme, a good memory cue for later recall of words. Chants are usually done to finger plays or body actions. Thus sensory experiences provide memory cues for later recall of words.

Children as young as one to two years old may begin to chant using nonsense syllables. These children are usually unable to sing accurately at this age, but they enjoy musical sounds, especially the human voice. Between ages two and three, children often chant or sing to themselves at play—often in a monotone—and try to keep time to the beat of music they hear. By age three, youngsters can sing simple songs, play simple singing games like "Ring Around the Rosy," and move to the beat. Four- and five-year-olds have improved all around if they have had practice (Greenberg, pp. 23–26). They still may not pronounce all the words of the songs accurately, but what does it matter? Singing is for enjoyment, not perfection, during the early childhood years.

To teach your children songs and chants, you need to repeat them over and over again with the children every day. Sing morning greeting songs; transition songs; finger plays at circle time; singing games in the large motor area; songs for the seasonal holidays of Halloween and Thanksgiving; songs for rainy days, sunny days, and snowy days; songs about animals; and especially, songs and chants about the children themselves. Use nursery rhyme favorites of your own, and make up words to familiar tunes using the children's names whenever possible. Soon you will create an interested group of young singers. Records are fine for occasional use, but give your children a special cognitive memory boost by helping them learn their own words to songs and chants.

You do not need to be a good singer yourself. The children will never know the difference. If you cannot sing, chant with the children in unison or in a monotone. Research shows that children who have experienced nursery rhymes in the preschool years have fewer problems learning to read in later years than those who have not encountered nursery rhymes.

If You Have Not Checked This Item: Some Helpful Ideas

▪ Use Children's Names in Songs

Make up words to a familiar tune using children's names; for example,

> Where is Bridget?
> Where is Bridget?
> Here she is!
> Here she is!
> How are you this morning?
> How are you this morning?
> Nice to know,
> Nice to know. (Tune: "Are You Sleeping?")

Some other tunes you can use are the following:

> "Here We Go Round the Mulberry Bush"
> "Lazy Mary, Will You Get Up"
> "Row, Row, Row Your Boat"
> "Sing a Song of Sixpence"
> "This Old Man"
> "Three Blind Mice"
> "Twinkle, Twinkle, Little Star"

▪ Read a Book

Several good children's books may motivate your children to sing.

Lizard's Song by George Shannon (New York: Greenwillow Books, 1981) is about a lizard who sings a simple song about his home. His friend, a bear, tries to remember the song but keeps forgetting. The music is included, so the children can learn to sing the song and not forget.

The Banza by Diane Wolkstein (New York: Dial Press, 1981) is a Haitian folktale about a little goat with a banjo who sings a song that protects her from ten fat tigers. The children will soon be singing this song, as well, and may want to make their own banjos.

▪ Do Finger Plays

There are also several excellent finger play books you may want to use.

Finger Frolics by Liz Cromwell and Dixie Hibner (Livonia, MI: Partner Press, 1976) contains the words and actions to dozens of finger plays for seasons, holidays, animals, community helpers, and transportation.

Eye Winker, Tom Tinker, Chin Chopper by Tom Glazer (Garden City, NY: Doubleday & Company, 1973) contains fifty musical finger plays with piano arrangements and guitar chords.

CAN RECOLLECT AND ACT ON ☐
DIRECTIONS OF A SINGING GAME

Understanding Recollection

Recollection is the most advanced of the three aspects of memory. It is an information-retrieval process in which the brain groups or selects particular information and recalls it for use by the child. It includes recognition and recall but takes them a step further. The child's mind must not only recognize things and recall information, but it must also group information in a meaningful way for use.

To be successful at recollection, the child first must be able to locate things and events in space and time. Researchers involved with programming computers and creating artificial intelligence are very much concerned with information processing and retrieval. These researchers talk in terms of short-term memory, long-term memory, and attention. Short-term memory is the storage of information that is received visually or auditorily by the brain. If the information is understood and useful, it goes into long-term memory for storage. In order to receive any information at all, the person must attend. Attention refers to the sensory data that a person selects to process from all of the available incoming information (Schickedanz, Schickedanz, & Forsythe, p. 389).

Developing Attention

A young child has only limited attention. During the early years, the child seems able to see only one aspect of objects or situations at a time. Therefore, the child's thinking skills lack the full range of information necessary to provide understanding for many events. Her long-term memory, which is called upon when she must recollect and act upon the directions of a singing game, is not capable of holding as much information as a mature mind. You may not be able to check this item for all of your children. Many are only at the beginning of this mature memory process. You will need to provide many experiences for children to use their memories by following directions.

In order to follow even simple directions, children must first listen to and attend to the directions given. Sound games are good attention-getting activities to begin with. Children must listen to and understand the directions of the game; then they must use their auditory perception to accomplish the game successfully. For example, teachers can drop two different objects, one at a time, after children cover their eyes. The children are then asked to compare the sounds of the objects. First drop objects that sound completely different (e.g., a pen and a penny). Can the children tell the difference? Then drop two objects that are alike. Do the children recognize similar sounds? Next play different rhythm instruments. Can the children tell what they are? Can the children tell when you play the same instrument over again?

Singing games ask for the children to listen carefully to the words of the song and then follow the actions called for. Many singing games are on records. Some of these are concept games, such as "This Is a Song About Colors," in which each child represents a particular color. The song asks each color to stand up or sit down at various times. The teacher should play the record first, so the children can hear the directions before acting them out. After repeating this singing game many times, children will be able to recollect the directions well enough to sing and act out the song without the record.

Traditional singing games are nursery rhymes that are sung without records and acted out by the group. Familiar examples include

"Here We Go Round the Mulberry Bush"
"Do the Hokey Pokey"
"Go in and out the Windows"
"London Bridge Is Falling Down"
"The Farmer in the Dell"
"A Tisket, a Tasket"
"Ring Around the Rosy"
"The Grand Old Duke of York"
"Here We Go Looby Loo"
"This Is the Way We Go to School"
"Bluebird, Bluebird on My Shoulder"
"Where, Oh, Where Is Sweet Little Susy?"
"Pass the Shoe from Me to You"
"Skip to My Lou"

Children learn to recollect the directions by repeating the games over and over. Some children do not understand the words, but merely follow the other children around. Imitation like this is another effective learning method for young children.

Children can follow the prescribed motions in these games or make up their own motions. Most preschoolers, for instance, will not be able to skip in "Skip to My Lou." Let them make their own movements instead.

If You Have Not Checked This Item: Some Helpful Ideas

■ Make Up a Singing Game

Have the children make up new words to a singing game they already know and then act it out. For instance, instead of "The Farmer in the Dell," they could sing "The Keeper in the Zoo" and then act out the zoo animals that the keeper takes.

■ **Use a Music Book**

Music: A Way of Life for the Young Child by Kathleen M. Bayless and Marjorie E. Ramsey (Columbus, OH: Merrill Publishing Company, 1987) contains not only words and music to many singing games, but also chapters on music for children by age groups.

OBSERVING, RECORDING, AND INTERPRETING COGNITIVE DEVELOPMENT

Checklist results on cognitive development for Sheila, the girl who was recorded in the beginning chapters, are as follows:

Cognitive Development:
Classification and Seriation Checklist

✔ Recognizes basic geometric shapes
   Evidence: Can draw circles, squares, triangles
✔ Recognizes colors
   Evidence: Can name all the colors she uses
✔ Recognizes differences in size
   Evidence: Plays size matching games with ease
✔ Recognizes differences in musical tones
   Evidence: Can play simple tunes on xylophone
✔ Reproduces musical tones with voice
   Evidence: Sings songs with accuracy
___ Sorts objects by appearance
   Evidence: Does not play sorting games
✔ Arranges events in sequence from first to last
   Evidence: Can follow a cooking chart
✔ Arranges objects in series according to a rule
   Evidence: Arranges dolls from biggest to smallest

Cognitive Development:
Number, Time, Space, Memory Checklist

✔ Counts by rote to ten
   Evidence: Counts to 20 and beyond
✔ Counts objects to ten
   Evidence: Counts all children in class
✔ Knows daily schedule in sequence
   Evidence: Is first to note when next activity should start
✔ Knows what happened yesterday
   Evidence: Often talks about events from yesterday

_____ Can build a block enclosure
Evidence: Never plays with blocks
__N___ Can locate an object behind or beside something
__✔___ Recalls words to song, chant
Evidence: Knows many songs
_____ Can recollect and act on directions of singing game
Evidence: Does not participate in group games yet

When the classroom staff reviewed Sheila's entire checklist, they were not surprised to see her results on the two cognitive development sections. Sheila seemed to the staff to be a bright child with exceptional language and art skills, but she seemed to have difficulty in gaining access to the group. She preferred to play by herself, although often parallel to others. In fact, one of the staff members predicted that every one of the items for Sheila under cognitive development would be checked. The prediction was almost correct: only three items were unchecked. The staff member miscalculated on those items because Sheila does not play with sorting games nor blocks, and because she still does not participate in group activities. The items on sorting games and blocks are indicative of certain skills that all the staff felt Sheila was able to accomplish. They were probably correct. She did not play with blocks or do sorting games because of a personal preference and not because she could not do them.

Thus, it is important for staff members to look at the total picture when they observe and record a child's development, and in addition, to talk together about the results. Not every child will accomplish every item even though he or she could probably do it. All of us have personal preferences, even preschool children.

REFERENCES CITED

Cowan, Philip A. (1978). *Piaget with Feeling.* New York: Holt, Rinehart and Winston.

Donaldson, Margaret. (March 1979). "The Mismatch Between School and Children's Minds." *Human Nature.*

Greenberg, Marvin. (1979). *Your Children Need Music.* Englewood Cliffs, NJ: Prentice-Hall.

Holzman, Mathilda. (1983). *The Language of Children.* Englewood Cliffs, NJ: Prentice-Hall.

Johnson, Harriet M. (1974). "The Art of Block Building." In *The Block Book*, edited by Elisabeth S. Hirsch, pp. 9–24. Washington, DC: National Association for the Education of Young Children.

Osborn, Janie Dyson, and **D. Keith Osborn.** (1983). *Cognition in Early Childhood.* Athens, GA: Education Associates.

Schickedanz, Judith A., David I. Schickedanz, and **Peggy D. Forsythe.** (1982). *Toward Understanding Children.* Boston: Little, Brown, and Company.

Spitzer, Dean R. (1977). *Concept Formation and Learning in Early Childhood.* Columbus, OH: Merrill Publishing Company.

Winsor, Charlotte B. (1974). "Blocks as a Material for Learning Through Play— The Contribution of Caroline Pratt." In *The Block Book,* edited by Elisabeth S. Hirsch, pp. 1–8. Washington, DC: National Association for the Education of Young Children.

OTHER SOURCES

Bayless, Kathleen M., and **Marjorie E. Ramsey.** (1987). *Music: A Way of Life for the Young Child.* Columbus, OH: Merrill Publishing Company.

Beaty, Janice J. (1988). *Skills for Preschool Teachers.* Columbus, OH: Merrill Publishing Company.

Donaldson, Margaret. (1978). *Children's Minds.* New York: W. W. Norton & Company.

Kamii, Constance Kazuko. (1985). *Young Children Reinvent Arithmetic.* New York: Teachers College Press.

Moomaw, Sally. (1984). *Discovering Music in Early Childhood.* Boston: Allyn and Bacon.

Provenzo, Eugene F., Jr., and **Arlene Brett.** (1983). *The Complete Block Book.* Syracuse, NY: Syracuse University Press.

Schultz, Karen A., Ron P. Colarusso, and **Virginia W. Strawderman.** (1989). *Mathematics for Every Young Child.* Columbus, OH: Merrill Publishing Company.

LEARNING ACTIVITIES

1. Use section eight of the *Child Skills Checklist* as a screening tool to observe all of the children in your classroom for cognitive development in the areas of number, time, space, and memory. For which of your children did you check most of the items? How do these children fare on other areas of the checklist?

2. Make a graphic rating scale for block building, and observe all of your children in this area. How do the results compare with the checklist results for the eighth section? Can you draw any conclusions from this?

3. Try to find out how many of the children whom you have checked on the item "can build a block enclosure" can also locate an object that is beside something.

4. Play a singing game that your children already know, and record which children can recollect the actions.

5. Use one of the activities suggested under each item in this chapter with a child who needs help in cognitive development, and record the results.

10 Spoken Language

Spoken Language Checklist

- ☐ Speaks confidently in the classroom
- ☐ Speaks clearly enough for adults to understand
- ☐ Speaks in expanded sentences
- ☐ Takes part in conversations with other children
- ☐ Asks questions with proper word order
- ☐ Makes "no" responses with proper word order
- ☐ Uses past tense verbs correctly
- ☐ Plays with rhyming words

S poken language is one of the important skills that make us human beings. We assume, without much thought, that our children will learn to speak the native tongue before they enter public school. Language acquisition cannot be all that difficult, we reason; otherwise, how could a little child do it? After all, the child does not have to be taught; language acquisition just seems to happen. It is nothing to get excited about, we think, unless it does not happen on schedule.

As a matter of fact, the acquisition of a native language is one of the greatest developmental accomplishments and mysteries we may ever encounter involving the young child. It is a great accomplishment because the child starts from scratch with no spoken language at birth and acquires an entire native tongue by age six; sometimes the child acquires even more than one language if he is in a bilingual family. The acquisition of this complex skill is a great mystery because we are still not exactly sure how it takes place.

True, we may not show concern while all goes well, but we should learn all we can about the kinds of things that help or hinder the acquisition process in order to smooth the way. The years from age two to five are especially crucial in this process, when the child's vocabulary suddenly expands from 250 words to 2,000 words, and he learns the rules of putting words together properly to speak in complex sentences. During these years, the child is often in an early childhood program; thus, the language environment you provide can have a significant effect on his progress.

In order to support your children's language development, you must know at the outset how accomplished they already are as speakers. Using an observation screening device such as the eight spoken-language checklist items to assess each of your children at the beginning of the year is a good way to start. Then follow up with written or tape-recorded language samples of each child.

☐ SPEAKS CONFIDENTLY IN THE CLASSROOM

The first checklist item actually refers more to the child's emotional adjustment to the classroom than to his or her speaking abilities. A child must feel at ease in the strangeness of the classroom environment and among her peers in order to speak at all. The so-called nonverbal child is frequently one who lacks confidence to speak outside the confines of the home. The child may have a shy nature or may come from a family that uses little verbal communication. The child also, of course, may have a physical disability, such as a hearing impairment, that has interfered with language development.

Spend time assessing this child using the entire *Child Skills Checklist*. The areas of self-identity, emotional development, and social play are especially important. Does the child have trouble separating from her parents when she comes to the center? Can she do things for herself with any confidence? Does she seem happy? Does she play by herself or with others?

Set up a meeting with her parents, and discuss the checklist results with them. If the results point toward some type of disability, the parents will want to have the child tested further by a specialist. If the parents indicate that the child talks fluently at home, the nonverbal child in your classroom may be demonstrating her feelings of insecurity in a strange new environment.

Your principal task with the shy or uncommunicative child will be to help her feel comfortable in the classroom. Using pressure to get her to talk before she is at ease may well produce the opposite results. You and your co-workers will need to take special pains to accept the child as she is and to try to make her welcome in the classroom. You can invite her to join appropriate activities, but if she refuses, you need to honor her reluctance. It often takes a great deal of patience and forbearance on the part of an early childhood classroom staff to allow the shy child to become at ease in her own good time.

If the nonverbal child seems to feel comfortable with another child, you may be able to have that child involve her with the others. On the other hand, sometimes the only solution is to leave the nonverbal child alone. If your environment is a warm and happy one, she eventually should want to participate.

The environment must be free from stress. For many children, speaking in a group of peers is a new and untried experience. To help them feel at ease about speaking, you need to help them feel at ease about themselves by accepting them as they are. Show you accept them with smiles, hugs, and words of welcome and praise. Show you are happy to see them every day and want them to participate.

A child must feel at ease in the classroom in order to speak
with confidence.

In addition, you need to accept their language, no matter how
poorly pronounced or how ungrammatical it is. Language is a very personal
thing. It reflects not only the child's stage of development, but also his family's life style. You must be especially careful not to correct a child's language. Telling him he is saying a word wrong or using the wrong word is a
personal put-down. He will learn the correct form himself when the time is
right by hearing you pronounce the word correctly and by practicing it with
his peers.

A stress-free environment means that your classroom is free from
stressful situations for the young child. He should not be put on the spot and
forced to perform verbally, creatively, or in any other way. Offer him opportunities and encouragement, but do not force the shy or unsure child to speak.

If You Have Not Checked This Item:
Some Helpful Ideas

■ **Use a Prop for Security**

Many young children feel more secure when they have something in their
hands, especially something soft and cuddly with the quality of a security
blanket. You might want to keep several stuffed animals for children to

choose from and hold when feeling out of sorts. They are also helpful when children first come to the classroom and do not yet feel comfortable. Your nonverbal child may even end up talking to her animal. It may be the beginning of her verbal integration into the classroom.

▪ Use a Puppet

Almost every child likes the idea of putting a puppet on his hand. Have a box of various kinds of puppets, and let the shy child choose a different one every day if he wants. Preschool children tend to play with puppets as if the puppets are a part of themselves rather than a separate toy like a doll. Because puppets have mouths, children often first experiment by trying to bite someone with the puppet, in fun, of course. Later, the youngsters get the idea of having the puppet speak, perhaps in a whisper or in a different tone from their own voice. Shy children are often more willing to have a puppet speak for them than they are to speak for themselves. You might find yourself able to talk with a shy child's puppet through a puppet you put on your own hand.

Puppets can be played with alone, but they often lead naturally to involvement with other children. Thus, puppets are an excellent transition material to help the shy child integrate himself painlessly into the activities of the classroom. An excellent resource in this area is *The Magic of Puppetry: A Guide for Those Working with Young Children* by Peggy Davison Jenkins (Englewood Cliffs, NJ: Prentice-Hall, 1980).

▪ Read a Book

Louie by Ezra Jack Keats (New York: Scholastic Book Services, 1975) tells the story of inner city boy Louie, who has never been heard to speak a word. When he attends a neighborhood puppet show, he becomes entranced with the doll puppet Gussie, and he says his first word, "Hello."

Maria Teresa by Mary Atkinson (Chapel Hill, NC: Lollipop Power, 1979) is about an unhappy little Hispanic girl who moves from her home in New Mexico to a new school where no one can even pronounce her name. She solves her problem by making a sheep puppet that speaks only Spanish and sharing him with the class at show and tell. This book is somewhat advanced for preschoolers, but bilingual classes and kindergarteners should enjoy hearing the Spanish spoken by the puppet.

☐ SPEAKS CLEARLY ENOUGH FOR ADULTS TO UNDERSTAND

The pronunciation of the language, or articulation, may be another speech area of concern to the teacher of young children. When children first begin to speak, they try to imitate the speech sounds of those around them, but with limited success. As they listen and practice, their vocal organs become more adept at making the sounds of English consonants, vowels, and blends. At first, children may use only ten basic sounds: nine consonants and a single vowel. By the time they are completely mature speakers—usually by age seven—the children will have mastered forty to forty-four separate sounds (Eisenson, p. 75).

Most children with normal speech and hearing abilities are able by age four to produce most of these sounds. A few letters or blends such as *s, l, r, th,* and *sk* still give many children problems. Usually children substitute an easy sound for one they cannot pronounce: for example, "*pwease*" for "*please.*" By age seven or eight, even these difficulties have disappeared in most children, and the youngsters are able to articulate like mature adults. In fact, some children—more likely girls—may produce mature speech by age five.

Nevertheless, language development, like the other aspects of growth, is highly individualized. Some children normally will be more advanced than others. Others are normally slow developers. One study showed that about 10 percent of three-year-olds were slow language developers, but most of these outgrew their problems within a year (Caplan & Caplan, p. 40).

Articulation, the way children pronounce words, is difficult for the lay person to evaluate. While mispronouncing words is a common speech disorder, articulation problems with preschoolers tend to be developmental lags rather than disorders. Something may seem to be a disorder to you because you cannot understand the child, but the condition may be merely a delay in the child's normal development.

If you have doubts, call on a specialist to evaluate the child. All aspects of the child's speaking—not just his articulation—should be taken into account.

In the meantime, you and your co-workers will need to serve as good language models for the child, helping and supporting him in classroom activities, but taking care not to correct his speech. Modern linguists now realize that it is pointless for adults to try to correct a preschooler's speech by making him repeat words according to an adult standard that he is not yet ready to use. Correcting, in fact, is a negative response that tends to reinforce the unwanted behavior and makes the child feel there is something wrong with him personally. Instead of improving a child's language, correcting often makes the child avoid speaking at all in the presence of the corrector.

If the other children in your classroom can understand the child speaker, you should be encouraged. It often takes longer for an adult with set speech patterns to become used to a child's speech idiosyncrasies. Listen carefully, and try to pick up what meaning you can without embarrassing the inarticulate child by making him repeat everything over and over.

Occasionally a child who has been pronouncing words normally will slip back into a kind of baby talk. He or she may also display other similar signs such as thumb sucking and wetting. Since this tends to be an indication of an emotional upset, you will want to talk with the parents about the pressures in the child's life that may be affecting him or her adversely, causing the temporary regression. Is there a new baby in the family? A new family member? A death or divorce? Someone in the hospital? A move? Young children feel these emotional upheavals in their families as severely as adults. Sometimes slipping back to earlier speech patterns is the first indication of such stress on a child.

However, because they are in a group of other child speakers, most young children will quickly pick up or revert back to the speech patterns and word pronunciations they hear around them. Their brains are programmed to do such copying at this stage of their lives. Even non-English-speaking children will soon join the mainstream of language with continued exposure to mainstream speakers. The common mispronunciations of preschoolers should be overlooked. As soon as the development of their vocal apparatus allows them to, they will be pronouncing English words just like everyone else.

If You Have Not Checked This Item: Some Helpful Ideas

▪ Do Not Make a Fuss

Making a fuss about children's mispronunciation may cause more problems than it solves. As previously pointed out, a person's speech is highly personal. If the child is made aware that he or she is doing something wrong, the child may stop trying altogether. In the case of children who are going through a period of disequilibrium in their development and begin to stutter, calling attention to their problem tends to make it worse. Have patience and faith. Once through a stressful period, most children will continue their language development normally.

▪ Help the Child to Feel Accepted

Children want to talk like the others around them. Their pronunciation trouble may already make them feel out of place. You will need to show by your actions and words that you accept the child as she is, that you are happy to have her in the class, and that you will support and encourage her in all of her endeavors. Accepting the non-English-speaking child is just as important. Children from bilingual families may not speak English as the dominant language at home. Nevertheless, preschool-age children have the ability to learn English quickly when they are surrounded by English speakers. Your acceptance of both the way they speak their native language and the way they pronounce English is an important first step toward their success in learning English as a second language.

■ Help the Child Succeed at Something Else

All children need to experience success at this stage of their development. If they are having trouble speaking clearly, help them to be successful in something else. Perhaps they can finger paint or model with clay or play dough. Such art activities are also therapeutic for children under stress.

■ Try Singing

Sometimes children who have trouble saying words will be able to sing words. Do not single out such children, but include them with the others in your singing activities. Give verbal praise to your children for their singing, just as you do their block building. They will be happy you liked what they did, and they may be more inclined to want to do it again another day.

SPEAKS IN EXPANDED SENTENCES □

Young children ages three, four, and five are just at the stage when their speaking develops most rapidly. From the simple two-word sentences they uttered before age two, they are now suddenly able to expand the subjects and predicates of their sentences into longer, more complex thoughts. While their early communications included gestures—"Want more," they might have said while pointing at the milk bottle—they now speak in complete and expanded sentences, such as "I want some more milk," with no necessity for gestures.

How did this expanded language come about? Linguists are searching for answers by audiotaping infants' utterances, videotaping their interactions with their caregivers, and comparing infants' development with deaf children, children from other cultures, and children from a variety of backgrounds.

We know that soon after an infant walks, he talks. We also know that all human infants are predisposed to acquire their native language. Their brains are programmed to sort and store the information that will later be used in producing speech. Human infants give their attention to human voices, listening and then responding at first in babbles but as soon as possible in word sounds. Then, sometime between a year-and-a-half and two years of age, the infants realize that everything has a name. Immediately their vocabulary starts expanding as they begin to absorb the words for everything they see and touch.

This is the crucial time for meaningful caregiver intervention. The parent or caregiver can name objects and actions. The children will listen and try to imitate. The caregivers will listen to the children and respond; all of this interaction takes place in the natural give-and-take manner of parents playing with their children.

This is also the crucial time for an enriched physical environment and the child's freedom to explore it. Just as children must learn names for things, the youngsters also need to see, feel, hear, and try them out. The children will want to see the doggie, pet the doggie, and laugh at the doggie's funny antics with a rubber bone. Young children learn words by interacting with the things that are represented by words in their environment. The more things the child interacts with, the more words the child will have the occasion to learn, we might say, as long as support, encouragement, and good language models are also at hand.

Young children do not learn word meanings by having someone teach the meanings, but rather youngsters infer the meanings on the basis of hearing the words used in life experiences (Holzman, p. 65). Children hear a word being used and watch carefully what is going on while it is used. Their first words are names (like *mama, daddy, doggie, ball, bottle,* and *bed*) or other common words they hear (such as *byebye, no-no,* and *drink*).

At first, these words are used only in one way to mean one thing, but soon the infant discovers he can call, direct, demand, point out, play with, and ask things by the way he intones the word. "Ball" comes to mean "Here is the ball," "Where is the ball?" and "Get me the ball." By this time, he is putting two words together to make primitive sentences. "Mama ball" may mean "Mama get me the ball," "Mama see the ball," or "Mama find the ball." He is beginning to learn the rules for producing sentences. In the meantime, we would hope that Mama is responding not only by giving him the ball but by repeating the child's sentence back to him, just a bit expanded: "Oh, the ball. Here's the ball. Mama's got ball. See the ball? Baby want ball?"

Children seemed to be predisposed to learn language this way. Linguists find it surprising that adults and older children also seemed predisposed to teach children language this way. Observers watching mother-infant interactions soon picked up this behavior. The language behavior of the infant seemed to elicit the particular language behavior from the mother that was most appropriate to the infant's level of development. As the infant's ability improved, the mother's level of response expanded (Holzman, p. 87). Even more surprising is the fact that anyone playing with an infant seems to be able to adapt intuitively to the infant's language level.

Studies with four-year-old boys who had no younger brothers or sisters showed that the boys were able to adjust their language to a two-year-old with good language ability and another two-year-old with poorer skills in explaining how a toy worked. The boys listened to the toddlers responses to their own instructions and made adjustments intuitively (Holzman, pp. 107–108). This result may well indicate that not only are infants born with the method for acquiring their native language, but also that the speakers around them are endowed with a similar skill for helping them acquire language.

By around age two, children are able to use the proper word order consistently in their primitive sentences. As they suddenly blossom into pretend play at this time, a parallel expansion seems to occur in their language. Their sentences grow longer and more complex, and their vocabularies increase (McCormick & Schiefelbusch, p. 72). Once they have absorbed the basic rules for forming sentences, they are on their way, for they then will be able to produce sentences they have never heard. For most children, this mastery has occurred by age four.

Obviously, it is important for children to be involved with competent speakers of the native language. If youngsters do not hear the language used or do not engage with someone in speaking it during these crucial years, they may have difficulty acquiring it. Language tends to be an activity carried out by the left hemisphere of the brain. The brain is programmed to acquire language during the early years. Recent evidence seems to indicate that if language acquisition has not occurred before puberty (as in cases of extremely deprived children), it is too late for the young person ever to learn it except at a primitive level (Holzman, p. 100).

It is important for you to know which children in your class are speaking in the expanded sentences most three-, four-, and five-year-old children should be able to use. Some children who are not speaking in sentences may be the shy or ill-at-ease children who have the ability but not the confidence to speak in the classroom. Others may come from homes where language is not used so extensively. Still others may have physical or mental impairments and may need to be tested by a specialist. For these and all of your children, you will want to provide rich language opportunities that allow the youngsters to hear sentences spoken and to respond.

If You Have Not Checked This Item: Some Helpful Ideas

▪ Provide Dramatic Play Opportunities

Children's imaginative play is one of the best preschool activities to motivate and promote language growth in young children. Youngsters take on roles in which they must produce dialog. Even the shy, nonverbal child will learn by listening to the others. Be sure to schedule enough time for children to become involved in this pretending type of play. Take a role yourself in order to help the shy child join the others. But once he is involved, you should withdraw.

▪ Go on Field Trips

Children need many real experiences with their world in order to process and use information in thinking and speaking. Give the youngsters many new things to think and talk about by going on field trips. These out-of-class experiences do not have to be elaborate or to distant locations. Have one adult take three children down to the corner store to buy something. Take a small group on a walk around the block to see how many different sounds they can hear. Be sure to take a tape recorder along to record sounds to play back later.

Go on a field trip to a tree every week in the spring or fall to see how it changes. You may want to take along an instant print camera to record the experience and to motivate talk about the changes back in the classroom.

Listen to children's own interests about their world. Have they ever really explored the building they are in? Do they know where the heat is produced? Young children are fascinated by things like furnaces that adults take for granted. Take the children to see such things, and then listen to the sentences they produce.

☐ TAKES PART IN CONVERSATIONS WITH OTHER CHILDREN

If children feel comfortable in your classroom and have mastered the skill of speaking in expanded sentences, they also should be participating in conversations with the other children. As soon as they are able to converse with ease, their speaking ability will show even greater improvement from practice with their peers, some of whom may speak at a bit higher level. Once the basic rules of language are mastered, children improve in speaking most rapidly when in the presence of speakers whose abilities are just a bit higher than their own.

For this reason, it is important to have mixed age groups in preschool programs. The younger children learn language skills from the older ones. The older children have an excellent opportunity to practice their skills with someone a bit younger. As noted previously, even children seem to be able to adapt their language level intuitively to less mature speakers, thus enabling younger children to improve their speech.

Just as the infant is predisposed to acquire his own language in a particular manner, he also seems to bring with him in life a preprogrammed way to learn the rules of conversation. Researchers have noted that infants as young as ten weeks old are beginning to learn behaviors necessary for later conversation (Holzman, p. 3). For instance, in order to converse, speakers must listen to what someone says, speak one at a time, and then pause for the other speaker to have a turn.

Another interesting finding is that mothers seem to treat their baby's gestures, cries, coos, smiles, and babbling as meaningful contributions to a real conversation. An infant's arm may reach out toward her rattle. The mother responds by picking up and giving the rattle to the child, at the same time conducting the following conversation: "Oh, you want your rattle. Here it is. Your rattle." The baby takes the rattle and shakes it. The mother replies, "Yes, your rattle. Your nice rattle." The baby pauses to hear the mother say this, shakes the rattle, and smiles. Then the baby pauses to hear the mother's response: "Oh, you like your rattle. Shake your rattle." The baby shakes the rattle and pauses once more for the mother's response. The mother smiles, nods her head in approval, and says, "Shake, shake, shake." Thus, the rules for conversation are learned long before the child can speak.

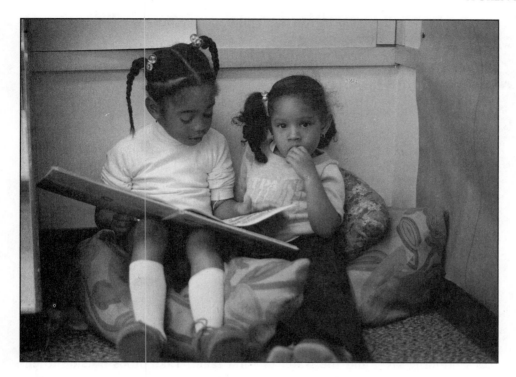

A child's speaking improves most rapidly when in the presence of another child whose speaking ability is just a bit more advanced than her own.

We may wonder who is reinforcing whom? The mother starts the conversation, but the baby listens and replies with her physical response, which makes the mother say the next thing, and so on. It takes two to talk in conservations. Children learn this from infancy, unless there is no one to talk to or no one who will listen. Parents who do not talk to their children during this preverbal period of development make a great mistake. Children need to hear their native language being addressed to them from the moment they are born if they are to be motivated to become fluent speakers themselves.

You have undoubtedly heard that one of the best things caregivers of preschoolers can do is to read to their children. This is true, but an even greater contribution to children's development is to converse with them, to listen and respond to them in conversational speech. Because many mothers intuitively treat preverbal youngsters as real contributors to conversations, the youngsters eventually become such. Caregivers who do not respond in this manner to infants and young children in fact may be causing delay in the youngster's language development.

You may have children who do not participate in peer conversations because they still are not confident enough. But an additional reason may be the one discussed above: the children may not have learned to converse naturally in their earlier years.

If You Have Not Checked This Item:
Some Helpful Ideas

■ Converse with Your Children

Spend time every day in conversations with small groups of children. One of the best times is at snack or lunch. Be sure an adult sits at each of the children's tables and helps to carry on a conversation. Talk normally about anything that interests you or the children. You do not have to be the "teacher" who is instructing them in the names of the fruits on the juice can. Instead, relax and enjoy your snack or meal with the children. Say the kinds of things you would at your own meal table at home: "Whew, isn't it hot today? I think summer is coming early. . . . What's that you say, Jamie, you like summertime best of all? . . . Me too. I love to swim and picnic. . . . You like to do that too, Jill? . . . Yes, you are lucky to live next to the park."

■ Encourage Dramatic Play

Children's own conversations often take place in dramatic play situations. Bring in props to encourage imaginative play in the housekeeping area, the block-building area, and the water or sand table. Take props outside to encourage dramatic play there too.

☐ ASKS QUESTIONS WITH PROPER WORD ORDER

This language skill is another good indication that your children's command of language is developing normally. Most children are able to ask questions as adults do by about age four. Before that, they go through a predictable sequence in learning to ask questions, just as they do in other areas of development (McCormick & Schiefelbusch, p. 74).

Children usually do not learn to ask questions until they have learned to answer them. Between a year-and-a-half and two years of age, when they are putting a few words together to form primitive sentences, they also ask their first questions if caregivers have been asking them questions first. The word order of these first questions is the same as a statement, but with a rising intonation at the end: "Bobbie drink milk?" meaning, "May Bobbie have a drink of milk?" or "Should Bobbie drink his milk?"

Next they begin to learn the use of the *wh* words at the beginning of questions, words like *what* and *where* and *who*: "Where Mama going?" meaning "Where is Mama going?" This type of question becomes quite popular because the adult generally responds, and suddenly the child realizes he has stumbled onto another way of controlling an adult—asking a question the adult will answer. This is not always true with mere statements. Since he delights in adult attention and their responses to things that he originates, he will often burst into a period of questioning. It is not only that he wants to know the answer, but also that he wants the adult's attention.

The next stage in learning to ask questions comes as he expands his sentences to include auxiliary verbs such as *can* and *will*. These questions, though, are often in inverted word order: "Where Daddy will go?" instead of "Where will Daddy go?"

The final stage is the expanded question in proper word order, which most children are able to ask at around four years: "Can I go with you?" "What are you doing?" or "Why doesn't the light go on?"

If you discover through your observation that certain children have not yet attained this level, what will you do? Will you sit down with them and teach them how to ask a question correctly? If you have been reading this text carefully, you know that the answer is "no." Young children do not develop language skills, nor most other developmental kinds of skills, by being taught formally. Then how do they learn? Just like they develop physical skills: they teach themselves proper word order by hearing the proper language forms spoken around them and by practicing it themselves when their physical and mental development has progressed to the point where it is possible for them to do so.

If You Have Not Checked This Item:
Some Helpful Ideas

■ Ask Questions Yourself

Since children do not ask questions correctly until they have learned to answer them, you need to include questioning in your activities with the children. Circle time is a good time for everyone to hear the proper word order of questions and to volunteer to answer the inquiries if so inclined. Even the children who are not at the point of answering questions in front of a group will learn by listening.

■ Ask Children to Help You Gather Information

You can ask a child to ask three or four other children for some information you need. For example, if you are planning a field trip, you might ask several children to go around asking others if their mothers would like to come along. This may not be the most accurate way to gather this information, but it is an excellent practice in questioning skills, and you can always check the accuracy of the information with the parents later.

■ Read a Book

A number of children's picture books have questions in the title or the text. Read these books with your children and give them a chance to answer the question asked or to make up similar questions of their own.

Where Does the Butterfly Go When It Rains? by May Garelick (New York: Scholastic Book Services, 1961) is a rhyming story about where various animals, birds, and insects go to get out of the rain. The book contains many questions that are asked and answered, with the exception of the question in the title. This format should motivate a discussion of how people find out such answers.

The 2 Ton Canary and Other Nonsense Riddles by Polly Cameron (New York: Coward, McCann & Geoghegan, 1965) is a wonderfully crazy riddle book full of riddle questions on every other page. Most are elephant jokes or animal riddles, such as "What is grey and has four legs and a trunk?" Answer: "A mouse on vacation." Many of the children may not have the cognitive understanding to get the point of the answers, but it really does not matter. The book's outlandish grey and red illustrations are so much fun, and the children love to repeat the riddle questions, which is the real point for reading it to the youngsters.

Hey, Riddle Diddle! by Rodney Peppe (New York: Puffin Books, 1971) is a more traditional riddle book in rhyming verses and questions, with clear illustrations that give clues to the answers. Children love to guess: "What has a face but cannot see?" Answer: "A clock."

☐ MAKES "NO" RESPONSES WITH PROPER WORD ORDER

As with questions, making "no" responses with proper word order is another sentence cue that can help you determine whether children are on target in their language development. By about four years of age, they should be producing statements containing negatives, just as adults do.

The child's development of negative sentences parallels that of questions because many questions must be answered in the negative. As soon as she understands the use of *yes* and *no*, the young child usually includes them in her utterances. *No* is especially popular when she finds out—probably to her great astonishment—that she can cause adults to respond with vigor when she says "no." Using *yes* has a lesser effect, so she delights in saying "no" no matter what she really means.

The discovery of the effect of using *no* happens at around two years of age. Much of the theme song of "the terrible two's" is based on the toddler's use of *no*. What would happen if adult caregivers refused to respond as they usually do to such negative declarations? What would happen if the adult caregivers just ignored the two-year-olds' "no" declarations? Why don't you try it and find out!

Once they understand the use of *no* and *not* at around two, children begin to tag these negatives onto simple phrases: "No do it," meaning "I won't do it"; or "Not more milk," meaning "I don't want any more milk."

By age three or three-and-a-half, many children have learned contractions: *don't, can't, won't, isn't, ain't.* Children often use contractions, though, in sentences with inverted word order: "Why me can't go out?" instead of "Why can't I go out?" (McCormick & Schiefelbusch, p. 75). Through hearing others speak with proper order and by practicing it themselves, children come to learn the mainstream manner of speaking. If they are not exposed to standard English in their homes, though, they will come to your center speaking the language or dialect used at home.

Again, it is not up to you to correct their speech. Instead, you will be providing them with many opportunities to listen to and engage in the speaking of standard English.

If You Have Not Checked This Item:
Some Helpful Ideas

▪ Have Question-and-Answer Discussions

At circle time or with a small group, ask "why" questions containing negatives such as "Why can't cats get down out of trees as easily as cats climb up?" "Why don't we usually see the moon in the daytime?" or "Why can't you ride a two-wheel bike as easily as you ride a trike?" Some of their answers should contain the proper use of negatives. Make up your own questions with negatives based on your children's interests.

▪ Read a Book

Pierre by Maurice Sendak (New York: Harper & Row, 1962) is a tiny "Nutshell Library" book that has a rhyming story about a little boy, Pierre, who "doesn't care." His parents ask him to do many things, all of which he refuses by saying, "I don't care."

USES PAST TENSE VERBS CORRECTLY ☐

Linguists have learned how children construct their own knowledge about language by listening to the particular errors children make at the various stages of their development. Because the errors are different from those of mature speakers, and because the young child's language is different from the language he has heard from an adult, we know that children learn language by methods other than pure imitation.

One common error that young children make is to put *-ed* at the end of all past tense verbs, whether the verbs are regular or irregular. A child hears adults in his environment saying "walked," "dressed," "looked," "hoped," "wanted," and "needed," and he somehow absorbs the fact that they are talking about past time, something that happened before. His brain stores this information as a new rule to be applied when you talk about something that happened in the past. Then he begins applying this rule to every past tense situation he talks about, without realizing there are many exceptions in English to the *-ed* for past tense rule.

TABLE 7. Language development

Age	Articulation	Expanded Sentences	Questions	Negative Responses
0–1	Pronounces first word near end of first year or beginning of second year	Uses one word to express different meanings		
1–2	Uses only ten basic sounds at first	Realizes everything has a name; expands vocabulary; speaks in two-word sentences	Asks first questions; uses same word order as for statements (e.g., "Bobby go?")	Uses *no* alone
2–3	Uses only ten basic sounds	Uses telegraphic speech (e.g., "Me go store")	Uses question words *what*, *where*, and *who*	Uses *no* and *not* tagged onto simple phrases
3–4	Has mastered most sounds but may have problems with a few: *s, l, r, th,* and *sk*	Uses proper word order consistently in statements	Uses *can* and *will* in questions, sometimes with inverted word order	Uses negative contractions *don't, can't, won't, isn't, ain't*; inverts word order sometimes
4–5	Has mastered most sounds but may have problems with a few: *s, l, r, th,* and *sk*	Has mastered basic rules for expanding sentences	Asks questions in adult manner	Produces negative statements in adult manner
5–6	Most children of this age speak in a mature adult manner.			

He says things like "I eated," "I runned," "She goed home," "I seed the man," and "My leg hurted"—forms he has never heard an adult say. From this construction we learn that children do indeed create their own grammar rules. The children do not create their own grammar rules from imitating mature speakers, because mature speakers do not talk this way. Because all children make these same errors in the same sequence and at about the same time during their language development period, we realize that the human brain must be preorganized to take in language information and sort it out like this. Applying a past tense rule like this to every past tense verb, even the irregular ones, is called *overgeneralizing*.

Children do the same thing with other general rules their brains have established. Once they learn that plurals are formed by adding -*s*, they say "boys" and "girls," but then they overgeneralize the rule, saying things like "tooths" instead of "teeth" and "foots" instead of "feet."

Children's brains seem to be programmed to absorb information about things, then to extract rules from the way the information seems to work, and finally to apply the rules to similar things. This procedure is called *inductive reasoning*. Preschool children who are allowed to play with computers learn to use the computers in the same way. The youngsters induce rules about how a computer program works from working with it. Then they play around with it, making mistakes, trying again, and finally figuring out what to do. This process is an effective method for self-learning. Perhaps this is the reason that adults, who generally think deductively, have trouble learning to use the computer, while children seldom do.

When children are at the overgeneralizing stage in language production, there is not much adults can do—or should do—to correct the youngsters. You can ask a child to say "ran" instead of "runned" over and over, but somehow it always comes out as "I runned home." To learn the proper formation of past tense verbs, the child will need more than just hearing verbs used correctly at this stage.

Be patient. When the brain matures, the child will discriminate more finely with word forms, just as she does with motor coordination. Provide her with a rich language environment where she will hear competent speakers and will participate in all kinds of speaking activities herself.

If You Have Not Checked This Item: Some Helpful Ideas

▪ Use Tape Recorders

Help children learn how to listen to and record tape cassettes on their own. Then provide the youngsters with some motivation for taping. You could start a story on the tape and ask an interested child to finish it. Have several tapes for as many as want to record. Play the tapes to a small group later. You might start the story with something like this: "As I was coming to school today, I heard a very strange noise. It sounded a little like a train. It sounded like it was coming around the corner. I felt like running away, but I didn't. Instead, I . . ."

▪ Use Toy Telephones

Have at least two toy telephones in your classroom for children to use for pretend conversations.

▪ Read a Book

Children eventually learn the correct English forms by hearing them spoken. Reading books or telling stories aloud is yet another way to fill the environment with the spoken language.

Cloudy with a Chance of Meatballs by Judi Barrett (New York: Atheneum, 1978) is a hilarious tall tale of a world where food falls from the sky. The story might motivate your children to make up their own tall tales. They may want to record their own stories.

☐ PLAYS WITH RHYMING WORDS

Just as they play with blocks, toys, and each other, children also play with words. Youngsters make up nonsense words, repeat word sounds, mix up words, say things backwards, make up chants, and repeat rhyming words. Most people pay little attention to this activity, as it seems so inconsequential. What we have not seemed to realize is that through this playful activity, children are once more at work creating their own knowledge. This time the content is language rather than cognitive concepts, and here the child is manipulating the medium (words) with his voice rather than his hands or body. Once again, he is structuring his experiences by finding out what words do and what he can do with them. Play is once more the vehicle because of the pleasure it gives him.

All children play with words, especially in the early stages of language development, but, of course, there are great individual differences in the amount of language play you will witness among your children. We do know that children who are involved in rhyming activities at an early age carry over this interest in poetry into adult life (Caplan & Caplan, p. 41), and that children who have had early experience with nursery rhymes are more successful later in reading than children who have not. It behooves us, then, to observe children's language play and to provide encouragement and support for all youngsters to become more involved with word play.

Although mothers often promote language play with their infants by playing word and action games with them, such as patty-cake and peek-a-boo, much language play is solitary. Children carry on monologs in which they manipulate sounds, patterns, and meanings of words. These three areas have, in fact, been identified by specialists as common types of word play (Schwartz, pp. 16–26).

Infants from six to eighteen months often "talk" to themselves before going to sleep, repeating rhythmic and rhyming sounds. The infants sound almost as if they are really talking, only with nonsense words. With older children, sound play contains more meaningful words, consonants, and blends. The children often repeat these words in nonsensical fashion: "Ham, bam, lamb, Sam, wham, wham, wham."

Pattern play is a common form of play that involves manipulating the structure of the language. The child begins with a pattern and then substitutes a new word each time he says it: "Bobby go out; Mommy go out; Daddy go out; doggie go out" or "Bite it; write it; light it; sight it; night it; fight it."

Meaning play is not as common among younger children, but it is really more interesting. Here the child interchanges real with nonsensical meanings or makes up words or meanings. An interesting example that Schwartz found was children doing water play with floating and sinking objects, and their telling the objects to "sink-up" (meaning "float") or "sink-down" (Schwartz, pp. 19–20).

Piaget describes much of the talk of three-to-five-year olds as egocentric. It is as if much of their speaking is not directed to anyone in particular but produced for their own pleasure. Some children go around muttering to themselves most of the day, especially when they are involved in an interesting activity. The muttering seems to disappear by the time they enter public school, but it may become inner speech instead (Caplan & Caplan, p. 41).

Are any of the children in your class engaged in word play? They will be if you sponsor or promote it. Do finger plays and body action chants with the children during circle time or for transitions between activities. Read children's poems and nursery rhymes to the youngsters. Use tape recorders to stimulate the children's own made-up rhymes.

If You Have Not Checked This Item: Some Helpful Ideas

■ Do Finger Plays

There are several good fingerplay books on the market containing the words and actions—and in some cases the music—to accompany the chant. You should also consider making up your own chants or listening to the children's word play and incorporating it into a chant for all to say.

Finger Frolics: Fingerplays for Young Children, compiled by Liz Cromwell and Dixie Hibner (Livonia, MI: Partner Press, 1976), is one of the best fingerplay books, with dozens of fingerplays about seasons, holidays, animals, and people.

Eye Winker, Tom Tinker, Chin Chopper: Fifty Musical Fingerplays by Tom Glazer (New York: Doubleday & Company, 1973) contains many of the traditional rhymes with piano arrangements and guitar chords.

■ Read a Book

Rhymes and Verses

There are many traditional nursery rhyme books on the market. Children still enjoy hearing and repeating nursery rhymes.

Mother Goose, illustrated by Aurelius Battaglia (New York: Random House, 1973), is a traditional Mother Goose with illustrations of medieval people and animals.

The Bedtime Mother Goose, with pictures by Ron Himler (New York: Golden Press, 1980), has some different rhymes with illustrations of Early American children.

Dogs and Dragons Trees and Dreams by Karla Kuskin (New York: Harper & Row, 1980) is one of a number of poetry books by this popular author. Long and short, rhyming and not, the poems in this collection are full of word plays, questions and answers, and humor. Children will enjoy listening and repeating the poems.

My Cat Likes to Hide in Boxes by Eve Sutton (New York: Viking Penguin, 1973) is a rhyming cumulative tale written in the format of "This is the House That Jack Built."

My Orange Gorange by Judith Fitzgerald (Ontario, Canada: Black Moss Press, 1985) is a nonsense poem by a little girl who cannot find a word to rhyme with orange.

Funny Words

Certain children's books are especially attractive to their audience because of one or two hilarious words. Children often go into spasms of laughter upon hearing them and want the book read to them again and again.

Mert the Blurt by Robert Kraus (New York: Simon & Schuster, 1980) is one. Little Mert cannot keep anything to himself; he goes around blurting out fanciful family secrets to a colorful host of neighbors.

The Surprise Party by Pat Hutchins (New York: Collier Books, 1969) is a delightfully mixed-up communication muddle like the game "Gossip." Here rabbit whispers to owl that he is having a party tomorrow and it is a surprise. The message is passed from one animal to another in such a garbled form that it truly is a surprise for all in the end. Children love the nonsensical phrases that the animals repeat, and they may want to try them on their own.

Pattern Play

My Name Is Alice by Jane Bayer (New York: E. P. Dutton, 1984) is an alphabet book containing a pattern verse for each letter, much like a jump-rope rhyme. For example: "A. My Name is Alice and my husband's name is Alex. We come from Alaska and we sell ants."

Meaning Play

Rugs Have Naps (But Never Take Them) by Charles Klasky (Chicago: Children's Press, 1984) is a book of nonsense phrases and illustrations with funny double meanings.

OBSERVING, RECORDING, AND INTERPRETING SPOKEN LANGUAGE

The checklist results for Sheila were much like the teachers in her classroom had predicted. Every item was checked except for "takes part in conversations with other children." Although Sheila spoke to other children, it was rarely in the form of conversation, but more often a command or a complaint. Because Sheila showed evidence of "speaks confidently in classroom," the staff members felt that Sheila eventually would join the other children in classroom activities, including conversation. In fact, Sheila's language skill could be used to help her become involved with the others. The teachers made plans for Sheila to tell several other children, one at a time, how to use the computer program "Stickybear ABCs" that the center had recently acquired.

REFERENCES CITED

Caplan, Theresa, and **Frank Caplan.** (1983). *The Early Childhood Years: The 2 to 6 Year Old.* New York: Putnam Publishing Group.

Eisenson, Jon. (1976). *Is Your Child's Speech Normal?* Reading, MA: Addison-Wesley Publishing Company.

Holzman, Mathilda. (1983). *The Language of Children.* Englewood Cliffs, NJ: Prentice-Hall.

McCormick, Linda, and **Richard L. Schiefelbusch.** (1984). *Early Language Intervention.* Columbus, OH: Merrill Publishing Company.

Schwartz, Judith I. (1981). "Children's Experiments with Language." *Young Children,* 36(5), 16–26.

OTHER SOURCES

Beaty, Janice J. (1988). *Skills for Preschool Teachers.* Columbus, OH: Merrill Publishing Company.

Berk, Laura E. (1985). "Why Children Talk to Themselves." *Young Children,* 40(5), 46–52.

Honig, Alice Sterling. (1988). "Humor Development in Children." *Young Children,* 43(4), 60–73.

Lindfors, Judith Wells. (1987). *Children's Language and Learning.* Englewood Cliffs, NJ: Prentice-Hall.

LEARNING ACTIVITIES

1. Use the ninth section of the *Child Skills Checklist* on spoken language as a screening tool to observe all of the children in your classroom. Which children seem to need help in more than one of the items? How do these children fare in the various areas of cognitive development?

2. Choose a child who seems to be having difficulty with spoken language, and observe him or her on three different days, doing a running record of his language activities. Compare the results with the checklist results. How do you interpret the evidence you have collected? Are there any pieces of evidence that are still missing about this child's language performance?

3. Choose a child whom you have screened as needing help in several of the checklist items, and carry out one or more of the activities listed. Record the results.

4. Teach the children a fingerplay or rhyming game. How did the children perform, especially those whom you noted as needing help in this area?

5. Do a tape-recorder activity with a small group of children. Have them tape-record their own words and then play them back. They may want to tell about themselves, tell a story, or say a verse.

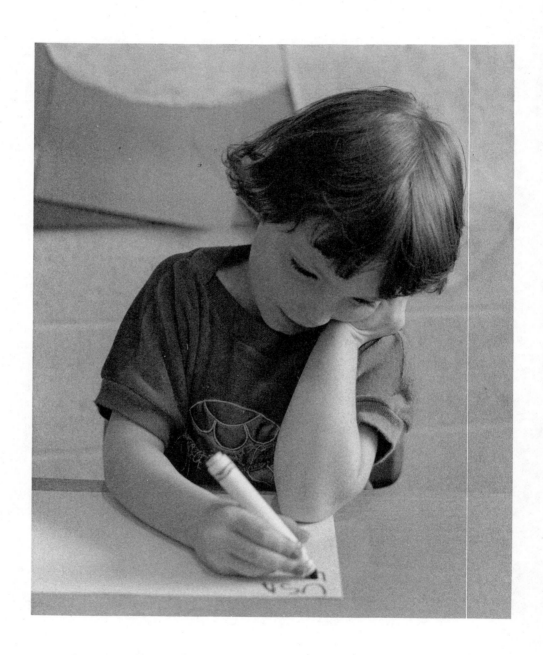

11 Written Language

Written Language Checklist

☐ Pretends to write by scribbling horizontally
☐ Includes features of real letters in scribbling
☐ Identifies own written name
☐ Identifies classroom labels
☐ Knows some alphabet letters
☐ Prints real letters
☐ Prints letters of name
☐ Prints name correctly in linear manner

W hy should a chapter on children's written language be included in a book on observing the development of young children? Surely learning to write has little to do with child development, does it? Furthermore, teaching children to write should come later when children are in first grade, shouldn't it? The answers to all of these questions are quite different today than they would have been as recently as fifteen years ago.

Enough research about the beginnings of writing and reading, about children's perceptual development, and how children make sense of their world through playful exploration has since been completed to change our minds forever about the way children develop and how we can best support their growth.

We know now that written language is an outgrowth of the same urge that drives children to express themselves orally and even pictorially. We also know that, given the proper tools and support, all children everywhere go through the same sequence of stages in teaching themselves to write. Yes, writing is indeed a natural part of a child's development. The fact is that "learning to write is largely an act of discovery," as one specialist puts it (Temple, Nathan, & Burris, p. 2). The term used to describe the child's natural development of writing (and reading) is *emergent literacy*.

Thus, writing joins language, thinking, emotional, social, and motor skills as another aspect of development that the child can arrive at on his own by playfully interacting with the materials in his environment, once his physical and mental maturity have made that possible.

This does not mean that writing development always occurs naturally. Many children come from families with few toys, let alone the tools for writing. Children need to practice writing just as they do speaking if they are to become proficient. Without a tool to write with or something to write on, they can do little more than make marks on steamy windows or scratches in the dirt.

On the other hand, this does not mean that we should sit down with the preschool child and formally teach him or her how to write, any more than we should formally teach him how to walk and talk. Instead, we should fill his environment with examples of written language, serve as models by doing a great deal of writing and reading in the presence of the child, and provide him with the tools and encouragement to attempt writing on his own.

Can any of your children print their names? Do any of them pretend to write, perhaps at the easel, by scribbling rows of markings? Make an assessment of the children in your classroom by using the eight items of the checklist on written language. Then set up a writing table or writing area, complete with a variety of writing tools, and watch what happens.

☐ PRETENDS TO WRITE BY SCRIBBLING HORIZONTALLY

The first natural attempts by young children to write are usually scribbles. Initial scribbling is also true with art, of course. Yet children as young as three years seem to recognize the difference between writing scribbles and drawing scribbles. In fact, some children do drawing scribbles on one part of a paper and writing scribbles that "tell about the picture" on another part (Vukelich & Golden, p. 4).

The two kinds of scribbles look completely different. Writing scribbles are done in a horizontal linear manner across the page, something like a line of writing. The children who make writing scribbles seem to understand that writing is something that can be read, and they sometimes pretend to read their pretend writing, known also as *linear mock writing* (Temple, Nathan, & Burris, p. 29). This is the first step in the natural acquisition of writing. Once their scribbles have become horizontal lines instead of circular markings or aimless meanderings, they are indicating they understand that writing is something different from drawing.

Their first scribbles do not resemble letters at all. The children, in fact, seem to be trying to copy only the broad general features of the writing system: that it is arranged in rows across a page and that it consists of a series of loops, tall sticks, and connected lines that are repeated. Only later will children differentiate the finer features of the system: the letters.

Where have they acquired this knowledge of written language so early in life? Look around you. They, like all of us, are surrounded by written material—in newspapers and magazines, on television advertising, on the labels of food products, in letters in the mail, in the stories read to them, on signs on stores, on bumper stickers on cars, and on mottos on T-shirts. The printed word is everywhere.

Some families, of course, encourage their children to print their own names at an early age, and family members even take time to write out the stories their children make up. Some children have older brothers or sisters who bring written material home from school. These children see family members engaged in writing or reading and want to become involved themselves.

Observe to discover which of your children do pretend writing, this first step in the writing process; which ones have progressed beyond this beginning; and which have not started.

If You Have Not Checked This Item: Some Helpful Ideas

■ Set Up a Writing Area

Most children will not ask to become involved in writing if there is no sign of writing in their environment. Set up a special writing table with all of the implements, and you will soon have a group of budding writers.

For paper it is best to use unlined sheets. Children will be placing their scribbles and pretend letters all over the page, and lined paper may inhibit this free-form exploration of how writing works. Use typing paper or stationery, as well as tablets and pads of different sizes and colors. You may want to have an individual notebook for each child with his or her name on the front.

For writing tools, you will want to include a variety. We sometimes think of pencils first, but research with beginning writers shows that pencils are the most difficult of all writing implements to manipulate effectively (Lamme, p. 22). Children themselves choose colored felt-tip markers as their favorites. You should also include colored chalk and a small chalkboard, crayons, and a few pencils, in addition to the markers. It is not necessary to have only the large primary-sized pencils. Some preschoolers have great difficulty handling these thick pencils and much prefer to use regular pencils. Put out a variety of writing tools, and children will find out on their own what is best for them.

Some children choose pencils from the beginning and seem to be able to handle these implements well. These children may well be ready for some direction on how to hold the pencil properly. If they grip it too tightly or bear down too hard, they will probably tire easily and may lose interest (Lamme, p. 23).

Voluntary and not enforced participation in writing activities should, of course, be the rule in your program. Some children need to develop better eye-hand coordination before they engage in writing. They might learn more from painting at the easel or playing with the utensils you have

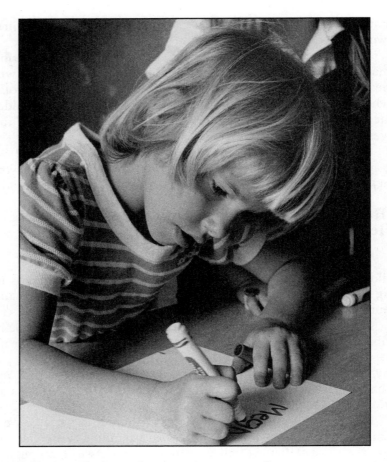

Preschool children teach themselves to write most easily
with felt-tip markers and unlined paper.

put out at the water or sand tables instead. If the youngsters can build a tall
block tower without its toppling over, can drive a nail straight into a piece of
wood, or can use a pair of scissors with ease, their eye-hand coordination is
probably developed enough for them to use a writing implement.

☐ INCLUDES FEATURES OF REAL LETTERS IN SCRIBBLING

Just as an infant's babbling finally begins to take the sound of real talking, so
a child's first linear scribblings eventually begin to look like real writing. For
many children, the lines of their scribbles become somewhat jagged and finally take on features of real letters such as straight, curved, or intersecting
lines, although no real letters are formed (Schickedanz, p. 243). This ad-

vanced scribbling happens as a natural developmental sequence when children have the freedom and opportunity to experiment with writing on their own. Teaching, in fact, has no effect whatsoever at this point.

Children extract the elements of writing from their environment and play around with these elements using markers and paper. Once again, youngsters are manipulating the medium (writing) until they have learned how to handle it, what it can do, and what they are able to do with it. Just as children do when they first learn to climb stairs, put together a puzzle, or ride a trike, they want to practice over and over. Many children fill pages with this pretend writing and take great satisfaction in doing so. This activity provides wonderful practice for them in learning to control the writing tool as well.

Children sometimes think their scribbling is something much more meaningful. If this is writing, as some children reason that it must be, then someone who knows how to read should be able to read it. Often they will take a piece of pretend writing to an adult and ask the grown-up to read it. How should you respond? Be honest about it. "Oh, Sharon, your writing is beginning to look almost real. Can you tell me what it says?" Some children really have a story in mind when they do their pretend writing, and they will be able to tell it to you. Others think that their "words" must speak only to someone who can read.

Observe to see which of your children are at this stage in their experimental writing. What can you do to help them progress further?

If You Have Not Checked This Item: Some Helpful Ideas

■ Support the Children's Efforts

You need to praise the children for their efforts in all the writing they do, just as you praise them for their art. Mount samples of their writing on the wall, just as you do for the children's art. You also may want to save samples of this stage of their writing, keeping it in a folder or the scrapbook you are making to show each child's accomplishments. Be sure to date these samples so that you will be able to compare them with later samples.

■ Use Sand or Salt Trays or Finger Painting

Put out small trays of sand or salt in your writing area so that children can practice "writing" with their fingers. It is easy to "erase" this writing by simply shaking the tray. Finger painting on tabletops or paper also gives the children practice doing linear pretend writing with their fingers.

■ Encourage Children to Write Messages

Children can write messages in pretend scribbling (mock linear writing) to other children, to their parents, or to you. Have youngsters write notes to their parents inviting them to visit the classroom or write a block-corner sign asking other children to leave their buildings standing. If you want (or if the children ask), you can write the real words under the mock writing. This is not necessary, though. Most children know what their scribbled messages say, and they can tell this to the message recipients. Specialists who are studying young children's emergent literacy call these early writing attempts *personal script*, while mature writing is known as *conventional script*. By using these terms, you can avoid telling children their writing is "wrong" or "nothing but scribbles."

☐ IDENTIFIES OWN WRITTEN NAME

If we want children to become involved with written language on their own, we must provide many examples of it throughout the preschool classroom. Because the principal focus of children of this age is themselves, a good place to begin with written language is with their own names. Children may not be ready to recognize written names at the beginning of the year, so it may be better to start with pictorial symbols at first.

Mount a different symbol on each child's cubby. The symbols can be various single-colored geometric shapes: red, green, blue, or yellow stars, circles, squares, and triangles. Or you can use peel-off labels with pictures of animals, birds, or flowers as a symbol for each child. Once the children are familiar with their own particular symbols, you should include their printed names on their signs. Use both upper- and lowercase letters and not just capitals. They will be using both forms later on in school and should learn how their names look printed the proper way.

At this point, the children may be identifying their name signs by either or both the symbol and the written name. Eventually you should remove the symbol altogether, so that they will become familiar with the look of their names alone. This familiarity does not mean the youngsters actually identify the individual letters at first. Children tend to look for whole configurations. Youngsters are often able to identify their own names and those of several others just by "the way they look."

Use children's name labels and tags to mark their cubbies, toothbrushes, cots, table places at meal time, science collections, and block-building structures. Children's names also can be written on the tags they hang to select their free choice activity areas. Print individual names on artwork, personal scrapbooks, puzzles made of the children's photos, and other personal possessions or products created in your class.

Talk about the children's names. Encourage the youngsters to identify their own name tags. Mix up the place cards at your lunch tables so that children will have to search for their seats. Put name tags on the chairs or floor space at circle time, so that children will have the fun and practice of searching out their places again.

How many of your children can identify their names? This is the important first step before they actually print their names.

If You Have Not Checked This Item: Some Helpful Ideas

■ Use Alphabet Blocks, Magnetic Letters

Let children play as they want with alphabet blocks and magnetic letters at first. Then you can start a game called "Whose letter (or name) is this?" Pick out the first letter of someone's name. Then spell the entire name with alphabet blocks or magnetic letters, and see if anyone can recognize the whole name.

■ Read a Book

Andy, That's My Name by Tomie dePaola (Englewood Cliffs, NJ: Prentice-Hall, 1973) can be read to the children to motivate them to make their names from alphabet blocks just as Andy does.

■ Use Computer Software

If you have a computer in your classroom that children are allowed to "play" with, then a commercial "name" program might be appropriate. (For other ideas, see "Chapter 4: The Computer as an Alphabet Book" in *The Computer as a Paintbrush: Creative Uses for the Personal Computer in the Preschool Classroom* by Janice J. Beaty and W. Hugh Tucker [Columbus, OH: Merrill Publishing Company, 1987].)

IDENTIFIES CLASSROOM LABELS ☐

Children may learn to write their names but still know very little about the concept of symbolization, that words are symbols representing things. Children need to have many meaningful experiences with print in their everyday lives. Printed signs, labels, and charts in your classroom can give them this experience.

In addition to labeling the children's cubbies and seats with their names, you should have each activity area labeled with its name. Other labels can include job charts, attendance charts, experience charts, weather charts, and recipe charts; names of animal and fish pets; pictures of community helpers, homes, and buildings in the block area; first aid kit and emergency directions; records of children's height, of how much their plants have grown, of how far children can jump, of which children have pets at home; stories the children have made up; favorite songs and fingerplays; signs for the play supermarket. There are many, many opportunities for using printed material in your classroom. Be sure these labels and signs are mounted at the children's eye level.

From this exposure, children will learn several things, including

1. Written words convey messages that can be read.
2. Writing is arranged in horizontal rows. (Be sure you do not use vertical labels.)
3. Writing is made up of letters.
4. Some letters are repeated, but never more than two together. (Temple, Nathan, & Burris, p. 51)

Obviously such concepts are internalized subconsciously, and you do not need to point them out. Your role is to fill the environment with printed material. The children's interaction with printed material will make certain impressions on their minds. Some youngsters will realize, just as they did when they first learned to talk, that everything has a name and that this name can be written.

To find out which of your children understand that written words convey meaning, ask them to point to the part of the story you are reading that tells what is happening. Some still may point to the picture on the page instead of the words. You may want to run your finger under the words you are reading to a small group from time to time, so that the children will see that you are using the words to tell the story, not the pictures.

If You Have Not Checked This Item: Some Helpful Ideas

■ Write Down What Children Are Doing

Encourage children to tell you about the art work they are doing, the block buildings they are constructing, the dramatic play situations they are involved with. You can write down their explanations for them to keep in a scrapbook of their own. Take instant print pictures of children engaged in activities and mount them in an album with labels or words the children have used to describe what they are doing.

■ Make Group Experience Charts

When some of the children have done something together, ask them to dictate their description of it to you, and write the dictation for all to see on an experience chart. Telling about a field trip, a holiday, or a special class occasion could prompt such written dictations, as could the dramatic play roles that the children are creating in the dress-up area.

■ Be a Writing Model Yourself

Do a lot of writing in the presence of the children. If they see that writing is important to you, they will want to do it too. If you are doing checklist recording or running records in their presence, children will often want to use your pen and paper to do some pretend writing themselves. Do not give up your writing tools, but be sure instead you have a well-equipped writing table to which they can be directed. Serving as a writing model will almost always stimulate certain of your children to try their own hand at writing.

■ Read Many Stories

You should read at least one story daily to small groups or individuals. Reading to the total group is not as satisfactory because not everyone gets to sit close to the teacher and see the pictures and words of the story.

■ Have a Class Mailbox

Put your written communications to children or their parents in a class mailbox. You can have a child take the mail out every day and, with your help, distribute it. You may want to make a field trip to the post office or have a mail carrier visit and talk to your class.

You should plan on writing one note to each child on a weekly basis. It should be simple and nice: "Rob, I love your new sneakers!" or "Shirl, thanks for helping Carol today." When the note is delivered to the child, one of the adults in the class can help him or her to read it. This modeling behavior on your part should stimulate children to want to write notes to classmates or answer your notes on their own. The children will need help, which you or your co-workers can provide.

KNOWS SOME ALPHABET LETTERS ☐

This checklist item, like the previous ones, refers to children's natural development of writing and not to their formal learning of the alphabet by being taught by an adult. Children do learn alphabet letters on their own just by being surrounded by the letters. The youngsters' own names are often the first source. The children may learn to say the letters in their names soon after they recognize their name sign. Many children will then be able to identify those particular letters wherever they see the letters.

Reciting or chanting the ABCs is not the same. Just as children can chant the numbers from one to ten but not understand what any of the numbers mean, so preschoolers often chant the alphabet without the slightest idea of what they are saying, as previously mentioned. Programs like "Sesame Street," of course, teach children the letter names, and some youngsters may have learned letters from this technique, although it is a more passive and formal method.

Others may have learned alphabet letters from a personal computer at home or in the classroom. A number of software programs feature alphabet games for children two to six years of age. In many ways computers are superior to television as a learning tool because children are actively and playfully involved in their own learning. Computers should be used playfully with young children, rather than in formal lessons. Children should be free to use a classroom computer during free choice period, just as they use blocks, dolls, or the water table.

Have alphabet games on the shelves of your manipulative area; alphabet letters mounted on the wall at children's eye level; alphabet books in the book area; and wooden, plastic, sandpaper, or magnetic letters available for the children to choose to play with. But do not teach the alphabet formally. You will find that if you have filled the children's environment with writing, there will be no need to teach the alphabet formally.

In recognizing alphabet letters, children progress through a particular sequence, just as they do in learning to make speech sounds naturally. The first distinctive feature children seem to recognize is whether the line that makes the letter is straight or curved. Letters that are round, such as *O* and *C*, are distinguished first. Then letters with curved lines, such as *P* and *S*, are noted. Next curved letters with intersections, such as *B* and *R*, are distinguished from curved letters without intersections, like *S* and *J*. Letters with diagonal lines, such as *K* and *X*, are among the last to be recognized (Schickedanz, p. 311). This pattern follows the one we noted in Chapter 8, that young children have difficulty distinguishing shapes with diagonal lines, as well.

This is the natural progression. Your children, of course, may learn some letters out of sequence because they occur in their names. Youngsters still, however, may have difficulty when it comes to writing certain letters.

If You Have Not Checked This Item: Some Helpful Ideas

■ Read an Appropriate Alphabet Book

There are many good alphabet books on the market, but you first will need to review any you plan to use with your children to see if the books are appropriate to the youngsters' age level. Some alphabet books are for very young children. Looking at the simplicity of the pictures may help you to determine the age level. If there are pictures of children in the book, are the children in the book the age of yours?

Some alphabet books are too sophisticated for young children. These books display the talent of the artist, but they do not teach the letters. Other alphabet books are confusing because of the unfamiliar objects used as illustrations. Alphabet books are most effective if they

1. Use both upper- and lowercase letters;
2. Have simple illustrations that children can recognize;
3. Use illustrations with only one common name (not *cat/kitten* or *rabbit/bunny*, for instance);

4. Use words starting with a single consonant (*cow, sail, ball*) rather than a blend (such as *church, ship,* or *brown,* for instance);
5. Have a theme, a simple story, or rhyming verses.

These books are more effective if read to one or two children at a time rather than a group. The children need to sit close to the teacher to identify the objects being named and to see the shapes of the letters. Have the books on your bookshelves so children can look at the books by themselves. Chall's extensive study on learning to read in America found that children's ability to identify letters was an important predictor of reading achievement in first and second grades (Chall, p. 141).

■ **Use Alphabet Software in Your Computer**

See p. 287 and p. 296 in this chapter.

■ **Have Alphabet Soup**

Serve alphabet soup for lunch, and see if the children can identify any of the letters.

■ **Have Fun with Pretzels**

Have pretzels for snack sometime, and see what letters your children can make by breaking off pieces before eating the pretzels.

PRINTS REAL LETTERS   □

Young children may begin making a few real letters even before the youngsters can name them. Often these letters are from the children's own names. The children may have seen the teacher or their mother write their names on their art products or other possessions. If children have the opportunity and the materials, they usually try to imitate an adult's writing of their names.

The children's first attempts are usually flawed. Youngsters make the same mistakes in writing letters that they do in recognizing letters—they often overlook the letter's distinguishing features. Development of children's written language, just as their other aspects of development, progresses from the general to the particular. Until their visual perception becomes fine-tuned enough, they will have difficulty making letters that are accurate in all the details.

Let the children practice on their own. Pointing out errors is not really productive, just as it was not in their development of spoken language. In time their errors will become less frequent as the children refine their perception of individual letters and gain control over their writing tools.

One of the children's problems in printing letters has to do with their orientation in space. Children are often able to get the features of the

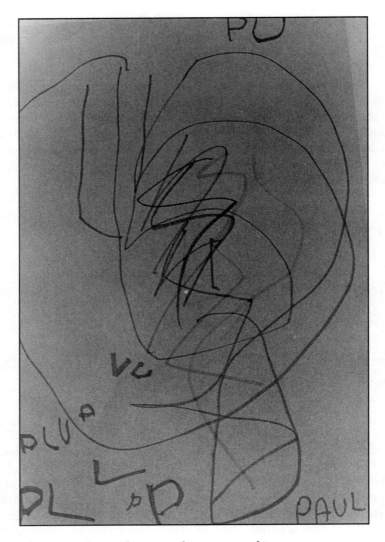

A child who has seen the teacher write his name on his art products often tries to imitate the letters.

letters accurate, but not the orientation of the letters. Some letters the children reverse, and some letters they even write upside down. Occasionally their letters are facing the right direction, but just as often their printing may be a complete mirror image of the real thing. We often wonder if children really see the letters like that.

Part of the answer may lie in the fact that the orientation of other kinds of things—that is, the direction they face—makes no difference in identifying them. For instance, a cup is a cup no matter whether the handle is pointing toward a person or away from her. A flashlight may be lying horizontally or standing on end, but it is still a flashlight. Objects, in other words, do not change their identity because they face a different direction.

But letters do. Letters made with the same features are completely different depending on the direction their curved lines face and whether their straight lines are at the top or bottom. If children are not used to paying attention to the direction certain features face, imagine the trouble they will have identifying and printing the letters *d, b, p,* and *q.* All four are made with the same curved and straight lines. It may take many years for children to get these details straight. Children often reverse letters even into the elementary grades.

One of the problems in children's playing with three-dimensional letters is the fact that they can be reversed or turned upside down. If you have such letters in your writing area, be sure to have real alphabet letters mounted on the nearby wall at the children's eye level so that the youngsters can easily see the proper orientation. Magnetic letters are better than letter blocks or plastic letters in this respect. At least the magnetic letters cannot be reversed when placed on a metal backing.

Another detail children sometimes overlook when they first print letters is whether the letters are open or closed, the difference between *O* and *C.* This visual discrimination problem may have to do with children's perception of space and their difficulty in making enclosures (discussed in Chapter 9). The youngsters, in fact, may not really see this detail at first. With practice and maturity, these problems resolve themselves unless the child has a learning impairment. Your best strategy is to fill the environment with words, letters, and occasions to write, as well as to support and encourage the children's own attempts at writing. But do not "teach" them.

If You Have Not Checked This Item: Some Helpful Ideas

■ Make Letters Personal

Children always learn in a more meaningful way if the subject is somehow connected to them. Help children to recognize the first letter in their own first name by playing games with it. You can have letter cards on string necklaces that the youngsters can hang around their necks. Let the children find their own letters. Then ask the youngsters if they can find any other child with a letter like theirs. Be sure to have enough similar letters, and make them big enough so that everyone can see them easily.

■ Have Many Writing Practice Activities

Trays with sand or salt on the bottom are fun to write in and easy to erase by shaking the tray. The Etch-a-Sketch picture board can be used by mature children with good eye-hand coordination to make letters. Some computer programs allow children to draw letters. Can your children form letters out of cooked spaghetti?

Children also like to trace around cardboard cut-out letters. Be sure that the face of the letters is distinctive from the underside, so that the letters will have the proper orientation.

▪ Have Alphabet Cards

Let children play with alphabet cards having a picture of an object on them. In that way, the youngsters will be seeing the letter in the proper orientation. The object on the card will also give them a clue to the name of the letter. It is best to have cards showing both upper- and lowercase letters. Then children will see that each letter can be written in two different ways. It is not helpful for children to use only capital letters, since they will need to write in lowercase in the elementary grades.

▪ Use a Primary Typewriter or a Computer

If you have access to either a primary typewriter or a computer, consider yourself fortunate. Children love to play with letters and words that they can type. Do not give youngsters formal lessons on either instrument. These machines should be used by children in a natural and spontaneous way, just as all of your writing tools are. In other words, children will teach themselves.

☐ PRINTS LETTERS OF NAME

Children may start printing their names before they make other letters. These last two checklist items sometimes, in fact, appear out of sequence with some children who show evidence of learning written language in the natural process described here.

Let the children learn to print their names on their own. You may be surprised at their initial production. Their names may contain all of the proper letters, but in different sizes, pointed in different directions (both backward and upside down), ordered in no particular sequence, and scattered around the paper as if they are dangling in three-dimensional space instead of lying flat on a two-dimensional surface.

Watch how children print naturally. Children experiment with writing just as they do with block building to find out which way works best for them. They may print the first letter of their names in the middle of the paper, then turn the paper half-way around and print the next letter. They may turn the paper again for the following letters, or keep it straight and print the remaining letters on the parts of the paper with the most space. If you find your children from the outset printing their names in a linear manner with the letters in the proper sequence, you will know they have probably had practice at home.

The example of initial word writing described here points up the concepts that children need to acquire before they can write successfully.

1. Words start at the left side of the paper and go right.
2. Words are written in a linear manner with all of the letters in a row.
3. The letters in words follow one another in sequence.

You understand that the children eventually will learn these concepts spontaneously without being taught formally, just by being surrounded by writing and by trying it out on their own. Do not expect your children to learn to write properly all at once. When they first write their names, they concentrate on making the letters and have little concern for the placement of the letters. Correct orientation and placement may not come until their cognitive concept of position in space is more developed.

Let them explore writing their names any way they want. If they come to you and ask you to write their names as a model for them to follow, you of course can print their names in a linear manner in upper- and lower-case letters at the top of a sheet of paper. The children may still be unable to copy this model, but it gives them another opportunity to see the proper form for writing. Follow the children's lead. Do not impose your own time-table on teaching children to write their names. Some children may learn it quickly on their own because of their maturity and practice. Others may not learn it at all for another year or so.

It is better for children to learn to write their names with a beginning capital letter and the rest in lowercase. Words appear this way in print, and the children will be required to write like this in elementary school. It is no more difficult for the youngsters to learn lowercase than uppercase. The three-dimensional letters they use in play, the alphabet books, cards, and letters on the wall also should contain both upper- and lowercase letters. Too often children are taught to write their names in capital letters only. Using only uppercase makes it very confusing when children reach the elementary grades and have to unlearn this incorrect method.

Have the children who can write their names, or even the first letter of their names, sign their paintings and other classroom products. Youngsters are used to having an adult do this signing. It gives children great satisfaction to do it for themselves. You may want to write the names of those who cannot yet do it for themselves with a capital and lowercase letters so that they will have a model to follow.

If You Have Not Checked This Item: Some Helpful Ideas

■ Write Greeting Cards

Make large greeting cards on newsprint at least once a week to send to various people on all sorts of occasions. You might send a thank-you note to the mail carrier for visiting your class, a congratulations card to one of your families that has a new baby, a Halloween card to the grandmother who volunteers in your program, or a have-a-nice-day card to your bus driver. Have the class help you to make up a message that you can write at the top of the paper with colored felt-tip markers. Then let the children sign their names underneath. Those who have not yet learned to write letters can sign with scribbles, and you can print their names underneath if they want you to do so. Fold up your giant cards, and send them in manila envelopes.

■ Use Computer Name Games

Several companies put out computer software for children two to six years of age that includes name games. *Kindercomp* by Spinnaker has a set of games that includes names, drawing, matching, letters, and numbers. *Stickybear ABC, Numbers, Shapes,* and *Opposites* are four learning game programs by Weekly Reader. *Nine Learning Games* and *Early Games* by Counterpoint Software include letters, names, drawing, colors, shapes, and sizes.

These games and others are found on the shelves of computer stores. Try out these games before you purchase any to make sure they are appropriate for your children. As mentioned before, you should allow children to experiment and learn on their own with the computer, just as you let them learn on their own how to build with unit blocks.

☐ PRINTS NAME CORRECTLY
IN LINEAR MANNER

The last of the checklist items is also the last to appear in children's development of written language. Not all of your children will progress to this stage until kindergarten. They may not be able to print words in a linear manner from left to right until a horizontal baseline shows up in their paintings. Some five- and six-year-olds continue to have difficulty reaching this stage.

Directionality is also a problem in the words of beginning writers, just as it is with their letters. Adults take for granted that words start at the left and go to the right. Young children have not established that directional perspective at first. They may print a word such as *book* by starting with a *b* in the middle of the page and going either way: "ꙕoobook." They may be merely manipulating the medium (letters) like they do with paint and unit blocks to find out how it works.

We know, however, that young children do not start out with a Euclidean or plane-geometry frame of reference, knowing that there is a single horizon or baseline and that things are located along straight lines or formed into shapes with angular corners. They seem to operate instead from the viewpoint of *topology,* a fluid point of view that sees various shapes as being the same so long as their boundaries are unbroken. A square can be a circle or a triangle if the perimeter is considered fluid like a rubber band. It may be for this reason that three- and four-year-olds find it next to impossible to follow instructions to "line up in a straight line." Where is the line? It is in whatever direction each child happens to be facing at the moment. One wonders if nine months of floating in a mother's womb could have created this frame of reference!

Children may write words from top to bottom or from right to left as easily as from left to right. Most youngsters go through a stage of writing their names backwards in a perfect mirror image. Children seem to see things from a number of different perspectives, in fact, before they finally learn a single linear orientation.

You may think that lined paper would help them to establish this baseline. During these early formative years the children's experiments with letters and words just do not fit between lines, and the youngsters are better off with unlined paper. Later in elementary school as they learn to control their pencil movements and refine their perceptions of letters and words, a line can be very helpful to the children.

There are three common processes children use when they begin writing words: tracing, copying, or generating their own words (Temple, Nathan, & Burris, p. 47). When they are exploring writing on their own, children may use any or all of these methods. Tracing is the easiest method and some children seem to do it spontaneously. When a teacher or parent writes these children's names on a piece of paper, the youngsters trace over the name again and again. Then the children try writing the same thing on another part of the paper.

Other children copy their names from a paper or words from a classroom label onto another sheet of paper or a chalkboard. The farther away the words are, the more difficult it is for the children to copy the words. If you see children trying to copy words from a distant part of the room, suggest that they move closer.

No matter how children do it, we should applaud their beginning efforts at writing, just as we do their initial attempts at block building, painting, or riding a trike. We should provide many opportunities for them to practice on their own, and we should serve as writing models ourselves. Every time children see you writing in the classroom, they will want to write too. If you have a writing table available, they can join you in this important communication skill that we now know is possible for them to acquire naturally.

If You Have Not Checked This Item: Some Helpful Ideas

■ **Play Linear Games**

Have children try to line up objects in a row: dominoes, toy cars or people, blocks, Lego building blocks. If children have magnetic letters, let them see how many rows they can make.

■ **Make Place Cards**

Have the children who are able to, make their own place cards for mealtime. Perhaps they can help other children to do theirs.

OBSERVING, RECORDING, AND INTERPRETING WRITTEN LANGUAGE

Although young children develop written language at the same time and in much the same manner that they develop spoken language, we realize that the same emphasis has not been placed on the natural development of children's written language by the adults around them. Therefore, there may be children who can produce writing but have not practiced it. If you screen your entire class using the *Child Skills Checklist* items on written language, you may find certain children who show skills in printing letters and even words.

Compliment these children on their accomplishments, and provide them with writing tools, paper, and opportunities to continue this development. Encourage other children who have few checkmarks in the written language area to try their own hand at printing letters and words. Follow up with a second screening using the checklist later in the year. Do you find that more of the children now have checkmarks? Do you find that your classroom now offers children more opportunities for writing?

REFERENCES CITED

Chall, Jeanne. (1967). *Learning to Read: The Great Debate.* New York: McGraw-Hill Book Company.

Lamme, Linda Leonard. (1979). "Handwriting in an Early Childhood Curriculum." *Young Children, 35*(1), 20–27.

Schickedanz, Judith A. (1982). "The Acquisition of Written Language in Young Children." In Bernard Spodek (Ed.), *Handbook of Research in Early Childhood Education,* pp. 242–263. New York: The Free Press.

Temple, Charles A., Ruth G. Nathan, and **Nancy A. Burris.** (1982). *The Beginnings of Writing.* Boston: Allyn and Bacon.

Vukelich, Carol, and **Joanne Golden.** (1984). "Early Writing: Development and Teaching Strategies." *Young Children, 39*(2), 3–8.

OTHER SOURCES

Cratty, Bryant. (1986). *Perceptual and Motor Development in Infants and Children.* Englewood Cliffs, NJ: Prentice-Hall.

Sampson, Michael R. (1986). *The Pursuit of Literacy: Early Reading and Writing.* Dubuque, IA: Kendall Hunt Publishing Company.

Schickedanz, Judith A. (1986). *More than ABCs: The Early Stages of Reading and Writing.* Washington, DC: National Association for the Education of Young Children.

Schickedanz, Judith A., David I. Schickedanz, and **Peggy D. Forsythe.** (1982). *Toward Understanding Children.* Boston: Little, Brown and Company.

LEARNING ACTIVITIES

1. Use the tenth section of the *Child Skills Checklist* on written language as a screening tool to observe all of the children in your classroom. Compare the children with checks at the higher levels of written language with their results in spoken language. Can you draw any conclusions?

2. Set up a writing table with paper and writing tools, and make a running record of how children use it on three different days.

3. Observe and make a running record of children using a typewriter or computer on three different days. How do they go about teaching themselves how to use the instrument? Do you see them changing what they are doing on the basis of their learning something about how the instrument works? Do they learn from their mistakes?

4. Read an appropriate alphabet book to an individual or small group of children. Let them try to match the letters in the book with letters from a set of magnetic or plastic letters.

5. Find out what other words the children who write their names can identify or write. What other activities might you plan for them?

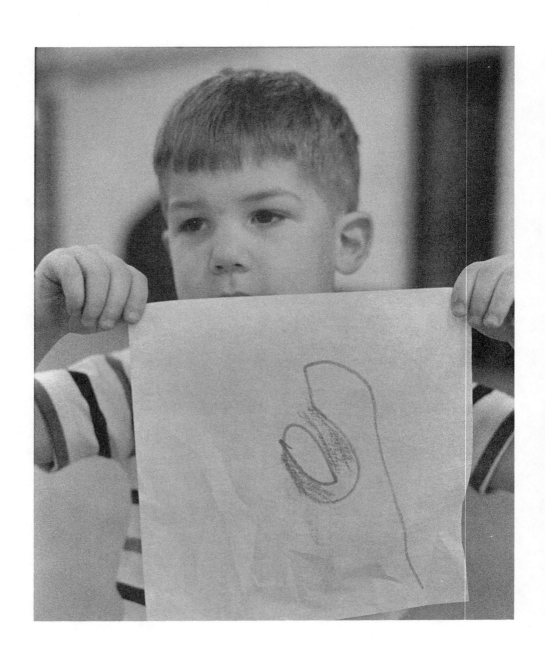

12 Art Skills

Art Skills Checklist

☐ Makes random marks or covers paper with color
☐ Scribbles on paper
☐ Forms basic shapes
☐ Makes mandalas
☐ Makes suns
☐ Draws human as circle with arms and legs attached
☐ Draws animals, trees
☐ Makes pictorial drawings

This chapter on the development of children's art skills and the following chapter on the development of imagination focus on the growth of creativity in young children. Too often creativity is not included when the major aspects of children's development—emotional, social, physical, cognitive, and language—are discussed. Yet it is as notable a drive in the development of the young human being as thinking or speaking.

The unfolding of the creative urge in the young child is a joy to behold for most sensitive early childhood caregivers. To help foster and not suppress such development is just as important here as it is for speaking and thinking skills. Yet we somehow equate creativity with special talent that not everyone displays; therefore, we downplay or ignore the development of creativity as more of a frill than a necessity for getting along in life.

In downplaying or ignoring creativity, we deprive the developing human of a basic aspect of his or her expressional capacities. Every child, surprising as it may seem, has the capacity to become an artist, a musician, a writer, or an inventor—if his interests carry him in that direction and if his caregivers and teachers give support and not control for his urge. The fact that not many people become artists is evidence of society's low priority for creativity and high priority for conformity.

Creativity connotes originality and novelty. To create, one brings into existence a new form of some kind. Creative people have original ideas, do things in new and different ways, see things from unique and novel perspectives. Creative people do not imitate; they do not follow the crowd. In a word, they are nonconformists.

Who are they? Artists, inventors, poets, writers, actors, musicians, interior decorators, chefs, architects, clothing designers, to name a few, and

301

young children. They are all people who follow their own bent and who use their ingenuity to design something new. Young children are naturally creative because everything they do, make, or say is completely new to them. They explore, experiment, put things together, take things apart, and manipulate things in ways no adult would ever think of, and the youngsters behave this way because they do not know any better.

Children come into the world uninhibited and with an entirely fresh point of view, their own. They continue to follow its bent until "they learn better," until they learn how society expects them to behave. Only those youngsters with strong enough psyches or strong enough outside support to resist society's inhibitions become the artists or creators whom we value as adults.

Could the children in your classroom become such creative adults? If their natural-born creativity is supported and valued by the adults around them and if it is given an opportunity to blossom and grow, the children will have the chance to escape the smothering pressure to conform and to be able to enrich their own lives and those of others with the products of their talent.

This chapter on creative development deals with art skills, not only because art is an important curriculum area in most early childhood programs, but also because many early childhood caregivers need help in restructuring their art programs. Too many activities in such programs suppress rather than support creativity.

The chapter just as well could deal with the development of science skills, which are also dependent on children's natural exploratory bent. Science, however, at the preschool level has somehow escaped the controlled approach that many teachers take with art. It seems good for children to explore plants and animals in all sorts of ways. But drawings should be done only in the manner prescribed by adults, because, of course, "adults know better."

This traditional point of view needs to be challenged. We need to step back and take a good look at the development of creativity. When does creativity appear in human beings? What are its characteristics? What can we do to help it grow? How can we keep from suppressing it?

This chapter looks at an eight-step developmental sequence in drawing skills that appear in all children everywhere in the world in the same order. Even blind children exhibit the beginning steps of the sequence until the youngsters' lack of visual feedback discourages them from continuing. You will note that this sequence is similar to the steps children take in developing physical skills, cognitive skills, and even writing skills.

It is obvious that the brain is programmed to accomplish all kinds of development in this particular order, from the general to the specific, as youngsters have the opportunity and materials to interact with their environment in a playful manner and thus discover what it and they are able to do.

MAKES RANDOM MARKS OR ☐
COVERS PAPER WITH COLOR

During the first year of life, children really do not draw. If they have access to a crayon, they are more apt to put it into their mouths than to put a mark on a paper. Around the age of thirteen months, according to Piaget, children's first scribbling begins (Lasky & Mukerji, p. 9). The first marks they make are usually random. These marks have more to do with movement, in fact, than with art. The toddler is surprised to find that a crayon, a pencil, or a paint brush will make marks. The youngsters are often captivated by watching the lines that their movements can make on a surface. The surface is not always paper, much to their caregiver's dismay. Children will mark on walls, table-tops, or anything else that will take a mark.

We need to be careful about scolding the child for her mistake. She was only investigating the properties of a strange new implement; she had no idea she was damaging anything. We want her to understand that the exploring and the marking were all right to do, but not on the walls and table. Harsh punishment at this stage may abort the budding creator's continued exploration of art. Have her help you clean off the marks with a child-sized sponge, give her a tablet to mark on, and put a newspaper under it to control slips.

This first stage of art skill development is purely mechanical and manipulative. The child is gaining control over the art tool whether it is a crayon, paint brush, pencil, felt-tip marker, or chalk. The child makes random marks or covers the paper with color without using eye control. Even blind children make the same kind of random marks. The urge to express oneself through drawing seems to be inborn, because young children with no art materials will make marks anyway on frosty windows or in the dirt.

Older children in your program who have had no access to art supplies or who have been suppressed in their attempts at home, still go through these same checklist stages, but more quickly. It will take these children far less time to learn manipulation of the materials, for instance. The youngsters soon will be into scribbling.

If You Have Not Checked This Item:
Some Helpful Ideas

> ■ **Have Art Materials Available
> During Free Choice Period**

Creativity blooms only when children have the freedom to try things on their own. Have paints available at one or two easels all the time. Have colored chalk and a small chalkboard, sets of watercolor felt-tip pens, sets of primary crayons, soft pencils, and various kinds of drawing paper available on low shelves next to art tables. Let children select and use their own materials in a spontaneous manner.

> ■ **Make Only Positive Comments**
> **on Children's Art Efforts**

Beginning drawers will often produce art that is smudgy and uninteresting from an adult point of view. Refrain from negative comments. You need to know that the children are not trying to draw a picture, but only to manipulate the medium. Your comments should reflect this: "You really worked hard in art this morning, Jeff. I'm glad you enjoy it so much."

☐ SCRIBBLES ON PAPER

From about two years of age through ages three and four (and sometimes later, depending on the child), an individual will mark on paper in a scribbling manner. At first the scribbles may be endless lines done in a rhythmic, manipulative manner. Eventually, the child will use eye control as well as hand/arm movement to make her scribbles and direct their placement on the paper. One scribble often is placed on top of another until the paper is a hodgepodge of lines and circles. Painters may cover over their painted scribbles with layers and layers of paint before they are finished. These scribbles are different from the writing scribbles, as noted in Chapter 11.

The product she has produced has little meaning to the child at first, for she is not trying to create something, but merely experimenting by moving colors around on a paper. The process is important to her, not the product. Adults, however, think of art mainly in terms of creating a product. Their response to scribbling is often either to dismiss it as unimportant and worthless or to ask children to tell them what they have drawn. Once children learn that adults expect this sort of information, the youngsters often begin naming their scribbles. This behavior does not mean that they really had anything in mind when they began moving the brush or crayon around on the paper. Our comments should focus on their efforts in the process of drawing, not on the imperfect products they first create.

Scribbling is hardly worthless. It is the first step in the self-taught process of learning to draw. In many respects, scribbling is the equivalent of babbling in the child's learning to speak. We support children in their babbling and congratulate them when they finally make sounds that seem to be words. Think what might happen to their language development if we forced them to stop making such worthless sounds, just as some adults force children to stop wasting their time making "worthless" scribbles.

Children work hard at scribbling. Only they know when a scribbled drawing is finished. Actually, not the drawing, but the process is finished. Some youngsters go over and over and over the lines they have made, almost as if they are practicing the way to make a straight or curved line. Their early products seem to show a greater proportion of vertical lines, especially in easel paintings (Smith, p. 301). But the children are able to make multiple horizontal lines, diagonal lines, and curved lines as well. Back and forth the youngsters work, sometimes changing their hand direction when they get tired and sometimes even changing hands. While two-year-olds place one scribble on top of another, three- and four-year-olds frequently put a single scribble on one paper (Kellogg, p. 18).

Rhoda Kellogg, who has collected and analyzed hundreds of thousands of children's drawings from around the world, has identified twenty scribbles that children make. Not all children make all twenty. Individuals tend to concentrate on a few favorites and to repeat them in many variations. The fact that all children everywhere produce the same twenty scribbles spontaneously—and no others—seems to indicate, though, that this early form of art somehow must be inborn in the human species.

Kellogg considers these scribbles to be "the building blocks of art" (Kellogg, p. 15). The individual's scribble "vocabulary" most easily can be read in his finger painting. He will draw his designs with one or more fingers, and then erase them before starting over. Because they do not pile up one on top of the other as with opaque paint or crayons, it is easier to see which of the twenty basic scribbles he favors.

It is not necessary for the early childhood teacher to identify a child's scribbles, only that he or she understands the importance of scribbles in the sequence of art skills development. Many children continue to go back to scribbles even when they have progressed beyond them to shape drawings. This is a perfectly natural progression. All child development tends to occur in a spiral rather than a straight line. We can expect children to appear to slip back even while they are moving forward.

If You Have Not Checked This Item: Some Helpful Ideas

■ Provide Controllable Materials

Beginners will not be able to progress much beyond scribbling unless they can control the materials. Be sure to provide fat, kindergarten-sized crayons for children to grip well. Children can use thin crayons, too, but sometimes the youngsters bear down so hard that they break the thin ones. Mix your tempera paints with just enough water to make them creamy but not drippy. Cut off the ends of long easel paintbrushes so that youngsters can manipulate the brushes easily. Wrap the ends of colored chalk with masking tape to help gripping and prevent smearing.

In the beginning, provide easel painters with contrasting colors rather than complementary colors in order to prevent muddy results. Children have more control when they start with only two contrasting colors instead of several different kinds. Avoid putting together red and green, yellow and purple, or blue and orange. Haskell recommends any of the following combinations instead:

1. Yellow with blue or red or green or brown
2. Orange with green or purple or brown or red
3. White with blue or red or green or purple (Haskell, p. 74)

▪ Be Nondirective

Allow children to explore and experiment with paint and chalk, finger paint and crayons, and felt-tip markers and pencils completely on their own. Put the materials out for their use during free play, or have materials invitingly placed on low shelves near art tables for the youngsters' own selection.

☐ FORMS BASIC SHAPES

As children's physical and mental development progresses and they are able to control the brush and paint more easily, their scribbles begin to take on the configuration of shapes. Kellogg has identified six basic shapes in children's early art: rectangle (including square), oval (including circle), triangle, Greek cross (+), diagonal cross (×), and odd shape (a catchall) (Kellogg, p. 45). These shapes do not necessarily appear separately, but rather they are mixed up with scribbles or with one another.

If children have had the freedom to experiment with art as toddlers, they usually begin to make basic shapes spontaneously by age three. Children's perceptual and memory skills help them to form, store, and retrieve concepts about shapes quite early if they have had appropriate experiences (see Chapter 8). The particular shapes a child favors seem to evolve from his own scribbles. Attempts at making ovals and circles usually appear very early. This form seems innately appealing to young humans everywhere, perhaps because of their preferred attention to the human face.

Circular movements in their scribbling eventually lead them to form an oval. Then the youngsters often repeat it, going round and round over the same shape. Visual discrimination of the shape and muscle control of the brush or crayon finally allow them to form the shape by itself instead of intertwined within a mass of scribbles. Memory comes into play as well, allowing the children to retrieve the oval from their repertory of marks and to repeat it another day.

The child's capacity to draw shapes, therefore, seems to emerge from his capacity to control the lines he makes in his scribbling. In other words, he makes one of the basic shapes because he remembers it from creating it spontaneously in his scribbling, not because he is copying the shape from his environment. As he experiments, he stumbles onto new ways to make new shapes. Certain ones seem more appealing, however, and individual children return to them again and again.

Three- and four-year-olds first create rectangles by drawing a set of parallel vertical lines and then adding horizontal lines at the top and bottom, rather than drawing a continuous line for a perimeter (Smith, p. 301). We understand why when we remember the problem children first have trying to make an enclosure with blocks (see Chapter 9). Thus, we see why it is important to give children many opportunities and much time to practice. The children are teaching themselves to draw, just as they taught themselves to block build, walk, talk, think, speak, and write.

If You Have Not Checked This Item: Some Helpful Ideas

- **Provide Materials Children Can Use on Their Own**

Easels should always be available. They are one of the best motivators for spontaneous drawing that you can have. Children soon find out that all they need for painting is to put on a smock and go to the easel. There is no need to get out paints, for they are already mixed and waiting. There is no need to ask for help or direction from the teacher. If an easel is unoccupied during free choice time, they can go and paint at it.

For children who are experienced easel painters, it is always good to challenge them with a new activity. Perhaps they would like to try flat table painting with paints in a muffin tin. Or you might make a table easel with two sections of cardboard taped together to form an inverted *V* over a table. Paper can be fastened to it with tacks or masking tape. Paint can be mixed and waiting in muffin tins or jars taped to the table so they will not tip over.

MAKES MANDALAS □

The next step in the sequence of children's self-taught art skills involves combining two of the shapes they have made. Kellogg has observed and written a great deal about this behavior. The Greek cross (+) and the diagonal cross (×) are favorite shapes. These are often combined with an oval or rectangle to make what is called a *mandala*. Mandalas do not necessarily stand alone on a sheet of paper but are usually repeated by children in a balanced way. Groups of these shapes or others form the bulk of art for three- and four-year-old children.

Pictorial drawing eventually evolves out of particular combinations of shapes. One of the first representations to occur in children's art is the human being. This representation seems to evolve naturally from the child's first experiments with an oval shape combined with a cross inside it (the mandala), which leads to an oval with lines radiating from its rim (the sun), and which later evolves into an oval with two lines for arms, two for legs, and small circles inside the large head/body oval for eyes (the human).

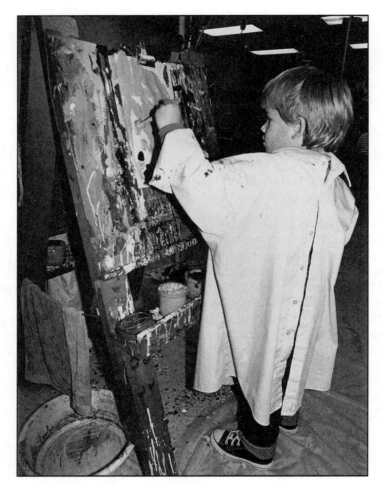

Having easels available at all times motivates
spontaneous painting. .

From mandalas to suns to humans is the natural sequence found
in much of children's spontaneous art. Watch for this development in the
children in your program. Talk to parents about the spontaneous way art
skills develop in children if youngsters are given the freedom to explore on
their own. Both you and the parents may want to save children's scribbling
and early shape drawings to see if you can identify the sequence of their
development. Be sure to date the art.

Because the shape combination called the mandala is a key part
of this sequence, it is treated as a separate checklist item for observers to
look for. The circle with the cross inside is a symbol found throughout
the world. In Oriental religions it is the symbol of the cosmos. Obviously,
young children are producing it spontaneously without any notion of its

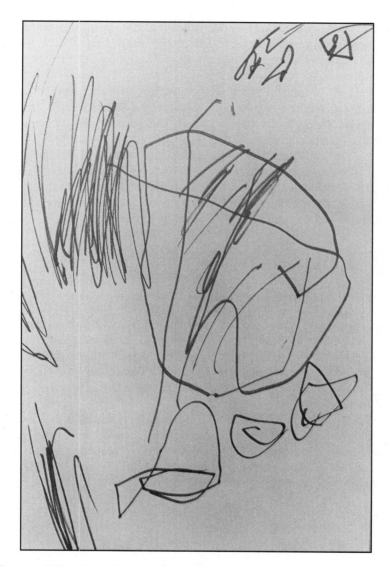

As children scribble, they often combine shapes such as the
circle and the cross to form a natural mandala.

symbolic meaning. Nevertheless, there must be an inborn appeal for such a
shape for it to appear as a natural sequence in children's art. Kellogg feels
that its overall balance is what makes it so appealing to the human species
(Kellogg, p. 68).

Early scribblings show many examples of crossed lines as well as
ovals and rectangles. It seems only natural that children eventually would experiment by trying to put the two together. Many scribbles show early attempts at placing a cross over a circle, possibly because children make

scribbles this way, one on top of the other. As children gain control of their implements and remember how to make the shapes they like, a shape like the mandala emerges naturally. If this shape is appealing to them, they will repeat it endlessly.

Perhaps this method reveals how early man came to include the mandala in his repertoire of symbols. Circles and squares with crosses inside them are found throughout the world in the rock-writing petroglyphs and pictographs of ancient man.

Not all children make mandalas, but most of them do. These basic shape combinations are never really lost once they have become a part of a person's art vocabulary. Take a look at the doodles adults make in a nonthinking, spontaneous fashion. You yourself still may draw the mandalas you first discovered as a child!

If You Have Not Checked This Item: Some Helpful Ideas

▪ Provide Variety in Your Art Materials

Not all children may enjoy painting at an easel. You should include other possibilities as often as possible. Finger painting is one. It can be done on a smooth paper, a tabletop, or a cookie sheet. Paper finger paintings can be hung to dry and are thus preserved if the child wants to save them. Tabletop finger paintings can also be preserved before the table is cleaned, by pressing a paper onto them and rubbing the paper.

The finger paint itself can be made from liquid starch that is poured onto paper with powder paint shaken into it, from wallpaper paste mixed with water and poster paint to the proper consistency, or with soap powder mixed with a little water and paint powder. Soap powder can also be whipped until stiff and used as white paint against colored construction paper.

☐ MAKES SUNS

A combination of an oval with lines radiating from its rim is often the next step in the child's natural sequence of drawing a pictorial representation. We call this shape combination a "sun" because it looks like the symbol adults use to represent the sun. Children do not call their sun-shape a sun unless adults or more experienced peers first give it the name. The youngsters are not drawing a sun, merely experimenting with shapes. If this combination appeals to them, they will repeat it many times. When they finally do begin to draw pictorially, they sometimes will call this figure a spider.

Although the figure seems quite simple to draw, the sun does not appear spontaneously in children's drawings in the beginning. Two-year-olds can make curved and straight lines, but children rarely produce suns before age three (Kellogg, p. 74).

The sun figure may well emerge from the children's experimentations with the mandala figure. Most of children's early attempts at sun figures include some kinds of marks in the center of the figures, either lines, dots, or ovals. Once the children have begun to make a sun with a clear center, they have progressed beyond the mandala to something new. These early suns with center marks are not forgotten, however. When children begin to draw "sun faces," their first humans, they include the center marks for eyes, nose, and mouth.

We see sun figures in primitive rock art as well. Early man must have followed the same sequence in his progression to artistic representation.

If You Have Not Checked This Item: Some Helpful Items

■ Draw with Chalk

Colored chalk is very appealing to children if they can grip it and control for its smeariness. Wrap the upper end with foil or masking tape to make gripping easier. Soft, thick chalk is preferred. Regular-sized chalk breaks too easily with the pressure some children apply. Chalk should first be used dry for children to become used to its properties. Then you can wet either the paper or the chalk for a richer effect. Use either a water-sugar solution (4 parts warm water to 1 part sugar) or liquid starch, and apply it to the paper for children to draw on with dry chalk. Or use the liquid as a dip for children to wet the chalk but draw on a dry surface. Many children like the rhythm of dipping and drawing (Haskell, p. 45). Dry chalk marks on paper can also be smeared around to create different effects.

■ Draw with Felt-Tip Pens

Water soluble felt-tip pens are always favorites with children. They seem to be able to control these more easily than paint brushes or crayons. The pens' thick size and smooth marking ability make them especially well-suited to preschool art. Some marking pens have brush-tip rather than felt-tip points. These have the spreading capacity of water color paint. It is not necessary or even desirable to give each child an entire set of pens of all colors. Give the youngsters only a few colors at a time until they express the need for more.

■ Keep Art Activities Spontaneous

Do not use pictures, figure drawings, or models for your children to copy. This is not how spontaneous art develops. Even children who have reached the pictorial stage do not need to copy. You will find that they draw what they know rather than what they see.

☐ DRAWS HUMAN AS CIRCLE WITH ARMS AND LEGS ATTACHED

One of the first pictorial figures that young children draw is a person. They draw it as an oval or circle with two lines coming out of the bottom for legs, a line from either side for arms (sometimes these are omitted), circles or dots inside the head circle for eyes and sometimes a nose and mouth. All children everywhere seem to draw their first humans in this spontaneous manner. They are known in the art world as "tadpole" drawings because of the resemblance.

To adults unfamiliar with children's sequence of development, these are strange humans indeed: all head and no body, with arms and legs attached to the head. Surely children age three and four can see that a person's arms and legs are attached to the body and not the head. Adult concepts about art, however, are entirely different from those of young children. All along, adults have felt that the product of children's art, the drawing or painting, is the most important thing. As a matter of fact, to the young child, it is the process that is more important. In the beginning, they are not drawing a picture but developing a skill.

Their production of a human is the transition to pictorial drawing for most young children. The method they apply is the same one they used for making shapes and symbols. They draw *what they know how to make*, not what they see. Out of their practice with mandalas and suns comes this sun-face human with a few of the sun's rays for arms and legs.

It is not surprising, in fact, that their first people are all face. We remember that even infants attend to this image most of all. The human brain seems to be programmed to take in details about faces. This, after all, is the most important part of the human being.

As children first create their circle humans, they do not always repeat their drawings exactly the same. All children make armless humans at one time or another, even though the youngsters may have drawn arm lines earlier. This behavior does not indicate the children are regressing or are cognitively immature. It may appear only because the proportion of two parallel legs to head is more appealing alone than with arms sticking out at the sides. Children rarely draw legless humans (Kellogg, p. 101). This behavior may also result from the brain's tendency to overgeneralize in early categories. Later details will be more discriminating.

Without a great many examples of a single child's drawings, it is risky to try to determine where he or she stands in this developmental sequence. Schools or psychologists who try to evaluate a child's maturity on the basis of only one drawing of a person (such as the Draw-a-Person Test) are basing their findings on extremely sketchy information. Kellogg found that one-third of 2,500 public school children who were asked to "draw a man" each day for five days, drew such different humans that their scores on the Draw-a-Man Test varied by as much as 50 percent (Kellogg, p. 191).

As children have more practice drawing their early people, they often add hair or hats, hands or fingers, and feet or toes. The additions may be lines, circles, or scribbles. The children may identify their persons as being themselves or someone else. The actual size of the person named in the drawing is usually not considered by young children. Instead, they often draw the most important person in the picture as the biggest. The so-called stick figure is not a part of spontaneous children's art; the figure seems to be learned by children at age five or six by copying the work of adults or older peers (Kellogg, p. 108).

Eventually, children will add a body to their head drawings. They often do this by drawing two extremely long legs and putting a horizontal line part way up between them. You may remember that this is the common method they used earlier to draw rectangles. The youngsters often will draw a belly button in the middle of the body. By this time, they frequently are drawing other pictorial representations, as well. These representations, as you will note, are based on the children's previous experience, showing once again how development proceeds in a continuous sequence from the general to the specific so long as children have the freedom to learn naturally.

If You Have Not Checked This Item: Some Helpful Ideas

■ Record Children's Stories About Their Drawings

Some children verbalize a great deal about their drawings. Others do not. You should take your lead from the child. If he or she likes to tell you stories about the people in the drawings, you may want to record these. Children may want to have their stories displayed along with their art on the classroom walls. On the other hand, they may want to make a scrapbook of their art or to take their art home. If children do not want to talk about their art products, you can support them best by comments like "You surely put a lot of effort into your drawing today, Sheila."

Keep in mind that much of children's early art is not pictorial, so there really are not any stories to tell about it, unless, of course, adults press children to make up something.

DRAWS ANIMALS, TREES ☐

Animals

Once children have discovered the way to draw a person, they will often begin drawing animals as well. Youngsters' first animals are hard to distinguish from humans. It is obvious the animals are based on the same practiced form: a head with eyes, nose, and mouth, and a body with arms sticking out from the sides and legs coming out from the bottom. Often the animal is facing front like a person and seems to be standing on two legs. The two ears sticking up straight from the top of the head are what makes the drawing an animal instead of a person. Sometimes these are pointed like a cat's ears and sometimes they are circular like a mouse's ears. This is a transitional animal.

Eventually, the young artist will find a way to make his animal horizontal with an elongated body parallel to the bottom of the paper, four legs in a row from the bottom of the body, a head at one end, and often a tail at the other end. The features of the face are still positioned in a frontal pose and not a profile. Most animal head profiles do not appear in children's drawings until around age five years or later.

In fact, many children do not draw animals until they go to kindergarten at age five. This behavior—or lack of it—may be due to their progress in their own developmental sequence, but drawing animals is also influenced by the kindergarten curriculum. Often kindergarten teachers give children outline animals to copy, which may, in fact, short-circuit the youngsters' spontaneous development. Kellogg believes many teachers seem to feel that a child's self-taught system differs too widely from adult drawing and that the child, therefore, needs to be taken in hand and taught how to draw "correctly" (Kellogg, p. 114). Children often abandon art in elementary school because of lack of teacher approval for their natural art.

Trees

The first trees are also transitional drawings based on the human figure children have taught themselves to draw. The first trees look like armless humans with two long legs for the trunk and a circular head for the treetop, which often contains small circles or dots that may be leaves but look more like fruit. The trees are not drawn to size. They may be similar in height to the humans in the picture or even smaller. A few four-year-olds may draw trees, but most children are five years old before they begin drawing trees.

As children have practice on trees, more details evolve. The tops of some trees resemble the sun, with the rays being branches and with balls at the ends of the branches being leaves. Other children make branches coming out from the trunk like arms on a human. The first flowers are also drawn to a familiar model: a sun with a stem.

The children in your classroom may not have advanced to this level. In this case, you should leave the checklist item blank. Given the freedom to develop art skills spontaneously, children will make their own progress as individuals. It is not your role to push the youngsters ahead, but to provide materials, time, and support so that the children may make their own progress according to their own biological timetables.

If You Have Not Checked This Item: Some Helpful Ideas

■ Add New Art Activities

Your children may want to try drawing with liquid glue from a plastic squeeze bottle. They may want to draw with a pencil or other marker first and then follow the lines with glue. Or they can try the glue without guidelines. Because glue is transparent when it dries, you may want to add food coloring to the bottles. This liquid glue is a much more free-flowing medium; children will need to play with it for awhile to see how it works and how to control it. They will need to squeeze and move the bottle at the same time, a trick of coordination that may be difficult for some. Do not expect pictorial designs from glue drawing.

MAKES PICTORIAL DRAWINGS ☐

A few of the children in your classroom may begin doing pictorial drawings at age three and a few more at age four. Do not expect all of the youngsters to make such drawings. Let them progress through their own sequences of development at their own individual rates. Those who do draw pictorially will be using the previously discussed repertory of figures that they have developed. Their drawings will be representations and not reproductions, for the young child draws what he knows, not what he sees. This principle is especially apparent in children's spontaneous drawings at age six, when many youngsters go through a stage of so-called x-ray drawings that show both the inside and outside of objects at the same time. The children's drawings show things as the youngsters know them, rather than just what can be seen. People are shown inside drawings of houses that are seen from the outside, for example.

The children in your classroom probably will not have reached this stage, nor will they have developed a baseline in their drawings much before age five. Objects are still free-floating on their art papers, just as their first spontaneous letters are (see Chapter 11). This different perspective used by young children is sometimes used by adult artists as well.

Children also interpret their pictorial drawings differently from adults. Often youngsters do not start out to draw a particular thing. Instead, they describe their art more by the way it turns out than by what they had in mind. The way it turns out may have more to do with the materials they are using than anything else. Runny paint in easel drawings may remind the youngsters of smoke, rain, or fire, for instance.

On the other hand, the children purposefully may make a picture of the post office that the class visited on a field trip. The picture will look, of course, just like the building shape they have learned to do spontaneously and not at all like the post office itself. Children first draw buildings by combining mostly rectangular shapes in various ways and not by looking at buildings. The drawing often has a door in the middle and at least two square windows above it. Roofs may be flat or pointed and often have a chimney with smoke coming out. The drawing catches the essence of the building, not the reality. Some four-year-olds also draw cars and trucks, as well as boats and planes. Often it is hard to tell the difference between early cars and trucks.

Once children have a repertory of figures that the adults around them seem to accept, children will begin to put the figures together into scenes. The size and color of their objects will not be realistic. The more important the object or person, the larger the child will make it. Colors will have little relation to the objects being depicted. Colors depend more upon the particular brush the child happens to pick up or a color the child happens to favor at the moment. Objects will be free-floating, as mentioned, and not anchored to a baseline, but the effect will be balanced and pleasing, nevertheless.

Those children who verbalize about their art may tell you things about their drawings that have little to do with what your eyes seem to show you. The youngsters must be speaking about an inner vision of their world, you decide. You are right, of course. From these inner visions come creative ideas, you remember. Support this beginning urge toward creativity in all of the children by giving it the freedom to grow spontaneously.

If You Have Not Checked This Item: Some Helpful Ideas

■ Encourage Children to Draw About Field Trips

Not all of your children can or want to draw pictorially. But for those who do, you can suggest they draw a picture about a trip you have taken together. Children find it satisfying to be able to represent things they know about. They can tell about the things in words, have you write down their words, or record their words on tape. But it is also good to make a drawing or build a block structure about new things they have encountered. Their products help you as a teacher to find out what is important to them and how they conceptualize the new ideas they have gained.

■ Have the Children Draw About Things in Their Repertory

If you know the children can draw people, houses, trees, and animals, you may want to ask them to draw a picture of their house and family. Those who want to, can have you write down their story about the drawing.

TABLE 8.   Development of art skills

Age	Art Skill
1–2	Makes random marks on paper Begins scribbling
2–3	Makes scribbles one on top of the other May cover paper with layers of color
3–4	May put a single scribble on a paper Makes basic shapes
4–5	Combines two shapes, often the circle and the cross to make mandala Draws suns Draws human as circle with arms and legs
5–6	Draws head of animals in profile Draws trees Makes pictorial drawings Includes baseline in pictures

OBSERVING, RECORDING, AND INTERPRETING ART SKILLS

Screen all of your children using the eight items of the *Child Skills Checklist* for art skills. If you find that most of your three- and four-year-olds have not progressed beyond the random marks or scribbles stages, ask yourself if your program has allowed the children the opportunity and freedom to pursue art on their own. Do you have at least one easel in the classroom? Do you have an art area where children can get their own supplies and do their own work without the teacher's directions? Give children this opportunity and freedom to explore and experiment with art on their own. Then do a second screening using the eight checklist items to see if more checks appear under "Art Skills."

REFERENCES CITED

Haskell, Lendall L. (1979). *Art in the Early Childhood Years.* Columbus, OH: Charles E. Merrill Publishing Company.

Kellogg, Rhoda. (1970). *Analyzing Children's Art.* Palo Alto, CA: National Press Books.

Lasky, Lila, and **Rose Mukerji.** (1980). *Art: Basic for Young Children.* Washington, DC: National Association for the Education of Young Children.

Smith, Nancy R. (1982). "The Visual Arts in Early Childhood Education: Development and the Creation of Meaning." In Bernard Spodek (Ed.), *Handbook of Research in Early Childhood Education*, pp. 295–317. New York: The Free Press.

OTHER SOURCES

Beaty, Janice J. (1988). *Skills for Preschool Teachers.* Columbus, OH: Merrill Publishing Company.

Bos, Bev. (1978). *Don't Move the Muffin Tins: A Hands-Off Guide to Art for the Young Child.* Roseville, CA: Turn the Page Press.

Jenkins, Peggy Davison. (1980). *Art for the Fun of It: A Guide for Teaching Young Children.* Englewood Cliffs, NJ: Prentice-Hall.

LEARNING ACTIVITIES

1. Use section eleven of the *Child Skills Checklist* on art skills as a screening tool to observe all of the children in your classroom. Compare the children with checks at the higher levels in the sequence of art skill development with their checks in cognitive development, Chapter 8, especially in the recognition of basic geometric shapes, colors, and differences in size. Can you draw any conclusions from this comparison?

2. Based on your screening survey, choose one or two children who have not shown much interest or development in art, and try to involve them in an art activity. Use one of the other checklist areas in which they have shown interest and skill, as the basis for the art activity. Record the result.

3. Set up your art area so that children can use it without adult help or direction. Record by running record what happens in this area on three different days.

4. Carry out one of the suggested art activities from the chapter with a group of children who show interest. Compare their results with their checklist standings in art skills. What can you conclude from this?

5. Save the art products of one of your children over a six-month period. Be sure to date them. How do they compare with the sequence of art skill development discussed here?

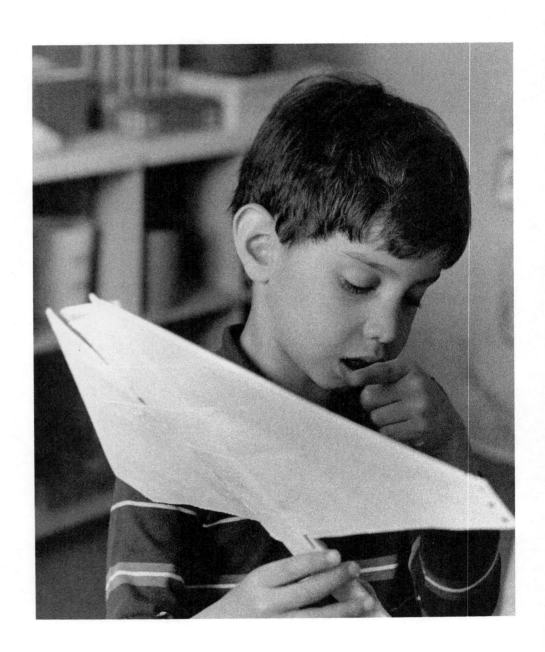

13 Imagination

Imagination Checklist

☐ Pretends by replaying familiar routines
☐ Needs particular props to do pretend play
☐ Assigns roles or takes assigned roles
☐ May switch roles without warning
☐ Uses language for creating and sustaining plot
☐ Uses exciting, danger-packed themes
☐ Takes on characteristics and actions related to role
☐ Uses elaborate and creative themes, ideas, details

A second important aspect of creativity in young children is their development of imagination. For young children, imagination is the ability to pretend or make believe, to take a role other than their own, to create fanciful situations, or to act out a fantasy of their own making. It is an activity that most children seem to engage in a great deal before the age of seven. It is a type of play that many adults fail to see as significant in the development of the child because they do not understand it. But early childhood specialists have come to recognize imagination as one of the most effective means for promoting the development of the young child's intellectual skills, social skills, language, and, most especially, creativity (Smilansky, p. 12).

One of the basic tools for creating is imagining, the ability to see a picture in our mind's eye. This ability allows us to tap into memories of the past and reform them as possibilities for the present or future. Children's make-believe relies heavily on this capacity to draw on such internal images and to create new ones. The Singers, who have done extensive research and writing on children's imaginative play, believe that imagining is essential to the development of intellectual and language skills as well. Children remember ideas and words they have actually experienced because the youngsters can associate the ideas with pictures in their minds (Singer & Singer, p. 6). This association reveals why it is so important for children to have many real experiences. Otherwise, there are few images stored in the youngsters' brains for them to draw on.

A number of adults who have been identified as creative report that they engaged in a great deal of daydreaming and fantasy play as children

321

(Singer, p. 228). This finding is not surprising when we realize that imaginative play relies heavily on the creative skills of the young child. She must utilize previous experiences in new and different ways. She extracts the essence of a familiar experience, such as getting ready for bed, and applies it creatively to a pretend activity, such as putting to bed her doll who does not want to go. She may then take the role of the doll herself as well as that of the mother losing patience with the stubborn dollie.

The child experiments with the situation, playing it this way one time and that way another. If a peer joins in, there is another point of view to be reckoned with. If the original player strays too far from her role, she may lose it to a player with more definite ideas on how a mother should act. Or she may switch to a different role herself and try on yet another set of characteristics. She learns to recall fragments of past experiences and combine them in novel ways, adding original dialog, fresh nuances to her characterizations, and new directions to her plots. No playwright ever had better practice.

In addition to being her own creative playwright, she is also the actor, the director, the audience for other actors, and an interactor with others, whether she plays her role or steps out of it to make aside-like comments on the progress of the spontaneous play. Just as with every other aspect of her development, she is creating her own knowledge when she has the freedom to participate in imaginative play.

This time the knowledge is about real life and the other actors in it: how they behave, how they respond to stressful situations, how they carry out their work roles, how they speak, and how they interact with one another. Adult observers of imaginative play find that most of the make-believe play of children is centered around "the social problems of adults with whom children have close contacts" (Smilansky, p. 21). Common themes include the family and home, doctors and hospitals, work and professions, school, and dramatizations of escape, rescue, and superheroes.

Playing at life is not the inconsequential activity many adults seem to think it is. Children who have had extensive practice doing imaginative play are often those who are most successful in life as adults. Many disadvantaged children who have not been allowed or encouraged to engage in such play are also at a disadvantage as adults, for they have missed an important grounding in social, intellectual, and creative skills.

Chapter 4 discusses imaginative play as it applies to the development of children's social skills in solitary, parallel, and group play. This chapter looks at the same phenomenon in relation to the development of creativity in young children. To discover where the children in your classroom stand in the sequence of their development, make an assessment of each child by using the eight items of the *Child Skills Checklist* as you observe children pretending in the dramatic play area, at the water table, in the block corner, at the wood bench, with science materials, at the easels, or on the playground.

You will find that young children pretend about everything they do, both alone and with others. Tap into this rich vein of creativity in young children yourself, and you may see life and the world from a completely new and fresh perspective: the *what if* point of view. This "what if" perspective is the true magic of childhood, children's belief that they can make life anything they want it to be.

Adults know from the hard facts of reality that life cannot be changed so easily, or can it? What if we also believed we could really make life anything we wanted it to be? Does believing make it so? Children act as if this idea were true. Is there a way we can help them develop into adults who will actually be able to make their adult lives come out the way they want them to be? Is there a way we can preserve the "child" in ourselves so that we can do the same? Take a hard look at the developmental sequence in imaginative play that follows to see what you need to do to keep this spark alive in children and to rekindle its essence in your own life.

PRETENDS BY REPLAYING ☐ FAMILIAR ROUTINES

This checklist item describes the earliest of the imaginative play behaviors in young children. Incredibly enough, it appears as early as one year of age (Smilansky, p. 10). By age eighteen months, infants may go through the imaginary routine of feeding themselves with an empty spoon and cup, and even saying "Yummy!" The Singers believe that this tendency to play or replay past events through imagery is one of the basic capacities of the human brain (Singer & Singer, p. 3).

Two-Year-Olds

By two years of age, most normal children spend a great deal of time at home or in a toddler program replaying fragments of everyday experience if given the chance. Pieces of familiar routines are repeated over and over with little change or little effort to expand them into a longer sequence. The toddler will put the baby to bed by putting the doll in the cradle, covering it, and saying "Nite-nite." Then the toddler will pick up the doll and begin the routine all over again. Once a particular routine is established with a two-year-old, it seems to become quite rigid, almost like a ritual (Segal & Adcock, p. 92).

Words are not all that important in the pretending of two-year-olds, however. The youngsters use them sparingly, mainly to accompany actions or for sound effects. Actions are the main ingredients of the imaginative play of two-year-olds. Once these youngsters get an idea for pretend play, they try to put it into action immediately. They do not set the stage with words or search for appropriate props.

Props may be used, though, if they are available. Two-year-olds use props realistically, for the most part. Dishes are used for eating, not usually as a steering wheel or a flying saucer. Because these youngsters are also impulsive in their behavior, props can influence the type of pretend play they engage in. A toy broom can inspire them to sweep, for instance, even though they had no previous plans for cleaning. They do not need props to pretend, however. Some two-year-olds may even carry on their play with invisible props.

The imaginative play of these youngsters is mainly centered around chores and routines such as eating, going to bed, caring for the baby, getting their hair washed, turning on television, shopping, visiting grandma,

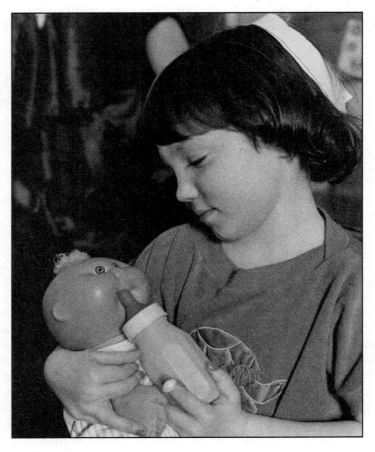

Doll play is a frequent activity for both boys and girls of this age, but older children often depend more on their imaginations than on props.

driving the car, and getting gas for the car. Two-year-olds are very serious about their play, and they take offense if adults make fun of their sometimes comical mode of pretending.

Doll play is also a frequent activity for both boys and girls of this age. Dolls are usually undressed, laid in a box or bed, and covered completely over with a piece of cloth in a very ritualized routine (Caplan & Caplan, p. 143).

The play of two-year-olds is frequently solitary and rarely involves more than one other player. They and their agemates have not yet developed the social skills for coming together in a common endeavor. When two children this age play together, one usually imitates the other. However, others will join in if they see one child doing something, and sometimes a wild melee ensues. The pretend play of children this young is brief at best, and it suddenly may disintegrate into running and squealing if other children are around.

Older children who have not done much imaginative play may start in this manner in your center. Their maturity usually carries them on quickly to a more advanced level.

If You Have Not Checked This Item: Some Helpful Ideas

■ Read a Book

Books with talking animal characters or human characters who use their imaginations to behave in unusual ways may stimulate your children to do likewise.

Bubble, Bubble by Mercer Mayer (New York: Four Winds Press, 1973) is a small-format wordless picture book that features a little boy who buys a magic bubble maker. He blows a wild assortment of bubble figures until his creatures begin to turn on him and he has to blow new creatures to scare away the old ones. Children must make up their own story to go along with the pictures. Two-year-olds will enjoy first having the adult make up a story and then trying to make up a story themselves. Because it is a small book in which every picture must be seen, you should read it only to one or two at a time.

If you use *Bubble, Bubble* in your program, be sure to have a bubble pipe and soap available for children to create their own inventions afterwards.

■ Have Appropriate Props Available

Knowing that the youngest children pretend mainly about familiar household routines, you should have eating, cleaning, and sleeping props available in your dramatic play area. Put out all kinds of baby dolls and their beds as well.

☐ NEEDS PARTICULAR PROPS
TO DO PRETEND PLAY

Three-Year-Olds

If three-year-olds have had a chance to pretend when they were two, they gradually develop new skills and interests in their imaginative play. The fragments of familiar routines that occupied the children earlier become more extended and less rigid as the youngsters mature. Three-year-olds begin to think a bit about the pretending they are about to do, rather than just acting on a sudden impulse. This forethought leads them to preplanning the play by finding or gathering certain props. In fact, some three-year-olds cannot proceed with the play until the right prop is found.

The rigidity expressed by many two-year-olds in their ritualistic manner of pretending is thus carried over by many three-year-olds in their insistence on particular props in order to play. Three-year-olds may feel they need a particular hat, costume, doll, or steering wheel in order to carry out a role. Many times the object is the basis for the play, but not so much on impulse as with the two-year-olds. Three-year-olds very much enjoy dressing up and playing a role, and they have a much broader concept of how to do it.

Props very well may serve the children as an instrument for getting out of themselves. Because three-year-olds are still strongly self-centered, they may need a prop in order to break away from their own point of view. Just as shy children can lose themselves in speaking through a hand puppet or from behind a mask, three-year-olds may need the extra impetus of an object that is outside of themselves to get them started in pretending to be someone else.

Some three-year-olds are very much into imaginary play of a different sort at home. They have an imaginary playmate or invisible friend. This is the most common age for children to invent such a friend. Research finds that first-born children who do not have many playmates may use their imaginations to create such a companion (Segal & Adcock, p. 10). This research gives additional evidence that pretending is an innate activity with young humans.

Such invisible companions, however, serve a different purpose from the pretend play in nursery school. They are invented companions for children who have none, loving friends for children who do not receive love from those around them, or protectors for children who need someone to support them. When children come to a preschool program, they usually leave their imaginary friends behind, often permanently. Once the children are occupied with real peers, they have little need for a made-up friend.

Family activities are still a large part of three-year-olds' pretend play in preschool programs, with dress-up in the housekeeping area, doll play, hospital play, and community helpers play included. Three-year-olds also enjoy driving cars and trains, flying jet planes, and being firefighters. These themes are carried out in dramatic play, block building, table block games, clay and paint creations, the water table, the woodworking bench, singing, creative movement, puppets, and toy telephone activities—anywhere and everywhere children gather.

If You Have Not Checked This Item: Some Helpful Ideas

■ Have a Variety of Props Available

In the large motor area have large wooden riding trucks, wagons, and a wheelbarrow, as well as large hollow blocks and floorboards for building child-sized structures. Put out a full-length mirror in the dress-up area. Include costume jewelry, scarves, handbags, wallets, belts, vests, shoes, aprons, all kinds of hats, doctor's equipment, goggles, binoculars, badges, umbrellas, and canes. An assortment of men's and women's clothes in teenage size is often easier for young children to handle.

■ Make Your Own Special Props

There is no need to spend a great deal of money equipping your dramatic play area because you can make your own props as needed. The excellent book *Be What You Want to Be! The Complete Dress-Up and Pretend Craft Book* by Phyllis and Noel Fiarotta (New York: Workman Publishing Company, 1977) gives directions for making from discarded materials such props as a telephone, cash register, typewriter, wigs, mustaches, hats, magnifying glass, screwdrivers, gas pump, musical instruments, cameras, ship's helm, barber shop pole and supplies, restaurant supplies (including fake food), florist shop supplies (including potted plants), bakery supplies (including fake cakes), plumbing equipment, shoe repair materials, firefighting equipment, and more. Obviously, it is beyond the capabilities of many three-year-olds to make these props on their own. However, the youngsters can assist adults in their preparation and will love it.

■ Read a Book

A whole series of books three-year-olds may relate to tells of the adventures of three-year-old Anthony and his "invisible" friend, Blackboard Bear. *We're in Big Trouble, Blackboard Bear* by Martha Alexander (New York: Dial Press, 1980) is a recent addition to the series. In this book, the bear goes out at night when Anthony is sleeping and causes all sorts of mischief at the neighbors' house. The bear, like Anthony, is able to restore things to rights with his drawing skill on the blackboard. Children will also enjoy *Blackboard Bear; And My Mean Old Mother Will Be Sorry, Blackboard Bear;* and *I Sure Am Glad to See You, Blackboard Bear.*

☐ ASSIGNS ROLES OR TAKES ASSIGNED ROLES

Three-year-olds usually find it is more fun when several children play together. You will have checked on this previously in your observations concerning social play. This item signals the beginning of peer play for most children. Pretend episodes usually do not last long in the beginning because most children of this age are not yet flexible when it comes to differences of opinions. This inflexibility sometimes shows up when it comes to who will play what role.

Many three-year-olds try to control imaginative play by assigning the roles. The dominant child takes the role he or she wants and assigns the others, who may or may not agree. Most children this age want their own role. As their creativity blossoms through this type of play, their solutions to role assignment problems are often highly creative and something an adult would not have thought of. Listen to your children to see how they resolve such problems.

The role of mother is a favorite one for girls of this age. What would you have done when all four of the girls playing together wanted to be the mother and no one would give in? After a few minutes of discussion—or rather argument—it became clear to the four that Janie, who spoke up first about being the mother, would not change, nor would the other three, and a different solution needed to be found. The girls accepted the fact that there could be only one mother in the household, but they could not agree that the other girls would be sisters or babies or grandmothers. Suddenly one of the girls said, "We'll all be other mothers who are visiting Janie this morning," and they were.

Three-year-olds who are playing pretend roles at home often will act the same way in assigning roles, even to adults. "I'll be the mother and you be the baby" is a role reversal commonly proposed by a child to her mother. Go along with the role reversal if you are the adult, and you will enjoy observing how your child plays your role.

Here is a typical role assignment situation played by three-year-olds and recorded in a running record.

> Sherry is in the play grocery store holding a box of cereal. She hands box to child playing role of cashier, walks back to grocery shelves, picks up box, and puts it in grocery cart. "Here's our groceries, Mother," she says to Ann, who is standing nearby.
>
> Sherry picks up bag filled with groceries and carries it to play house. She walks back to grocery store. "I'm gonna be mother," she says loudly to herself. She picks up several boxes off shelf and walks to cashier, who puts groceries in bag. "Mother, it's time to go home," she says to Ann. Ann gives no response but pays for her groceries. "There are no more groceries. We have to leave now," says Sherry. She still gets no response from Ann. "I'm the mother and you're the grandmother. I'm not a little kid," she says to Ann. No response.

They walk to house together. She puts her bag down and helps Ann with hers. "We have to unload everything now." They start to unpack all the groceries. "Oh, no, daughter," she says to Ann, "when it's cleanup time we have to pick all this up." Both girls laugh.

Since Ann was originally the director of this play episode and Sherry had evidently agreed to the role of daughter by taking it, it is interesting to see what strategy Sherry now uses to get out of an unwanted role. First, she states loudly but to herself that she is going to be the mother. Since she receives no response, she retains her daughter role at first, but then she states outright to Ann that she is the mother and Ann can be the grandmother. Sherry still gets no response. Silence does not necessarily give consent among young children. Silence may only mean that the challenged child does not want to engage in an argument, not that she agrees to give up her role. Sherry tries calling Ann daughter, but Ann refuses to get involved verbally, so the role problem is still unresolved before cleanup time ends the play.

Another imaginative play episode previously recorded in Chapter 1 shows children who are late three- and four-year-olds engaged in the type of role assignment problem being discussed here.

Katy is playing by herself with plastic blocks, making guns; she walks into other room.

K: Lisa, would you play with me? I'm tired of playing by myself.

They walk into other room to slide & climbing area.

K: I am Wonder Woman.

L: So am I.

K: No, there is only one Wonder Woman. You are Robin.

L: Robin needs a Batman because Batman and Robin are friends.

All this takes place under slides and climber. Lisa shoots block gun which Katy has given her. Katy falls on floor.

L (to teacher): We're playing superfriends and Wonder Woman keeps falling down.

Katy opens eyes, gets up, and says:

K: Let's get out our batmobile and go help the world.

She runs to other room and back, making noises like a car.

L: Wonder Woman is died. She fell out of the car.

She falls down.

K: It's only a game, wake up. Lisa, you be Wonder Woman, I'll be . . .

L: Let's play house now.

Katy begins sliding down the slide.

K: We have a lot of superfriends to do.

(She says this while sliding.)

K: Robin is coming after you!

(She shouts this to Lisa, running from slide into other room.)

Lisa has gone into the housekeeping area and says to Katy:

L: Katy, here is your doll's dress.

(It was lost yesterday.)

John joins the girls.

L: I'm Wonder Woman.

K: I'm Robin.

J: I'm Batman. Where is the batmobile?

K: It's in here.

They run into the other room, and Katy points under the slide, telling John what the batmobile can do. Then all run to the other room and back again.

K: John, we are not playing superfriends any more.

This typical pretending episode illustrates perfectly the kind of role assignment and switching so characteristic of children this age. It is obvious from the children's easy agreement that they have played together before and therefore accept certain conditions. Katy is the director here and assigns the roles. She takes the role of Wonder Woman and assigns Lisa the role of Robin. Lisa really does not agree (we soon see), but she accepts her assignment. She probably has gone through this with Katy before and knows that if she plays along without making a fuss, her turn will come. It comes quite soon, in fact, when she notes that Katy seems to have abandoned the Wonder Woman role by suddenly getting out the batmobile and "going to help the world."

Here Lisa announces that she is Wonder Woman and has fallen out of the car and died. Katy agrees to her new role by saying: "It's only a game, wake up. Lisa, you be Wonder Woman." When John joins the game and takes the role of Batman, the girls do not object at first. But obviously they know how to get rid of unwanted players by announcing: "John, we are not playing superfriends any more."

Observe to discover what other creative ploys your children use to get peers to take role assignments or to get out of assigned roles they do not want and into ones they really want.

If your children are engaged in this kind of dramatic play, you will probably be checking this item. If you leave it blank, it means either that the child is not playing because he has not reached this level of group imaginative play or that he does not assign roles or accept assignments. If this is the case, he has probably not reached the group play level, because children who play together like this soon come to an understanding about role assignments.

If You Have Not Checked This Item: Some Helpful Ideas

■ **Read a Book**

A Lion for Lewis by Rosemary Wells (New York: Dial Press, 1982) is the story of dress-up play in the attic by two older children (five-year-olds) and little Lewis (age three), who always gets assigned to play the inferior roles and never a main character. He is the baby to the older children's mother and father, sick child to their doctor and nurse, and maid to their king and princess. Lewis eventually gets his way, however, much in the manner of real children, by finding something better that the older children really respect: Lewis finds a lion suit into which he climbs to turn the play upside down. It is the same kind of creative solution that real children use when they are blocked by their peers.

The development of creativity, as you can see, means much more than becoming an artist or a writer. Perhaps the most valuable lesson that children learn from imaginative play, in fact, is how to develop creative solutions to life's sticky interpersonal problems. What an exceptionally strong inducement that is for our promoting imaginative play in early childhood!

Much Bigger Than Martin by Steven Kellogg (New York: Dial Press, 1976) relates the typical younger sibling/older sibling problem in a highly imaginative way. The young narrator imagines in humorous detail all the things he will do to his older brother Martin when he makes himself much bigger. Nothing the young narrator tries seems to work, however, until he uses his creativity to make a pair of stilts.

MAY SWITCH ROLES WITHOUT WARNING ☐

The pretend play of three-year-olds is obviously more elaborate than that of two-year-olds. Because of their free-floating nature, the plots three-year-olds make up often shift from one event to another without much advance warning. We have witnessed this characteristic before in these children. They write the letters of their names or of words here and there on a sheet of paper, sometimes starting in the middle and working both forward and backward. The teacher also finds that when he asks preschoolers to line up in a straight line, he gets fifteen different versions of straightness.

Three-year-olds are not grounded on a common baseline as in Euclidean geometry, we remember. Thus their imaginative play also reflects their free-form thinking. They may start out playing superfriends, but the activity soon becomes house with hardly the blink of an eye. They seem to accept these abrupt shifts as a matter of course, since it is part of their nature.

Adults have more trouble trying to follow such thinking patterns. Our only current experience is with nighttime dreams, which may start out with one sequence but evolve into something entirely different when we subconsciously play around with a particular detail.

This type of easy shifting is characteristic of divergent thinking, the process in which individuals generate a variety of novel responses to a situation, or creative thinking, in other words. It is the opposite of what usually occurs—convergent thinking—in which individuals move toward a uniform response. Obviously, many more solutions to a problem are generated when we practice divergent thinking. For adults, practicing divergent thinking is difficult because we have been conditioned for so long to think in a stereotyped format acceptable to all.

The development of creativity calls on us to promote divergent thinking in young children and rekindle its use in our own lives. Divergent thinking is nonconformist in nature, and, therefore, somewhat threatening to adults' usual response of going along with the crowd. Most young children have not yet been conditioned to behave in an inhibited manner. Thus, they are more open to novel solutions in their imaginative play. If these solutions could be carried over into adult life, what creative possibilities for resolving interpersonal problems might ensue!

Three-year-olds not only move from one episode to another in their pretend play without much concern, but they also switch from one role to another without warning. Although adults are somewhat disconcerted by such illogical moves, peers seem to accept such switches as normal. "If you want to be someone else, that's your privilege" seems to be the unspoken rule. "However, you must work it out in an appropriate manner if you want others to continue playing with you" seems to be the rest of the peer contract.

The previous checklist item discussed the assignment of roles by one child and the taking of them by others. Children seem to learn early how to get out of roles they do not want and into roles they do want without disrupting the play.

This behavior may be an illustration of the interesting findings by Gottman and Parkhurst. They found that the friendships of three- and four-year-olds were characterized by the playing of extended fantasy roles and that children of this age took particular care to avoid disagreements. When squabbling broke out among them, the children had great difficulty de-escalating it. Therefore, they seemed to create a "climate of agreement" for one another in which they explained or played away disagreements immediately because of their awareness that disagreements had "unmanageable, adverse consequences for their friendships" (Damon, p. 141).

If we look back at the pretend play episode with Katy, Lisa, and John, it is evident that all three know who is who and what is going on even though they are sliding down the slide, running back and forth from one room to the other, and even switching the roles three times. Katy is Wonder Woman, Robin, then someone unnamed. Lisa is Robin and then Wonder Woman. John is Batman and then excluded from the play.

This format is typical of the play of three- and four-year-olds. Their ability to handle such role assignments and switches with a nonchalance or sensitivity that prevents squabbles is a positive result of imaginative play that has seldom been pointed out. Not all children are able to play this way. Neither are all three- and four-year-olds able to participate in group play at this level. But those who have been allowed the freedom and given the support to engage in such play can reach this level. Are they eventually the adults in our society who know "instinctively" how to get along with others? We would like to think so.

If You Have Not Checked This Item: Some Helpful Ideas

■ Allow Children to Settle Their Own Play Problems

Unless the players are physically hurting one another, it is better to allow them to settle their own problems. For them to experience a squabble that gets out of hand is important in their learning how to play with one another, as Gottman and Parkhurst discovered.

■ Read a Book

Your Turn, Doctor by Carla Perez and Deborah Robison (New York: Dial Books for Young Readers, 1982) is a marvelously illustrated, hilarious story about a turn-about for the little girl Gloria and her doctor, who is about to give her a physical exam. Gloria refuses, and instead she gives the exam to her doctor. Your children who are forever engaged in playing doctor will love the story, but it is also a book every doctor who deals with a young child should know by heart!

USES LANGUAGE FOR CREATING □
AND SUSTAINING PLOT

While two-year-olds do most of their pretending without much language, three-year-olds depend upon language to set the scene and sustain the action. If three-year-olds are playing by themselves, they often will talk to themselves about what is happening. They also will speak for the characters—all of them. If the youngsters are playing with other children, they often use a great deal of dialog to carry out their ideas. This behavior promotes their improved use of language and dialog with others. In addition, it provides yet another opportunity for them to express creativity in the fresh and novel way they use words.

Words direct what the children do, the way the youngsters act, who the characters are, the unfolding of the plot, and the way the children resolve conflict. Children involved in pretending who do not have the language skills of the more advanced players are able to listen and eventually imitate the advanced players' use of language. Everyone involved gets excellent practice in improving speaking skills, trying out new words, and using familiar language in new ways.

One of the new ways for some children is the use of language to express feelings. The characters in these spontaneous make-believe situations need to express how they feel about what is happening to them. Many children have trouble putting their feelings into words. Younger children prefer to "act out" rather than speak out. This type of imaginative play gives them the opportunity to learn how to express feelings.

The youngsters, in fact, are projecting their feelings by expressing what a character feels. Even if the character is a doll, a puppet, or an inanimate figure of a person or an animal, the children have yet another opportunity to speak. Three-year-olds are often more comfortable expressing the feelings of toy people than their own. The youngsters like to take their dolls or stuffed animals to the doctor's office, to listen to these pretend people express their fears, and to comfort them. In doing so, the children sort out their own impressions about the situation and try out their own sometimes novel ideas for resolving problems.

Smilansky has found three main functions of language in this sort of dramatic play: imitating adult speech, imagining the make-believe situation (mainly dialog), and managing the play. In this regard, language serves to explain, command, and direct the action (Smilansky, p. 27).

If you listen carefully to the actors in imaginative play, you will note that they carry out all three of these functions. They definitely imitate adult speech. You practically can hear yourself speaking if you are the parent or the teacher of any of these children. Children also bring imagery to life in the characterizations that they express through dialog. Finally, someone in the group, usually the self-assigned director, is forever stepping outside her role to explain or reaffirm what is going on.

If inner imagery allows the child to pretend in the first place, then talking aloud allows him to expand the meaning of what he visualizes. He not only hears himself speaking, but he also receives feedback from the reactions of others. This feedback helps him to revise and refine ideas and word use. Until he arrives at the point where he can create and sustain the action of pretend situations through language, he will miss the value of using his imagination in this manner. Eventually he must use mainly language and not just imagining in thinking. Thus imaginative play serves as a sort of transitional activity for the preschool child to learn spoken words for his internal images.

Creative adults, especially writers, need to be able to express their imagery in words like this. Mental pictures are not enough. Many writers admit to experiencing rich fantasy lives as children. Providing a variety of opportunities for pretending in the preschool setting may help your children to become such creative adults.

If You Have Not Checked This Item: Some Helpful Ideas

■ Have the Children Read Wordless Picture Books

Most wordless books illustrate their plots in a clear sequence of pictures. Although the pictures tell the story, the child needs to express the action and dialog in words as she reads the book. This gives her excellent practice for doing the same activity in imaginative play. Wordless books are designed for children of various ages and developmental levels. Some are simple; others are extremely complex and sophisticated. Be sure to go through a book ahead of time to see if it is suitable for a particular child.

The Midnight Adventures of Kelly, Dot, and Esmeralda by John S. Goodall (New York: Atheneum, 1972) is a small-format book containing full-page color illustrations with half-page illustrations between them. The reader turns the half page to reveal a surprising aspect of both full pages. For instance, the half page facing the child is often a door. He turns it to reveal a double-page spread of the interior of a house. This format is an excellent device to encourage anticipation and imagining of what is hidden behind the half page. Goodall has written many books using the same format. (See his *Porky Pig* series.)

In *The Midnight Adventures of Kelly, Dot, and Esmeralda*, the plot revolves around the adventures of a teddy bear named Kelly, a doll called Dot, and a mouse named Esmeralda, who come to life when the clock strikes midnight. They soon enter a picture hanging on the wall and begin their trip through a fantasy land of talking animals, carnival people, and an animal-tamer cat who kidnaps Esmeralda. An exciting and danger-filled escape episode brings the book to a satisfying conclusion. Children can try out dialog to express the feelings of the adventuresome trio, as well as descriptive words to set the scene and follow the action.

■ Use Hand Puppets

Have a variety of hand puppets available for the children: animals, characters from books, community helpers, adults, and children figures. A puppet theater made from a cardboard carton can help to motivate the children's use of puppets as play actors. You may need to put on a puppet show yourself to set the stage, so to speak, for your children's dramas. Younger children tend to use puppets as an extension of their arms, using their mouths for pretend biting rather than for speaking, as mentioned previously. Your modeling behavior can show the children a better way to use puppets. It is not necessary to have a puppet theater in the beginning, but your more advanced pretenders may expand their repertory of imaginative play if a puppet theater is available.

☐ USES EXCITING, DANGER-PACKED THEMES

Four-Year-Olds

Most four-year-olds do everything in a more exuberant out-of-bounds manner than three-year-olds, including pretending. Four-year-olds are more noisy, active, and aware of things outside of themselves. They are fascinated with matters of life and death, and they begin to use such themes more often in their imaginative play. Superheroes and other television characters show up in their pretending. Bad guys are captured. Good guys are rewarded. People get shot and killed.

Many four-year-olds use exciting, danger-packed themes in their dramatic play.

Adults look askance and blame television. They feel that TV watching surely must be bad for young children. By the age of four, children are viewing an average of four hours of television a day. Surely this television viewing must affect their pretending and imaginations. Research carried on by the Singers, however, resulted in findings contrary to what they had expected. The Singers found no relationship of statistical significance between watching television and imaginary play. Pretending neither increased nor decreased as a result of watching television.

The strongest correlation the Singers found was between the amount of television watched and overt aggression in the classroom. How true, agree nursery school teachers without perhaps realizing that four-year-olds have always exhibited aggression in their play. The real reason for the increased aggression may well be that sitting and watching television like this for long periods of time does not help young children discharge their energy and aggressive feelings (Segal & Adcock, p. 138).

Four-year-olds are extremely active and must have daily opportunities to discharge this pent-up energy. It is only natural for this energy to take the form of aggressive character roles from the television programs the children watch. Ask adults who were raised before the days of television what form their wildest pretending took, and you will hear tales of cowboys and Indians, cops and robbers, or American soldiers and Nazis.

Group play comes into its own when children reach age four. When they first get together, however, it often degenerates into a wild sort of play without plot or dialog, almost a regression from their previous role playing (Segal & Adcock, p. 98). This wildness seems to be a natural progression in their learning to get along with one another. The establishment and recognition of dominance is dealt with in such rough-and-tumble play. Children also develop coping skills as they focus on the sometimes aggressive actions and reactions of peers. Out of these interactions comes a sense of common group purpose that sets the stage for the more organized play to follow.

Teachers can help, not by preventing wild play, but by redirecting its energy into the exciting, danger-packed themes that four-year-olds favor. Doctor play, always a favorite, can involve taking sick or injured patients to the hospital in an ambulance with a loud siren. One teacher found that her children needed help organizing and elaborating on their ambulance plot. They had built an ambulance out of large blocks. Now what could they do? This time, the teacher decided to play a role herself. A running record of an observation of four-year-old Jessica includes the following:

> Jessica runs to climber, climbs up and sits on top. Teacher, who is trying to involve children in dramatic play, suggests they use the climber as their hospital. They are building an ambulance out of large blocks. Jessica climbs down and begins stacking blocks one on top of the other. She sits and watches others finish by putting on paper plates to use as headlights. She picks up plate and tapes it to rear of ambulance.
>
> Jessica runs to table to get felt-tip marker. "I want the yellow marker. Lots of yellow." She gets marker. "What am I gonna write on? I want to color something. I'll color the wheels black." Jessica drops yellow marker and picks up black one. She colors in back wheel with marker. "I want to color something yellow." Teacher suggests steering wheel. She does it.
>
> Jessica runs and climbs in block ambulance. "I'm the driver." She uses her plate as steering wheel. "I wanna be the patient." Jessica gets up and lies down in middle of ambulance. She gets carried to "the hospital" by teacher and other children. She lies by the climber and pretends to be sick, moaning and groaning. Other children leave, but she stays.

Then she gets up and runs to table where teacher is helping children to make doctor bags. Teacher asks her what name she wants on her bag. She answers, "I want to be a nurse, not a doctor." Teacher asks what tools a nurse uses. She answers, "Nurses help, they don't use tools. Doctors use tools." Teacher asks, "What does your mother use when you are sick?" She answers, "I don't know."

Jessica takes bag and runs back to ambulance with bag on arm, smiling. She yells, "Lisa, lay down, you're the patient." Jessica sits in front seat and drives ambulance using paper plate steering wheel. She hops up again and runs to teacher, asking her to be the doctor. She jumps up and down, urging teacher to hurry. "Hurry, we're ready," she repeats. Teacher comes and helps carry Lisa to the hospital.

The teacher noted that more children participated in this particular role play than any others she had witnessed. An ambulance had gone by on the street outside earlier in the morning, siren blaring, and the children who saw it were excited but alarmed. This event prompted their building of the block ambulance. But the teacher's own participation in the play certainly stimulated the extra number of children to become involved. The teacher's idea for extending the play by helping the children make doctor bags added immensely to the drama. The running record, however, caught four-year-old Jessica just as she normally acted, always on the run.

Jessica's rather stereotyped answers about doctors is also typical of this age. Gender roles seem to become more rigid, with girls insisting on playing the mother, waitress, or teacher, while boys often want to play father, driver, policeman, or superhero. Same-gender groups form about this time, with girls' play becoming more relaxed and verbal, and boys' play faster paced and more aggressive (Segal & Adcock, p. 101).

Block play, for instance, may get out of hand with four-year-olds. It sometimes disintegrates into throwing when adults are not around, or even when they are. Try to change the direction of the block play by giving the players a new task involving excitement or mystery: "Where is the mysterious tunnel I saw on the floor this morning, boys? What, you didn't see it? I'm surprised. I thought you had x-ray vision. I could see it right through the rug. You don't believe me? Well, maybe if you make your own tunnel, you'll be able to see the mystery tunnel, too. Jeff, you and Lennie know how to build tunnels. Maybe you could make a mystery tunnel at one end of the rug, and Rod and Kennie could make a mystery tunnel at the other end. If the tunnels came together in the middle, you'd all be able to run your cars through one long tunnel. What do you think?"

If you observe that individual children who are four years old have not started playing with exciting, danger-packed themes, it may be that they are less mature than the others or may need more practice. How do they compare with other four-year-olds in motor skills, for instance? Obviously, it is not appropriate to push such children into something they are not interested in. Provide them with many opportunities to engage in play themes of their own interests. You will know what some of these are from your observations and conversations with such youngsters.

If You Have Not Checked This Item: Some Helpful Ideas

- **Read a Book**

Come Away from the Water, Shirley by John Burningham (New York: Thomas Y. Crowell, 1977) is a marvelous example of the imaginative life of a four- or five-year-old girl who accompanies her mother and father to the beach. While they sit in their beach chairs and give her directions on the left side of the book's double-spread pages, Shirley and her dog engage in an imaginary pirate ship adventure on all of the right-hand pages. While her mother is telling her not to stroke that dog, "Shirley, you don't know where he's been," the opposite page shows Shirley being forced to walk the plank on the pirate ship while her dog bites the pirate's leg. Shirley's imaginary adventures are wordless, giving the children a chance to make up their own dialog and descriptions.

- **Have Big Building Supplies**

Four- and five-year-olds like to build big structures to play in. Have the youngsters use hollow wooden blocks if possible. Or bring in wooden packaging crates you get from a wholesaler. Cardboard cartons, plastic milk carton carriers, scrap boards, and lumber can be used for building huts, forts, houses, boats, race cars, and fire engines. Play houses also can be purchased commercially, made out of pup tents, made by covering a card table with a blanket, or produced by hanging sheets over lines strung in a corner of the room.

TAKES ON CHARACTERISTICS □ AND ACTIONS RELATED TO ROLE

Four-year-olds have more experience than three-year-olds when it comes to creating a role in their pretend play. Because they desperately want to participate in the adult world, four-year-olds try out all sorts of adult roles: mother at work, father at work, doctor, nurse, bus driver, astronaut, waiter, fast-food cook, gas station attendant, mail carrier, firefighter, truck driver, train conductor, or crane operator. In addition, four-year-olds play their roles with many more realistic details. They select props more carefully, dress up more elaborately, and carry out the role with more appropriate dialog and actions.

If you listen carefully to four-year-olds when you are observing them doing imaginative play, you will be able to learn a great deal about their understanding of the people and situations in their world. In addition, you may gain quite a respect for their use of creativity in developing their roles. Even the mundane roles of mother, father, brother, and baby are played with new twists and novel solutions to problems. Dialog is expanded, and the players even express emotions quite eloquently where appropriate.

Language is used more than ever before to set the scene and create the mood. Because the players are beginning to make greater distinctions between real and pretend, they often make aside-like comments about things that are not real, just pretend, so that you, their peers, and even they themselves understand what is real and what is pretend.

Four-year-olds are also more flexible about taking different roles. Children who would not take a bad guy's role at age three may play it to the hilt at age four.

Observe your children carefully as they pretend in the dramatic play area, in the block corner, at the water table, and on the playground. Are they playing roles with greater realism than before, using expanded dialog, showing more emotion, and almost becoming the character? If so, you should mark this item on the checklist.

If You Have Not Checked This Item: Some Helpful Ideas

■ Have Many Sets of Flannelboard Characters

Children can use cutout characters from their favorite storybooks to play with on a flannelboard. Obtain an extra paperback copy of the book, cut out the characters, and mount them on cardboard with sandpaper backing. Keep the characters in a manila envelope with a copy of the book inside. Then children can look at pictures from the story when they play. The youngsters can act out scenes from the book if they want, or they can have the characters participate in brand-new adventures. This activity is good practice in role playing with characters the children already know. A child can play by herself or with another child. More than two children at the same flannelboard is a bit crowded. Keep more than one small flannelboard in the book area, if you want this to be a popular activity. Flannelboards can be made by mounting flannel or felt to a piece of cardboard folded in two and hinged at the top so that it stands easily on a table.

Some favorite storybooks in paperback from which you may want to cut out characters are

Will I Have a Friend? by Miriam Cohen (New York: Collier Books, 1967). The characters include Jim and his preschool friends.

Corduroy by Don Freeman (New York: Viking Press, 1968). The characters are a girl, her mother, and a teddy bear named Corduroy.

Whistle for Willie by Ezra Jack Keats (New York: Puffin, 1977). The characters include Peter, his mother and father, and his dog Willie.

Where the Wild Things Are by Maurice Sendak (New York: Scholastic Book Services, 1963). The characters are a little boy named Max and the wild things.

Strega Nona by Tomie dePaola (Englewood Cliffs, NJ: Prentice-Hall, 1975). The characters include Strega Nona, the Grandma Witch; Big Anthony; the Magic Pot; and the townspeople.

The Three Billy Goats Gruff by Paul Galdone (New York: Clarion Books, 1973). The characters are the little Billy Goat Gruff, the middle Billy Goat Gruff, the big Billy Goat Gruff, and the troll.

■ Read a Book

Reading a book where the main character is a child who uses his imagination to take on the characteristics and actions of a particular role is another method for motivating children to pretend. In *The Train* by David McPhail (Boston: Little, Brown and Company, 1977), Matthew, who loves trains, dreams that he is involved in fixing a real train, as well as helping the stationmaster, the conductor, and the engineer.

USES ELABORATE AND CREATIVE □ THEMES, IDEAS, DETAILS

Four-Year-Olds

The themes that four-year-olds use in their pretending are many of the same ones they used at age three, only much expanded. The youngsters still enjoy playing house. Both boys and girls play with dolls and take roles in the housekeeping corner. Doll play now includes dressing as well as undressing, but the central action usually involves putting the doll to bed. Many girls of this age prefer playing with little girl dolls rather than baby dolls. Play with dollhouses, however, is still too detailed to hold the interest of most four-year-olds. They like the dolls more than the houses. Even block structures are not played with as much as they will be played with at age five. At age four, the pretending takes place during the process of building, rather than with the finished product afterwards.

Doctor play is at its peak at age four, and it will seldom be as popular again. All kinds of themes involving community helpers are used, especially after a visit by a community helper or a field trip to a work site. Superheroes are popular, as we have seen, especially television characters. Monsters sometimes appear, but they are still a bit too scary for four-year-olds to handle.

Five-Year-Olds

The pretend play of older four-year-olds and of five-year-olds is characterized by the elaborate nature of the drama, no matter whether the theme is a common one or an invented adventure. Five-year-olds add all kinds of details through their dialog, dress-up, props, and imaginations. Their play gets so involved, in fact, that it even can be carried over from one day to the next. The players remember where they left off the day before and can start right in again.

There is much more talk during pretend play, as well, because five-year-olds have a better command of the language. With their improved language usage, they clarify ideas and talk out problems. Concerns about sickness, accidents, and death are dealt with more realistically in the imaginative play of five-year-olds. Although the youngsters like to use props, those with a high level of fantasy can pretend without props.

Boys and girls begin playing more in groups of the same gender by this time. This structure changes the nature of the play somewhat, with girls' play becoming more calm and boys' play becoming more active. Girls still prefer to play house, but boys more often play superhero or monster. Groups are often larger than before as friendships expand and children learn how to get along with more than one or two peers.

Five-year-olds like to build big buildings and then play inside the structures. Imaginative play is at its height just before and during this period. After children enter first grade and games-with-rules become the norm, make-believe play begins to wane. It is not at all prevalent among children much after age seven.

By about age seven, a cognitive change that allows more abstract thinking has taken place within the child. What happens to pretending? We speculate that it does not disappear at all but becomes a part of the inner self to be tapped by adults in their daydreaming as well as in their generation of creative ideas. Those adults who experienced a rich fantasy life as children may be the fortunate possessors of the skill to play around with ideas in their heads, just as they did with props and toys in the nursery school as children.

As you observe the children in your classroom on the last of the checklist items, you may want to make a list of the themes the children are using in their play. What can you do to add to this list? Put out more props? Read more stories? Help the children make more costumes? Take children on more field trips so that the youngsters will have additional real experiences to draw from? All of these activities are good ideas. Try them, and see how your children respond.

If You Have Not Checked This Item: Some Helpful Ideas

■ Read a Book

Children love to hear about *Owliver* by Robert Kraus (New York: Windmill & Dutton, 1974), the little owl who liked to pretend. Owliver first pretends he is an orphan, but when his mother and father object, he pretends to be an actor. This time his father objects and gives him doctor and lawyer toys to encourage more serious interests. His mother, however, gives him acting lessons, including tap dancing. He fools them both, of course, by growing up to become . . . a fireman!

TABLE 9. Development of imagination

Age	Child's Pretend Play Behavior
1–2	Goes through pretend routines of eating or other brief actions, in some cases
2–3	Replays fragments of everyday experience (e.g., putting baby to bed) Repeats routine over and over in ritualistic manner Uses realistic props (if uses props at all)
3–4	Insists often on particular props in order to play May have imaginary playmate at home Uses family, doll-play, hospital, cars, trains, planes, and firefighting themes Assigns roles or takes assigned roles May switch roles without warning
4–5	Uses exciting, danger-packed themes (e.g., superheroes, shooting, and running) Is more flexible about taking assigned roles during play Uses more rigid gender roles (e.g., girls as mother, waitress, or teacher; boys as father, doctor, or policeman)
5–6	Plays more with doll house, block structure Includes many more details, much dialog Carries play over from one day to next sometimes Plays more in groups of same gender

OBSERVING, RECORDING, AND INTERPRETING IMAGINATION

Information from the running record on Sherry found on page 328 can be transferred to the checklist.

Imagination Checklist

N Pretends by replaying familiar routines
Evidence: Sherry at three years old is beyond this.

✓ Needs particular props to do pretend play
Evidence: Uses props such as actual boxes and bags in grocery play

✓ Assigns roles or takes assigned roles
Evidence: Took role as daughter but later tried to assign this role to Ann

✓ May switch roles without warning
Evidence: Changed role from daughter to mother without warning

✓ Uses language for creating and sustaining plot
Evidence: Talked constantly during grocery plot

Uses exciting, danger-packed themes

✓ Takes on characteristics and actions related to role
Evidence: Got groceries off shelf, put them in bag, went to cashier, took groceries home, unpacked

✓ Uses elaborate and creative themes, ideas, details
Evidence: Carried out detailed actions in grocery store plot

The information from the running record that was transferred to the checklist shows Sherry as a mature player in this imaginative role. The only blank on her checklist ("Uses exciting, danger-packed themes") is more typically observed in a four-year-old, especially a boy. Since imaginative play is an area of strength and confidence for Sherry, her teacher should consider using a dramatic play activity to help Sherry in a checklist area that needs strengthening. For example, Sherry has shown little development in the area of written language. Perhaps she could copy a sign for the grocery store or pretend to write out a grocery list of things to buy. All children's development is interrelated. We should thus be sure to use strengths from other areas of a child's development when we design an individual plan to strengthen a child's particular need.

REFERENCES CITED

Caplan, Theresa, and **Frank Caplan.** (1983). *The Early Childhood Years: The 2 to 6 Year Old.* New York: Putnam Publishing Group.

Damon, William. (1983). *Social and Personality Development.* New York: W. W. Norton & Company.

Segal, Marilyn, and **Don Adcock.** (1981). *Just Pretending: Ways to Help Children Grow Through Imaginative Play.* Englewood Cliffs, NJ: Prentice-Hall.

Singer, Dorothy G., and **Jerome L. Singer.** (1977). *Partners in Play: A Step-by-Step Guide to Imaginative Play in Children.* New York: Harper & Row.

Singer, Jerome L. (1973). *The Child's World of Make-Believe: Experimental Studies of Imaginative Play.* New York: Academic Press.

Smilanksy, Sara. (1968). *The Effects of Sociodramatic Play on Disadvantaged Preschool Children.* New York: John Wiley & Sons.

OTHER SOURCES

Beaty, Janice J. (1988). *Skills for Preschool Teachers*. Columbus, OH: Merrill Publishing Company.

Bergen, Doris (Ed.). (1988). *Play as a Medium for Learning and Development*. Portsmouth, NH: Heinemann.

Paley, Vivian Gussin. (1984). *Boys and Girls: Superheroes in the Doll Corner*. Chicago: University of Chicago Press.

LEARNING ACTIVITIES

1. Use the twelfth section of the *Child Skills Checklist* on imagination as a screening tool to observe all of the children in your classroom. Compare the children with checks at the higher levels in the sequence of imagination development with their checks in social play and language development. Can you draw any conclusions from this comparison?

2. Choose a child who has displayed high-level skills in imagination and make a running record of him or her on three different days. What new details did you learn about the child's pretending?

3. Look over the activities suggested, and choose one for use with one of the children whom you have screened as needing help in this area. Carry out the activity you have prescribed for the child. Record the results.

4. Take a field trip with your children to a site of interest where they can see and meet people at work in a special field. Put out appropriate props in your dramatic play area after you return, and record what kinds of pretend play take place. Is the play any different from what went on previously? If so, how do you account for this?

5. Carry out one of the book activities from this chapter with one child or a small group, and see if it stimulates any pretending. How could you extend this pretending?

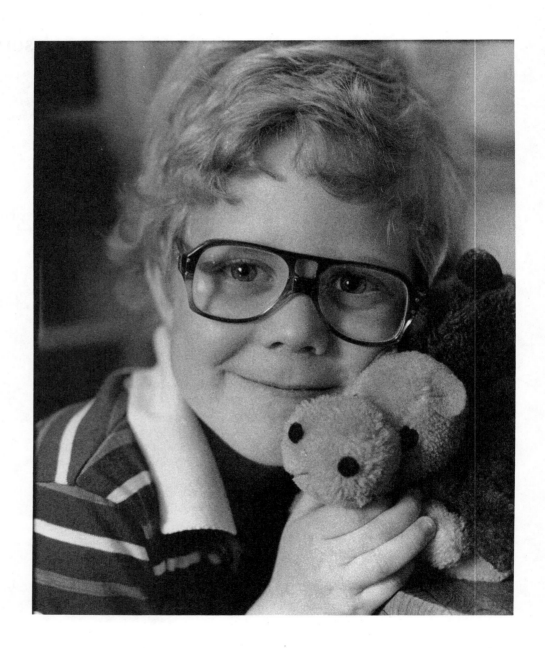

14 Observation of the Whole Child

A s you have studied the twelve separate areas of child development included in this observational program, you may have noted that each of the aspects follows a similar pattern in the growth of the child, from the general to the specific. Children learn to control large muscles before they achieve small motor control. Children recognize overall patterns of cognitive discrimination before the details become clear, speak single words to include whole categories of things before they learn the names for each, draw a circle to represent a person before they learn to add the details, and pretend in stereotyped roles about mothers and fathers before they add the personal touches identifying specific family members.

This book has proceeded in the opposite direction: specific categories of development were detailed first. We have looked in some depth at self-identity, emotional development, social play, prosocial behavior, large motor development, small motor development, cognitive development (classification and seriation; number, time, space, and memory), spoken language, written language, art skills, and imagination.

Now it is time to look at the whole picture. The child is, of course, a whole being whose development in these areas is proceeding simultaneously. Once you understand the details of this growth, it is possible to make an overall assessment of the developmental skills that each of your children possesses by using the *Child Skills Checklist* as a whole. From such an assessment, it is possible to draw a total picture of the child in order to make individual plans that will promote continued development.

TEACHER OR STUDENT TEACHER AS OBSERVER

In order to draw a total picture of the child, you must step out of your role of caregiver and into the role of objective observer. Do this role changing in your classroom as unobtrusively as possible. Have another staff member take over your duties for a particular period while you observe a single child using the checklist as your guide. Many teachers find that using a clipboard or notebook for backing, with a pencil or pen attached on a string, is a convenient way to record while you sit or stand. Keep away from the activities but as close as possible to the child whom you are observing. Try not to become involved with the children.

If the children ask what you are doing, you can reply that you are busy writing this morning. If they want you to join their activity, you can

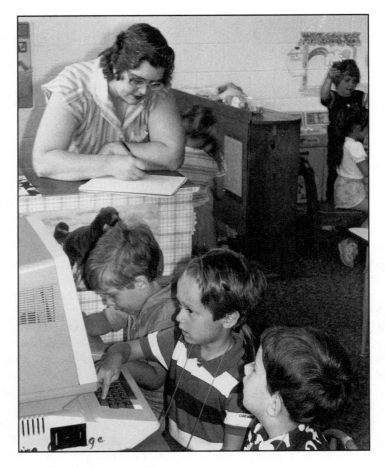

In order to record a total picture of a child, you must step out of your role as teacher and into the role of objective observer.

politely refuse, saying that you have things to write and that you will join them later. If a child wants to use your pencil, you can show him that it is attached to the clipboard and suggest that he should use a pencil in the writing area. Children will soon try to imitate you, and you had better attach a pencil to a notebook in the writing area, for the children will want their materials to be just like yours.

How long should you spend? It is a good idea to observe using the checklist for at least half an hour at a time. You should be familiar with the various items by now and not have to spend too much time flipping the pages back and forth to locate an item. You may find, as many observers do, that it is difficult to step back in a busy classroom and keep your concentration for much longer than half an hour at a time. Yet it is important for you to see as much of the child's involvement in all aspects of the program as possible. The solution is to make a number of observations at different times on different days.

Making a reliable overall assessment of a single child is not possible based on only one observation. You should have as much information as you can gather from as many different days, different activities, and different points of view as possible. The best overall records are a compilation made by all of the classroom staff. Have each person put a date by the items she has observed. She may want to indicate her checkmarks with a symbol or her initials if you are using the same checklist for all your observations.

Try to avoid making eye contact with the child you are observing. If he or she looks your way, you can look around at the other children. Children are much more observant than we often give them credit for. In spite of your best efforts, the child you are observing will often pick up the fact that you are watching him or her if you keep at it long enough. Most children soon forget about the scrutiny they are undergoing and continue their participation in their activity. If you find, however, that your child seems uncomfortable by your presence and even tries to get away, you should break off your observation. Try again another day, or let another staff member or another student observe that particular child.

How should you begin? You may want to learn something about a particular child in a certain area of development to start. Perhaps he has difficulty getting involved with the others in the pretend play during free choice period. Plan to begin your observation during this period. You will want to look at the items on social play. Other checklist areas that can often be seen at the same time as social play include the items on self-identity, emotional self-control, prosocial behavior, spoken language, and imagination.

Circle the checklist area you are observing, and place a checkmark for each item you see the child performing or an *N* for the items you have no opportunity to observe. Leave the item blank if neither of the above conditions apply. This means that the child has the opportunity to perform the item but does not do it.

Many observers also like to make notes after each item, jotting down the action the child performs (or does not perform) that prompted them to check the item (or leave it blank). If you use the checklist on more than one day in a cumulative manner, be sure to put the date after each item, as well.

The time of your next observation may be determined by the areas you have not had the opportunity to observe. For self-identity, for instance, you will want to observe the child when he arrives in the morning, especially at the beginning of the year. The second area, emotional development, needs to be observed during lunch or snack time, toileting, and nap time.

The checklist is not a test. You should not need to ask children questions about whether they recognize certain colors, for instance. The youngsters' performance on the items should become evident as you observe the children in their natural play activities. Set up activities that will engage the children in the areas you are interested in observing. Be sure these activities are spontaneous and not forced. If a child does not get involved in art skills although art activities are available every day, you should circle this area and leave the items blank. Do not use *N*, or no opportunity to observe, when the child has the opportunity to participate in art activities but, in fact, chooses not to. You will want to note, though, after the art skill items that "easel painting and table activities of cutting and pasting are available, but Robbie does not get involved in art."

USE OF THE *CHILD SKILLS CHECKLIST*

Sample Checklist

The checklist on pages 351–357 was used to observe a four-year-old boy, Robbie, whom the teacher was concerned about because he seldom joined the others in their play. She observed Robbie on three different days. Note how even short evidence statements add significant information.

Interpretation of Checklist Results

When the teacher, Carol J., had finished observing Robbie on three different days for about half an hour each time, she had a much better idea of Robbie's strengths as well as his areas needing strengthening. Her observation confirmed that Robbie did not usually play with other children, but seemed to prefer to do things on his own. He seemed to be quite independent, making choices on his own, defending his rights, being enthusiastic about the things he chose to do, and smiling much of the time. She chuckled about his characteristic tuneless humming as he busily engaged himself in block building or racing little cars. She always could tell where Robbie was by his humming.

Child Skills Checklist

Name: _Robbie_   Observer: _Carol J._

Program: _Riverside Head Start_   Dates: _10/5, 10/7, 10/8_

Directions:
Put a ✔ for items you see the child perform regularly.
Put *N* for items where there is no opportunity to observe.
Leave all other items blank.

Item	Evidence	Date
1. Self-Identity		
_____ Separates from parents without difficulty	*Upset when mother leaves*	10/5
✔ Does not cling to classroom staff excessively	*Plays by himself*	10/5
✔ Makes eye contact with adults		10/5
✔ Makes activity choices without teacher's help	*Goes directly to activity area*	10/5
_____ Seeks other children to play with		
_____ Plays roles confidently in dramatic play		
✔ Stands up for own rights	*Will not let others take his toys. Shows anger*	10/7
✔ Displays enthusiasm about doing things for self	*Hums a happy tune*	10/5
2. Emotional Development		
✔ Allows self to be comforted during stressful time	*Lets teacher hold him*	10/5
✔ Eats, sleeps, toilets without fuss away from home		
N Handles sudden changes/startling situations with control		

Item	Evidence	Date
_____ Can express anger in words rather than actions	*Sometimes hits when angry. No words*	10/5
___✔___ Allows aggressive behavior to be redirected		
___✔___ Does not withdraw from others excessively		10/5
___✔___ Shows interest/attention in classroom activities	*Likes blocks especially*	10/8
___✔___ Smiles, seems happy much of the time		
3. Social Play		
___N___ Plays by self with or without objects		
___✔___ Plays by self in pretending-type activities	*Pretends with small cars, people*	10/8
___N___ Plays parallel to others with or without objects		
___✔___ Plays parallel to others in pretending-type activities	*Pretends with car*	10/8
___✔___ Plays parallel to others constructing or creating something	*Builds garage for car*	10/8
_____ Plays with a group with or without objects		
_____ Plays with a group in pretending-type activities		
_____ Plays with a group constructing or creating something		
4. Prosocial Behavior ___✔___ Shows concern for someone in distress	*Comes over to child who is crying*	10/5

Item	Evidence	Date
__N__ Shows delight for someone experiencing pleasure		
_____ Shares something with another		
__N__ Gives something of his or her own to another		
_____ Takes turns with toys or activities	*Has trouble with favorite toys*	10/8
__✔__ Waits for turn without a fuss		
__✔__ Helps another do a task	*Helps Nat with building*	10/8
__N__ Helps another in need		
5. Large Motor Development		
__✔__ Walks down steps alternating feet		
__✔__ Runs with control over speed and direction	*Likes to run*	10/5
__✔__ Jumps over obstacle, landing on two feet		
__✔__ Hops forward on one foot		
__✔__ Climbs up and down climbing equipment with ease	*Good control*	10/5
__N__ Moves legs/feet in rhythm to beat		
__N__ Claps hands in rhythm to beat		
__N__ Beats drum alternating hands in rhythm to beat		

Item	Evidence	Date
6. Small Motor Development		
___✓___ Shows hand preference (which is _right_)		10/5
___✓___ Turns with hand easily (knobs, lids, eggbeaters)	_Likes water play_	10/7
_____ Pours liquid into glass without spilling		
_____ Unfastens and fastens zippers, buttons, Velcro tabs		
___✓___ Picks up and inserts objects with ease	_Puzzles_	10/5
_____ Uses drawing/writing tools with control		
_____ Uses scissors with control		
___N___ Pounds in nails with control	_Not available_	10/5
7. Cognitive Development: Classification and Seriation		
___N___ Recognizes basic geometric shapes		
___✓___ Recognizes colors	_Tells colors of clothes_	10/8
___✓___ Recognizes differences in size		
___N___ Recognizes differences in musical tones		
___N___ Reproduces musical tones with voice		
___✓___ Sorts objects by appearance	_Plays table games_	10/8
___N___ Arranges events in sequence from first to last		
___N___ Arranges objects in series according to a rule		

Item	Evidence	Date
8. Cognitive Development: Number, Time, Space, Memory		
✔ Counts by rote to ten		10/8
✔ Counts objects to ten		10/8
✔ Knows the daily schedule in sequence		10/8
✔ Knows what happened yesterday		10/8
✔ Can build a block enclosure	*Good with blocks*	10/8
✔ Can locate an object behind or beside something		10/8
N Recalls words to song, chant		
N Can recollect and act on directions of singing game		
9. Spoken Language		
Speaks confidently in classroom	*Speaks very softly*	10/5
✔ Speaks clearly enough for adults to understand		10/5
✔ Speaks in expanded sentences		10/5
Takes part in conversations with other children	*Not usually*	10/5
Asks questions with proper word order		
Makes "no" responses with proper word order		

Item	Evidence	Date
_____ Uses past tense verbs correctly		
__N__ Plays with rhyming words		
10. Written Language		
_____ Pretends to write by scribbling horizontally		
_____ Includes features of real letters in scribbling		
__✓__ Identifies own written name		10/7
__✓__ Identifies classroom labels		10/7
__✓__ Knows some alphabet letters	*Letters of his name*	10/7
_____ Prints real letters		
_____ Prints letters of name		
_____ Prints name correctly in linear manner		
11. Art Skills		
__✓__ Makes random marks or covers paper with color	*Not often*	10/7
_____ Scribbles on paper		
_____ Forms basic shapes		
_____ Makes mandalas		

Item	Evidence	Date
_____ Makes suns		
_____ Draws human as circle with arms and legs attached		
_____ Draws animals, trees		
_____ Makes pictorial drawings		
12. Imagination ____N____ Pretends by replaying familiar routines		
____✓____ Needs particular props to do pretend play	Cars, people	10/8
_____ Assigns roles or takes assigned roles	Doesn't often play with others	10/8
_____ May switch roles without warning		
____✓____ Uses language for creating and sustaining plot	Talks to himself	10/8
____✓____ Uses exciting, danger-packed themes	With cars & people	10/8
____✓____ Takes on characteristics and actions related to role	Motorcycle driver	10/8
____N____ Uses elaborate and creative themes, ideas, details		

Being happy and smiling were especially important clues to Carol about the overall status of any child in her class. Robbie demonstrated few negative behaviors, in fact, except for his quick temper when other children tried to interfere with his activities. Carol had tried to get him to express his feelings in words, but without success. Now she noted that he really did not speak very much at all. Somehow she had missed that important aspect of his behavior because he seemed content and, possibly, because he did vocalize . . . if only to hum.

Now she noted that although she could understand him if she listened closely, his speaking skills were not at the level of the other four-year-olds. She began to wonder if this might be the reason he did not get involved in playing with the others. Because dialog and conversation are so much a part of make-believe play, a child without the verbal skills might feel out of place, she reasoned.

She had a strong hunch that Robbie was highly creative. Watching him build elaborate roads for his race car and talk to himself as he played alone or parallel to the others, he seemed to invent all kinds of situations for the miniature people he played with. She noted that creativity certainly did not show up in his art skills, but she reasoned that his difficulty with small motor skills may have caused him to avoid painting, drawing, and cutting.

In looking for areas of strength, Carol picked out his enthusiasm and good self-concept, his large motor skills, his cognitive skills, and his imaginative play. His special interests seemed to be block building, water play, and all kinds of outdoor play. She felt he was a bright boy who used his cognitive ability in playing by himself rather than by joining others. Areas needing strengthening included language; small motor skills; using writing, drawing, and painting tools; control of his temper; and, especially, playing with the other children.

Sharing Checklist Results

In order to confirm her interpretation of the *Child Skills Checklist* observation, Carol shared the results with the two other classroom workers. They were also surprised about how little Robbie verbalized and that they too had not noticed this fact previously. What had they missed about the other children, they wondered? One of them decided to observe Robbie on her own, using the checklist to see how her results compared with Carol's. The teacher assistants were fascinated by the details Carol had gleaned in a very short time and by the way she had interpreted Robbie's inability to join in group play.

Carol decided to set up a meeting with Robbie's mother to share her findings and talk about how Robbie behaved at home. As always, she featured the positive aspects of Robbie's development and behavior, hoping to use them in helping Robbie improve in the areas where he needed strengthening. Robbie's mother was very interested in Carol's observation. She told

Carol that Robbie was the youngest of three brothers, and he did not seem to have the language skills at age four that his older brothers had shown. She also noted that Robbie preferred to play alone, but she had never considered that his speaking skills might be the cause.

She told how all three boys invented their own games because they had few toys at home. As a single working parent she had all she could do to provide for their food and clothing needs. When Carol suggested that Robbie might like to continue water play at home in the sink with empty containers, his mother thought this was a fine idea and also a way that he might help her with the dishes! She was especially pleased that Carol felt Robbie was bright on the basis of his water play games and block building in the center. She asked Carol for other ideas for making up games with household throwaway items. Carol offered to lend her a booklet of ideas. When Carol also mentioned that the center liked to send home picture books for parents to read to their children, Robbie's mother said she thought Robbie would like this a lot. She wanted to come back in a few weeks and see how Robbie was doing, to which Carol agreed with pleasure.

Planning for Individuals
Based on Checklist Results

Once the observation has been completed, the classroom staff can make plans for the individual child by using his areas of strength to help build on his areas needing strengthening. These can be listed on a learning prescription along with particular activities to help the child. Activities to help children improve in each checklist item are, of course, described at the end of discussion about the item. (See the learning prescription that Carol formulated to help Robbie, page 360. See Appendix B, page 371, for a reproducible copy of the form.)

After Carol and her staff had agreed upon Robbie's most important strengths and areas needing strengthening, they discussed what activities they could set up to involve Robbie in helping himself improve in the three areas listed. They decided to ask him to help a new boy, Russ, to learn to use the outside climber because Robbie was so good at it. Talking and helping one other child should not be so difficult for Robbie in the beginning as playing with a larger group.

The staff looked at the activities on spoken language listed in Chapter 10, and they decided to use puppets as a possible way for Robbie to get more involved in speaking with others. Carol would read the book *Louie* to Robbie and a small group of children; she would then give each of them a puppet that the staff had prepared from paper bags. The staff decided to give Robbie's puppet a name—Ron, the Race Car Driver. Carol then would use her own puppet to engage the children in talking through their puppets. Once they got the idea, she would extract herself from the pretending and let them play on their own.

```
┌─────────────────────────────────────────────────────────────────┐
│                    Learning Prescription                          │
│                                                                   │
│  Name  Robbie                             Date  10/12             │
│                                                                   │
│              Areas of Strength and Confidence                     │
│  1.  Good self-concept, happy, helpful                            │
│  2.  Creative in block building, water play                       │
│  3.  Good large motor skills on outside equipment                 │
│                                                                   │
│                 Areas Needing Strengthening                       │
│  1.  Learn to play with others                                    │
│  2.  Develop better speaking skills                               │
│  3.  Improve small motor coordination                             │
│                                                                   │
│                      Activities to Help                           │
│  1.  Ask Robbie to help new boy learn to use climber              │
│  2.  Read "Louie" and give him puppet to play with                │
│  3.  Do medicine dropper, water & food colors in muffin tin       │
└─────────────────────────────────────────────────────────────────┘
```

She decided to do this during the activity period every day with small groups of children, always trying to include Robbie. She hoped Robbie and the others would like the activity enough to make other puppets on their own. This would also involve Robbie with small motor and art skills. She also decided to work on Robbie's problem of learning to control his temper through the puppet play by having her own puppet get angry and hit her, and asking the others to help her puppet express anger differently.

In case Robbie did not get involved in making his own puppet, she thought the medicine dropper activity with colored water in a muffin tin should interest him because of his fascination with water play. The staff decided to try these activities for a week and discuss the results at their planning session the following week. They also decided to do a similar observation for each of the children as time permitted and to make a similar learning prescription.

USE OF THE CHECKLIST BY PRESERVICE TEACHERS AND STUDENT TEACHERS

Preservice and student teachers can use the *Child Skills Checklist* in a similar manner, making a series of observations of a single child until all of the items have been noted. In order to interpret the checked items or blanks, the observer then should read the particular chapters that discuss these areas.

It is especially helpful for the preservice teacher to make a written report or case study that includes an interpretation of the child's development in each of the twelve principal checklist areas. Such a report should include not only specific information from the observations, but also whatever inferences and conclusions the observer can draw from the data.

In Robbie's case, the observer will want to read Chapter 2 on self-identity, for example, to find out what it could mean when the child has difficulty separating from the mother and why the child seems happy but still does not play with other children. Without a great deal of information, an outside observer often is not able to interpret child observations with the confidence of the classroom staff. However, certain inferences and conclusions can be offered based on the data collected, and the outside observer may even make an important contribution to the understanding of a particular child because of her fresh perspective.

In addition to the written interpretation of each of the twelve checklist areas, the observer needs to summarize the overall development of the child in some detail. A learning prescription similar to the one Carol did for Robbie should be done, followed by an explanation for the activities prescribed.

Case studies such as this can be helpful not only to the preservice or student teacher, but also to the supervising classroom teacher, as well as the parent of the child observed. Supervising teachers need to set up case conferences with individual parents (to which student observers are invited) to discuss their reports.

OBSERVATION OF EACH CHILD

It is important to observe each of your children in this kind of detail during the year. Teachers report that they are able to learn more about each child by stepping back and making a focused observation like this than by simply having the child in their program for an entire year. It is an eye-opening experience to look at one child in-depth from an observer's point of view, rather than from the perspective of a busy teacher involved with the activities of many other lively youngsters.

Child-development college students report that this type of in-depth look at a real child makes textbooks and courses come alive. Parents, too, benefit from the information gained by objective observations. Not only do the parents learn new activities to use with their children at home, but they often also become involved in the fascinating drama of how their own children develop, why their children act the way they do, and how they, as parents, best can help their children to realize their full potentials.

Observing the development of young children is thus a teaching as well as a learning technique that should benefit all of its participants—teachers, students, children, and parents—because it outlines each aspect of child development carefully, objectively, and positively. Promoting development in young children works best when it is focused on an assessment of their strengths. When you know the strengths of each child in every aspect of development, you will be able to design your program to meet an individual's needs as the children in your classroom work and play together, creating their own unique selves.

Appendixes

363

Child Skills Checklist

Name: _____ Observer: _____

Program: _____ Dates: _____

Directions:
Put a ✓ for items you see the child perform regularly.
Put N for items where there is no opportunity to observe.
Leave all other items blank.

Item	Evidence	Date
1. Self-Identity		
_____ Separates from parents without difficulty		
_____ Does not cling to classroom staff excessively		
_____ Makes eye contact with adults		
_____ Makes activity choices without teacher's help		
_____ Seeks other children to play with		
_____ Plays roles confidently in dramatic play		
_____ Stands up for own rights		
_____ Displays enthusiasm about doing things for self		
2. Emotional Development		
_____ Allows self to be comforted during stressful time		
_____ Eats, sleeps, toilets without fuss away from home		
_____ Handles sudden changes/ startling situations with control		

Item	Evidence	Date
_____ Can express anger in words rather than actions		
_____ Allows aggressive behavior to be redirected		
_____ Does not withdraw from others excessively		
_____ Shows interest/attention in classroom activities		
_____ Smiles, seems happy much of the time		
3. Social Play		
_____ Plays by self with or without objects		
_____ Plays by self in pretending-type activities		
_____ Plays parallel to others with or without objects		
_____ Plays parallel to others in pretending-type activities		
_____ Plays parallel to others constructing or creating something		
_____ Plays with a group with or without objects		
_____ Plays with a group in pretending-type activities		
_____ Plays with a group constructing or creating something		
4. Prosocial Behavior		
_____ Shows concern for someone in distress		

Item	Evidence	Date
_____ Shows delight for someone experiencing pleasure		
_____ Shares something with another		
_____ Gives something of his or her own to another		
_____ Takes turns with toys or activities		
_____ Waits for turn without a fuss		
_____ Helps another do a task		
_____ Helps another in need		
5. Large Motor Development _____ Walks down steps alternating feet		
_____ Runs with control over speed and direction		
_____ Jumps over obstacle, landing on two feet		
_____ Hops forward on one foot		
_____ Climbs up and down climbing equipment with ease		
_____ Moves legs/feet in rhythm to beat		
_____ Claps hands in rhythm to beat		
_____ Beats drum alternating hands in rhythm to beat		

Item	Evidence	Date
6. Small Motor Development		
_____ Shows hand preference (which is _____)		
_____ Turns with hand easily (knobs, lids, eggbeaters)		
_____ Pours liquid into glass without spilling		
_____ Unfastens and fastens zippers, buttons, Velcro tabs		
_____ Picks up and inserts objects with ease		
_____ Uses drawing/writing tools with control		
_____ Uses scissors with control		
_____ Pounds in nails with control		
7. Cognitive Development: Classification and Seriation		
_____ Recognizes basic geometric shapes		
_____ Recognizes colors		
_____ Recognizes differences in size		
_____ Recognizes differences in musical tones		
_____ Reproduces musical tones with voice		
_____ Sorts objects by appearance		
_____ Arranges events in sequence from first to last		
_____ Arranges objects in series according to a rule		

Item	Evidence	Date
8. Cognitive Development: Number, Time, Space, Memory		
_____ Counts by rote to ten		
_____ Counts objects to ten		
_____ Knows the daily schedule in sequence		
_____ Knows what happened yesterday		
_____ Can build a block enclosure		
_____ Can locate an object behind or beside something		
_____ Recalls words to song, chant		
_____ Can recollect and act on directions of singing game		
9. Spoken Language		
_____ Speaks confidently in classroom		
_____ Speaks clearly enough for adults to understand		
_____ Speaks in expanded sentences		
_____ Takes part in conversations with other children		
_____ Asks questions with proper word order		
_____ Makes "no" responses with proper word order		

Item	Evidence	Date
_____ Uses past tense verbs correctly		
_____ Plays with rhyming words		
10. Written Language		
_____ Pretends to write by scribbling horizontally		
_____ Includes features of real letters in scribbling		
_____ Identifies own written name		
_____ Identifies classroom labels		
_____ Knows some alphabet letters		
_____ Prints real letters		
_____ Prints letters of name		
_____ Prints name correctly in linear manner		
11. Art Skills		
_____ Makes random marks or covers paper with color		
_____ Scribbles on paper		
_____ Forms basic shapes		
_____ Makes mandalas		

Item	Evidence	Date
_____ Makes suns		
_____ Draws human as circle with arms and legs attached		
_____ Draws animals, trees		
_____ Makes pictorial drawings		
12. Imagination		
_____ Pretends by replaying familiar routines		
_____ Needs particular props to do pretend play		
_____ Assigns roles or takes assigned roles		
_____ May switch roles without warning		
_____ Uses language for creating and sustaining plot		
_____ Uses exciting, danger-packed themes		
_____ Takes on characteristics and actions related to role		
_____ Uses elaborate and creative themes, ideas, details		

Learning Prescription

Name _____ Date _____

Areas of Strength and Confidence

1. _____

2. _____

3. _____

Areas Needing Strengthening

1. _____

2. _____

3. _____

Activities to Help

1. _____

2. _____

3. _____

Index of Activities

Index of Children's Books

General Index

383